UNCONSTRAINED FACE RECOGNITION

International Series on Biometrics

Consulting Editors

Professor David D. Zhang

Department of Computer Science
Hong Kong Polytechnic University
Hung Hom, Kowloon, Hong Kong

email: csdzhang@comp.polyu.edu.hk

Professor Anil K. Jain

Dept. of Computer Science& Eng.
Michigan State University
3115 Engineering Bldg.
East Lansing, MI 48824-1226, U.S.A.
Email: jain@cse.msu.edu

In our international and interconnected information society, there is an ever-growing need to authenticate and identify individuals. Biometrics-based authentication is emerging as the most reliable solution. Currently, there have been various biometric technologies and systems for authentication, which are either widely used or under development. The International Book Series on Biometrics will systematically introduce these relative technologies and systems, presented by biometric experts to summarize their successful experience, and explore how to design the corresponding systems with in-depth discussion.

In addition, this series aims to provide an international exchange for researchers, professionals, and industrial practitioners to share their knowledge of how to surf this tidal wave of information. The International Book Series on Biometrics will contain new material that describes, in a unified way, the basic concepts, theories and characteristic features of integrating and formulating the different facets of biometrics, together with its recent developments and significant applications. Different biometric experts, from the global community, are invited to write these books. Each volume will provide exhaustive information on the development in that respective area. The International Book Series on Biometrics will provide a balanced mixture of technology, systems and applications. A comprehensive bibliography on the related subjects will also be appended for the convenience of our readers.

Additional titles in the series:

PALMPRINT AUTHENTICATION *by David D. Zhang;* ISBN: 1-4020-8096-4
HUMAN-COMPUTER INTERFACE *by Antonio J. Colmenarez, Ziyou Xiong and Thomas S. Huang;* ISBN: 1-4020-7802-1
FACIAL ANALYSIS FROM CONTINUOUS VIDEO WITH APPLICATIONS TO COMPUTATIONAL ALGORITHMS FOR FINGERPRINT RECOGNITION *by Bir Bhanu and Xuejun Tan;* ISBN: 1-4020-7651-7

Additional information about this series can be obtained from our website:
http://www.springeronline.com

UNCONSTRAINED FACE RECOGNITION

by

Shaohua Kevin Zhou
Siemens Corporate Research, Princeton, NJ, USA

Rama Chellappa
University of Maryland, College Park, MD, USA

Wenyi Zhao
Sarnoff Corporation, Princeton, NJ, USA

Springer

Shaohua Kevin Zhou
Integrated Data Systems Dept.
Siemens Corporate Research
755 college Road East
Princeton, NJ 08540

Dr. Rama Chellappa
Univ. Maryland College Park
Center Automation Research
College Park, MD 20742-3275

Wenyi Zhao
Sarnoff corp.
Vision Technologies Lab
201 Washington Road
Princeton, NJ 08540

UNCONSTRINED FACE RECOGNITION

By Shaohua Kevin Zhou, Rama Chellappa and Wenyi Zhao

ISBN-13: 978-1-4419-3890-9
e-ISBN-13: 978-0-387-29486-5

Printed on acid-free paper.

springeronline.com

Dedicated to Professor Azriel Rosenfeld
(1931-2004)

Contents

Preface

Although face recognition has been actively studied over the past decade, the state-of-the-art recognition systems yield satisfactory performance only under controlled scenarios and recognition systems degrade significantly when confronted with unconstrained situations.

Examples of unconstrained conditions include illumination and pose variations, video sequences, expressions, aging, and so on. Recently, researchers have begun to investigate face recognition under unconstrained conditions. For example, as video sequence becomes ubiquitous due to advances in digital imaging devices and the advent of the Internet era, face recognition based on video sequences is gaining more attention. Face recognition under illumination and pose variations remains a big challenge to researchers.

The goal of this book is to provide a comprehensive review of unconstrained face recognition, especially face recognition from video, and to assemble descriptions of novel approaches that are able to recognize human faces under various unconstrained situations. The underlying theme of these approaches is that, unlike conventional face recognition algorithms, they exploit the inherent characteristics of the unconstrained situation and gain improvements in recognition performance when compared with conventional algorithms. For instance, generalized photometric stereo combines physics-based illumination model with statistical modeling to address face recognition under illumination variation. Simultaneous tracking and recognition employs the temporal information embedded in a video sequence and thus improves both tracking accuracy and recognition performance.

The book is organized into five parts: I) Fundamentals, preliminaries, and reviews; II) Face recognition under variations; III) Face recognition via kernel learning; IV) Face tracking and recognition from video; and V) Future directions. Part I, consisting of two chapters, addresses fundamental issues of face recognition, especially under unconstrained scenarios, and provides necessary background for following the discussions in subsequent parts and an up-to-date survey of unconstrained face recognition. Part II, consisting of four chapters, presents face recognition approaches that are able to handle variations due to illumination, pose, and aging. Part III, consisting of two chapters, studies face recognition from a viewpoint of an appearance manifold whose nonlinearity is characterized via two kernel learning methods: computing probabilistic distances in reproducing kernel Hilbert space and matrix-based kernel methods. Part IV, consisting of three chapters, presents adaptive visual tracking, simultaneous tracking and recognition, and a unifying framework of probabilistic identity characterization. A detailed description of the organization and the contents of each chapter are given in Section 1.2.

The book is accessible to a wide audience since only elementary level of linear algebra, probability and statistics, and signal processing is assumed. Graduate students and researchers unfamiliar with face recognition can use the book to quickly comprehend the state-of-the-art of unconstrained face recognition. Also the book serves as a starting point for them to embark research on face recognition. Instructors can use the book as a textbook or for supplementary reading for graduate courses on biometric recognition, human perception, computer vision, or relevant seminars. Professional practitioners of face recognition and other biometrics can use the book as a reference and directly extract interested algorithms for their applications.

We are indebted to numerous friends and colleagues that made the book possible. We first thank Guarav Aggarwal for providing materials on illumination-invariant face recognition in the presence of multiple light sources and Narayanan Ramanathan for writing the part of face recognition across aging progression. Most of the work was done when SKZ and WZ were at the Center for Automation Research (CfAR), University of Maryland. SKZ thanks his then lab colleagues: Amit Roy-Chowdhury, Naresh Contoor, Jian Li, Jian Liang, Haiying Liu, Amit Kale, Gang Qian, Jie Shao, Namrata Vaswani, Zhanfen Yue, and Qinfen Zheng.

SHAOHUA KEVIN ZHOU, RAMA CHELLAPPA, AND WENYI ZHAO

PART I

FUNDAMENTALS, PRELIMINARIES AND REVIEWS

Chapter 1

FUNDAMENTALS

Identifying people from faces is an effortless task for humans. Is it the same for computers? This is the central issue defining the field of automatic face recognition [22, 23, 24, 25, 26, 27, 28, 29, 134] (also referred to as face recognition in the present book), one of the most active research areas in the emerging field of biometrics.

Over the past decade, face recognition has attracted substantial attention from various disciplines and seen a tremendous growth in the literature. Below, we present an overview of face recognition from the biometric, experimental, and theoretical perspectives.

1.1 Overview

1.1.1 Biometric perspective

Face is a biometric [33]. As a consequence, face recognition finds wide applications in authentication, security, and so on. One potential application is in the recently deployed US-VISIT system [32] by the Department of Homeland Security (DHS), collecting vistors' fingerprints and face images.

Biometric signatures enable automatic identification of a person based on physiological or behavioral characteristics [31, 30]. Physiological biometrics are biological/chemical traits that are innate or naturally grown, while behavioral biometrics are mannerisms or traits that are learned or acquired. Table 1.1 lists commonly used biometrics. Some introductory discussions on biometrics may be found in [30, 31, 33, 34].

Biometrics technologies are becoming the foundations of an extensive array of highly secure identification and personal verification solutions. Compared with conventional identification and verification methods based on personal identification numbers (PINs) or passwords, biometrics technologies offer some

Type	*Examples*
Physiological biometrics	Body odor, DNA, face, fingerprint, hand geometry, iris, pulse, retinal
Behavioral biometrics	Face, gait, handwriting, signature, voice

Table 1.1. A list of biometrics.

unique advantages. First, biometrics are individualized traits while passwords may be used or stolen by someone other than the authorized user. Also, a biometric is very convenient since there is nothing to carry or remember. In addition, biometric technology is becoming more accurate and inexpensive.

Among all biometrics listed in Table 1.1, face biometric is unique because face is the only biometric belonging to both physiological and behavioral categories. While the physiological part of the face biometric has been widely researched in the literature, the behavioral part is not yet fully investigated. In addition, as reported in [35, 36], face has advantage over other biometrics because it is a natural, non-intrusive, and easy-to-use biometric. For example [35], among the six biometrics of face, finger, hand, voice, eye, and signature in Figure 1.1, the face biometric ranks first in the compatibility evaluation of a machine readable travel document (MRTD) system on the basis of six criteria: enrollment, renewal, machine-assisted identity verification requirements, redundancy, public perception, and storage requirements and performance. Probably the most important feature of a biometric is its ability to collect the signature from non-cooperating subjects.

Besides applications related to identification and verification such as access control, law enforcement, ID and licensing, surveillance, etc., face recognition is also useful in human-computer interaction, virtual reality, database retrieval, multimedia, computer entertainment, etc. See [29, 48] for a review of face recognition applications.

1.1.2 Experimental perspective

Face recognition mainly involves the following three tasks [61]:

- Verification. The recognition system determines if the query face image and the claimed identity match.

- Identification. The recognition system determines the identity of the query face image by matching it with a database of images with known identities, assuming that the identity of the quest face image is inside the database.

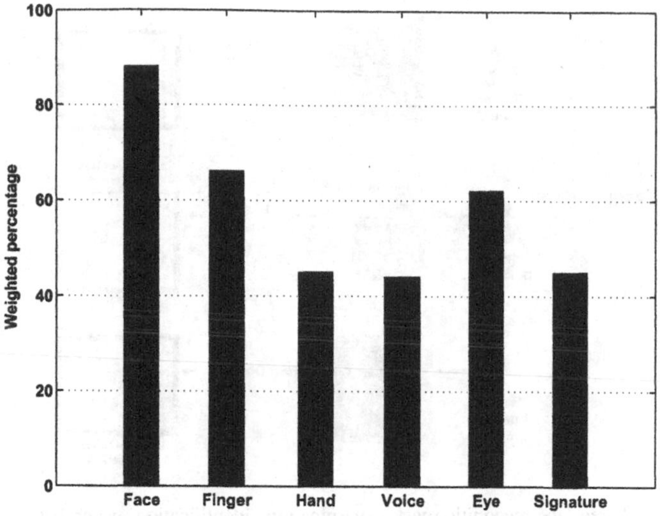

Figure 1.1. Comparison of various biometric features based on MRTD compatibility (from [35]).

- Watch list. The recognition system first determines if the identity of the query face image is in the stored watch list and, if yes, then identifies the individual.

Figure 1.2 illustrates the above three tasks and corresponding statistics used for evaluation. Among three tasks, the watch list task is the most difficult one.

The present book focuses only on the identification task. In the face recognition literature, there is a face recognition test protocol FERET [60] widely followed by researchers for evaluating the performance of face recognition systems. FERET stands for 'facial recognition technology'. In most experiments discussed in this book, we also follow the FERET protocol.

The FERET protocol assumes the availability of the following three sets, namely a training set, a gallery set, and a probe set. The training set is provided for the recognition algorithm to learn the characteristic features. The gallery and probe sets are used in the testing stage. The gallery set contains images with known identities and the probe set with unknown identities. The algorithm associates descriptive features with images in the gallery and probe sets and determines the identities of the probe images by comparing their associated features with features associated with gallery images.

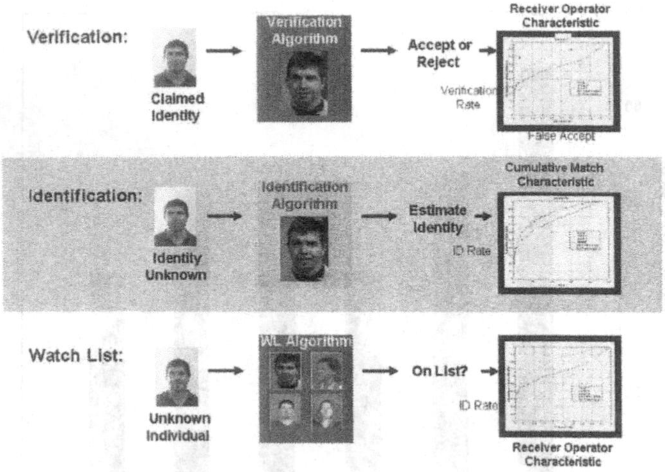

Figure 1.2. Three face recognition tasks: verification, identification, watch list (courtesy of P.J.Phillips [61]).

1.1.3 Theoretical perspective

Face recognition is by nature an interdisciplinary research area, tied to many research fields, ranging from pattern recognition, computer vision, graphics, and image processing/understanding to statistical computing and machine learning. In addition, automatic face recognition designs are often guided by the psychophysical and neural studies. A good summary of research on face perception is presented in [29, 37, 40]. We now focus on the theoretical implications of pattern recognition for the special task of face recognition.

We present a three-level hierarchy for understanding the face recognition problem, as shown in Figure 1.3. The three levels characterize general patterns, visual patterns, and face patterns, each associated with a corresponding theory of recognition. Accordingly, face recognition approaches can be grouped into three categories.

General pattern and pattern recognition

General pattern lays the foundation of the hierarchy. Because face is first a general pattern, any pattern recognition theory [7] can be directly applied to a face recognition problem. In general, a vector representation is used in pattern recognition. A common way of deriving a vector representation from a 2D face image, say of size $M \times N$, is through a 'vectorization' operator that stacks the pixels as an $MN \times 1$ vector. Obviously, given an arbitrary $MN \times 1$ vector, it can be decoded into an $M \times N$ image by reversing the above 'vectorization'

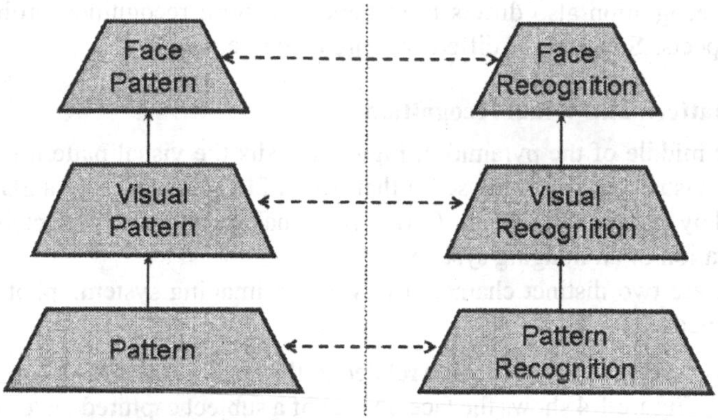

Figure 1.3. A hierarchy of face pattern and face recognition.

operator. Such a vector representation corresponds to the holistic representation mentioned in the psychophysics literature [38, 39].

Subspace methods are pattern recognition techniques widely invoked in various face recognition approaches. Two well-known appearance-based recognition schemes are the principal component analysis (PCA) [12, 50] and linear discriminant analysis (LDA) [7]. Principal component analysis performs an eigen-decomposition of the covariance matrix and consequently minimizes the reconstruction error in the mean square sense. Linear discriminant analysis minimizes the within-class scatter while maximizing the between-class scatter. The PCA approach used in face recognition is called the 'Eigenface' approach [64]. The LDA approach used in face recognition is called the 'Fisherface' approach [44] since LDA is also commonly referred to as Fisher discriminant analysis. LDA for face recognition was also independently proposed in [47]. Further PCA and LDA are combined (LDA after PCA) as in [67] to yield an improved recognition scheme. Other subspace methods such as independent component analysis (ICA) [22, 43, 243], local feature analysis (LFA) [253], probabilistic subspace [56, 57, 58], multi-exemplar discriminant analysis [70] have been used in face recognition. A comparison of these subspace methods is reported in [58, 68]. Other than the subspace methods, classical pattern recognition tools such as neural networks [53], learning methods [59], and evolutionary pursuit/genetic algorithms [54] have also been applied to face recognition.

One concern in a general pattern recognition problem is the 'curse of dimensionality' since usually M and N themselves are quite large. Practical face recognition systems store only a small number of samples per subject. This further worsens the 'curse of dimensionality' problem.

Face recognition also differs from general pattern recognition problem in many aspects. Some of the differences are discussed below.

Visual pattern and visual recognition

In the middle of the pyramid in Figure 1.3 sits the visual pattern layer. A face is a visual pattern in the sense that it is a 2D appearance of a 3D object captured by an imaging system. Certainly, visual appearance is affected by the configuration of an imaging system.

There are two distinct characteristics of the imaging system: photometric and geometric.

- Photometric characteristics are related to the light sources distributed in the scene. Figure 1.4 shows the face images of a subject captured under varying illumination conditions. Numerous models have been proposed to describe the illuminating phenomenon. In addition to coding information such as light source direction and intensity, an illumination model also characterizes the object surface material properties.

- Geometric characteristic deals with the camera properties and the relative positioning of the camera with respect to the object. Camera properties include camera intrinsic parameters and camera imaging models. The imaging models widely studied in the computer vision literature are orthographic, scaled orthographic, and perspective models. Because the perspective model requires depth information, the orthographic or scaled orthographic model is used more often in the face recognition community. The relative positioning of the camera and the object results in pose variation, a key factor determining how the 2D appearances are produced. Figure 1.4 shows the face images of one object captured at different poses.

Understanding photometric and geometric characteristics has been a long standing problem in the computer vision literature, which is mostly reflected by researches in visual recognition under illumination and pose variations. A comprehensive review of the visual recognition literature is beyond the scope of the book. However, face recognition methods that address the photometric and geometric characteristics are still at a nascent stage of development and much more work needs to be done.

Approaches to face recognition under illumination variation are usually treated as extensions of research efforts on illumination models. For example, if a simplified Lambertian reflectance model ignoring shadow pixels [150, 161, 168] is used, a rank-3 subspace can be constructed to cover the appearances arbitrarily illuminated by a distant point source. Similarly low-dimensional subspaces [143, 144] can be found using a Lambertian model with attached shadows. Face recognition can be performed by checking if a query face image lies in the object-specific illumination subspace. To generalize from the

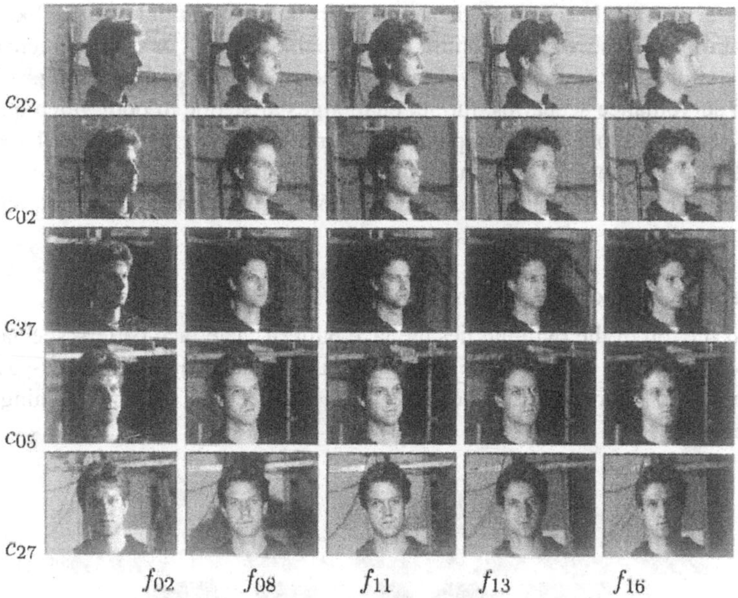

Figure 1.4. One PIE [85] individual under different illumination and poses.

object-specific illumination subspace to a class-specific illumination subspace, bilinear models are used in [84, 214, 95]. Most face recognition approaches across pose variation use view-based appearance representation [73, 76, 81]. Face recognition across illumination and poses is more difficult when compared to recognition with the presence of either pose or illumination variation. Of the many proposed approaches in the literature including [72, 77, 96], the 3D morphable model [72] yields the best recognition performance. The feature-based approach [51] is reported to be partially robust to illumination and pose variations.

An important feature of a visual pattern is its presence in video. The ubiquitousness of video sequences calls upon recognition algorithms based on videos. Because a video sequence is a collection of still images, face recognition from still images can be applied on a frame-by-frame basis. However, an important property of a video sequence is its temporal dimension. Recent psychophysical and neural studies [39, 41] demonstrate the role of movement in face recognition: Famous faces are easier to recognize when presented in moving sequences than in still photographs, even under a range of different types of degradations. Computational approaches utilizing such temporal information include [112, 123, 124, 129, 206, 133]. Figure 1.6 shows the results of face tracking in a video sequence captured in an office environment [109]. Clearly, due to free movement of the human face and an uncontrolled environment, issues like illumination and pose variations still exist. Localizing faces or face segmentation in a cluttered environment in video sequences is also very challenging.

In surveillance scenarios, further challenges arise due to poor video quality and low resolution. For example, the face region can be as small as 15×15, while most feature-based approaches [51, 72] need as many as 128×128 pixels. However, video provides multiple observations linked by their temporal continuity.

Face pattern and face recognition

At the top of the pyramid lies the face pattern. The face pattern specializes the visual pattern by letting the object be a human face. Therefore, face-specific properties or characteristics should be taken into account when performing face recognition.

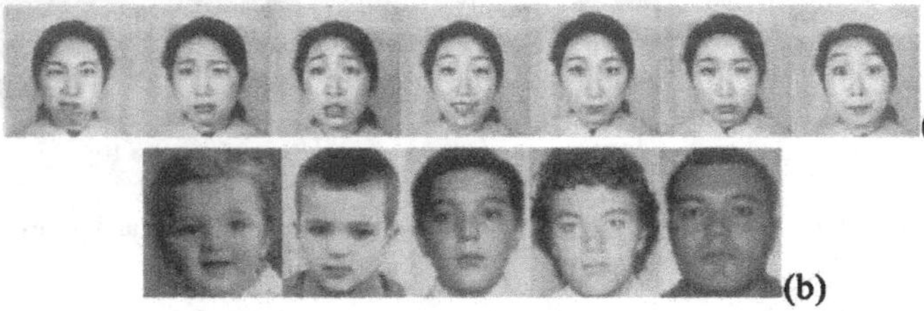
(a)
(b)

Figure 1.5. (a) Appearances of one individual with different facial expressions (from [55]). (b) Appearances of one individual at different ages (from [136]).

- *Deformation.* Humans express emotions through facial expressions, yielding nonrigid deformations of facial images. The non-rigidity is of very high degree of freedom and exacerbates the recognition task. Figure 1.5(a) shows the face images of a person exhibiting different expressions. While face expression analysis has attracted a lot of attention [45, 62, 63], recognition under expression variation has not been fully explored.

- *Aging.* Face appearances vary significantly with aging and such variations are specific to an individual. As a result, theoretical modeling of aging [136] is very difficult. Figure 1.5(b) shows the face images of a person at different ages.

- *Face surface.* One speciality of face surface is its bilateral symmetry. Symmetry constraint has been widely exploited in [162, 93, 95]. In addition, surface integrability is an inherent property of any surface, which has also been used in [149, 168, 213, 95].

- *Self-similarity.* There is a strong visual similarity among face images of different individuals. Geometric positioning of facial features such as eyes, noses, mouths, etc. are alike across individuals. Early face recognition approaches in the 70's [26, 49] used the distances between feature points to describe the face and achieved some success. Also, face surface materials properties are similar within the same race. As a consequence of visual similarity, the 'shapes' of the face appearance manifolds belonging to different subjects are similar. This is the basis of approaches [57, 58, 70] that attempt to capture the 'shape' characteristics by constructing the so-called intra-person space.

- *Makeup, cosmetic, etc.* There factors are specific to an individual and so are unpredictable. The effect of glasses has been studied in [44]; effects induced by other factors have not been widely investigated.

Face appearances of the same individual under variations in illumination, pose, deformation, aging, etc. lie in a nonlinear manifold. Figure 1.6 visualizes such a manifold by projecting the appearances of the top row into top three principal components. Manifold characterization can be done in various ways. One way is to embed a manifold in a low-dimensional space [251, 256]. The other way is to learn the nonlinearity using machine learning techniques [9, 21, 65, 263, 268, 270, 272, 276, 277, 278].

1.2 Unconstrained Face Recognition

State-of-the-art face recognition systems yield satisfactory performance under controlled conditions. To be specific, the face images are typically acquired in frontal views and are often illuminated by a frontal light source. These conditions pose strong restrictions on patterns possibly acquired. In other words, the clustering nature of the produced patterns (usually tightly clustered) is amenable for classical pattern analysis. Therefore, most face recognition approaches lie in the first level of the hierarchy. Unfortunately, recognition performance degrades significantly when face recognition systems are presented with patterns that go beyond these controlled conditions.

Recently, researchers have begun to investigate face recognition under unconstrained conditions. Examples of unconstrained conditions include illumination and pose variations, video sequences, expressions, aging, and so on. In general, recognition approaches addressing the second and third levels of the hierarchy can be considered to be addressing the unconstrained face recognition problem.

In this book, we present several unconstrained face recognition approaches. The book is organized as follows. Part I presents fundamentals, preliminaries, and reviews of face recognition. Parts II, III and IV discuss numerous face

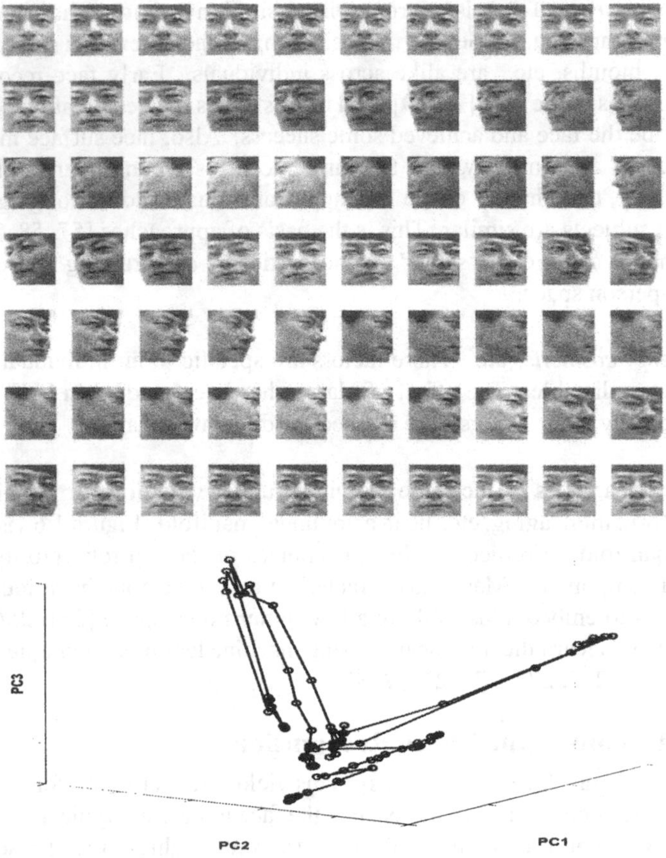

Figure 1.6. Face appearances in a video sequences, forming a nonlinear manifold.

recognition algorithms: Part II on *Face Recognition under Variations*, Part III on *Face Recognition via Kernel Learning*, and Part IV on *Face Tracking and Recognition from Videos*. Summary of the book and future directions are presented in Part V.

1.2.1 Face recognition under variations

Part II of the book studies face recognition under illumination, pose, and aging variations, which are related to the second level of Figure 1.3. In Chapter 3, we present a general theory of *symmetric shape from shading* that overcomes the challenges present in traditional shape from shading(SFS) algorithms. In Chapter 4, we present a *generalized photometric stereo* algorithm for recognizing faces under illumination variation and then in Chapter 5 an *illuminating light field* algorithm for recognizing faces under illumination and pose variations. Chapter 6 addresses issues related to *facial aging*.

Chapter 3 studies the SFS, that is to infer the 2.5D structure of a object from its shading information/image [151, 153, 10]. This is an ill-posed problem in general. To reduce the ill-posedness of SFS, we impose symmetry cue for symmetric objects by introducing the self-ratio image. This concept can be used to develop a new SFS algorithm referred to as symmetric SFS. We prove that unlike typical SFS, the symmetric SFS has a unique (global) solution which can be simultaneously obtained at each point under the assumption of a C^2 surface. We then outline several computational algorithms to recover both shape and albedo and present experimental results. In addition, a model-based symmetric source-from-shading algorithm is presented for improved source estimation. Finally, we discuss the extensions of symmetric SFS and applications of symmetry cue for image synthesis and view-synthesis of face images.

Most photometric stereo algorithms employ a Lambertian reflectance model with a varying albedo field and involve the appearances of only one object. The recovered albedos and surface normals are *object-specific* and hence appearances not belonging to the object cannot be easily handled. In Chapter 4, we generalize photometric stereo algorithms to handle all appearances of all objects in a class, in particular the human face class, by assuming that albedos and surface normals of all objects in the class be rank-constrained, i.e. lie in a subspace. Rank constraints lead to a factorization of an observation matrix that consists of exemplar images of different objects under different illuminations. To fully recover the subspace bases or *class-specific* albedos and surface normals, we employ integrability and face symmetry constraints and propose a linearized algorithm that takes into account the effects of the varying albedo field. We then apply the generalized photometric stereo algorithm for recognizing faces under illumination variations. We obtain good recognition results using the PIE database that contains images illuminated by a single light source [94, 95]. By a careful treatment of the nonlinearity of the Lambertian model, we successfully extend our algorithm to perform face recognition in the presence of multiple illumination sources.

The *illuminating light field* algorithm presented in Chapter 5 is an image-based method for face recognition across different illumination and different poses, where the term image-based means that no explicit prior 3D models are used. As face recognition under illumination and pose variations involves three factors, namely identity, illumination, and pose, generalizations in all these three factors are desired. The *illuminating light field* approach is able to generalize in identity and illumination and handle a given set of poses. The proposed approach derives an identity signature that is illumination- and pose-invariant, where the identity is tackled using subspace encoding, the illumination is characterized using a Lambertian reflectance model, and the given set of poses is treated as a whole. Experimental results using the PIE database demonstrate the effectiveness of the proposed approach [97, 96].

Chapter 6 presents two topics related to facial aging: age estimation and face recognition across aging progression. Age estimation is solved using a general technique called image based regression using boosting methods. The proposed boosting regressor [260] overcomes various challenges in an image based regression problem, such as appearance variance, multiple outputs, and storage and computation requirement. For face recognition across aging progression, two similarity functions are proposed to match facial images taken at different ages. The first one is a classifier based on a Bayesian framework, following the spirit of [56]. The second one is a direct similarity function across different age groups based on eigen-analysis.

1.2.2 Face recognition via kernel learning

As mentioned earlier, the visual pattern lies in a nonlinear manifold, which is further complicated by face-specific characteristics. Nonlinear data modeling is an important research topic in machine learning. While linear techniques such as PCA and LDA utilize first- and second-order statistics, higher-order statistics play essential roles in nonlinear data modeling. Kernel learning methods (or kernel methods) are able to capture the higher-order statistical information.

In the core of kernel learning methods lie two important components: a learning algorithm using linear geometry and a nonlinear feature space induced by a kernel function. Such a space is referred to as a reproducing kernel Hilbert space (RKHS) [18, 19, 21] in the literature. Kernel methods are linear learning algorithms operating on the nonlinear feature space. In Part III, we introduce two kernel learning methods: *probabilistic distances in RKHS* and *matrix-based kernel subspace analysis*

Probabilistic distance measures are important quantities in many research areas. For example, the Chernoff distance (or the Bhattarchayya distance as its special example) is often used to bound the Bayes error in a pattern classification task and the Kullback-Leibler (KL) distance is a key quantity in information theory literature. However, computing these distances is a difficult task and analytic solutions are not available except under some special conditions. One popular example is the Gaussian density. The Gaussian density employs only up to second-order statistics and its modeling capacity is linear and hence rather limited. In Chapter 7, we enhance this capacity through a nonlinear mapping from original data space to RKHS, which is implemented using kernel embedding. Using this nonlinear mapping, we study these probabilistic distances from a different perspective whose feasibility and efficiency are demonstrated using experiments on synthetic and face recognition examples [277].

It is a common practice that a matrix, the *de facto* image representation, is first converted into a vector before fed into subspace analysis or kernel method; however, the conversion ruins the spatial structure of the pixels that defines the image. In Chapter 8, we propose two kernel subspace methods that are directly based on the matrix representation, namely matrix-based kernel principal component analysis (matrix KPCA) and matrix-based kernel linear discriminant component analysis (matrix KLDA). We show that, through an extended Gram matrix, the two proposed matrix-based kernel subspace methods generalize their vector-based counterparts and contain richer information. Our experiments on face recognition under illumination and pose variations [278] also confirm the advantages of the matrix-based kernel subspace methods over the vector-based ones.

1.2.3 Face tracking and recognition from videos

Video sequences are becoming ubiquitous due to the advances in digital imaging devices and the advent of internet era. A face in video sequences presents further challenges to recognition algorithms besides those common to face recognition from still images.

In Chapter 9, we present an approach called *adaptive visual tracking* that incorporates appearance-adaptive models in a particle filter to realize robust visual tracking. Tracking needs modeling of inter-frame motion and appearance changes whereas recognition needs modeling of appearance changes between frames and gallery images. In conventional tracking algorithms, the appearance model is either fixed or rapidly changing, and the motion model is simply a random walk with fixed noise variance. Also, the number of particles is typically fixed. All these factors make the visual tracker unstable. To stabilize the tracker, we propose the following features: an observation model arising from an adaptive appearance model, an adaptive velocity motion model with adaptive noise variance, and an adaptive number of particles. The adaptive-velocity model is derived using a first-order linear predictor based on the appearance difference between the incoming observation and the existing particle configuration. Occlusion analysis is implemented using robust statistics. Experimental results [206, 200, 201] on tracking visual objects in long outdoor and indoor video sequences demonstrate the effectiveness and robustness of our tracking algorithm.

In Chapter 10, recognition of human faces using a gallery of still images and a probe set of videos is systematically investigated using a probabilistic framework called *simultaneous tracking and recognition*. In still-to-video recognition, where the gallery consists of still images, a time series state space model is proposed to fuse temporal information in a probe video, which simultaneously characterizes the kinematics and identity using a motion vector and an identity variable, respectively. The joint posterior distribution of the motion vector and the identity variable is estimated at each time instant and then propagated to the next time instant. Marginalization over the motion vector yields a robust estimate of the posterior distribution of the identity variable. A computationally efficient sequential importance sampling (SIS) algorithm is presented for estimating the posterior distribution. Empirical results demonstrate that, due to the propagation of the identity variable over time, a degeneracy in posterior probability of the identity variable is achieved to give improved recognition. Experiments performed [122, 123, 124, 125, 126, 127, 128] using images/videos with pose/illumination variations illustrate the effectiveness of this approach for the still-to-video scenario with appropriate model choices.

In Chapter 11, we present the most general framework for characterizing the face identity in a single image or a group of images with each image containing a transformed version of the object. In terms of the transformation, the group is made of either still images or frames of a video sequence. The face identity signature is either discrete- or continuous-valued. This framework referred as *probabilistic identity characterization* integrates all the evidence of the set and handles the localization problem, illumination and pose variations through subspace identity encoding. Issues and challenges arising in this framework are addressed and efficient computational schemes are given. All instances of face recognition algorithms are be interpreted in the most general framework [131].

Chapter 2

PRELIMINARIES AND REVIEWS

In this chapter, we first present some mathematical preliminaries on various topics needed for the development of the book, beginning with a glossary of notations. We then review related literature on (i) face recognition under illumination and/or pose variations and (ii) face recognition from multiple still images or video sequences (including visual tracking).

2.1 Preliminaries

We begin by introducing some notations commonly used throughout the book and then present basic introductions to several relevant research topics, including Lambertian illumination model, subspace analysis, kernel method, regression, state space time series, and particle filter.

2.1.1 Notation

We denote a scalar by a, a vector by $\mathtt{a}$, and a matrix with p rows and q columns by $\mathtt{A}_{p\times q}$, and a block matrix by $\mathcal{A}$. The matrix transpose is donate by $\mathtt{A}^{\mathsf{T}}$, the pseudo-inverse by $\mathtt{A}^{\dagger}$. The matrix L_r-norm is denoted by $||.||_r$.

The following special notations are introduced for brevity, convenience, and emphasis of special structure.

- Concatenation notations: $\Rightarrow$ and $\Downarrow$.

  $\Rightarrow$ and $\Downarrow$ mean horizontal and vertical concatenations, respectively. For example, we can represent an $n \times 1$ vector $\mathtt{a}_{n\times 1}$ and its transpose by

  $$\mathtt{a} = [a_1, a_2, ..., a_n]^{\mathsf{T}} = [\Downarrow_{i=1}^{n} a_i], \;\; \mathtt{a}^{\mathsf{T}} = [a_1, a_2, ..., a_n] = [\Rightarrow_{i=1}^{n} a_i].$$

  Similarly, we can represent a matrix $\mathtt{A}_{p\times q}$ by

  $$\mathtt{A} = [\mathtt{a}_1, \mathtt{a}_2, ..., \mathtt{a}_q] = [\Rightarrow_{i=1}^{q} \mathtt{a}_i]$$

where each $\mathtt{a}_i$ is a $p \times 1$ vector.

We can use $\Rightarrow$ and $\Downarrow$ to concatenate matrices to form a block matrix $\mathcal{A}$. For instance, given a collection of matrices $\{\mathtt{A}_1, \mathtt{A}_2, \ldots, \mathtt{A}_n\}$ of size $p \times q$, we construct a block matrix of size $p \times nq$ as

$$\mathcal{A}_{p \times nq} = [\Rightarrow_{i=1}^{n} \mathtt{A}_n].$$

Given a collection of matrices $\{\mathtt{A}_{11}, \mathtt{A}_{12}, \ldots, \mathtt{A}_{1n}, \ldots, \mathtt{A}_{mn}\}$ of size $p \times q$, we construct a block matrix of size $pm \times qn$ as

$$\mathcal{A}_{mp \times nq} = [\Downarrow_{i=1}^{m} [\Rightarrow_{j=1}^{n} \mathtt{A}_{ij}]\ ].$$

and a block matrix of size $p \times qmn$

$$\mathcal{A}_{p \times qmn} = [\Rightarrow_{i=1}^{m} [\Rightarrow_{j=1}^{n} \mathtt{A}_{ij}]\ ].$$

- Kronecker (tensor) product: $\otimes$.
  It is defined as

$$\mathtt{A}_{p \times q} \otimes \mathtt{B}_{m \times n} = [\Downarrow_{i=1}^{p} [\Rightarrow_{j=1}^{q} a_{ij}\mathtt{B}]\ ]_{pm \times qn}.$$

  Note that the two matrices can be of different sizes.

- Hadamard (element-wise) product: $\circ$.
  It is defined as

$$\mathtt{A}_{m \times n} \circ \mathtt{B}_{m \times n} = [\Downarrow_{i=1}^{m} [\Rightarrow_{j=1}^{n} a_{ij} b_{ij}]\ ]_{m \times n}.$$

  Note that the two matrices must be of identical size.

- Vectorization operator: $vec(.)$.
  It converts a $p \times q$ matrix to a $pq \times 1$ vector by arranging all the elements of the matrix according to a fixed order, say a lexicographic order. In other words,

$$vec(\mathtt{A})_{pq \times 1} = [\Downarrow_{i=1}^{p} [\Downarrow_{j=1}^{q} a_{ij}]\ ].$$

- Gram matrix. The dot product matrix (or Gram matrix) of two matrices $\mathtt{A}_{p \times q} = [\Rightarrow_{i=1}^{q} \mathtt{a}_i]$ and $\mathtt{B}_{p \times q} = [\Rightarrow_{j=1}^{q} \mathtt{b}_j]$ is given as

$$\mathtt{A}_{p \times q}^{\mathsf{T}} \mathtt{B}_{p \times q} = [\Downarrow_{i=1}^{q} [\Rightarrow_{j=1}^{q} \mathtt{a}_i^{\mathsf{T}} \mathtt{b}_j]\ ].$$

- Identity matrix $\mathtt{I}_m$ of size $m \times m$.

- Diagonal matrix $\mathtt{D}[d_1, d_2, \ldots, d_m]$ of size $m \times m$ whose diagonal elements are $\{d_1, d_2, \ldots, d_m\}$.

- Normal distribution $\mathtt{N}(\mathbf{x}; \mu, \Sigma)$ with mean μ and covariance matrix Σ.

2.1.2 Lambertian illumination model

Many illumination models have been proposed in the literature. In the face recognition community, a Lambertian imaging model with a varying albedo field is mostly used. In the Lambertian illumination model, an image pixel h is represented as

$$h = \max(\rho\, \mathtt{n}^{\mathsf{T}} \mathtt{s}, 0) = \max(\mathtt{t}^{\mathsf{T}} \mathtt{s}, 0), \tag{2.1}$$

where ρ is the albedo at the pixel, $\mathtt{n} = [\hat{a}, \hat{b}, \hat{c}]^{\mathsf{T}}$ is the unit surface normal vector at the pixel, $\mathtt{t}_{3\times1} = \rho\mathtt{n}$ is the product of albedo and surface normal, and $\mathtt{s}$ (a 3×1 unit vector multiplied by its intensity) specifies a distant illuminant. If the pixel is not directly facing the light source, it satisfies $\mathtt{t}^{\mathsf{T}}\mathtt{s} < 0$ or $h = 0$. This is called an *attached shadow*. Another kind of shadow is *cast shadow*. Cast shadow is generated at a certain pixel when the light source is blocked by other pixels. This is related to the geometry of the object. Figure 2.1 gives an illustration of the Lambertian illumination model.

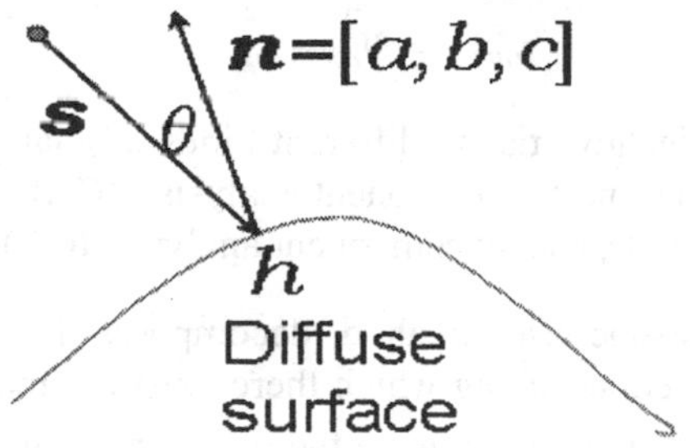

Figure 2.1. Illustration of Lambertian illumination model.

An image $\mathtt{h}$ is a collection of d pixels $\{h_i, i = 1, ..., d\}$. By stacking all the pixels into a column vector, we have

$$\begin{aligned} \mathtt{h}_{d\times1} &= [\Downarrow_{i=1}^{d} h_i] - [\Downarrow_{i=1}^{d} \max(\mathtt{t}_i^{\mathsf{T}} \mathtt{s}, 0)] \\ &= \max(\mathtt{T}_{d\times3}\, \mathtt{s}_{3\times1}, 0), \end{aligned} \tag{2.2}$$

where the $\mathtt{T}$ matrix encodes the 'product' of the albedo and the surface normal for all pixels. We call the $\mathtt{T}$ matrix as the *object-specific albedo-shape* matrix.

Another useful parameterization of the Lambertian model uses surface shape gradients. Suppose that $p_{(x,y)}$, $q_{(x,y)}$ are the shape gradients, i.e., partial derivatives of the depth map $z_{(x,y)}$.

$$h = \rho cos(\theta) = \rho \frac{1 + pP_s + qQ_s}{\sqrt{1 + p^2 + q^2}\sqrt{1 + P_s^2 + Q_s^2}} \tag{2.3}$$

where θ is the angle between the outward normal to the surface $\vec{n} = (p, q, 1)$ and the negative illumination vector $-\vec{L} = (P_s, Q_s, 1)$ which represents the direction opposite to the distant light source.

2.1.3 Subspace analysis

Subspace analysis is often used in pattern recognition, signal processing and computer vision problems as an efficient method for both dimensionality reduction and finding the direction of the projection with certain properties. For example, in the context of face recognition [29], one attempts to find some basis vectors in that space serving as directions of projection, and hopefully the projected data are clustered according to their class labels.

The basic framework of subspace analysis is as follows. Suppose we have a d-dimensional random vector $\mathtt{x}$ where d is very large, we attempt to find m basis vectors ($m < d$) forming a projection matrix $\mathtt{U}_{d\times m}$, such that the new representation $\mathtt{z}$ defined below satisfies certain properties.

$$\mathtt{z}_{m\times 1} = \mathtt{U}^{\mathsf{T}}_{d\times m}\mathtt{x}_{d\times 1}.$$

Different properties give rise to different kinds of analysis methods. Two popular methods are principal component analysis (PCA), linear discriminant analysis (LDA) and independent component analysis (ICA).

- PCA [12], an unsupervised method, decomposes the available data into uncorrelated directions, along which there exist the maximum variations. In other words, it tries to minimize the reconstruction error $||\mathtt{U}\mathtt{U}^{\mathsf{T}} - \mathtt{X}||_2$, where $\mathtt{X} = [\Rightarrow_{n=1}^{N} \mathtt{x}_n]$ encodes the training data set.

$$\mathtt{U} = \arg\min_{\mathtt{U}} ||\mathtt{U}\mathtt{U}^{\mathsf{T}} - \mathtt{X}||_2.$$

  To this end, a total scatter matrix $\hat{\Sigma} = \mathtt{X}\mathtt{X}^{\mathsf{T}}$ is defined and the optimal matrix $\mathtt{U}$ is formed by the eigenvectors corresponding to the m largest eigenvalues of $\hat{\Sigma}$.

- LDA [7], a supervised method, exploits the class label information and attempts to maximize the between-class scatter while minimizing the within-class scatter. In LDA [7], two scatter matrices are defined: between-class scatter matrix Σ_B and within-class scatter matrix Σ_W [7]. The following cost function $J(\mathtt{U})$ is maximized.

$$\mathtt{U} = \arg\max_{\mathtt{U}} \frac{||\mathtt{U}^{\mathsf{T}}\Sigma_B\mathtt{U}||_2}{||\mathtt{U}^{\mathsf{T}}\Sigma_W\mathtt{U}||_2}.$$

- ICA [43, 243], an unsupervised method, finds the projection directions along which the data are statistically independent. Often, a contrast function that measures the independence is minimized.

2.1.4 Kernel method

PCA and LDA are linear methods that utilize first- and second-order statistics. Therefore, their effectiveness is diminished when confronted with highly nonlinear data structures. To enhance their modeling capability, kernel PCA (KPCA) [272] and kernel LDA (KLDA) [263, 268] have been proposed in the literature. These kernel methods enhance the modeling capability by nonlinearly mapping the data from the original space to a very high dimensional feature space, the so-called RKHS. The nonlinear mapping enables implicit characterization of higher-order statistics. The key idea of kernel methods is to avoid the explicit knowledge of the mapping function by evaluating the dot product in the feature space using a kernel function.

In the core of kernel methods lies a kernel function. Let $\mathcal{E}$ be a set. A two variable function $k(\alpha, \beta)$ on $\mathcal{E} \times \mathcal{E}$ is a *reproducing kernel* if for any finite point set $\{\alpha_1, \alpha_2, ..., \alpha_n\}$ and for any corresponding real numbers $\{c_1, c_2, ..., c_n\}$, the following condition holds:

$$\sum_{i=1}^{n} \sum_{j=1}^{n} c_i c_j k(\alpha_i, \alpha_j) \geq 0.$$

The most widely used kernel functions in the literature [18, 19, 21] are defined on a vector space, that is $\mathcal{E} = \mathcal{R}^p$. For example, two popular kernel functions based on vector inputs are the radial basis function (RBF) and the polynomial kernels. Their definitions are as follows [18, 19, 21]. $\forall \mathrm{x}, \mathrm{y} \in \mathcal{R}^p$,

$$k(\mathrm{x}, \mathrm{y}) = \exp\{-\theta^{-1}||\mathrm{x} - \mathrm{y}||^2\}, \quad k(\mathrm{x}, \mathrm{y}) = \{\mathrm{x}^\mathsf{T}\mathrm{y} + \theta\}^d.$$

The kernel function k can be interpreted as a dot product between two vectors in a very high-dimensional space, i.e., the RKHS $\mathcal{H}_k$. In other words, there exists a nonlinear mapping function $\phi : \mathcal{R}^p \rightarrow \mathcal{H}_k = \mathcal{R}^f$, where $f > p$ and f could even be infinite, such that

$$k(\mathrm{x}, \mathrm{y}) = \phi(\mathrm{x})^\mathsf{T}\phi(\mathrm{y}).$$

This is the so-called 'kernel trick', which is also illustrated in Figure 2.2.

Given a set of training data $\{\alpha_1, \alpha_2, ..., \alpha_n\}$, the Gram matrix characterizes complete information for the kernel method. The Gram matrix $\mathrm{K} = [k(\alpha_i, \alpha_j)]$ is an $n \times n$ matrix whose ij^{th} element equals to $k(\alpha_i, \alpha_j)$.

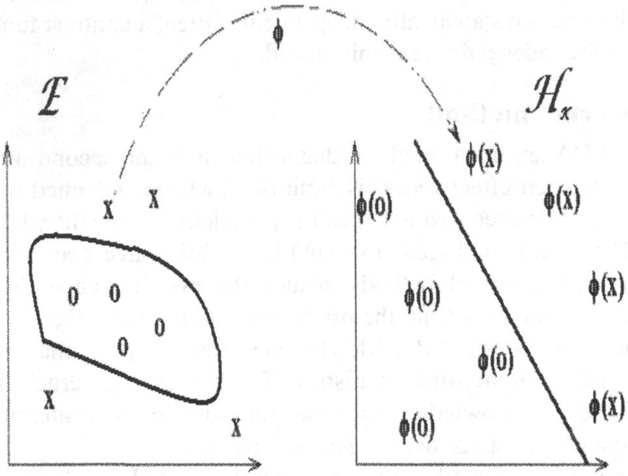

Figure 2.2. Illustration of 'kernel trick': The nonlinear decision boundary in the original space $\mathcal{E}$ becomes linear in the RKHS $\mathcal{H}_k$.

2.1.5 Regression

Regression finds the solution to the following minimizing problem:

$$\hat{g}(x) = \arg\min_{g \in \mathcal{G}} \mathcal{E}_{p(x,y)}\{L(y(x), g(x))\}, \tag{2.4}$$

where $\mathcal{G}$ is the set of allowed output functions, $\mathcal{E}_{p(x,y)}$ takes the expectation under the distribution $p(x, y)$, and the $L(\circ, \circ)$ function is the loss function that penalizes the deviation of the regressor output $g(x)$ from the true output $y(x)$. We assume that $x \in \mathcal{R}^d$ and $y(x) \in \mathcal{R}^q$.

In practice, it is impossible to compute the expectation since the distribution $p(x, y)$ is unknown. Given a set of training examples $\{(x_n, y(x_n));\ n = 1, 2, \ldots, N\}$, the cost function $\mathcal{E}_{p(x,y)} L(y(x), g(x))$ is approximated as the training error $J(g) = N^{-1} \sum_{n=1}^{N} L(y(x_n), g(x_n))$.

If the number of samples N is infinitely large, the above approximation is exact by the law of the large number. Unfortunately, a practical value of N is never large enough, especially when dealing with image data and high-dimensional output parameter. A more severe problem is *overfitting*: given a limited number of training examples, the function $g(x)$ can be easily and *arbitrarily* constructed to yield a zero training error. Therefore, additional regularization constraints are used. The combined cost function is given as (ignoring the scaling factor N^{-1})

$$J(\mathrm{g}) = \sum_{n=1}^{N} L(\mathrm{y}(\mathrm{x}_n), \mathrm{g}(\mathrm{x}_n)) + \lambda R(\mathrm{g}),$$

where $\lambda > 0$ is the *regularization coefficient* that controls the degree of regularization and $R(\mathrm{g})$ is the regularization term. Regularization often imposes certain smoothness on the output function or reflects the belief of some prior knowledge of the output.

Popular regression algorithms are data-driven in the sense that the output function are directly related to the training data inputs. Examples of data-driven regressors include nonparameteric kernel regression (NPR), linear methods and their nonlinear kernel variants such as kernel ridge regression (KRR), support vector regression (SVR), etc.

Nonparametric kernel regression (NPR)

Nonparametric kernel regression (NPR) [9] is a smoothed version of k-nearest-neighbor (kNN) regression. The kNN regressor approximates the conditional mean, an optimal estimate in the L^2 sense. NPR takes the following form:

$$\mathrm{g}(\mathrm{x}) = \frac{\sum_{n=1}^{N} h_\sigma(\mathrm{x}; \mathrm{x}_n)\mathrm{y}(\mathrm{x}_n)}{\sum_{n=1}^{N} h_\sigma(\mathrm{x}; \mathrm{x}_n)},$$

where $h_\sigma(\circ; \mathrm{x}_n)$ is a kernel function. The most widely used kernel function is the RBF kernel

$$h_\sigma(\mathrm{x}; \mathrm{x}_n) = exp(-\frac{||\mathrm{x} - \mathrm{x}_n||^2}{2\sigma^2}).$$

The RBF kernel has a noncompact support. Other kernel functions with compact supports such as the Epanechnikov kernel can be used too.

In general, when confronted with the scenario of image based regression, NPR, albeit smooth, tends to overfit the data and to yield a low bias and a high variance.

Kernel ridge regression (KRR)

Kernel ridge regression (KRR) [9] assumes that the multiple-output regression function takes a linear form:

$$\mathrm{g}(\mathrm{x}) = \sum_{n=1}^{N} \alpha_n k(\mathrm{x}; \mathrm{x}_n),$$

where $k(\mathrm{x}; \mathrm{x}_n)$ is a reproducing kernel function and α_n is a $q \times 1$ vector that weights the kernel function. The solution to the multiple-output KRR is

$$\mathrm{g}(\mathrm{x}) = \mathrm{Y}(\mathrm{K} + \lambda\mathrm{I})^{-1}\kappa(\mathrm{x}),$$

where $\mathrm{Y}_{q\times N} = [\Rightarrow_{i=1}^{N} \mathrm{y}(\mathrm{x}_i)]$ is the training output matrix, $\mathrm{K}_{N\times N} = [k(\mathrm{x}_i; \mathrm{x}_j)]$ is the Gram matrix for the training data, and

$$\kappa(\mathrm{x})_{N\times 1} = [\Downarrow_{n=1}^{N} k(\mathrm{x}; \mathrm{x}_n)].$$

In general, when a linear kernel is used, KRR tends to underfit the data and yields a high bias and a low variance. Using the nonlinear kernel function often gives enhanced performance. One computational difficulty of KRR lies in inverting the $N \times N$ matrix $\mathrm{K} + \lambda \mathrm{I}$.

Support vector regression (SVR)

Support vector regression (SVR) [21] is a robust regression method. Its current formulation works for *single output* data, i.e. $q = 1$. SVR minimizes the following cost function

$$\frac{1}{2}||\mathrm{w}||^2 + C\sum_{n=1}^{N} |y(\mathrm{x}_n) - g(\mathrm{x}_n)|_\epsilon,$$

where $|\circ|_\epsilon$ is an ϵ-insensitive function, $g(\mathrm{x}) = \sum_{n=1}^{N} w_n k(\mathrm{x}; \mathrm{x}_n)$ with $k(\mathrm{x}; \mathrm{x}_n)$ being a reproducing kernel function and w_n its weight, and $\mathrm{w} = [\Downarrow_{n=1}^{N} w_n]$. Because some of the coefficients w_n, which can be found through a quadratic programming procedure, are zero-valued, the samples x_n associated with nonzero weights are called support vectors.

SVR strikes a good balance between bias and variance tradeoff and hence is very robust. Unfortunately, directly applying SVR to the multiple-output regression problem is difficult.

2.1.6 State space time series model and particle filter

State space time series models [17] are widely employed to represent video data. Two important components of state space modeling are state transition and observation models whose most general forms can be defined as follows:

$$\textit{State transition model:}\ \theta_t = \mathrm{f}_t(\theta_{t-1}, \mathrm{u}_t), \tag{2.5}$$

$$\textit{Observation model:}\ \mathrm{y}_t = \mathrm{g}_t(\theta_t, \mathrm{v}_t), \tag{2.6}$$

where u_t is the system noise, $\mathrm{f}_t(.,.)$ characterizes the kinematics, v_t is the observation noise, and $\mathrm{g}_t(.,.)$ models the observer.

The key quantity that characterizes the time series is the posterior distribution $p(\theta_{1:s}|\mathrm{y}_{1:t})$. Depending on the relation between s and t, we solve three different problems: *filtering* if $s = t$, *prediction* if $s > t$, and *smoothing* if $s < t$. In face tracking and recognition problems, we mostly consider the filtering problem and how to solve it.

General particle filter algorithm

Given the state transition model in (2.5) characterized by the state transition probability $p(\theta_t|\theta_{t-1})$ and the observation model in (2.6) characterized by the likelihood function $p(\mathrm{y}_t|\theta_t)$, the problem is reduced to computing the posterior probability $p(\theta_t|\mathrm{y}_{1:t})$. The nonlinearity and non-Normality in (2.5) and (2.6) make the standard Kalman filter [1] ineffective. The particle filter is a means of approximating the posterior distribution $p(\theta_t|\mathrm{y}_{1:t})$ by a set of weighted particles $\mathcal{S}_t = \{\theta_t^{(j)}, w_t^{(j)}\}_{j=1}^J$ with $\sum_{j=1}^J w_t^{(j)} = 1$. It can be shown [248] that $\mathcal{S}_t$ is *properly weighted* with respect to $p(\theta_t|\mathrm{y}_{1:t})$ in the sense that, for every bounded function $\mathrm{h}(.)$,

$$\lim_{J\to\infty} \sum_{j=1}^J w_t^{(j)} \mathrm{h}(\theta_t^{(j)}) = \mathrm{E}_p[\mathrm{h}(\theta_t)]. \tag{2.7}$$

Given $\mathcal{S}_{t-1} = \{\theta_{t-1}^{(j)}, w_{t-1}^{(j)}\}_{j=1}^J$ which is properly weighted with respect to $p(\theta_{t-1}|\mathrm{y}_{1:t-1})$, we first resample $\mathcal{S}_{t-1}$ to reach a new set of samples with equal weights $\{\theta_{t-1}^{'(j)}, 1\}_{j=1}^J$. We then draw samples $\{\mathrm{u}_t^{(j)}\}_{j=1}^J$ for u_t and propagate $\theta_{t-1}^{'(j)}$ to $\theta_t^{'(j)}$ by (2.5). The new weight is updated as

$$w_t \propto p(\mathrm{y}_t|\theta_t) \tag{2.8}$$

The complete algorithm is summarized in Figure 2.3. This algorithm was first introduced to the vision community by Isard and Blake [183] (called the CONDENSATION algorithm) to deal with a contour tracking problem.

Initialize *a sample set* $\mathcal{S}_0 = \{\theta_0^{(j)}, 1)\}_{j=1}^J$ *according to prior distribution* $p(\theta_0)$.
For $t = 1, 2, \ldots$
  For $j = 1, 2, \ldots, J$
    Resample $\mathcal{S}_{t-1} = \{\theta_{t-1}^{(j)}, w_{t-1}^{(j)}\}$ *to obtain a new sample* $(\theta_{t-1}^{'(j)}, 1)$.
    Predict *the sample by drawing* $\mathrm{u}_t^{(j)}$ *for* u_t *and computing* $\theta_t^{(j)} = \mathrm{f}_t(\theta_{t-1}^{'(j)}, \mathrm{u}_t^{(j)})$.
    Compute *the transformed image* $\mathrm{z}_t^{(j)} = \mathcal{T}\{\mathrm{y}_t; \theta_t\}$.
    Update *the weight using* $w_t^{(j)} = p(\mathrm{y}_t|\theta_t^{(j)}) = p(\mathrm{z}_t^{(j)}|\theta_t^{(j)})$.
  End
  Normalize *the weight using* $w_t^{(j)} = w_t^{(j)} / \sum_{j=1}^J w_t^{(j)}$.
End

Figure 2.3. The general particle filter algorithm.

Often in time series, we are interested in deriving the best estimate $\hat{\theta}_t$ given the observations up to now. For example, the state estimate $\hat{\theta}_t$ can either be the minimum mean square error (MMSE) estimate,

$$\hat{\theta}_t = \theta_t^{mmse} = \mathrm{E}[\theta_t|\mathrm{y}_{1:t}] \approx J^{-1} \sum_{j=1}^J w_t^{(j)} \theta_t^{(j)}, \tag{2.9}$$

where E the expectation operator, the maximum a posteriori (MAP) estimate,

$$\hat{\theta}_t = \theta_t^{map} = \arg\max_{\theta_t} \mathrm{p}(\theta_t|\mathbf{y}_{1:t}) \approx \arg\max_{\theta_t} w_t^{(j)}, \tag{2.10}$$

or other forms based on $p(\theta_t|\mathbf{y}_{1:t})$.

Variations of particle filter

Sequential Importance Sampling (SIS) [237, 248] draws particles from a *proposal distribution* $q(\theta_t|\theta_{t-1}, \mathbf{y}_{1:t})$ and then for each particle a proper weight is assigned as follows:

$$w_t \propto p(\mathbf{y}_t|\theta_t)p(\theta_t|\theta_{t-1})/q(\theta_t|\theta_{t-1}, \mathbf{y}_{1:t}). \tag{2.11}$$

Selection of the proposal distribution $q(\theta_t|\theta_{t-1}, \mathbf{y}_{1:t})$ is usually dependent on the application. We here focus on the extentions used in the vision literature. In the ICondensation algorithm [184] which fuses low-level and high-level visual cues in the conventional Condensation algorithm [183], the proposal distribution, a fixed Gaussian distribution for low-level color cue, is used to predict the particle configurations, then the posterior distribution of the high-level shape cue is approximated using SIS. It is interesting to note that two different cues can be combined together into one state vector to yield a robust tracker, using the co-inference algorithm [198] and the approach proposed in [196]. In the chapter on visual tracking, we also use a prediction scheme but our prediction is based on the same visual cue i.e. the appearance in the image, and it is directly used in the state transition model rather than used as a proposal distribution.

2.2 Reviews

In this section, we review two important topics in unconstrained face recognition: (i) face recognition under illumination, pose, and/or aging variations and (ii) face recognition from multiple still images or video sequences (including visual tracking).

2.2.1 Face recognition under illumination, pose and/or aging variations

We first characterize the three factors of illumination, pose, and identity in the context of face recognition under illumination and pose variations. We then address approaches on face recognition under illumination and/or pose variances. We also give a brief review of facial aging.

Identity, illumination, and pose

Three factors are involved in face recognition under pose and illumination variations, namely illumination, pose, and identity. Using the human face images as examples, we now address issues involved in each of the three factors by fixing the other two.

- *Illumination.* Various illumination models are available in the literature, ranging from models for highly specular objects such as mirrors to models for matte objects. Mostly objects belong to the latter category and are described by Lambertian reflectance models for their simplicity. Early shape from shading approaches [10] assumed a constant albedo field. However, this assumption is violated at locations such as eyes and mouth edges. For the human face, the Lambertian reflectance model with a varying albedo field provides a reasonable approximation [75, 84, 144, 168, 95]. The Phong illumination model also has application [72]. Later, we adopt the Lambertian reflectance model with a varying albedo field to model the effect of illumination.

- *Pose.* The issue of pose essentially amounts to a correspondence problem. If dense correspondences across poses are available and if a Lambertian reflectance model is further assumed, a rank-1 constraint is implied because theoretically, a 3D model can be recovered and used to render novel poses. However, recovering a 3D model from 2D images is a difficult task. There are two types of approaches for recovering 3D models from 2D images: model-based and image-based. Model-based approaches [72, 215, 224, 226] require explicit knowledge of prior 3D models, while image-based approaches [190, 194, 218, 219, 221] do not use prior 3D models. In general, model-based approaches [72, 215, 224, 226] register the 2D face image to 3D models that are given beforehand. In [215, 226], a generative face model is deformed through bundle adjustment to fit 2D images. In [224], a generative face model is used to regularize the 3D model recovered using the Structure from motion (SfM) algorithm. In [72], 3D morphable models are constructed based on many prior 3D models. There are mainly three types of image-based approaches: SfM [190, 194], visual hull [218, 221], and light field rendering [219, 216] methods. The SfM approach [190] works with sparse correspondence and does not reliably recover the 3D model amenable for practical use. The visual hull methods [218, 221] assume that the shape of the object is convex, which is not always satisfied by the human face, and also require accurate calibration information. The light field rendering methods [219, 216] relax the requirement of calibration by a fine quantization of the pose space and recover a novel view by sampling the captured data that form the so-called light field. Later in 5, we propose an image-based method with no prior 3D models used. It handles a given set of views through an analysis analogous to the light field concept. However, no novel poses are rendered.

- *Identity.* One straightforward method to describe the identity is through discrete class labels. However, using this discrete description it is impossible to establish a link between objects used in the training and testing stages in terms of the identity. An alternative way is to associate the labels with continuous-valued features, which are regarded as an identity signatures. One good example is to use subspace encoding [50, 64], where linear generalization is assumed to incorporate the fact that all human faces are similar. Once the subspace basis are learned from the training set, they are used to characterize the gallery/probe set, thus enabling the required generalization capability.

Face recognition under illumination variation

Face recognition under illumination variation is a very challenging problem. The key is to successfully separate the illumination source from the observed appearance. Once separated, what remains is illuminant-invariant and appropriate for recognition. In addition to illumination variation, various issues embedded in the recognition setting make recognition even more difficult. We follow the FERET recognition protocol introduced in [60]. Assuming the availability of the following three sets, namely one training set, one gallery set, and one probe set, the recognition algorithm learns from the training set the characteristic features, associates descriptive features with the objects in the gallery set, and determines the identity for the objects in the probe set. Different recognition settings can be formed in terms of identity and illumination overlaps among the training, gallery, and probe sets. The most difficult setting, which is the focus of Chapter 4, is obviously the one in which there is no overlap at all among the three sets in terms of both identity and illumination, except the identity overlap between the gallery and probe sets. In this setting, generalizations from known illumination to unknown illumination and from known identities to unknown identities are particularly desired.

Existing approaches can be grouped into three streams: subspace methods, reflectance-model methods, and 3D-model-based methods. (i) The first approach is very popular for the recognition problem. After removing the first three eigenvectors, PCA was reported to be more robust to illumination variation than the ordinary PCA or the 'Eigenface' approach [64]. The 'Fisherface' approach [44, 77] used LDA to handle illumination variations. In general, subspace learning methods are able to capture the generic face space and thus recognize new objects not present in the training set. The disadvantage is that subspace learning is actually tuned to the lighting conditions of the training set; therefore if the illumination conditions are not similar among the training, gallery, and probe sets, recognition performance may not be acceptable. (ii) The second approach [144, 75, 161, 84, 90, 93] employs a Lambertian reflectance model with a varying albedo field, mostly ignoring both attached and cast shadows. The main disadvantage of this approach is the lack of generalization from known objects to unknown objects, with the exception of [84, 90]. In [84], Shashua and Raviv used an ideal-class assumption. All objects belonging to the ideal class are assumed to have the same shape. The work of Zhang and Samaras [90] utilized the regularity of the harmonic image exemplars to perform face recognition under varying light. (iii) The third approach employs 3D models. The 'Eigenhead' approach [71] assumes that the 3D geometry (or 3D depth information) of any face lies in a linear space spanned by the 3D geometry of the training ensemble and uses a constant albedo field. The morphable model approach [72] is based on a synthesis-and-analysis strategy. It is able to handle both illumination and pose variations with illumination directions specified. The weakness of the 3D model approaches is that they require 3D models and complicated fitting algorithms.

Face recognition under pose variation

As mentioned earlier, pose variation essentially amounts to a correspondence problem. Unfortunately, finding correspondences is a very difficult task and, therefore there exists no subspace based on an appearance representation when confronted with pose variation. Approaches to face recognition under pose variation [75, 76, 81] avoid the correspondence problem by sampling the continuous pose space into a set of poses, *v.i.z.* storing multiple images at different poses for each person at least in the training set. In [81], view-based 'Eigenfaces' are learned from the training set and used for recognition. In [75], a denser sampling is used to cover the pose space. However, as [75] uses object-specific images, appearances belonging to a novel object (i.e. not in the training set) cannot be handled. In [76], the concept of light field [219] is used to characterize the continuous pose space. 'Eigen' light fields are learnt from the training set. However, the implementation of [76] still discretizes the pose space and recognition can be based on probe images at poses in the discretized set. One should note that the light field is not related to variation in illumination.

Face recognition under illumination and pose variations

Approaches to handling both illumination and pose variations include [72, 77, 88, 89, 94]. The approach [72] uses 3D morphable models to characterize the human faces. Both geometry and texture are linearly spanned by those of the training ensemble consisting of 3D prior models. It is able to handle both illumination and pose variations. Its only weakness is a complicated fitting algorithm. Recently, a fitting algorithm more efficient than suggested in [72] is proposed in [83]. In [77], the Fisher light field is proposed to handle both illumination and pose variations, where the light field is used to cover the pose variation and the LDA to cover the illumination variation. Since discriminant analysis is just a statistical analysis tool which minimizes the within-class scatter while maximizing the between-class scatter and has no relationship with any physical illumination model, it is doubtable if discriminant analysis is able to generalize to new lighting conditions. Instead, this generalization may be inferior because discriminant analysis tends to overly tune to the lighting conditions in the training set. The 'Tensorface' approach [88, 89] uses a multilinear analysis to handle various factors such as identity, illumination, pose, and expression. The factors of identity and illumination are suitable for linear analysis, as evidenced by the 'Eigenface' approach (assuming a fixed illumination and a fixed pose) and the subspace induced by the Lambertian model, respectively. However, the factor of expression is arguably amenable for linear analysis and the factor of pose is not amenable for linear analysis. In [94], preliminary results are reported by first warping the albedo and surface normal fields at the desired pose and then performing recognition as usual.

Facial aging

While studying the role played by these external factors in affecting face recognition is crucial, it is important to study the role played by natural phenomenon such as facial aging. Aging effects on human faces manifest in different forms in different ages. While aging effects are manifested more in terms of changes in the cranium's shape during one's younger years, they are manifested more in terms of wrinkles and other skin artifacts during one's older years. Here, we provide a brief overview of the literature on facial aging.

Pittenger and Shaw [140] characterized the growth of human faces as a viscal-elastic event and proposed shear & strain transformations to model the changes in the shape of face profiles due to growth. They studied the effects of shear and strain transformations on the perceived age. O'Toole et al. [139] applied a standard facial caricaturing algorithm to three dimensional models of faces and reported an increase in the perceived age of faces when facial creases were exaggerated into wrinkles and a decrease when such creases were de-emphasized.

Lanitis et al. [136] proposed a method for simulating aging effects on face images. On a database of age progressive images of individuals each under 30 years of age, they used a combined shape-intensity model to represent faces. They modeled age as a quadratic function of the PCA coefficients extracted from the model parameters. They reported results on experiments such as estimating the age of an individual from his/her face image; simulating aging effects on face images etc. In [137], Lanitis *et al.* used a similar framework as defined in [136] on a similar data set and evaluated the performance of three age classifiers: the first was a quadratic function of the model parameters; the second was based on the distribution of model parameters; and the third was based on supervised and unsupervised neural networks trained on the model parameters.

Tiddeman et al. [141] developed a model for aging face images by transforming facial textures. Face images were represented in terms of 2D shape vectors and pixel intensities. They developed prototype faces by averaging the 2D shape vectors and pixel intensities across a set of face images under each age group. To age a face image, they superimposed the difference in 2D shape vectors and pixel intensities of the prototype faces on to the face image. Further, they simulated wrinkles in face images by employing locally weighted wavelet functions at different scales and orientations and thereby enhanced the edge amplitudes. Their experimental evaluation reported significant increase in the perceived age of subjects. Wu et.al. [142] came up with a dynamic model to simulate wrinkles in 3D facial animation and skin aging. They represented skin deformations as plastic-visco-elastic processes and generated permanent wrinkles through a simulation of inelastic skin deformations. Givens et.al. [135] analyzed the role of various co-variates such as age, gender, expression, facial hair etc in affecting recognition and noted that older faces were easily recognized by three face recognition algorithms.

2.2.2 Face recognition from multiple stills or videos

In this section, we review related literature on face recognition from multiple still images, or from video sequences. Since visual tracking is an integrated part in video-based recognition, we also briefly review the literature on tracking in the end.

Three properties

It is obvious that multiple still images or a video sequence can be regarded as a single still image in a degenerate manner [103, 107, 117, 119, 120]. More specifically, suppose that we have a single-still-image-based FR algorithm $\mathcal{A}$ (or the base algorithm) by some means, we can construct a recognition algorithm based on multiple still images or a video sequence by combining multiple base algorithms denoted by $\mathcal{A}_i$'s. Each A_i takes a different single image as input, coming from the multiple still images or video sequences. The combination rule can be ad hoc chosen to be additive, multiplicative, and so on.

However, the fused algorithms completely neglect additional properties possessed by multiple still images or video sequences, which are not present in a still image. In particular, three properties manifest themselves, which motivated various approaches recently proposed in the literature.

1 [$P1$: **Set of observations**]. This property is directly utilized by the fused algorithms. One main disadvantage may be the *ad hoc* nation of the combination rule. However, theoretical analysis based on a set of observations can be principally derived. For example, a set of observations can be sum-

marized using quantities like matrix, probability density function, manifold, etc. Hence, corresponding knowledge can be utilized to match two sets.

2 [*P*2: **Temporal continuity/Dynamics**]. Successive frames in the video sequences are continuous in the temporal dimension. Such continuity, coming from facial expression, geometric continuity related to head and/or camera movement, or photometric continuity related to changes in illumination, provides an additional constraint for modeling face appearance. In particular, temporal continuity can be further characterized using kinematics. For example, facial expression and head movement when an individual participates certain activity result in structured changes in face appearance. Modeling of such a structured change (or dynamics) further regularizes FR.

3 [*P*3: **3D model**]. This means that we are able to reconstruct a 3D model from a group of still images and a video sequence. Recognition can then be based on the 3D model. Using the 3D model provides possible invariance to pose and illumination.

Clearly, the first and third properties are shared by multiple still images and video sequences. The second property is solely possessed by video sequences.

Below, we review various face recognition approaches utilizing these properties in one or more ways. Generally speaking, the newly designed algorithms are better in terms of recognition performance, computational efficiency, etc.

P1: Approaches utilizing set of observations

Four rules of summarizing a set of observations have been presented. In general, different data representations are utilized to describe multiple observations and corresponding distance functions based on the presentations are invoked for recognition.

One image or several images

Algorithms designed by representing a set of observations into one image or several images and then applying the combination rules are essentially still-image-based and hence are not reviewed here.

Matrix

Yamaguchi *el al.* [121] proposed the so-called *Mutual Subspace Method* (MSM) method. In this method, the matrix representation is used and the similarity function between two matrices is defined as the angle between two subspaces of the matrices (also referred to as principal angle or canonical correlation coefficient). Suppose that the columns of $\mathtt{X}$ and $\mathtt{Y}$ represent two subspaces $\mathtt{U_X}$ and $\mathtt{U_Y}$, the principle angle θ between the two subspaces is defined as

$$\cos(\theta) = \max_{\mathtt{u} \in \mathtt{U_X}} \max_{\mathtt{v} \in \mathtt{U_Y}} \frac{\mathtt{u}^T \mathtt{v}}{\sqrt{\mathtt{u}^T \mathtt{u}}\sqrt{\mathtt{v}^T \mathtt{v}}}. \tag{2.12}$$

It can be shown that the principle angle θ is equal to the largest singular value of the matrix $\mathtt{U}_\mathtt{X}^\mathtt{T}\mathtt{U}_\mathtt{Y}$ where $\mathtt{U}_\mathtt{X}$ and $\mathtt{U}_\mathtt{Y}$ are orthogonal matrices encoding the column bases of the $\mathtt{X}$ and $\mathtt{Y}$ matrices, respectively.

In general, the leading singular values of the matrices $\mathtt{U}_\mathtt{X}^\mathtt{T}\mathtt{U}_\mathtt{Y}$ defines a series of principal angles $\{\theta_k\}$'s.

$$\cos(\theta_k) = \max_{\mathtt{u}\in\mathtt{U}_\mathtt{X}} \max_{\mathtt{v}\in\mathtt{U}_\mathtt{Y}} \frac{\mathtt{u}^\mathtt{T}\mathtt{v}}{\sqrt{\mathtt{u}^\mathtt{T}\mathtt{u}}\sqrt{\mathtt{v}^\mathtt{T}\mathtt{v}}} \tag{2.13}$$

subject to:

$$\mathtt{u}^\mathtt{T}\mathtt{u}_i = 0, \mathtt{v}^\mathtt{T}\mathtt{v}_i = 0,\ i = 1, 2, \ldots, k-1. \tag{2.14}$$

Yamaguchi *el al.* [121] recorded a database of 101 individuals posing variation in facial expression and pose. They discovered that the MSM method is more robust to noisy input image or face normalization error than the still-image-based method that is referred to as conventional subspace method (CSM) in [121]. The similarity function of the MSM method is more stable and consistent than that of the CSM method.

Wolf and Shashua [275] extended the computation of the principal angles into the RKHS. Kernel principal angles between two matrices $\mathtt{X}$ and $\mathtt{Y}$ are then based on their 'kernelized' versions $\phi(\mathtt{X})$ and $\phi(\mathtt{Y})$. A 'kernelized' matrix $\phi(\mathtt{X})$ of $\mathtt{X} = [\mathtt{x}_1, \mathtt{x}_2, \ldots, \mathtt{x}_n]$ is defined as $\phi(\mathtt{X}) = [\phi(\mathtt{x}_1), \phi(\mathtt{x}_2), \ldots, \phi(\mathtt{x}_n)]$. The key is to evaluate the matrix $\mathtt{U}_{\phi(\mathtt{X})}^\mathtt{T}\mathtt{U}_{\phi(\mathtt{Y})}$ defined in RKHS. In [275], Wolf and Shashua showed the computation using the 'kernel trick'.

Another contribution of Wolf and Shashua [275] is that they further proposed a positive kernel function taking matrix as input. Given such a kernel function, it can be readily plugged into a classification scheme such as a support vector machine (SVM) [18]. Face recognition using multiple still images, coming from a tracked sequence, were studied and the proposed kernel principal angels slightly outperforms other non-kernel versions.

Zhou [278] systematically investigated the kernel functions taking matrix as input (also referred to as matrix kernels). More specifically, the following two functions are kernel functions.

$$k_\bullet(\mathtt{X}, \mathtt{Y}) = tr(\mathtt{X}^\mathtt{T}\mathtt{Y}),\ k_\star(\mathtt{X}, \mathtt{Y}) = det(\mathtt{X}^\mathtt{T}\mathtt{Y}), \tag{2.15}$$

where tr and det are matrix trace and determinant. They are called as matrix trace and determinant kernels. Using them as building blocks, Zhou [278] constructed more kernels based on the column basis matrix, the 'kernelized' matrix, and the column basis matrix of the 'kernelized' matrix.

$$k_{\mathtt{U}\bullet}(\mathtt{X}, \mathtt{Y}) = tr(\mathtt{U}_\mathtt{X}^\mathtt{T}\mathtt{U}_\mathtt{Y}),\ k_{\mathtt{U}\star}(\mathtt{X}, \mathtt{Y}) = det(\mathtt{U}_\mathtt{X}^\mathtt{T}\mathtt{U}_\mathtt{Y}), \tag{2.16}$$

$$k_{\phi\bullet}(\mathtt{X}, \mathtt{Y}) = tr(\phi(\mathtt{X})^\mathtt{T}\phi(\mathtt{Y})),\ k_{\phi\star}(\mathtt{X}, \mathtt{Y}) = det(\phi(\mathtt{X})^\mathtt{T}\phi(\mathtt{Y})), \tag{2.17}$$

$$k_{U_{\phi\bullet}}(X, Y) = tr(U_{\phi(X)}^T U_{\phi(Y)}),\ k_{U_{\phi\star}}(X, Y) = det(U_{\phi(X)}^T U_{\phi(Y)}). \tag{2.18}$$

Probability density function (PDF)

Shakhnarovich *et al.* [118] used multivariate normal density for summarizing face appearances and the Kullback-Leibler (KL) divergence or relative entropy for recognition. The KL divergence between two Gaussian densities $p_1 = N(\mu_1, \Sigma_1)$ and $p_2 = N(\mu_2, \Sigma_2)$ can be explicitly computed as

$$\begin{aligned} KL(p_1||p_2) &= \int_{\mathbf{x}} p_1(\mathbf{x}) \log \frac{p_1(\mathbf{x})}{p_2(\mathbf{x})} d\mathbf{x} \\ &= \frac{1}{2} log(\frac{|\Sigma_2|}{|\Sigma_1|}) + (\mu_1 - \mu_2)^T \Sigma_2^{-1} (\mu_1 - \mu_2) \\ &\quad + \frac{1}{2} tr(\Sigma_1 \Sigma_2^{-1}) - \frac{d}{2}, \end{aligned} \tag{2.19}$$

where d is the dimensionality of the data. One disadvantage of the KL divergence is that it is asymmetric. To make it symmetric, they used $KL(p_1||p_2) + KL(p_2||p_1)$. Shakhnoarovich *et al.* [118] achieved better performance than the MSM approach by Yamaguchi *el al.* [121] on a dataset including 29 subjects.

Other than the KL divergence, probabilistic distance measures such as Chernoff distance and Bhattacharyya distance can also be used. The Chernoff distance is defined and computed in the case of normal density as:

$$\begin{aligned} J_C(p_1, p_2) &= -\log\{\int_{\mathbf{x}} p_1^{\alpha_2}(\mathbf{x}) p_2^{\alpha_1}(\mathbf{x}) d\mathbf{x}\} \\ &= \frac{1}{2}\alpha_1\alpha_2(\mu_1 - \mu_2)^T [\alpha_1\Sigma_1 + \alpha_2\Sigma_2]^{-1} (\mu_1 - \mu_2) \\ &\quad + \frac{1}{2} \log \frac{|\alpha_1\Sigma_1 + \alpha_2\Sigma_2|}{|\Sigma_1|^{\alpha_1} |\Sigma_2|^{\alpha_2}}, \end{aligned} \tag{2.20}$$

where $\alpha_1 > 0, \alpha_2 > 0$ and $\alpha_1 + \alpha_2 = 1$. When $\alpha_1 = \alpha_2 = 1/2$, the Chernoff distance reduces to the Bhattacharyya distance.

In [265], Jebara and Kondon proposed probability product kernel function

$$k(p_1, p_2) = \int_{\mathbf{x}} p_1^r(\mathbf{x}) p_2^r(\mathbf{x}) d\mathbf{x},\ r > 0. \tag{2.21}$$

When $r = 1/2$, the kernel function k reduces to the so-called Bhattacharyya kernel since it is related to the Bhattacharyya distance. When $r = 1$, the kernel function k reduces to the so-called expected likelihood kernel. In practice, we can simply use the kernel function k as a similarity function.

However, the Gaussian assumption can be ineffective when modeling the nonlinear face appearance manifold. In [277] (also Chapter 7), Zhou and Chellappa modeled the nonlinearity through a different approach: kernel methods.

Since a nonlinear function is used, albeit in an implicit fashion, Zhou and Chellappa [277] investigated their uses in a different space. To be specific, analytic expressions for probabilistic distances that account for nonlinearity or high-order statistical characteristics of the data are derived. On a dataset involving subjects presenting appearances with pose and illumination variations, the probabilistic distance measures performed better than their non-kernel counterparts.

Recently, Arandjelović and Cipolla [98] used resistor-average distance (RAD) for video-based recognition.

$$RAD(p_1, p_2) = (KL(p_1||p_2)^{-1} + KL(p_2||p_1)^{-1})^{-1}. \tag{2.22}$$

Further, computation of the RAD was conducted on the RKHS to absorb non-linearity of face manifold. Some robust techniques such as synthesizing images to account for small localization errors and RANSAC algorithms to reject outliers were introduced to achieve improved performance. They [99] further extended their work to use the symmetric KL divergence distance between two mixture-of-Gaussian densities.

Manifold

Fitzgibbon and Zisserman [104] proposed to compute a joint manifold distance to cluster appearances. A manifold is captured by subspace analysis which is fully specified by a mean and a set of basis vectors. For example, a manifold $\mathcal{P}$ can be represented as

$$\mathcal{P} = \{\mathtt{m}_p + \mathtt{B}_p\mathtt{u} | \mathtt{u} \in \mathcal{U}\} \tag{2.23}$$

where $\mathtt{m}_p$ is the mean and $\mathtt{B}_p$ encodes the basis vectors. In addition, the authors invoked affine transformation to overcome geometric deformation. The joint manifold distance between $\mathcal{P}$ and $\mathcal{Q}$ is defined as

$$\begin{aligned} d(\mathcal{P}, \mathcal{Q}) &= \min_{\mathtt{u},\mathtt{v},\mathtt{a},\mathtt{b}} ||T(\mathtt{m}_p + \mathtt{B}_p\mathtt{u}, \mathtt{a}) - T(\mathtt{m}_q + \mathtt{B}_q\mathtt{v}, \mathtt{b})||^2 + \\ & \qquad E(\mathtt{a}) + E(\mathtt{b}) + E(\mathtt{u}) + E(\mathtt{v}), \end{aligned} \tag{2.24}$$

where $T(\mathtt{x}, \mathtt{a})$ transforms image $\mathtt{x}$ using the affine parameter $\mathtt{a}$ and $E(\mathtt{a})$ is the prior cost incurred by invoking the parameter $\mathtt{a}$.

In experiments, Fitzgibbon and Zisserman [104] performed automatic clustering of faces in feature-length movies. To reduce the lighting effect, the face images are high-pass filtered before subject to a clustering step. The authors reported that sequence-to-sequence matching presents a dramatic computational speedup when compared with pairwise image-to-image matching.

Identity surface is a manifold, proposed by Li *et al.* in [114], that depicts face appearances presented in multiple poses. The pose is parameterized by yaw α and tilt θ. Face image at (α, θ) is first fitted to a 3D point distribution model and an active appearance model. After pose estimation, the face appearance is warped to a canonical view to provide a pose-free representation from which a nonlinear discriminatory feature vector is extracted. Suppose that the feature vector is denoted by $\mathtt{f}$, the function $\mathtt{f}(\alpha, \theta)$ defines the identity surface that is pose-parameterized. In practice, since only a discrete set of views are available, the identity surface is approximated by piece-wise planes. The manifold distance between two manifolds $\mathcal{P} = \{\mathtt{f}_p(\alpha, \theta)\}$ and $\mathcal{Q} = \{\mathtt{f}_q(\alpha, \theta)\}$ is defined as

$$d(\mathcal{Q}, \mathcal{P}) = \int_\alpha \int_\theta w(\alpha, \theta) d(\mathtt{f}_q(\alpha, \theta), \mathtt{f}_p(\alpha, \theta)) d\alpha d\theta. \tag{2.25}$$

where $w(\alpha, \theta)$ is a weight function.

A video sequence corresponds to a trajectory traced out in the identity surface. Suppose that video frames sample the pose space at $\{\alpha_j, \theta_j\}$, the following distance $\sum_j w_j d(\mathtt{f}_q(\alpha_j, \theta_j), \mathtt{f}_p(\alpha_j, \theta_j))$ is used for video-based FR. In the experiments, 12 subjects were involved and a 100% recognition accuracy was achieved.

P2: Approaches utilizing temporal continuity/dynamics

Simultaneous tracking and recognition is an approach proposed by Zhou *et al.* [129] that systematically studied how to incorporate temporal continuity in video-based recognition. Zhou *et al.* modeled two tasks involved, namely tracking and recognition, in a probabilistic framework. A time series model is used, with the state vector (n_t, θ_t) where n_t is the identity variable and θ_t is the tracking parameter, and the observation $\mathbf{y}_t$ (i.e. the video frame). The time series model is fully specified by the state transition probability $p(n_t, \theta_t | n_{t-1}, \theta_{t-1})$ and the observational likelihood $p(\mathbf{y}_t | \theta_t, n_t)$. This is covered in detail in Chapter 10.

In the work of Zhou *et al.* [129], in addition to the case that the gallery consists of one still image per individual, they also extended the approach to handle video sequence in the gallery set. Representative exemplars are learned from the gallery video sequences to depict individuals. Then simultaneous tracking and recognition was invoked to handle video sequences in the probe set. Li and Chellappa [112] also proposed an approach somewhat similar to [129]. In [112], only tracking was implemented using SIS and recognition scores were subsequently derived based on tracking results.

Lee *et al.* [109] performed video-based face recognition using probabilistic appearance manifolds. The main motivation is to model appearances under pose variation, i.e., a generic appearance manifold consists of several pose manifolds. Since each pose manifold is represented using a linear subspace, the overall appearance manifold is approximated by piecewise linear subspaces. The learning procedure is based on face exemplars extracted from a video sequence. K-means clustering is first applied and then for each cluster principal component analysis is used for subspace characterization.

In addition, the transition probabilities between pose manifolds are also learned. The temporal continuity is directly captured by the transition probabilities. In general, the transition probabilities between neighboring poses (such as frontal pose to left pose) are higher than those between far-apart poses (such as left pose to right pose). Recognition also reduces to computing posterior distribution.

In experiments, Lee *et al.* compared three methods that use temporal information differently: the proposed method with learned transition matrix, the proposed method with uniform transition matrix (meaning that temporal continuity is lost), and majority voting. The proposed method with learned transition matrix achieved a significantly better performance than the other two methods. Recently, Lee and Kriegman [110] extended [109] by learning the appearance manifold from a testing video sequence in an online fashion.

Liu and Chen [115] used adaptive hidden Markov model (HMM) to depict the dynamics. HMM is a statistical tool to model time series. Usually, the HMM is denoted by $\lambda = (\mathtt{A}, \mathtt{B}, \pi)$, where $\mathtt{A}$ is the state transition probability matrix, $\mathtt{B}$ is the observation PDF, and π is the initial state distribution. Given a probe video sequence $\mathtt{Y}$, its identity is determined as

$$\hat{n} = \arg \max_{1,2,\ldots,N} = p(\mathtt{Y}|\lambda_n), \tag{2.26}$$

where $p(\mathtt{Y}|\lambda_n)$ is the likelihood of observing the video sequence $\mathtt{Y}$ given the model λ_n. In addition, when certain contains hold, HMM λ_n was adapted to accommodate the appearance changes in the probe video sequence that results in improved modeling over time. Experimental results on various datasets demonstrated the advantages of using the adaptive HMM.

Aggarwal *et al.* [100] proposed a system identification approach for video-based FR. The face sequence is treated as a first-order auto-regressive and moving averaging (ARMA) random process.

$$\theta_{t+1} = \mathtt{A}\theta_t + \mathtt{v}_t, \;\; \mathtt{y}_t = \mathtt{C}\theta_t + \mathtt{w}_t, \tag{2.27}$$

where $\mathtt{v}_t \sim \mathcal{N}(0, \mathtt{Q})$ and $\mathtt{w}_t \sim \mathcal{N}(0, \mathtt{R})$. System identification is equivalent to estimating the parameters $\mathtt{A}$, $\mathtt{C}$, $\mathtt{Q}$, and $\mathtt{R}$ from the observations $\{\mathtt{y}_1, \mathtt{y}_2, \ldots, \mathtt{y}_T\}$. Once system is identified or each video sequence is associated with its parameters, video-to-video recognition uses various distance metrics constructed based on the parameters. Promising experimental results (over 90%) were reported when significant pose and expression variations are present in the video sequences.

Facial expression analysis is also related to temporal continuity/dynamics, but not directly related to FR. Examples of expression analysis include [45, 62]. A review of face expression analysis is beyond the scope of this chapter.

P3: Approaches utilizing 3D model

There is a large body of literature on SfM. However, the current SfM algorithms do not reliably reconstruct the 3D face model. There are three difficulties in the SfM algorithm. The first lies in the ill-posed nature of the perspective camera model that results in instability of the SfM solution. The second is that the face model is not a truly rigid model especially when facial expressions and other deformations are present. The final difficulty is related to the input to the SfM algorithm. This is usually a sparse set of feature points provided by a tracking algorithm that itself has many flaws. Interpolation from a sparse set of feature points to a dense set is very inaccurate.

To relieve the first difficulty, orthographic and paraperspective models are used to approximate the perspective camera model. Under such approximate models, the ill-posed problem becomes well-posed. In Tomasi and Kanade [194], the orthographic model was used and a matrix factorization principle was discovered. The factorization principle was extended to the paraperspective camera model in Poelman and Kanade [223]. Factorization under uncertainty was considered in [175, 182].

The second difficulty is often resolved by imposing a subspace constraint on the face model. Bregler *et al.* [176] proposed to regularize the nonrigid face model by using the linear constrain. It was shown that factorization can be still be obtained. Brand [175] considered such factorization under uncertainty. Xiao *et al.* [228] discovered a closed form solution to nonrigid shape and motion recovery.

Interpolation from a sparse set to a dense depth map is always a difficult task. To overcome this, a dense face model is used instead of interpolation. However, the dense face model is only a generic model and hence may not be appropriate for a specific individual. Bundle adjustment [215, 226] is a method that adjust the generic model directly to accommodate the video observation. Roy-Chowdhury and Chellappa [224] took a different approach for combining the 3D face model recovered from the SfM algorithm with the generic face model. Jebara and Pentland [108] regularized the SfM using a parameterized face model built from a training set.

The SfM algorithm mainly recovers the geometric component of the face model, i.e., the depth value of every pixel. Its photometric component is naively set to the appearance in one reference video frame. Image-based rendering method, on the other hand, directly recovers the photometric component of the 3D model. Light field rendering [216, 219] in fact bypasses the stage of recovering the photometric of the 3D model but rather recovers the novel views directly. The light field rendering methods [216, 219] relax the requirement of calibration by a fine quantization of the pose space and recover a novel view by sampling the captured data that form the so-called light field. The 'eigen' light field approach developed by Gross *et al.* [76] assumes a subspace assumption of the light field. In Zhou and Chellappa [97] (described in detail in Chapter 5), the light field subspace and the illumination subspace are combined to arrive at a bilinear analysis. Another line of research relates to 3D model recovery using the visual hull methods [218, 221]. But, the visual hull method assumes that the shape of the object is convex, which is not always satisfied by the human face, and also requires accurate calibration information. Direct use of visual hull for FR is not found in the literature.

To characterize both the geometric and photometric components of the 3D face model, Blanz and Vetter [72] fitted a 3D morphable model to a single still image. The 3D morphable model uses a linear combination of dense 3D models and texture maps. In principle, the 3D morphable model can be fitted to multiple images. The 3D morphable model can be thought of as an extension of 2D active appearance model [212] to 3D, but the 3D morphable model uses dense 3D models. Xiao *et al.* [229] proposed to combine a linear combination of 3D sparse model and a 2D appearance model.

Although there is significant interest in recovering the 3D model, directly performing FR using the 3D model is a recent trend [101, 116, 102]. Blanz and Vetter [72] implicitly did so by using the combining coefficients for recognition. Beumier and Acheroy [101] conducted matching based on 2D sections of the facial surface. Mavridis *et al.* [116] used 3D+color camera to perform face recognition. Bronstein *et al.* [102] used a 3D face model for compensating the effect of facial expression in face recognition. However, the above approaches use the 3D range data as input. Because in this chapter we are mainly interested in face recognition from multiple still images or video sequence, a thorough review of face recognition based on 3D range data is beyond its scope.

Future approaches from multiple stills or videos

Thus far, we reviewed the approaches that utilize the three properties. Although they usually achieved good recognition performance, they have their own assumptions or limitations. For example, the Gaussian distribution used in Shakhnoarovich *et al.* [118] is easily violated by pose and illumination variations. The HMM used in Liu and Chen [115] poses a strong constraint on the change of face appearance that is not satisfied by video sequences that contain an arbitrarily moving face.

In this section, we forecast possible new approaches. These new approaches either arise from new representation for more than one still image or extend the capability of the existing approaches.

New representation

In the matrix representation, multiple observations are encoded using a matrix. In other words, each observation is an image that is 'vectorized'. The 'vectorization' operator ignores the spatial relationship of the pixels.

To fully characterize the spatial relationship, a tensor can be used in lieu of matrix. Here, a tensor is understood as a 3-D array. Tensor representation is used in Vasilescu and Terzopoulos [88] to learn a generic model of the face appearance for all humans, at different views, and under different illuminating conditions, etc. However, comparing two tensors has not been investigated in the literature.

In principle, the PDF representation is very general. But in the experiment, a certain parametric form is assumed as in Shakhnoarovich *et al.* [118]. Other PDF forms can be employed. The key is to find an appropriate density that can model the face appearance. The same problem appears in the manifold description. With advances in manifold modeling, FR based on manifold can be improved too.

Using the training set

The training set is usually used to provide a generic model of face appearances of all humans, while the images in the gallery set is related to an individualized model of face appearance belonging to the same person. If there are enough observations, one can build an accurate model of the face for each individual in the gallery set and hence the knowledge of the training set is not necessary. If the number of images is not sufficiently large, one should combine the knowledge of a generic model with the individualized model to describe the identity signature.

3D model comparison

As mentioned earlier, comparison between two 3D models has not been fully investigated yet. In particular, direct comparison of the geometric component of the 3D model is rather difficult because it is nontrivial to recover the 3D model in the first place and the correspondence between two 3D models cannot be easily established.

Current approaches [229] warp the model to the frontal view and use the frontal 2D face appearance for recognition. However, these approaches are very sensitive to illumination variation. Generalized photometric stereo [95] can be incorporated into these approaches for a more accurate model.

The most sophisticated 3D model is to use a statistical description. In other words, both the geometric component g and the texture component f have their distributions, say $p(g)$ and $p(f)$, respectively. Such distributions can be learned from multiple still images/video sequence. Probabilistic matching can then be applied for FR.

Utilizing more than one property

Most of the approaches reviewed earlier utilize only one of the three properties. However, these properties are not overlapping in the sense that more than one property can be unified to achieve further improvements.

Probabilistic identity characterization [131] proposed in Chapter 11 is an example of integrating the properties $P1$ and $P2$, where FR from multiple still images and FR from video sequences are unified in one framework.

Statistical 3D model is a combination of properties $P1$ and $P3$, where the PDF part of property $P1$ is used.

Visual tracking

Roughly speaking, previous work on visual tracking can be divided into two groups with no clearly defined boundaries: deterministic tracking and stochastic tracking. Our approach combines the merits of both stochastic and deterministic tracking approaches in a unified framework using a particle filter. We give below a brief review of both approaches.

Deterministic approaches usually reduce to an optimization problem, e.g., minimizing an appropriate cost function. The definition of the cost function is a key issue. A common choice in the literature is the sum of squared distance (SSD) used in many optical flow approaches [180]. In fact, using SSD is equivalent to using a model where the noise obeys an iid Gaussian distribution; therefore this case can also be viewed as stochastic tracking. A gradient descent algorithm is most commonly used to find the minimum. Very often, only a local minimum can be reached. In [180], the cost function is defined as the SSD between the observation and a fixed template, and the motion is parameterized as affine. Hence the task is to find the affine parameter minimizing the cost function. Using a Taylor series expansion and keeping only the first-order terms, a linear prediction equation is obtained. It has been shown that for the affine case, the system matrix can be computed efficiently since a fixed template is used. Mean shift [178] is an alternative deterministic approach to visual tracking, where the cost function is derived from the color histogram.

Stochastic tracking approaches often reduce to an estimation problem, e.g., estimating the state for a time series state space model. Early works [171, 177] used the Kalman filter or its variants [1]. However, this restricts the type of model that can be used. Recently sequential Monte Carlo (SMC) algorithms [6, 179, 245, 248], which can model nonlinear/non-Gaussian cases, have gained prevalence in the tracking literature due in part to the CONDENSATION algorithm [183]. Stochastic tracking improves robustness over its deterministic counterpart by its capability for escaping the local minimum since the searching directions are for the most part random even though they are governed by a deterministic state transition model. Toyama and Blake [195] proposed a probabilistic paradigm for tracking with the following properties: Exemplars are learned from the raw training data and embedded in a mixture density; the kinematics is also learned; the likelihood measurement is constructed on a metric space. However, as far as computational load is concerned, stochastic algorithms in general are more intense. Note that the stochastic approaches can often be formulated as optimization problems.

PART II

FACE RECOGNITION UNDER VARIATIONS

Chapter 3

SYMMETRIC SHAPE FROM SHADING

The basic idea of shape from shading (SFS) is to infer the 2.5D structure of a object from its shading information/image [151, 153, 10]. In order to quantitatively extract such information, we need to assume a reflectance model under which the image (the only measurement we have) is generated from the 3D depth map. There are many illumination models available, which can be broadly categorized into diffuse reflectance models and specular models [156]. Among these models, the Lambertian model is the most popular one for diffuse reflectance and has been used extensively in the computer vision community for the SFS problem. Furthermore, in most SFS algorithms, the Lambertian model with known constant albedo is assumed (or the value of constant albedo can be easily extracted). Hence the goal of most SFS algorithms is to recover depth $z[x, y]$ or its partial derivatives (p, q) from shading information (image intensity I) using a standard image irradiance equation. Some SFS algorithms also include source-from-shading (estimation of the light source direction). Zhang et. al. divide SFS algorithms into four groups: minimization approaches, propagation approaches, local approaches and linear approaches [169]. Minimization approaches obtain the solution by minimizing an energy function. Propagation approaches propagate shape information from a set of surface points (e.g., singular points) to the whole image. Local approaches derive shape based on the assumption of surface type. Linear approaches compute the solution based on the linearization of the reflectance map.

The nature of SFS, inferring the 2.5D structure from limited observations (image intensities), makes it an ill-posed problem in general. This is sometimes reflected in an interesting phenomenon: many SFS algorithms can recover a 'good' depth map for re-rendering the given image at the same lighting and viewing angles, but not good enough for rendering images at different lighting or viewing angles[10]. However it is very attempting to apply SFS in many applications. For example, in face recognition we can apply SFS to infer the face shape information, and therefore simultaneously solve problems due to illumination and pose variations [29]. The advantage of SFS-based methods is that only one single input image is required when compared to other approaches proposed to solve the illumination and pose problems in face recognition. In addition, the soft facial skin makes SFS an appealing choice compared to other passive 3D recovery methods such as stereo where image correspondence needs to be established.

In order to handle complex face images, we describe a varying-albedo Lambertian model. This makes the SFS problem even more difficult. In this chapter, we examine the issues of traditional SFS algorithms and present a well-conditioned SFS algorithm by imposing the symmetry cue embedded in symmetric objects (e.g., face objects). The symmetry cue has also proven to be a powerful constraint in many face recognition methods, e.g., image synthesis for the illumination problem [91] and view-synthesis for the pose problem [75, 92]. An efficient implementation of these methods would be to store only the prototype images in the database and all testing images are converted/synthesized into the prototype images for facial ID matching. A *prototype image* I_p is defined as the frontal-lighted image of an frontal-view object.

This chapter is organized as follows [93]: The following section proposes using a varying-albedo Lambertian model and shows that it is a more realistic model. Section 3.1 addresses the symmetry cue and introduces the self-ratio image. Section 3.2 presents a general theory of symmetric SFS. In Section 3.3 we propose several computational algorithms to recover both shape and albedo and present experimental results. In addition, a model-based symmetric source-from-shading algorithm is presented for improved source estimation. In Section 3.4, we discuss the extensions of symmetric SFS and applications of symmetry cue for image synthesis and view-synthesis of face images.

3.1 Symmetry Cue: Improved Model and Unique Solution

3.1.1 Issues of traditional SFS

There exist two issues with traditional SFS algorithms: the first is whether there exists a unique solution and the second is how complex a surface could be dealt with.

Uniqueness issue

There exist many potential applications of SFS in various fields including computer vision, computer graphics, robotics, and pattern recognition etc. Unfortunately, SFS is an ill-posed problem in general [209]. To overcome this short-coming, additional constraints have been proposed. For example, the smoothness constraint on shape is the most commonly used [10]. One drawback of such a method is that it tends to over-smooth surface patches that have complex structure. More recent approaches drop this constraint and replace it with a physically meaningful constraint known as surface integrability [10, 149, 213].

In theory, the uniqueness in SFS can be achieved by directly exploiting the existence of a singular point, i.e., the brightest point ($I = 1$ and $P_s = 0, Q_s = 0$) [86, 148]. Uniqueness can also be guaranteed by enforcing the boundary condition (solutions to (p,q) on the boundary) if they are available [152]. The way to prove the uniqueness or construct a SFS algorithm (of propagation type) is to first identify the condition at the singular point or on the boundary and then propagate these solutions to the whole image. Following this basic idea, two similar approaches have been implemented [148, 147]. However in a recent survey paper [169], it has been shown that the algorithm by Bichsel and Pentland is outperformed by other two energy minimization approaches that do not guarantee a unique solution.

Model sufficiency issue

So far, we have focused on the uniqueness issue of SFS algorithms based on the assumption that the underlying physical model is Lambertian and the albedo is known and constant. The main reason why such a model is so popular in SFS literature is its simplicity. However, the widely used constant-albedo Lambertian model is just an approximate model for most objects in real world. And often the approximation is not good for real objects, for example, a human face. Human faces appear different not only due to the differences in the underlying 3D bone structures, but also due to the differences in texture. Moreover, different parts of a human face have different textures. Should we enforce a constant-albedo model on face objects and try to solve the SFS problem, poor depth estimates result since the depth parameter estimate needs to accommodate both depth and varying albedo. One proposed alternative is to segment out the cheek region and apply SFS to this region only with the assumption of constant albedo in this region. This approach would leave some region unresolved. Furthermore, we would like to have a direct method that explicitly models the albedo variation. As obtaining a unique solution to the SFS problem in general is difficult, we adopt a simple varying albedo Lambertian model which has been suggested before for problems other than SFS [154, 165]. We believe that this model has modest complexity, yet sufficient to represent many man-made and natural objects.

Conceptually, adopting a better reflectance model in SFS certainly helps us to solve real problems. But from earlier discussions on the uniqueness issue, we know that adding albedo as a free parameter makes SFS even more difficult to solve. Hence we need additional constraints such as symmetry and integrability.

3.1.2 The symmetry cue

Symmetry is very useful information that can be exploited in many computer vision problems including SFS for fully or partly symmetric objects [220]. Here we describe a direct method for incorporating this important cue: using self-ratio images [93]. By directly imposing the symmetry constraint, we prove that we can achieve a unique global solution which consists of unique local solutions at each point simultaneously obtained using the intensity information at that point and the surrounding local region under the assumption of a C^2 surface. This is different from existing propagation approaches which propagate the unique (known or easily obtained) solutions at singular points or on the boundary to other points. Independent of our research, a recent paper [162] presented a shape reconstruction method for symmetric objects exploring symmetric information. This method is based on integrating geometric and photometric information. It can be categorized as a propagation approach since it propagates the self-correspondence function over the whole image from a given pair of self-corresponding points. Though it offers a solution for general configuration of lighting and viewing conditions, a constant-albedo Lambertian surface was assumed.

In summary, imposing symmetry cue not only allows us to have improved modeling for symmetric objects but also guarantees a unique solution to the symmetric SFS problem.

3.1.3 The Lambertian model

As mentioned earlier, the most commonly used model in SFS literature is the Lambertian surface with constant albedo. However, it is not sufficient for many objects in real world. To illustrate this point, we use human face as an example. First, we demonstrate that SFS based on constant-albedo assumption does not recover the image (and the depth) accurately. Second, we show that a varying-albedo model is much better by comparing images synthesized under various illuminant directions using constant and varying albedos.

To facilitate our discussion, let us review some standard definitions used in SFS. The key equation is the *image irradiance equation* [151]:

$$I[x,y] = R(p[x,y], q[x,y]) \tag{3.1}$$

where $I[x,y]$ is the image intensity of the scene, R is the reflectance map, and $p[x,y], q[x,y]$ are the shape gradients (partial derivatives of the depth map $z[x,y]$). With the assumption of Lambertian surface reflection and a single, distant light source, we have

$$I = \rho \cos\theta,$$

or

$$I = \rho \frac{1 + pP_s + qQ_s}{\sqrt{1 + p^2 + q^2}\sqrt{1 + P_s^2 + Q_s^2}} \tag{3.2}$$

where θ is the angle between the outward normal to the surface $\vec{n} = (p, q, 1)$ and the negative illumination vector $-\vec{L} = (P_s, Q_s, 1)$ which represents the direction opposite to the distant light source, and ρ is the albedo. The surface orientation can also be represented using two angles, slant and tilt. Similarly the light source can be represented by illuminant direction slant and tilt. Even though the adoption of these angle terms as the standard in SFS literature is unfortunate since they are not mnemonic and frequently confused [10], we abide by the standard notations used in the SFS literature. More specifically, we use the angle terms *slant* and *tilt* exclusively for the illuminant direction throughout this book. The illuminant direction *slant* α is the angle between the negative $\vec{L}$ and the positive z-axis: $\alpha \in [0^0, 180^0]$; and the illuminant direction *tilt* τ is the angle between the negative $\vec{L}$ and the x-z plane: $\tau \in [-180^0, 180^0]$. To relate these angle terms to P_s and Q_s, we have $P_s = \tan\alpha\cos\tau$, $Q_s = \tan\alpha\sin\tau$.

SFS based on constant-albedo model

To test how efficient some of the existing SFS algorithms are for real objects such as faces, we applied three SFS algorithms to synthetic face images generated based on a constant-albedo Lambertian model, and more importantly real face images: (1) Zheng and Chellappa [170] (a minimization method based on the variational principle), (2) Wei and Hirzinger [164] (a minimization method based on radial basis expansion), and (3) Tsai and Shah [163] (a linear approach based on linearization of the local depth map). All these methods have been shown to be effective on many synthetic and a few real images. From our own experiments on real face images, we found that the simple linear approach [163] works best when a 3D generic face model is given as the initial shape. Possible reasons for the simple linear approach being the best are: 1) the Lambertian model with constant albedo is inherently inconsistent with real images which can be modeled much better as having a varying-albedo, causing systematic errors; 2) the linear (local) approach does not propagate errors, while the minimization approaches propagate errors, making algorithms walk away from a good solution, and 3) the underlying surface is complex but a good initial depth map is available.

In [170] the surface smoothness term usually employed in variational approaches was dropped. Instead, the image gradient constraint and surface integrability were imposed. This suggests that the algorithm can handle relatively complex surfaces and guarantees that the reconstructed surface is physically meaningful. Zheng and Chellappa [170] minimized the following energy function:

$$\iint \{[R(p,q) - I[x,y]]^2 + [R_x - I_x]^2] + [R_y - I_y]^2 + \mu[(p - z_x)^2 + (q - z_y)^2]\}dxdy$$

where R_x, R_y are the partial derivatives of the reflectance map R and μ is a weighting factor.

By decomposing the depth map $z[x,y]$ onto the radial basis functions Φ

$$z[x,y] = \sum_{k=1}^{N} w_k \Phi([x,y], t_k, s_k),$$

where t_k and s_k are the parameters of the basis functions, Wei and Hirzinger [164] transformed the problem of estimating (p,q) and z into that of estimating the parameters w_k. Estimation is then carried out by minimizing the energy function

$$\iint \{[R(p,q) - I[x,y]]^2 + \mu[s_1[x,y]z_{xx}^2 + s_2[x,y]z_{xy}^2 + s_3[x,y]z_{yy}^2]\}dxdy$$

where $s_i(x,y)$ $(i = 1,2,3)$ are empirical quadratic smoothness constraints which allow for integrating prior knowledge.

We have applied the local SFS algorithm [163] to dozens of real face images. The method is based on the linearization of the local depth z; hence the iteration at the n-th step is

$$z^n[x,y] = z^{n-1}[x,y] + \frac{-f(z^{n-1}[x,y])}{\frac{d}{dz[x,y]} f(z^{n-1}[x,y])},$$

where f is $I[x,y] - R(\frac{\partial z}{\partial x}, \frac{\partial z}{\partial y})$ and the partial derivatives are approximated by forward differences $\frac{\partial z}{\partial x} \approx z[x,y] - z[x-1,y]$ and $\frac{\partial z}{\partial y} \approx z[x,y] - z[x,y-1]$. In Figure 3.1, some of the best results using both synthetic and real face images is shown. In each case, we plot the given image (column 1) along with the recovered original image (column 2). In addition we plot the rendered prototype image (column 3) along with the real (approximate) prototype image (column 4). An ideal prototype image I_p can be expressed as:

$$I_p = \rho \frac{1}{\sqrt{1 + p^2 + q^2}}. \tag{3.3}$$

More results are presented in Figure 3.2 with the input image, recovered original image and the rendered prototype image arranged in the same row. Notice that large portions of the recovered images are unsatisfactory as the method does not render face-like images. An image size of 96×84 is used in these examples.

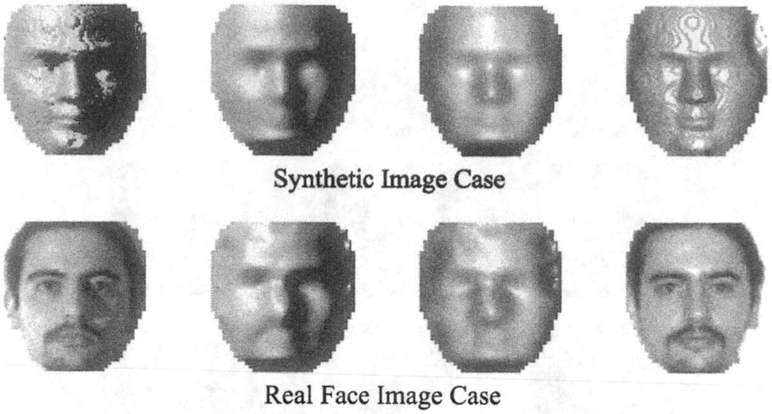

Figure 3.1. One of the best results obtained using the linear (local) SFS algorithm: First column: original input images; second column: recovered original images; third column: recovered prototype image; fourth column: real prototype image.

Most traditional SFS algorithms do not generate reliable depth estimates for real face images. There are two reasons behind this: 1) the complex shape of face objects making regularization-based SFS algorithms inappropriate; 2) the presence of regions with different albedos (reflecting properties) from various parts (cheek, lip, eye, eyelid, etc.) of face objects making the constant albedo assumption used in most SFS algorithms invalid.

A varying-albedo model

To overcome the constant albedo issue in modeling objects such as faces, we propose a varying-albedo Lambertian model, i.e., ρ is now a function $\rho[x, y]$. To show that varying-albedo Lambertian model is a better model, we compare the image synthesis results obtained using constant albedo and varying albedo assumptions. In Figure 3.3, image synthesis results are compared one-by-one, i.e., a pair of images (in the same column) are synthesized exactly the same way except that one is using a constant-albedo model and the other is using a varying-albedo model. To obtain a realistic albedo we use a real face image and a generic 3D face model (one example in Figure 3.10). To align this 3D model to the input image, we normalize both of them to the same size with two eye pairs kept in the same fixed positions. Because the input image and model are not from the same object, we can see that some parts of the synthesized images are not perfect, for example, around the nose region. The same 3D model will be used throughout this chapter and we will see similar behavior. This model has also been used for model-based synthesis for recognition [91].

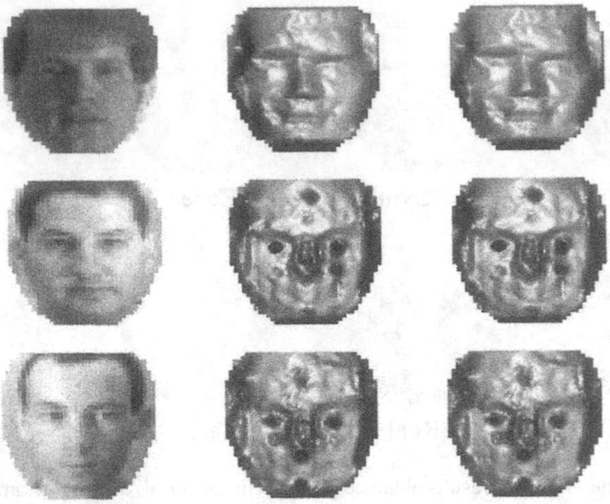

Figure 3.2. Some of the results obtained using the local SFS algorithm. First column: input images; second column: recovered images; third column: recovered prototype images.

It is worth noting that even the varying-albedo Lambertian model may not be sufficient due to the following reasons: 1) a real surface reflectance consists of both specular and diffuse components, 2) in practice the assumption of a single distant light source is not valid, and 3) the existence of noise in the image. Nevertheless Figure 3.3 clearly suggests that the varying-albedo model is much more realistic. However it introduces another unknown factor, the albedo $\rho[x, y]$. To cancel this additional parameter, we use the *self-ratio image*, described in the next sub-section.

3.1.4 Self-ratio image: the albedo-free image

Let us assume that we are dealing with a symmetric surface from now on. Obviously the background should be excluded since it need not be symmetric. Our definition of a symmetric surface is based on the following two equations (with an easily-understood coordinate system):

$$z[x, y] = z[-x, y], \tag{3.4}$$

and

$$\rho[x, y] = \rho[-x, y]. \tag{3.5}$$

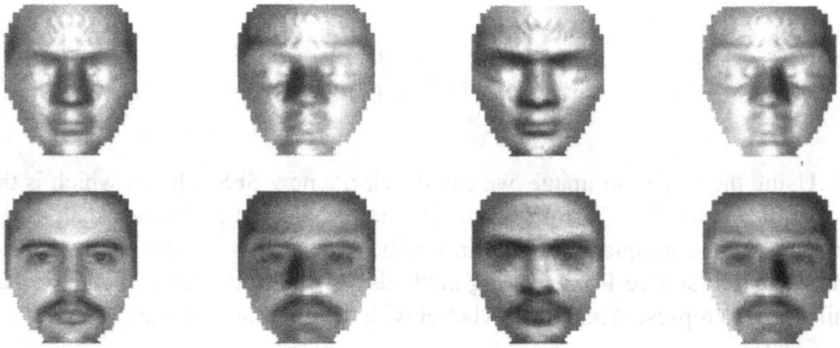

Figure 3.3. Image synthesis comparison under various lighting conditions. First row: constant-albedo Lambertian model; second row: varying-albedo Lambertian model.

One immediate property of a symmetric (differentiable) surface is that it has both anti-symmetric and symmetric gradients:

$$\begin{aligned} p[x,y] &= -p[-x,y] \\ q[x,y] &= q[-x,y] \end{aligned} \tag{3.6}$$

We introduce the concept of *self-ratio image* to cancel the effect of varying albedo. The idea of using two aligned images to construct a ratio has been explored by many researchers [154, 165, 84]. Here we extend the idea to a single image [93]. Let us substitute Eqs. (3.5), (3.6) into the equations for $I[x,y]$ and $I[-x,y]$, and then add them, giving

$$I[x,y] + I[-x,y] = 2\rho \frac{1 + qQ_s}{\sqrt{1+p^2+q^2}}. \tag{3.7}$$

Similarly we have

$$I[x,y] - I[-x,y] = 2\rho \frac{pP_s}{\sqrt{1+p^2+q^2}}. \tag{3.8}$$

The above symmetric relations have also been explored by other researchers [162]. To simplify the notation, let us define $I_+[x,y] = \frac{I[x,y]+I[-x,y]}{2}$ and $I_-[x,y] = \frac{I[x,y]-I[-x,y]}{2}$. Then the *self-ratio image* r_I can be defined as

$$r_I[x,y] = \frac{I_-[x,y]}{I_+[x,y]}, \tag{3.9}$$

which has a very simple expression

$$r_I[x, y] = \frac{pP_s}{1 + qQ_s}. \tag{3.10}$$

Using the self-ratio image, we can develop a new SFS scheme which is the topic of Section 3.2. The new SFS scheme has elegant properties such as the existence of a unique solution. In addition, self-ratio images help improve model-based source-from-shading methods. In summary, the self-ratio image allows us to represent real images better with the guarantee of a unique solution.

3.2 Theory of Symmetric Shape from Shading

In this section we show the main result of symmetric SFS. That is, there exists a unique solution to the symmetric SFS problem. Significantly, the unique global solution consists of unique local solutions at each point simultaneously obtained using the intensity information at that point and the surrounding local region under the assumption of a C^2 surface. To proceed, we start from the easiest case when the constant albedo is known. We then extend to the case where both the constant albedo and shape are unknown. Finally, we show that there exists a unique solution in the case of non-constant (piece-wise constant) albedo. In all cases, degenerate conditions, including special surfaces, lighting configurations and shadow points where point-wise symmetric SFS recovery can not be carried out, are indicated.

3.2.1 Basic notations

Denoting the right-hand-side of Eq. (3.10) as the *self-ratio symmetric reflectance map* $r_R(p, q)$, we arrive at the following *self-ratio image irradiance equation*:

$$r_I[x, y] = r_R(p[x, y], q[x, y]). \tag{3.11}$$

We refer the problem of recovering the shape information of a symmetric object using image irradiance equation (Eq. (3.1)) and self-ratio image irradiance equation (Eq. (3.11)) as symmetric SFS.

Explicit use of the symmetric property reduces the number of unknowns by half as suggested by Eqs. (3.5) and (3.6). In terms of the reflectance map, symmetric SFS has two reflectance maps $R(p, q)$ and $r_R(p, q)$ while SFS only has one $R(p, q)$. Figure 3.4 compares the two reflectance maps; one has a nonlinear structure and another has a linear structure (except on the singular point of a rational function).

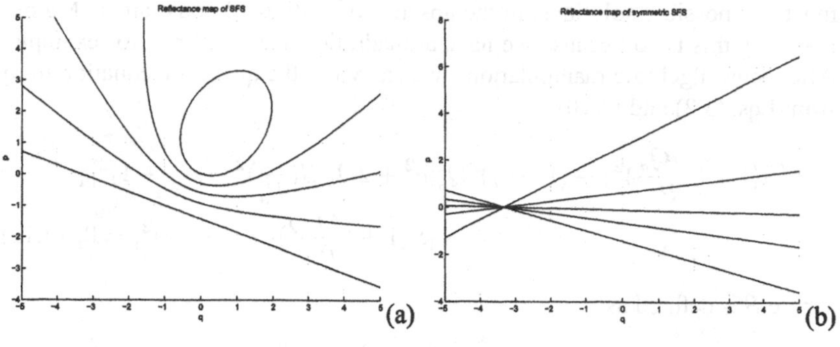

Figure 3.4. Comparison of reflectance maps: $\rho = 1$, $P_s = 0.3$ and $Q_s = 0.7$. The plot in (a) is the regular SFS reflectance map $R(p, q)$) while the plot in (b) is the symmetric reflectance map $r_R(p, q)$.

3.2.2 Symmetric SFS with constant albedo

When the albedo is constant across the whole image plane, symmetric SFS is a well-posed problem. More specifically, the shape information can be uniquely recovered at each point locally. In the following discussion, we first assume that the constant albedo value is known, and then discuss how to recover this unknown value.

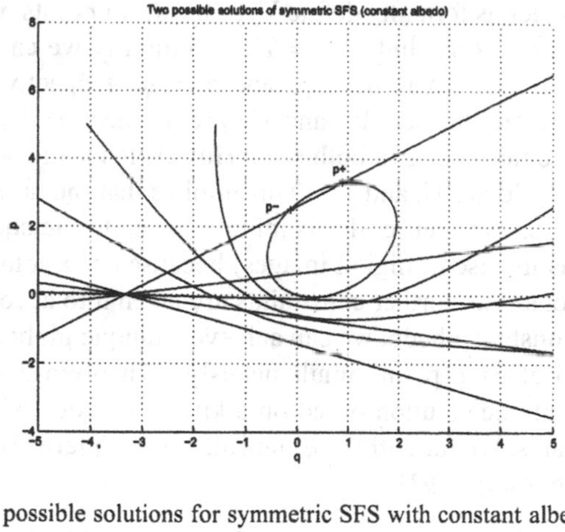

Figure 3.5. Two possible solutions for symmetric SFS with constant albedo. This is a direct result of combining plots (a) and (b) in Figure 3.4.

Since symmetric SFS has two reference maps (Figures 3.4(a) and (b)), it is obvious that the true solution to (p, q) must lie at the intersection of these two maps (Figure 3.5). Having at most two intersections implies that there are at most two possible solutions, in the absence of additional constraints. Mathematically this is so because we have a quadratic equation for q, for example. After some algebraic manipulations, we can write the quadratic equation for q from Eqs. (3.2) and (3.10)

$$[S(1+(\frac{r_I Q_s}{P_s})^2)-(1+r_I)^2Q_s^2]q^2+2Q_s[S(\frac{r_I}{P_s})^2-(r_I+1)^2]q$$
$$+[S(1+(\frac{r_I}{P_s})^2)-(1+r_I)^2]=0, \quad (3.12)$$

where S is defined as

$$S=(1+P_s^2+Q_s^2)(I/\rho)^2. \quad (3.13)$$

Note that once q is obtained, p is uniquely determined based on Eq. (3.10). To simplify the notation, we write the coefficients of second order, first order and the constant item of Eq. (3.12) as a, b and c. Now let us denote the two possible solutions for q as $q_+ = T1+T2$ and $q_- = T1-T2$, where $T1$, $T2$ are defined as $-\frac{b}{2a}$ and $\frac{\sqrt{b^2-4ac}}{2a}$ respectively.

For convenience, we can label a point based on the possible solutions for q at this point, for example, as V_- and/or V_+. It is possible that $q_+ = q_-$ at this point, i.e. Eq. (3.12) has double roots. In this case, we can give it a special label, for example, V_0. It should be clear that a point could have 2 labels V_- and V_+ ($q_- \neq q_+$), or one special label V_0 ($q_- = q_+$). To describe all the points in a image, let us formally define V_0 as the set of points where Eq. (3.12) has double roots, i.e., $\{[x,y] | q[x,y] = T1\}$. Similarly we can define V_+ and V_- as the set of points where $q = q_+$ and $q = q_-$ respectively ($q_- \neq q_+$). We should emphasize that sets V_- and V_+ are not necessarily exclusive, i.e., an image point could belong to both sets. However, V_0 and V_- are exclusive in our definitions. So are V_0 and V_+. This implies that the number of possible global solutions for symmetric SFS is infinite (or up to the square of the total number of pixels in case of digital images) because each point could have up to 2 local solutions if no further constraints are taken into account.

In case of a constant albedo, we can achieve a unique global solution which can be obtained at each point simultaneously. Theorem 3.1 states that we can obtain this unique solution based on a known albedo. Theorem 3.3 then shows that we can solve for both (p, q) and albedo uniquely. For proof of these theorems, please refer to [93].

THEOREM 3.1 With a known constant albedo ρ, the symmetric SFS problem has a unique solution which consists of unique local solutions at each point simultaneously obtained using the intensity information at that point and the surrounding local region for a symmetric C^2 surface z excluding the following special conditions:

- the surface z cannot have the following special form

$$z(x', y') = F(x') + G(y'), \tag{3.14}$$

where the new coordinate system x'-y'-z' is obtained by rotating the x-y plane about the z-axis by τ.

- slant angle $\alpha = 0^0$: $P_s = 0$ and $Q_s = 0$. Here the image is the *prototype image* and only the regular SFS algorithms can be applied.

- tilt angle $\tau = 90^0$: $P_s = 0$, and $Q_s \neq 0$. Here regular SFS can be applied at all points.

Moreover symmetric SFS cannot be performed at a shadow point (including both attached-shadow and cast-shadow). Here only regular SFS can be applied to its symmetric counterpart $(-x, y)$ if it is not a shadow point.

Determining the albedo value

Up to now, we have assumed that the constant albedo value is already known, as in most existing SFS algorithms. What about the unknown constant albedo case? In some special cases, we cannot recover both shape and albedo. For example, when we have a planar surface, albedo and shape cannot be uniquely determined if the true angle θ_t is not zero degrees or the true albedo value is not 1: $\rho_t cos(\theta_t) = \rho cos(\theta)$. On the other hand, determining the albedo can be trivial. For example, if we assume the existence of brightest points (I_{max}), immediately we have $\rho = I_{max}$, and $p = P_s, q = Q_s$ at these points.

Excluding these special cases, we show that we can uniquely determine the albedo value based on the following Lemma (see [93] for the proof):

LEMMA 3.2 Excluding the special conditions listed in Theorem 3.1, usually there is only one choice of albedo value ρ_t (the true value) which can satisfy

$$C_a(\rho) = 0, \tag{3.15}$$

where $C_a(\rho)$ is defined as $\int\int_{R_0} |\frac{\partial p(\rho)}{\partial y} - \frac{\partial q(\rho)}{\partial x}| dxdy$. The exceptions can occur only when the following configuration is true:

$$2\frac{\partial r'_I}{\partial x'}|_{x=0} = \frac{1}{S'}\frac{\partial S'}{\partial x'}|_{x=0}$$

or when the surface satisfies

$$q|_{x=0} = \textit{constant}.$$

where all measurements S', r'_I are in the new coordinate system x'-y'-z' which is obtained by rotating the x-y plane about the z-axis by τ.

One simple example of special conditions is when the surface is a symmetric planar surface. Combining Lemma 3.2 and Theorem 3.1, we have proved the following theorem:

THEOREM 3.3 For symmetric SFS, we can recover both the constant albedo value and the partial derivatives (p, q) uniquely except in those special conditions listed in Lemma 3.2 and Theorem 3.1.

3.2.3 Symmetric SFS with varying albedo

When albedo is not constant across the whole image plane, the situation becomes complicated since we need to recover both (p, q) and $\rho[x, y]$ from just one image. At first glance, it seems that we can just use the self-ratio image irradiance equation (Eq. (3.11)) and the smoothness constraint to recover the shape information as in ordinary SFS. But using the self-ratio image irradiance equation alone may not be a good idea. This is because all line contours (corresponding to different r_I's) are passing through the singular point ($p = 0, q = -\frac{1}{Q_s}$ in Figure 3.4(b)), and the true solution may be far away from the singular point. More specifically, enforcing the local smoothness constraint, or equivalently finding the solution (p, q) at a point $[x, y]$ in the linear reflectance map r_I that is closest to all lines corresponding to the local neighborhood of $[x, y]$, may not be stable.

Piece-wise constant albedo field

However if the albedo field has a special form, that is the field can be divided into regions each having a constant albedo, then it is possible to recover both shape and piece-wise albedo information. Expanding Theorem 3.3 and using the assumption that ρ is piece-wise constant, we can prove the following theorem:

THEOREM 3.4 If the depth z is a C^2 surface and the albedo field is piece-wise constant, then both the solutions for shape (p, q) and albedo ρ are unique except in those special conditions listed in Theorem 3.1 and Lemma 3.2.

Proof: The piece-wise constant albedo field can be fully described in two parts: 1) the partition $\mathcal{P}$ of the 2D albedo field which divides the whole field into connected regions $R_i^{\mathcal{P}}$ each having a constant albedo value (neighboring regions cannot have the same albedo value), and 2) the albedo value $\rho_{R_i^{\mathcal{P}}}$ for each region $R_i^{\mathcal{P}}$. To prove the theorem, we also need the following facts:

- *p, q, r_I and S are continuous across the whole image plane except at shadow points. So are a, b, c and T_1, T_2.*
- *I is piece-wise continuous except at shadow points, i.e., continuous within each constant albedo region $R_i^{\mathcal{P}}$. If the whole image plane has just one albedo value, then I is continuous.*

The proof is in two steps: we first show that the partition of the albedo field is unique, and we then prove that we can recover the albedo value in each constant-albedo region uniquely and hence (p, q) uniquely. Refer to [93] for more detail.

Arbitrary albedo field

For an albedo field which is purely continuous, the problem becomes difficult and we leave it as an open issue for future research.

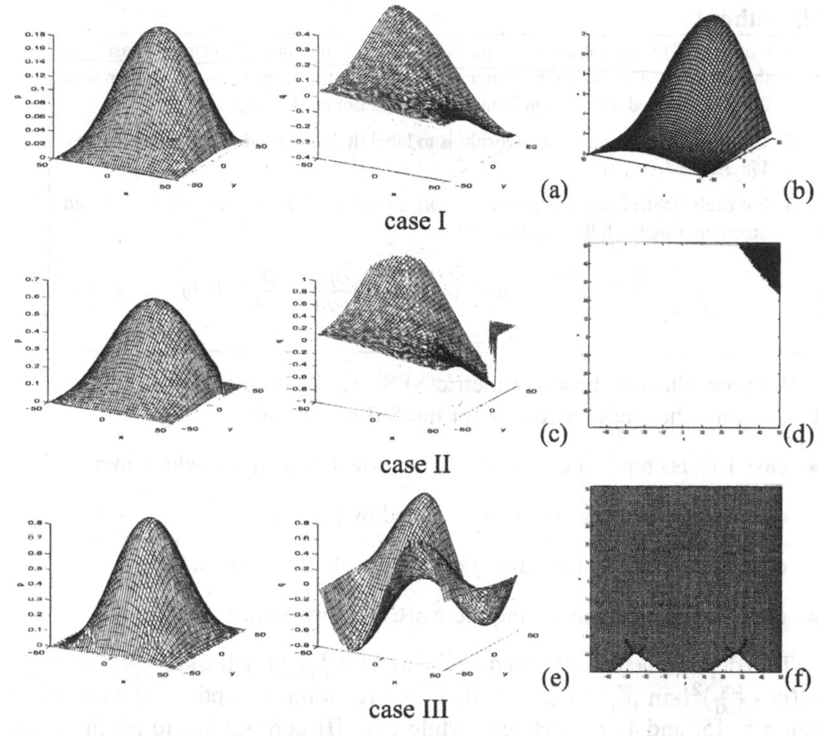

Figure 3.6. Simulation results for cases I, II and III (Algorithm I). The plots are arranged in rows with each row representing one case. All plots in the first column, i.e., the plots in (a), (c) and (e), are the recovered shape information (p, q). The plot in (b) is the underlying depth map of z_1, the plot in (d) is the shadow map (dark part), and the plot in (f) is the map for regions V_0, V_- and V_+. (The strange appearance of V_0 is due to the simple shrinking algorithm used to shrink the initial region V_0 based on the threshold. In ideal case, it would be just a curve with no branches. A similar appearance occurs in case IV (Figure 3.7).)

3.3 Symmetric SFS Algorithms and Experiments

In this section, we propose several simple computational algorithms to recover both shape and albedo based on the results derived in Section 3.2. We also carry out experiments using synthetic data and real images to test these algorithms.

3.3.1 Symmetric SFS with constant albedo

Albedo is known

Based on Theorem 3.1, we propose the following algorithm to perform shape recovery.

Algorithm I

1 Compute T_2 values at all image points and determine the zero locations based on thresholding. This procedure generates the V_0 set. If the set V_0 is empty, then step 2 can be omitted and the whole image plane is denoted by R_0.

2 Use component-connection algorithms to label the connected regions separated by V_0: R_i (i=$1, \ldots, m$).

3 For each labelled region R_i (i=$1, \ldots, m$), the choice between q_+ and q_- is based on comparing the following two values:

$$\int\int_{R_i} |\frac{\partial p_+}{\partial y} - \frac{\partial q_+}{\partial x}|dxdy \overset{?}{>} \int\int_{R_i} |\frac{\partial p_-}{\partial y} - \frac{\partial q_-}{\partial x}|dxdy \tag{3.16}$$

We now illustrate how symmetric SFS can be used to recover (p, q). We demonstrate the recovery results for the following cases:

- **case I** V_0 is empty and there are no shadow points in the whole image plane.
- **case II** V_0 is empty and there are shadow points.
- **case III** V_0 is not empty and there are no shadow points.
- **case IV** V_0 is not empty and there are shadow points.

Two depth functions are used: $z_1 = s_1(\cos \frac{x\pi}{100})(1 + 0.5 \sin \frac{y\pi}{100})^2$ and $z_2 = s_2(\cos \frac{x\pi}{100})^2(\sin \frac{y\pi}{100})$. Cases I, II, IV correspond to depth z_1 with scalar s_1 being 5, 15, and 40 respectively, while case III corresponds to depth z_2 with scalar s_2 being 25. The illumination angles in all cases are the same: $\alpha = 60^0$ and $\tau = 135^0$. In the examples which contain shadow points, we leave the shape information un-recovered at those shadow points and their symmetric counterparts.

Albedo is unknown

Based on Theorem 3.3, we have the following algorithm to recover both constant albedo and shape.

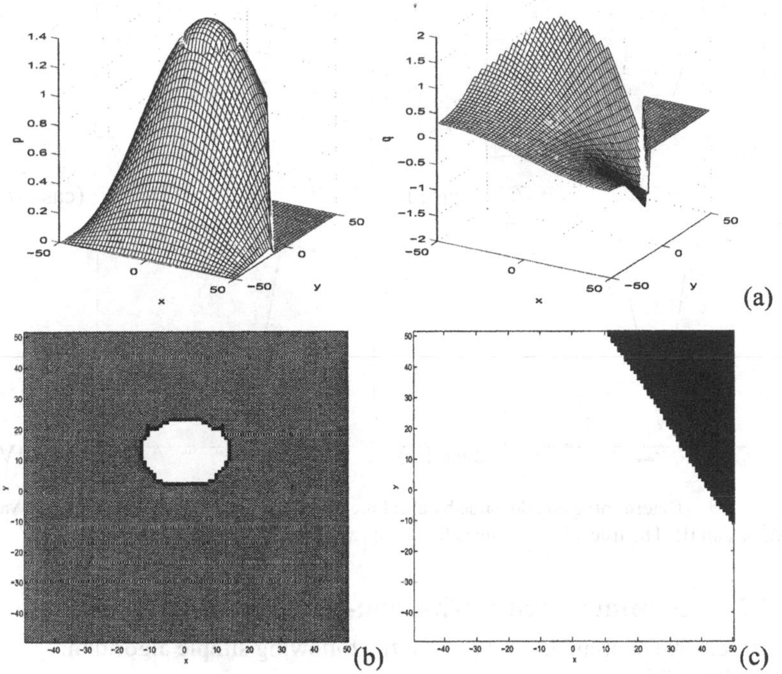

Figure 3.7. Simulation results for case IV (Algorithm I). The plot in (a) is the recovered shape information, the plot in (b) is the map for regions V_0, V_- and V_+, and the plot (c) is the shadow map (dark part).

Algorithm II

1 Hypothesize the value of the constant albedo ρ. For example, this can be done by simply sampling $[0, 1]$.

2 Apply Algorithm I with the hypothesized albedo value.

3 Compute $C_a(\rho)$: if $C_a(\rho) \leq$ threshold (theoretically this should be zero), we are done; otherwise, go to step 1 with a different hypothesis.

We verify this algorithm in the following simulations. The simulated data here are exactly the same as in previous experiments (Figs. 3.6 and 3.7) except that now the true albedo is 0.5 instead of 1. Figure 3.8 plots $\log(C_a(\rho) + 1)$ versus the hypothesized ρ values in all four cases. As can be seen, the minimum is always obtained at the true albedo value. Though ideally the minimum should be zero, in practice this is not the case due to numerical errors.

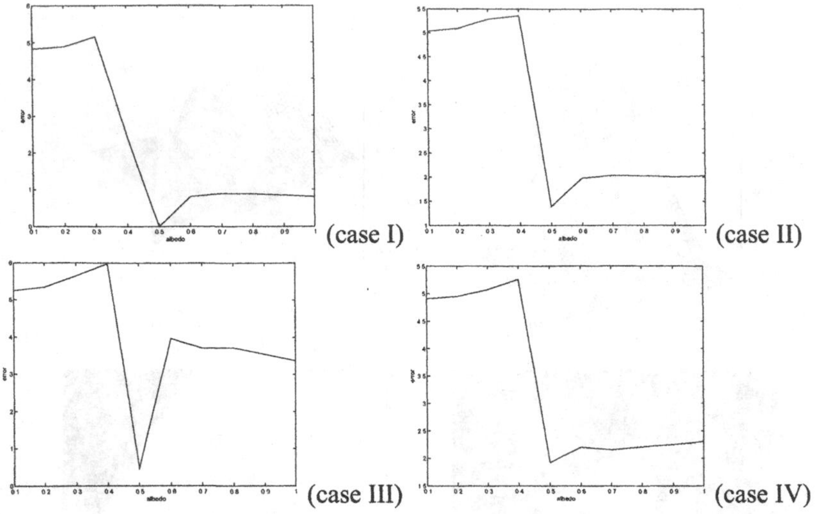

Figure 3.8. Determining albedo value by checking $\log(C_a(\rho) + 1)$ for a hypothesized ρ value (Algorithm II). The true albedo value is 0.5 in all cases.

3.3.2 Symmetric SFS with non-constant albedo

Based on Theorem 3.4, we present the following simple algorithm:

Algorithm III

1. Determine the partition $\mathcal{P}$ of the albedo field by finding the discontinuities of the image intensity field.
2. Hypothesize a possible value ρ_i for each region $R_i^{\mathcal{P}}$, and apply Algorithm I.
3. Compute $C_a(\rho[x,y])$ and $C_c(\rho[x,y])$ to determine if they are small enough so a different hypothesis is not needed. Here $C_c(\rho[x,y])$ is the measurement of surface discontinuity. $C_a(\rho[x,y])$ is a generalized version of $C_a(\rho)$ since $\rho[x,y]$ is not a constant any more:

$$C_a(\rho[x,y]) = \sum_i \int\int_{R_i^{\mathcal{P}}} |\frac{\partial p(\rho)}{\partial y} - \frac{\partial q(\rho)}{\partial x}| dxdy. \quad (3.17)$$

It should be noted that this simple algorithm is not robust since it depends on the assumption that discontinuities in image intensity only occur along the borders of the albedo partition, and in practice this is not true for digitized images of complex objects.

To verify this simple algorithm, we show a simple example (Figure 3.9) in which we first recover the simple albedo field (piecewise constant) and then recover the shape information. More specifically, we first use an image-histogram-based approach to segment the albedo field, and then apply algorithm

II to recover both shape and albedo. The simulated data here is very similar to depth function z_2, but we have a piece-wise constant albedo field with values 0.5, 0.8 and 1.

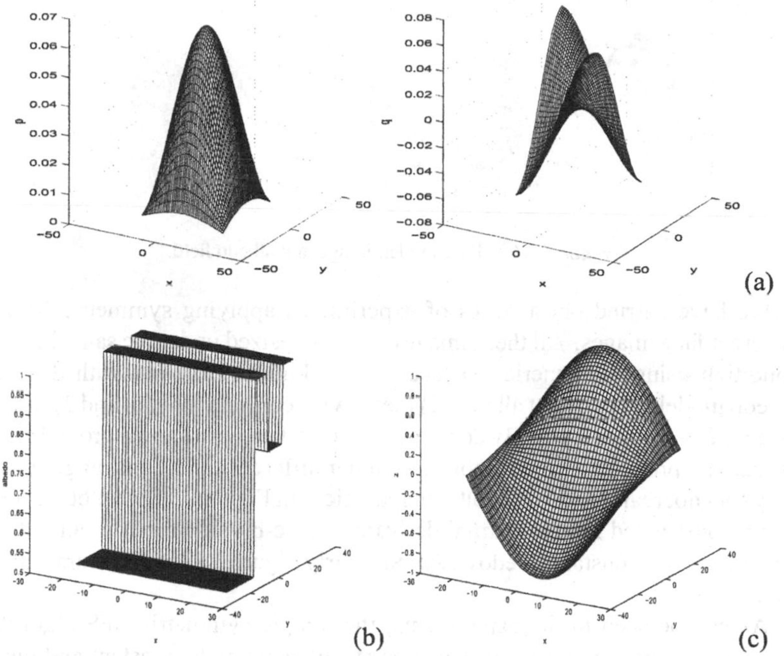

Figure 3.9. Simulation result for varying albedo symmetric SFS (Algorithm III). The plot in (a) is the recovered shape information (p, q), the plot in (b) is the recovered albedo field, and the plot in (c) is the true depth map.

3.3.3 Symmetric SFS for real complex images

We have proved that up to piece-wise-constant albedo case, we can recover both albedo and shape. And we have provided simulation results to demonstrate that capability. However, when it comes to real and complex objects, solving symmetric SFS is not trivial. A complex object could have both complicated shape and complex yet continuous albedo. From a theoretical point of view, we have not been able to prove the uniqueness of solution for such a general case. In other words, the proposed Algorithm III is not sufficient enough to handle these objects by recovering first the albedo and then the shape. To illustrate such a case, we plot in Figure 3.10 the albedo field computed using a real face image and a generic 3D model (the same pair is used in Figure 3.1). Clearly the albedo field is very complicated and we need to develop better algorithms. If the problem is somehow reduced to illumination-normalization, i.e., obtaining the prototype image from a given image, then it is possible without actually solving the shape information [91, 84].

Figure 3.10. Face model, image and albedo field.

We have carried out a series of experiments applying symmetric SFS to different face images. All these images are synthesized under the same lighting condition using the generic 3D face model (Figure 3.10) but with different albedo model: 1) constant albedo, 2) piece-wise constant albedo, and 3) natural face albedo (Figure 3.10). By constructing such data with known ground-truth, we can test proposed simple algorithms under different conditions ranging from easy (but not realistic) to difficult (but realistic). In Figure 3.11 we plot the input and reconstructed images, partial derivatives side-by-side for constant albedo and piece-wise constant albedo cases. Similarly Figure 3.12 is for natural albedo case.

As can be seen in the experiments, the simple symmetric SFS algorithm III is able to handle objects of complex (face) shape with constant and piece-wise constant albedos (Figure 3.11). And the results are perfect except in the shadow points (e.g., compare the original image and the reconstructed image in Figure 3.11(a),(b), and notice the reconstructed image (b) has unrecovered part due to the shadow map in Figure 3.11(d)) or their counterparts since we did not recover shape information at these points. However it is entirely possible to recover the shape information at these points by applying the regular SFS to their symmetric counterparts (if they are not shadow points) with known boundary conditions which are uniquely solved for using symmetric SFS [152]. A more practical and easy approach would be to interpolate information available. In the case of natural albedo field, algorithm III turns out to be not sufficient(Figure 3.12). The algorithm was able to recover a sensible piece-wise constant albedo field (Figure 3.12(b)) from the input image. But it is not equal to the original continuous albedo field (the right-most plot in Figure 3.10). The recovery of one partial derivative (right image in Figure 3.12(d)) is good compared to the true one (right image in Figure 3.12(c)). However, the re-

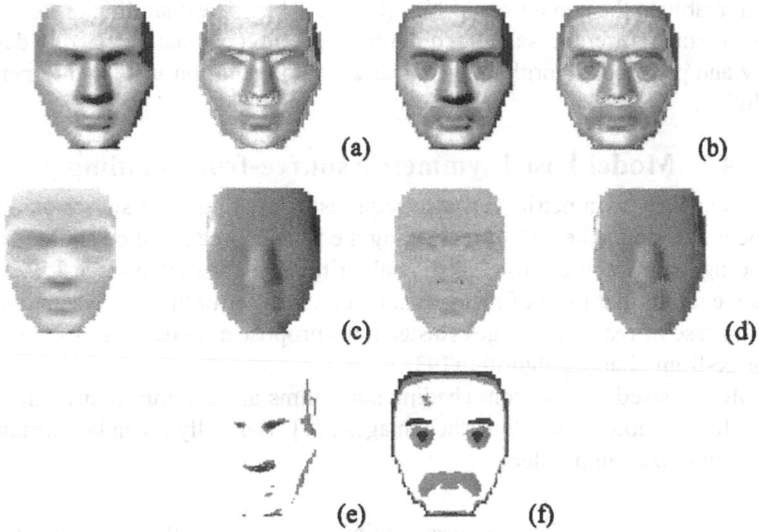

Figure 3.11. Face shape and image reconstruction results using symmetric SFS: the cases of constant albedo and piece-wise constant albedo. The plots in the first row are input images (left) and reconstructed images (right): (a) is for the constant albedo case, (b) is for the piece-wise albedo case. The plots in the second row are the true partial derivatives (c) and recovered partial derivatives (d). Plot (e) represents the shadow map in the input images which explains the holes in the reconstructed images. Plots (c), (d) and (e) are valid for both constant albedo and piece-wise constant albedo cases since they are the same. However, plot (f) is the recovered albedo filed only valid for the piece-wise constant albedo case.

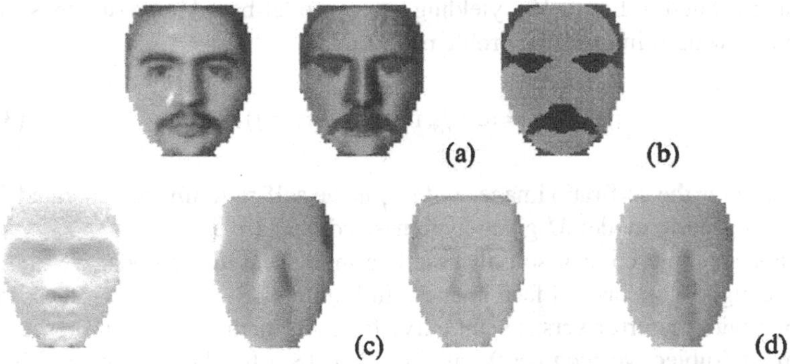

Figure 3.12. Face shape and image reconstruction result using symmetric SFS: the case of natural face albedo. The plots in (a) are input images (left) and reconstructed images (right). Plot (b) is the recovered albedo filed. The plots in the second row are the true partial derivatives (c) and recovered partial derivatives (d).

covery of the other partial derivative is not good. Hence the final result is not comparable to the previous two cases (Figure 3.11). The quantifiable algorithm performance differences among different cases suggest that we need to design new and practical algorithms which seek a good solution instead of a perfect solution.

3.3.4 Model-based symmetric source-from-shading

As in SFS, symmetric SFS also requires estimating light source as a pre-processing step. The task of recovering the light source is called source-from-shading. Many source-from-shading algorithms are available [155, 159, 170], but we found that most of them do not work well for both tilt and slant angles in the case of real face images. Instead, we propose a model-based symmetric source-from-shading algorithm [93].

Model-based source-from-shading algorithms are commonly used in practice, for example, in handling face images [71]. Basically it can be formulated as a minimization problem

$$(\alpha^*, \tau^*) = \arg_{\alpha,\tau} \min(I_M(\alpha, \tau)) - I)^2. \tag{3.18}$$

where I is the input image, and I_M is the image generated from a 3D generic shape M based on Lambertian model (Eq. (3.2)) with constant albedo given hypothesized α and τ. One advantage of using a 3D model is that we can take into account both attached-shadow and cast-shadow effects, which are not utilized in traditional statistics-based methods. Meanwhile, we notice that this method has one drawback, that is we are using a constant-albedo Lambertian model for objects such as face. We fix this problem by using the self-ratio image defined in Eq. (3.10), yielding a new model-based approach by solving the following minimization problem

$$(\alpha^*, \tau^*) = \arg_{\alpha,\tau} \min(r_{I_M}(\alpha, \tau)) - r_I)^2. \tag{3.19}$$

where r_I is the self-ratio image, and r_{I_M} is the self-ratio image generated from the 3D generic model M given hypothesized α and τ.

For a simple comparison of these two model-based methods, we ran both these algorithms on real face images. In Figure 3.13, we plot one face image along with the error-versus-slant curve for each method. As can be seen, the correct (subjective judgment) value of slant (8^0) has been recovered by the symmetric method (Eq. (3.19)). However, it is missed using (Eq. (3.18)). This new symmetric source-from-shading method has been successfully applied to more than 150 real face images as the pre-processing step prior to illumination-normalization for face recognition [91].

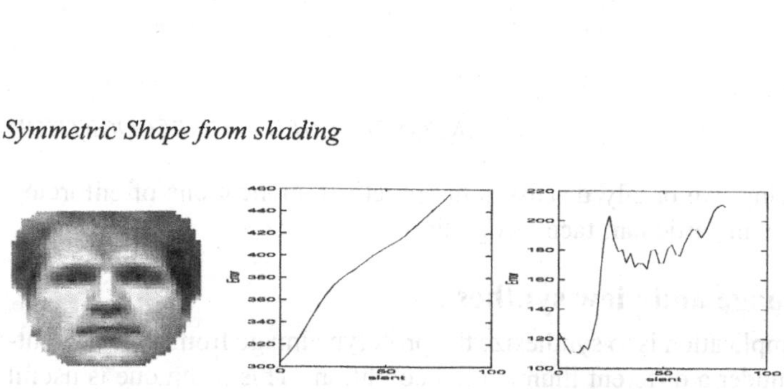

Figure 3.13. Comparison of model-based source-from-shading algorithms. The correct slant value was recovered using the algorithm (Eq. (3.19)) (right figure), while it was missed using algorithm (Eq. (3.18)) (middle figure).

3.4 Beyond Symmetric SFS

Using the self-ratio image, a new symmetric SFS scheme has been developed and proved to have a unique solution which can be obtained at each point simultaneously. The new symmetric SFS presented in this chapter has the following advantages over existing SFSs for symmetric objects:

- It not only has a unique solution for (p, q) but also a unique solution for albedo. Here the albedo can be either constant or piece-wise constant across the whole image plane. Significantly, the unique (global) solution can be obtained at each point simultaneously under usual conditions.

- Combining symmetric SFS and regular SFSs, unique solutions at shadow points can be obtained. More specifically, after recovering the unique solutions for (p, q) at lighted points, the regular SFS algorithms can be applied to the symmetric counterparts (which is lighted) of the shadow points. Since the boundary conditions (values at surrounding lighted points) are given, regular SFS is likely to be well-posed and have a unique solution [152].

- Compared to photometric stereo algorithms [166, 158], the registration problem of multiple images has been alleviated.

3.4.1 Statistical symmetric SFS

One interesting development along symmetric SFS is the so-called statistical symmetric SFS [74]. The relationship between this statistical symmetrical SFS and the symmetrical SFS proposed in this chapter is similar to the relationship between SFS and the statistical SFS [71]. Just as in [71], a sequence of laser-scanned range images of real human heads are used to transform the symmetric SFS problem into a parametric problem; hence, a more stable and easier-to-compute version of symmetric SFS.

So far we have been focusing on how to improve shape from shading by exploring the symmetry property of symmetric objects directly. The symmetry cue has also been applied successfully in other applications [91, 75, 92, 95].

In the following, we briefly discuss some practical applications of enforcing symmetry cue, in particular, face recognition.

3.4.2 Image and view synthesis

The first application is to synthesize the prototype image from a given front-view image under a different illumination condition. This technique is useful for improving the performance of existing face recognition systems when only one image is available [91]. Based on the assumption that all faces share a similar common shape, we can shorten the two-step procedure of obtaining the prototype image from a given image (1. given image to shape via SFS, 2. recovered shape to prototype image) to one direct step: image to prototype image with the aid of a generic 3D head model.

Comparing Eq. (3.7) and Eq. (3.3), we obtain

$$I_p[x,y] = \frac{K}{2(1+qQ_s)}(I[x,y] + I[-x,y]), \tag{3.20}$$

where K is a constant equal to $\sqrt{1+P_s^2+Q_s^2}$. This simple equation directly relates the prototype image I_p to $I[x,y]+I[x,-y]$ which is already available. It is worthwhile to point out that this *direct computation* of I_p from I offers the following advantages over the two-step procedure:

- There is no need to recover the varying albedo $\rho[x,y]$.
- There is no need to recover the *full* shape gradients (p,q).

The only parameter that needs to be recovered is the partial shape information q. Theoretically, we can use the symmetric SFS algorithm to compute this value. But as we discussed earlier, due to practical issues of using just one image, we approximate this value with the partial derivative of a 3D face model and use the self-ratio image equation (Eq. (3.9)) as a consistency checking tool [91]. A better way could be to deform the generic model based on image contour [106].

In Figure 3.14 we compare the results of rendering the prototype images using 1) local SFS and model-based source-from-shading and 2) direct computation based on SSFS plus a generic 3D face model and model-based symmetric source-from-shading. These results clearly indicate the superior quality of the prototype images rendered by direct computation.

For face object under out-of-plane rotation we can apply view-synthesis based on similar idea [92]. This can be done by first determining the 3D pose of the object and then rotating it back [106, 92]. In order to facilitate this procedure, we need the following lemma (see [92] for details):

LEMMA 3.5 Suppose that, after the underlying surface is rotated in the x-z plane about the y-axis by θ (anti-clock-wise), the partial gradients $(p[x,y], q[x,y])$

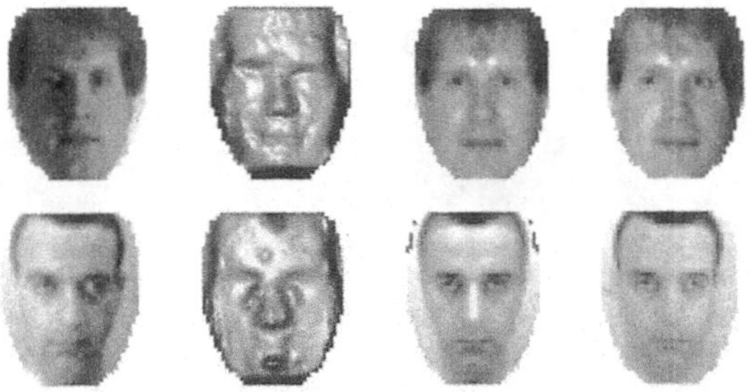

Figure 3.14. Image rendering comparison. All the original images are listed in the first column. The second column represents the prototype images rendered using the local SFS algorithm. Prototype images rendered with symmetric SFS are plotted in the third column. Finally, the fourth column represents real images which are close to the prototype images.

become $(p^\theta[x', y'], q^\theta[x', y'])$; then they are related by

$$\begin{aligned} p^\theta[x', y'] &= \tan(\theta + \theta_0) \\ q^\theta[x', y'] &= \frac{q[x,y]\cos\theta_0}{\cos(\theta+\theta_0)}, \end{aligned} \tag{3.21}$$

where $\tan\theta_0 = p[x, y]$.

In Figure 3.15, we illustrate the synthesized images under different rotations and illuminations (with a Lambertian model).

In [167], a method has been proposed to perform pose-normalization while the lighting condition is kept unchanged. For a given non-frontal view of a symmetric object under a non-frontal illumination, they first generate the mirror image of the object under the same illumination condition as the original view. They then apply view morphing technique to synthesis the frontal view image under the same illumination.

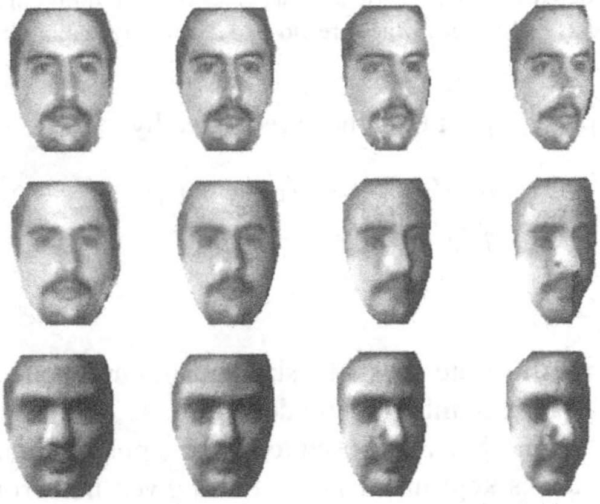

Figure 3.15. Rendering images under different rotations and illuminations using the generic face head. The images are arranged as follows: in the row direction (left to right) the images are rotated by the following angles: 5^0, 10^0, 25^0, and 35^0; in the column direction (top to bottom) images are illuminated under the following conditions: pure texture warping (no illumination imposed); ($\alpha = 0^0$); and ($\alpha = 30^0, \tau = 120^0$).

Chapter 4

GENERALIZED PHOTOMETRIC STEREO

We present a theory of generalized photometric stereo and its application to face recognition. In the first part, we present the generalized photometric stereo algorithm that is able to handle all appearances under different illuminations of all objects in a class, in particular the human face class, whereas the ordinary photometric stereo algorithm handles the appearances belonging to one object under different illuminations. In the second part, we evaluate this algorithm in its application to face recognition under illumination variation. Since this generalization is linear, the blending linear coefficients offer an illuminant-invariant identity signature.

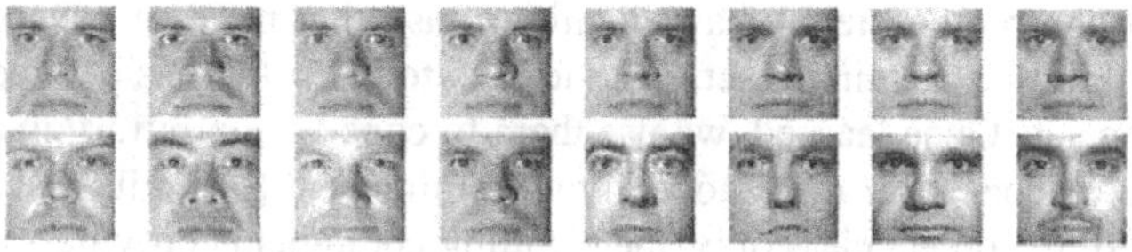

Figure 4.1. The top row displays an example of an *o*bject-specific ensemble, which contains images of one object under eight different light sources. This can be handled by the ordinary photometric stereo algorithm. The bottom row displays an example of a *c*lass-specific ensemble, which contains images of eight different objects illuminated by eight different lighting sources. This cannot be handled by the ordinary photometric stereo algorithm but can be handled by the proposed generalized photometric stereo algorithm. Imagery courtesy of [75].

Figure 4.1 motivates the proposed approach. The top row of Figure 4.1 displays one Yale object [75] under eight different light sources. This is an example of an *object-specific* ensemble. Photometric stereo algorithms [150, 161] take object-specific ensemble as input and recover the varying albedos and surface normals for the object, even assuming no knowledge of the illumination conditions. Here, by photometric stereo algorithm we mean any algorithm that utilizes a Lambertian reflectance model to describe the visual appearance and has a capability of recovering the albedos and surface normals involved in the reflectance model. However, ordinary photometric stereo algorithm cannot handle the images in the second row of Figure 4.1, where each image represents a different object under a different light source. This gives an example of a *class-specific* ensemble. The need to handle class-specific ensemble motivates us to propose a generalized photometric stereo approach.

As in ordinary photometric stereo algorithm, the generalized photometric stereo algorithm utilizes a Lambertain refletance model to represent the visual appearance. The significant difference between the ordinary and generalized photometric stereo algorithms lies in the image ensemble they analyze. The object-specific image ensemble that the ordinary photometric stereo algorithm analyzes consists of the appearances of one object under different illuminations while, in general, the class-specific image ensemble that the generalized photometric stereo algorithm analyzes consists of the appearances of different objects, with each object under a different illumination. Analysis of the latter image ensemble is very difficult. To further complicate the matter, the knowledge of the basis objects is also unknown and to be recovered. To this end, we introduce a *key assumption*: These different objects belong to one class (for example, the human face class) so that they are linearly spanned by a fixed number of basis objects. Generalized photometric stereo does not assume any knowledge of the lighting sources as well as the blending coefficients. Rather, the generalized photometric stereo approach actually recovers these parameters.

We evaluate the generalized photometric stereo algorithm in a face recognition application. The *key assumption* has two important implications. First, it fits with the requirement of a recognition task that needs a generalization capability built on a training set. The idea is to learn the basis objects from the training set. Once learned, we use them to cope with arbitrary images belonging to objects other than those in the training set. Secondly, because the bases are for the object class only, the blending coefficients provide an identity encoding that is invariant to illumination. We employ them for illumination-variant face recognition in the presence of a single light source, which results in good recognition performance. Up to now, the shadow pixels are excluded for computation. We further extend the above analysis to directly incorporate the nonlinearity in the Lambertian model that accounts for attached shadows. We validate this extension in the application of illumination-variant face recognition in the presence of multiple light sources.

Section 4.1 elaborates the generalized photometric stereo algorithm and addresses its issues and challenges. Sections 4.2 and 4.3 detail the face recognition setting and present experimental results using the PIE database. Section 4.2 focuses on face recognition in the presence of a single light source and Section 4.2 on multiple light sources.

4.1 Principle of Generalized Photometric Stereo

This section describes the generalized photometric stereo algorithm. We begin in Section 4.1.1 with a brief review of the related literature and highlight the advantages of the proposed approach. We list in Section 4.1.2 the setting and constraints. Then we present a method for recovering the albedos and surface normal for a class in Sections 4.1.3 and 4.1.4. Section 4.1.3 discusses the task of separating the illumination (*v.i.z.* finding the illuminant vector and the blending coefficient) from an arbitrary image, which is used in the recovery algorithm presented in Section 4.1.4.

4.1.1 Literature review and proposed approach

Recovery of albedos and surface normals has been studied in the computer vision community for a long time. Usually a Lambertian reflectance model, ignoring both attached and cast shadows, is employed. Early works from the SFS literature assume a constant albedo field: this assumption is not valid for many real objects and thus limits the practical applicability of the SFS algorithms. Early photometric stereo approaches also require the knowledge of lighting conditions, but such knowledge is hard to gather under uncontrolled scenarios. Recent research efforts [75, 150, 161, 84, 168, 93, 144, 143, 90] attempt to go beyond these restrictions by (i) using a varying albedo field, a more accurate model of the real world, and (ii) assuming no prior knowledge or requiring no control of the lighting sources. As a consequence, the complexity of the problem has also increased significantly.

If we fix the imaging geometry and only move the lighting source to illuminate one object, the observed images (ignoring the cast and attached shadows) lie in a subspace completely determined by three images illuminated by three independent lighting sources [161]. If an ambient component is added [168], this subspace becomes 4-D. If attached shadows are considered, the subspace dimension grows to infinity [145] but most of its energy is packed in a limited number of harmonic components, thereby leading to a low-dimensional subspace approximation [160, 144, 143]. However, all the photometric-stereo-type approaches (except [84, 90]) commonly restrict themselves to *object-specific* samples and cannot perform reconstruction using an ensemble of images belonging to different objects.

In this chapter, we present a generalized photometric stereo algorithm that is able to handle all appearances of all objects in a class, in particular the human face class. To this end, we impose a rank constraint (i.e. a linear generalization) on the albedos and surface normals of all human faces. We choose the human face as a working example because it naturally fits in our framework and is widely studied in the photometric stereo literature; however this does not pose any constraints in applying our algorithm to other appropriate cases.

We propose a rank constraint on the product of albedo and surface normal. The rank constraint enables us to accomplish a factorization of the observation matrix that decomposes a *class-specific* ensemble into a product of two matrices: one encoding the albedos and surfaces normals for a class of objects and the other encoding blending linear coefficients and lighting conditions. A *class-specific* ensemble consists of exemplar images of different objects with each under a different illumination, which is beyond what can be analyzed using bilinear techniques of [214]. Bilinear analysis requires exemplar images of different objects under the same set of illuminations. Because a factorization is always up to an invertible matrix, a full recovery of the albedos and surface normals is not a trivial task and requires additional constraints. We use two constraints: *surface integrability* and *face symmetry*.

The surface integrability constraint [10, 149, 213] has been used in several approaches [75, 168] to successfully recover albedo and shape. The symmetry constraint has also been employed in [162, 93] for face images. We present an approach to fusing these constraints to recover the *class-specific* albedos and surface normals, even in the presence of shadows. More importantly, this approach takes into account the effects of a varying albedo field by approximating the integrability terms using only the surface normals instead of the product of the albedos and the surface normals. Due to the nonlinearity embedded in the integrability terms, regular algorithms such as the steepest descent are inefficient. We derive a linearized algorithm to find the solution.

4.1.2 Setting and constraints

Photometric stereo

As reviewed in Chapter 2, an image, which a collection of d pixels $\{h_i, i = 1, ..., d\}$ that follow a Lambertian imaging model with a varying albedo field, can be written as

$$\mathtt{h}_{d\times 1} = \mathtt{T}_{d\times 3}\ \mathtt{s}_{3\times 1}. \tag{4.1}$$

In the above and for time being, we do not consider the shadow pixels and will deal with them later on. The index i corresponds to a spatial position $\mathtt{x} = (x, y)$. We will interchange both notations. For instance, we might also use $\mathtt{x} = 1, ..., d$.

In the case of photometric stereo, we have n images of the *same* object, say $\{\mathtt{h}_1, \mathtt{h}_2, \ldots, \mathtt{h}_n\}$, observed at a fixed pose illuminated by n different lighting sources, forming an *object-specific* ensemble. Simple algebraic manipulation gives:

$$\mathtt{H}_{d\times n} = [\Rightarrow_{i=1}^{n} \mathtt{h}_i] = \mathtt{T}[\Rightarrow_{i=1}^{n} \mathtt{s}_i] = \mathtt{T}_{d\times 3}\ \mathtt{S}_{3\times n}, \tag{4.2}$$

where $\mathtt{H}$ is the *observation matrix* and $\mathtt{S} = [\mathtt{s}_1, \mathtt{s}_2, \ldots, \mathtt{s}_n]$ encodes the information on the illuminants. Hence photometric stereo is rank-3 constrained.

Note that when shadow pixels are present, the above factorization is still valid if we are able to exclude them successfully.

The rank-3 constraint implies that, given at least three exemplar images for one object under three different independent illuminations, we can determine the identity of a new probe image by checking if it lies in the linear span of the three exemplar images. This requires capturing at least three images for one object in the gallery set, which might be prohibitive in practical scenarios. Note that in this recognition setting, there is no need for the training set; in other words, the training set is equivalent to the gallery set.

A typical recognition setting [60], however, assumes no identity overlap between the gallery set and the training set and often stores only one exemplar image for each object in the gallery set. However, the training set can have multiple images for one object. In order to generalize from the training set to the gallery and probe sets, we note that all images in the training, gallery, and probe sets belong to the same face class, which naturally leads to the rank constraint.

The rank constraint

The rank constraint is motivated by subspace analysis, which assumes that an image $\mathtt{h}$ is linearly spanned by basis images $\mathtt{h}_i$.

$$\mathtt{h} = \sum_{i=1}^{m} f_i \mathtt{h}_i. \tag{4.3}$$

Typically, the basis images are learned by PCA [64] using the images not necessarily illuminated from the same light source. This forces the learned basis images to cover variations in both identity and illumination, making it ineffective.

We impose the restriction of the same light source on the training images. As a consequence, the basis images can be expressed as

$$\mathtt{h}_i = \mathtt{T}_i \mathtt{s}. \tag{4.4}$$

because the basis image is a linear combination of the training images in PCA. Therefore, Eq. (4.3) becomes

$$\mathtt{h}_{d\times 1} = \mathtt{Ts} = \sum_{i=1}^{m} f_i \mathtt{h}_i = \sum_{i=1}^{m} f_i \mathtt{T}_i \mathtt{s} = \mathtt{W}_{d\times 3m}[\mathtt{f}_{m\times 1} \otimes \mathtt{s}_{3\times 1}], \tag{4.5}$$

where $\mathtt{W} = [\Rightarrow_{j=1}^{m} \mathtt{T}_j]$, $\mathtt{f} = [\Downarrow_{j=1}^{m} f_j]$, and $\otimes$ denotes the Kronecker (tensor) product. This leads to a two-factor bilinear analysis [214].

Because $\mathtt{s}$ is a free parameter, Eq. (4.5) is equivalent to imposing a rank constraint on the $\mathtt{T}$ matrix: any $\mathtt{T}$ matrix is a linear combination of some basis matrices $\{\mathtt{T}_1, \mathtt{T}_2, \ldots, \mathtt{T}_m\}$ coming from some m *basis objects*.

$$\mathtt{T}_{d\times 3} = \sum_{j=1}^{m} f_j \mathtt{T}_j. \tag{4.6}$$

Since the $\mathtt{W}$ matrix encodes all albedos and surface normals for a class of objects, we call it a *class-specific albedo-shape* matrix.

With the availability of n images $\{\mathtt{h}_1, \mathtt{h}_2, \ldots, \mathtt{h}_n\}$ for *different* objects, observed at a fixed pose illuminated by n *different* lighting sources, forming a *class-specific* ensemble, we have

$$\mathtt{H}_{d\times n} = [\Rightarrow_{i=1}^{n} \mathtt{h}_i] = \mathtt{W}[\Rightarrow_{i=1}^{n} (\mathtt{f}_i \otimes \mathtt{s}_i)] = \mathtt{W}_{d\times 3m}\mathtt{K}_{3m\times n}, \tag{4.7}$$

where $\mathtt{K} = [\Rightarrow_{i=1}^{n} (\mathtt{f}_i \otimes \mathtt{s}_i)]$. It is a rank-$3m$ problem, which combines the rank of 3 for the illumination and the rank of m for the identity.

One immediate goal is to estimate $\mathtt{W}$ and $\mathtt{K}$ from the observation matrix $\mathtt{H}$. The first step is to invoke an SVD factorization, $\mathtt{H} = \mathtt{U}\Lambda\mathtt{V}^{\mathsf{T}}$, and retain the top $3m$ components as $\mathtt{H} = \mathtt{U}_{3m}\Lambda_{3m}\mathtt{V}_{3m}^{\mathsf{T}} = \hat{\mathtt{W}}\,\hat{\mathtt{K}}$, where $\hat{\mathtt{W}} = \mathtt{U}_{3m}$ and $\hat{\mathtt{K}} = \Lambda_{3m}\mathtt{V}_{3m}^{\mathsf{T}}$. Thus, we can recover $\mathtt{W}$ and $\mathtt{K}$ up to an $3m \times 3m$ invertible matrix $\mathtt{R}$ with $\mathtt{W} = \hat{\mathtt{W}}\mathtt{R}$, $\mathtt{K} = \mathtt{R}^{-1}\hat{\mathtt{K}}$. Additional constraints are required to determine the $\mathtt{R}$ matrix. We will use the integrability and face symmetry constraints, both related to $\mathtt{W}$. In addition, the matrix $\mathtt{K}$ takes a special structure, i.e., each column vector of $\mathtt{K}$ is a tensor product between two vectors.

The integrability constraint

One common constraint used in SFS research is the integrability of the surface [149, 213, 168, 75]. Suppose that the surface function is $z = z_{(\mathbf{x})}$ with $\mathbf{x} = (x, y)$, we must have $\frac{\partial}{\partial x}\frac{\partial z}{\partial y} = \frac{\partial}{\partial y}\frac{\partial z}{\partial x}$. If given the unit surface normal vector $\mathtt{n}_{(\mathbf{x})} = [\hat{a}_{(\mathbf{x})}, \hat{b}_{(\mathbf{x})}, \hat{c}_{(\mathbf{x})}]^{\mathsf{T}}$ at pixel $\mathbf{x}$, the integrability constraint requires that

$$\frac{\partial}{\partial x}\frac{\hat{b}_{(\mathbf{x})}}{\hat{c}_{(\mathbf{x})}} = \frac{\partial}{\partial y}\frac{\hat{a}_{(\mathbf{x})}}{\hat{c}_{(\mathbf{x})}}. \tag{4.8}$$

Equivalently, with $\alpha_{(\mathbf{x})}$ defined as an integrability constraint term,

$$\alpha_{(\mathbf{x})} = \hat{c}_{(\mathbf{x})}\frac{\partial \hat{b}_{(\mathbf{x})}}{\partial x} - \hat{b}_{(\mathbf{x})}\frac{\partial \hat{c}_{(\mathbf{x})}}{\partial x} + \hat{a}_{(\mathbf{x})}\frac{\partial \hat{c}_{(\mathbf{x})}}{\partial y} - \hat{c}_{(\mathbf{x})}\frac{\partial \hat{a}_{(\mathbf{x})}}{\partial y} = 0. \tag{4.9}$$

If given the product of the albedo and the surface normal $\mathtt{t}_{(\mathbf{x})} = [a_{(\mathbf{x})}, b_{(\mathbf{x})}, c_{(\mathbf{x})}]^{\mathsf{T}}$ with $a_{(\mathbf{x})} = \rho_{(\mathbf{x})}\hat{a}_{(\mathbf{x})}$, $b_{(\mathbf{x})} = \rho_{(\mathbf{x})}\hat{b}_{(\mathbf{x})}$, and $c_{(\mathbf{x})} = \rho_{(\mathbf{x})}\hat{c}_{(\mathbf{x})}$, Eq. (4.9) still holds with $\hat{a}$, $\hat{b}$, and $\hat{c}$ replaced by a, b, and c, respectively. Practical algorithms approximate the partial derivatives by forward or backward differences or other differences with the inherent smoothness assumption. Hence, the approximations based on $\mathtt{t}_{(\mathbf{x})}$ are very rough especially at places where abrupt albedo variations exist (e.g. the boundaries of eyes, iris, eyebrow, etc.) since the smoothness assumption is seriously violated. We proceed to use $\mathtt{n}_{(\mathbf{x})}$ in order to remove this effect.

The face symmetry constraint

For a face image in a frontal view, one natural constraint is its symmetry about the central y-axis [93, 162]:

$$\rho_{(x,y)} = \rho_{(-x,y)}; \hat{a}_{(x,y)} = -\hat{a}_{(-x,y)}; \; \hat{b}_{(x,y)} = \hat{b}_{(-x,y)}; \; \hat{c}_{(x,y)} = \hat{c}_{(-x,y)}, \tag{4.10}$$

which is equivalent to, using $\mathbf{x} = (x, y)$ and its symmetric point $\bar{\mathbf{x}} = (-x, y)$,

$$a_{(\mathbf{x})} = -a_{(\bar{\mathbf{x}})}; \; b_{(\mathbf{x})} = b_{(\bar{\mathbf{x}})}; \; c_{(\mathbf{x})} = c_{(\bar{\mathbf{x}})}, \tag{4.11}$$

and is further equivalent to

$$\beta^2_{(\mathbf{x})} = \{a_{(\mathbf{x})} + a_{(\bar{\mathbf{x}})}\}^2 + \{b_{(\mathbf{x})} - b_{(\bar{\mathbf{x}})}\}^2 + \{c_{(\mathbf{x})} - c_{(\bar{\mathbf{x}})}\}^2 = 0. \tag{4.12}$$

We call $\beta_{(\mathbf{x})}$ as the symmetry constraint term.

If a face image in a non-frontal view, such a symmetry still exists but the coordinate system should be modified to take into account the view change.

4.1.3 Separating illumination

In this section, we temporarily assume that the class-specific albedo-shape matrix $\mathtt{W}$ is available and solve the problem of separating illumation, *v.i.z.*, for an arbitrary image $\mathtt{h}$, find the illuminant vector $\mathtt{s}$ and the coefficient $\mathtt{f}$. For convenience in performing tasks such as recognition, we also normalize the solution $\mathtt{f}$ to the same range.

The rank constraint gives rise to the basic equation $\mathtt{h} = \mathtt{W}\,(\mathtt{f} \otimes \mathtt{s})$. So, we convert the separation task to a minimization task of finding $\mathtt{f}$ and $\mathtt{s}$ to minimize the least square (LS) cost, i.e.,

$$\min_{\mathtt{f},\mathtt{s}} \mathcal{E}(\mathtt{f}, \mathtt{s}) = ||\mathtt{h} - \mathtt{W}\,(\mathtt{f} \otimes \mathtt{s})||^2, \tag{4.13}$$

Note that $\mathtt{f}$ and $\mathtt{s}$ can be recovered only up to a non-zero scalar; one can always multiply $\mathtt{f}$ by a non-zero scalar and divide $\mathtt{s}$ by the same scalar. Therefore, without loss of generality, we can simply pose an additional constraint: $\mathtt{1}^{\mathsf{T}}\mathtt{f} = 1$, where $\mathtt{1}_{m\times 1}$ is a vector of 1's.

One way to solve this is indicated in [84]. It is a two-step algorithm. First, $\mathtt{k}$ is approximated by $\mathtt{k} = \mathtt{W}^{\dagger}\mathtt{h}$, where $[.]^{\dagger}$ is the Moore-Penrose pseudo-inverse. Then $\mathtt{k} = \mathtt{f} \otimes \mathtt{s}$ is used to solve for $\mathtt{f}$ and $\mathtt{s}$, again using the LS approximation, i.e. finding $\mathtt{f}$ and $\mathtt{s}$ such that the cost $||\mathtt{k} - \mathtt{f} \otimes \mathtt{s}||^2$ is minimized. However, as pointed out in [84], the above algorithm is not robust since two approximations are involved.

Before we proceed to the actual separation algorithm, note that shadows in principle increase the rank (for the illumination only) to infinity. However, if those pixels are successfully excluded in our calculations, the rank for the illumination still remains to be 3 and the overall rank is $3m$.

In view of the above and considering the normalization requirement, we modify the optimization problem as

$$\textbf{[Problem A]} \quad \min_{\mathtt{f},\mathtt{s}} \mathcal{E}(\mathtt{f},\mathtt{s}) = ||\tau \circ (\mathtt{h} - \mathtt{W}\,(\mathtt{f} \otimes \mathtt{s}))||^2 + (\mathtt{1}^{\mathsf{T}}\mathtt{f} - \mathbf{1})^2, \quad (4.14)$$

where $\tau_{d\times 1}$ indicates the inclusion or exclusion of the pixels of the image $\mathtt{h}$ and $\circ$ denotes the Hadamard (or element-wise) product. For a pixel $\mathtt{x}$, $\tau(\mathtt{x}) = 1$ means to include the pixel $\mathtt{x}$ and $\tau(\mathtt{x}) = 0$ means to exclude the pixel $\mathtt{x}$.

Using the fact that Eq. (4.5) provides a series of sub-equations, which is linear in $\mathtt{f}$ if $\mathtt{s}$ is fixed and in $\mathtt{s}$ if $\mathtt{f}$ is fixed, we can design a simple iterative algorithm to solve the Problem A. Each iteration of the algorithm has three steps.

- *Step 1:* We solve for the LS estimate of $\mathtt{f}$, given $\mathtt{s}$ and τ.

$$\mathtt{f} = \begin{bmatrix} \mathtt{W_f} \\ \mathtt{1}^{\mathsf{T}} \end{bmatrix}^{\dagger} \begin{bmatrix} \tau \circ \mathtt{h} \\ 1 \end{bmatrix}; \quad \mathtt{W_f} = [\Rightarrow_{j=1}^{m} (\mathtt{T}_j\mathtt{s})]_{d\times m}. \quad (4.15)$$

- *Step 2:* We solve for the LS estimate of $\mathtt{s}$, given $\mathtt{f}$ and τ:

$$\mathtt{s} = \mathtt{W}_{\mathtt{s}}^{\dagger}(\tau \circ \mathtt{h}), \quad (4.16)$$

  where $\mathtt{W_s}$ can be similarly defined.

- *Step 3:* Given $\mathtt{f}$ and $\mathtt{s}$, we update τ as follows:

$$\tau = [\ |\mathtt{h} - \mathtt{W}\,(\mathtt{f} \otimes \mathtt{s})| < \eta\ ], \quad (4.17)$$

  where η is a pre-defined threshold. We typically set $\eta = 10$. The above is a Matlab operation which performs an element-wise comparison.

Note that in Eq. (4.15) and Eq. (4.16), additional saving in computation is possible. We can form dimension-reduced matrices $\mathtt{W}'_{\mathtt{f}}$ and $\mathtt{W}'_{\mathtt{s}}$ and vector $\mathtt{h}'$ and apply the primed version in Eq. (4.15) and Eq. (4.16). The matrices $\mathtt{W}'_{\mathtt{f}}$ and $\mathtt{W}'_{\mathtt{s}}$ and vector $\mathtt{h}'$ are formed from $\mathtt{W_f}$, $\mathtt{W_s}$, and $\mathtt{h}$, respectively, by discarding those rows corresponding to the excluded pixels.

The initial condition of s can be arbitrary. But, for fast convergence, we need good initial values. In our implementation, we estimate s using the algorithm presented in [170]. To initialize τ, we employ heuristics to distinguish pixels in shadows: their intensities are close to zero. In practice, we set those pixels whose intensities are smaller than a certain threshold as missing values. In addition, we also set those pixels whose intensities are above a certain threshold as missing values to remove pixels possibly in a specular region. This is only done for initialization as we update τ during iterations. This way of initializing τ is very important for deriving the final solution; an initialize of $\tau = 0$ always yields a zero cost function thus one has to avoid this attraction. We empirically found that our current way of initialization is very robust.

To test the stability of our algorithm, we perturb the initial conditions and find that our algorithm is very stable. It always reaches the same solution (up to the convergence error) regardless of initial conditions and generates a smaller residual than the algorithm in [84].

4.1.4 Recovering class-specific albedos and surface normals

The recovery task is to find from the observation matrix H the *class-specific albedo-shape* matrix W (or equivalently R), which satisfies both the integrability and symmetry constraints, as well as the matrices F and S. We decompose R as

$$\mathtt{R}_{3m\times 3m} = [\mathbf{r}_{a1}, \mathbf{r}_{b1}, \mathbf{r}_{c1}, \mathbf{r}_{a2}, \mathbf{r}_{b2}, \mathbf{r}_{c2}, \ldots, \mathbf{r}_{am}, \mathbf{r}_{bm}, \mathbf{r}_{cm}]$$

and treat the column vectors $\{\mathbf{r}_{aj}, \mathbf{r}_{bj}, \mathbf{r}_{cj};\ j = 1, ..., m\}$ as our computational 'units'. We also decompose the $\hat{\mathtt{W}}$ matrix that comes from SVD as $\hat{\mathtt{W}} = [\Downarrow_{\mathtt{x}=1}^{d} \hat{\mathtt{w}}_{(\mathtt{x})}^{\mathsf{T}}]$ where $\hat{\mathtt{w}}_{(\mathtt{x})}$ $(\mathtt{x} = 1, 2, \ldots, d)$ is a $3m \times 1$ vector and $\hat{\mathtt{w}}_{(\mathtt{x})}^{\mathsf{T}}$ is set to be the row corresponding to the pixel x in $\hat{\mathtt{W}}$. $\mathtt{W} = [\Downarrow_{\mathtt{x}=1}^{d} [\Rightarrow_{j=1}^{m} [a_{j(\mathtt{x})}, b_{j(\mathtt{x})}, c_{j(\mathtt{x})}]]] = \hat{\mathtt{W}}\mathtt{R}$, it is easy to show that

$$a_{j(\mathtt{x})} = \hat{\mathtt{w}}_{(\mathtt{x})}^{\mathsf{T}} \mathbf{r}_{aj},\ b_{j(\mathtt{x})} = \hat{\mathtt{w}}_{(\mathtt{x})}^{\mathsf{T}} \mathbf{r}_{bj},\ c_{j(\mathtt{x})} = \hat{\mathtt{w}}_{(\mathtt{x})}^{\mathsf{T}} \mathbf{r}_{cj};\ j = 1, \ldots, m. \quad (4.18)$$

As mentioned in Section 4.1.3, we must take into account attached and cast shadows. After setting them as missing values, we perform SVD with missing values [232] to find $\hat{\mathtt{W}}$. Other analyses dealing with missing value are available in [259, 255, 217].

In view of the above, we formulate the following optimization problem: Minimize over $\mathtt{R}_{3m\times 3m}$, $\mathtt{F}_{m\times n} = [\mathbf{f}_1, \mathbf{f}_2, \ldots, \mathbf{f}_n]$, and $\mathtt{S}_{3\times n} = [\mathbf{s}_1, \mathbf{s}_2, \ldots, \mathbf{s}_n]$ the cost function $\mathcal{E}$ defined as

$$\mathcal{E}(\mathtt{R}, \mathtt{F}, \mathtt{S}) = \frac{1}{2} \sum_{i=1}^{n} \sum_{\mathtt{x}=1}^{d} \tau_i(\mathtt{x}) \{h_{i(\mathtt{x})} - \hat{\mathtt{w}}(\mathtt{x})^{\mathsf{T}} \mathtt{R}(\mathbf{f}_i \otimes \mathbf{s}_i)\}^2$$

$$+\frac{\lambda_1}{2}\sum_{j=1}^{m}\sum_{\mathbf{x}=1}^{d}\{\alpha_{j(\mathbf{x})}\}^2+\frac{\lambda_2}{2}\sum_{j=1}^{m}\sum_{\mathbf{x}=1}^{d}\{\beta_{j(\mathbf{x})}\}^2,$$

$$= \mathcal{E}_0(\mathtt{R},\mathtt{F},\mathtt{S})+\lambda_1\mathcal{E}_1(\mathtt{R})+\lambda_2\mathcal{E}_2(\mathtt{R}), \qquad (4.19)$$

where $\tau_i(\mathbf{x})$ is an indicator function which takes the value one if the pixel $\mathbf{x}$ of the image $\mathbf{h}_i$ is not in shadow and zero otherwise, $\alpha_{j(\mathbf{x})}$ is the integrability constraint term based only on surface normals as defined in Eq. (4.9), and $\beta_{j(\mathbf{x})}$ is the symmetry constraint term as defined in Eq. (4.12). Alternatively, one could directly minimize the cost function over W, F, and S. This is in principle possible but numerically difficult as the number of unknowns depends on the image size, which can be quite large in practice.

As shown in [146], the recovered surface normal is up to a generalized bas-relief (GBR) ambiguity. To avoid trivial solutions such as a planar object, we normalize the matrix R by setting $||\mathrm{R}||_2 = 1$ where $||.||_2$ is a matrix norm. In this way, the surface normals we are recovering are versions up to a GBR ambiguity with respect to the true physical surface normals [75]. However, they are enough for tasks such as face recognition under illumination variation. Another ambiguity between $\mathbf{f}_j$ and $\mathbf{s}_j$ is a nonzero scale, which can be removing by normalizing $\mathbf{f}$ to same range: $\mathbf{f}_j^{\mathsf{T}}\mathbf{1} = 1$, where $\mathbf{1}_{m\times 1}$ is a vector of 1's.

To summarize, we perform the following task:

$$\min_{\mathrm{R,F,S}} \ \mathcal{E}(\mathtt{R},\mathtt{F},\mathtt{S}) \ \textit{subject to} \ ||\mathrm{R}||_2 = 1, \mathtt{F}^{\mathsf{T}}\mathbf{1} = 1. \qquad (4.20)$$

An iterative algorithm can be designed to solve Eq. (4.20). While solving for F and S with R fixed is quite easy, solving for R with F and S is very difficult because the integrability constraint terms involve partial derivatives of the surface normals that are nonlinear in R. Algorithms based on steepest descent are inefficient. We propose a linearized algorithm to solve for R, which is detailed in [95].

We now illustrate how to update $\mathtt{F} = [\mathbf{f}_1, \mathbf{f}_2, \ldots, \mathbf{f}_n]$, $\mathtt{S} = [\mathbf{s}_1, \mathbf{s}_2, \ldots, \mathbf{s}_n]$, and $\tau = [\tau_1, \tau_2, \ldots, \tau_n]$ with R fixed (or W fixed). First note that F, S, and τ are only involved in the term $\mathcal{E}_0$. Moreover, $\mathbf{f}_i$, $\mathbf{s}_i$ and τ_i are related to only the image $\mathbf{h}_i$. This becomes the same as the illumination separation problem defined in Section 4.1.3. The proposed algorithm is also iterative in nature. After running one iterative step to obtain the updated F, S, and τ, we update R again and this process is continued on until convergence.

Again, the same issue of initializing τ exists, that is, an initialize of $\tau = 0$ always yields a zero cost function and one has to avoid this situation. We use the same heuristics to initialize τ_i that corresponds to image i. Another issue is related to the integrability constraint. It should be noted that the integrability constraint is introduced only for regularizing the solution. We make no claim (and there is no guarantee) that the recovered matrices $\{T_j;\ j = 1, 2, \ldots, m\}$ must satisfy the integrability constraint. Further even if the matrices $\{T_j;\ j = 1, 2, \ldots, m\}$ satisfy the integrability constraint, their linear combination $\sum_{f=1}^{m} f_j T_j$ does not.

To demonstrate how the algorithm works, we design the following scenario with $m = 2$ so that the rank of interest is $2 \times 3 = 6$. To defeat the photometric stereo algorithm, which requires one object illuminated by at least three sources, and the bilinear analysis, which requires two fixed objects illuminated by at least three same lighting sources, we construct eight images by taking random linear combinations of two basis objects illuminated by eight different lighting sources. Figure 4.2 displays the two basis objects under the same set of eight illuminations and the synthesized images. The recovered class-specific albedo-shape matrix is also presented in Figure 4.2, which clearly shows the two basis objects. The quality of reconstruction is quite good except around the nose region. The reason might be that the two basis objects have quite distinct noses so that the nose part of their linear combinations is not visually good (for example the last image in the third row), which propagates to the recovery results of albedos and surface normals from these combination images. Our algorithm usually converges within 100 iterations.

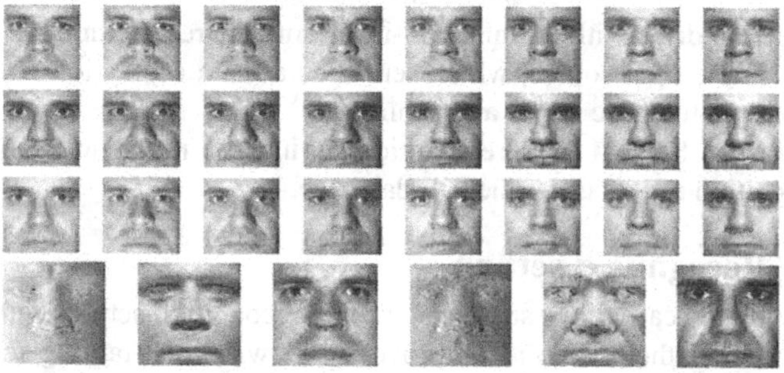

Figure 4.2. Row 1: The first basis object under eight different illuminations. Row 2: The second basis object under the same set of eight different illuminations. Row 3: Eight images (constructed by random linear combinations of two basis objects) illuminated by eight different lighting sources. Row 4: Recovered class-specific albedo-shape matrix W showing the product of varying albedos and surface normals of two basis objects (i.e. the three columns of T_1 and T_2) using the generalized photometric stereo algorithm.

One notes that the special case $m = 1$ of our algorithm can be readily applied to photometric stereo (with the symmetry constraint removed) to robustly recover the albedos and surface normals for one object.

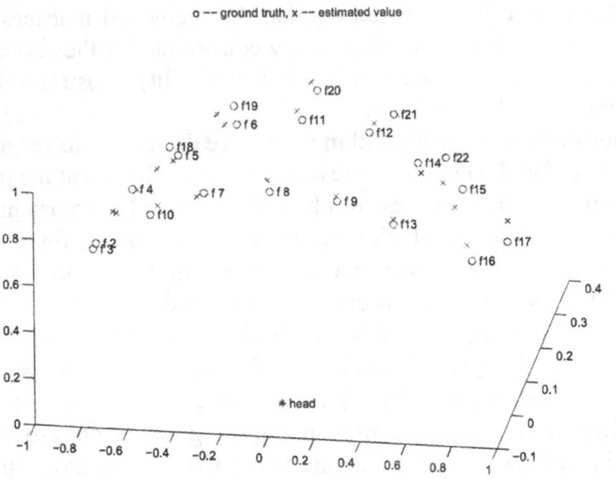

Figure 4.3. Right: Flash distribution in the PIE database. For illustrative purposes, we move their positions on a unit sphere as only the illuminant directions matter. 'o' means the ground truth and 'x' the estimated values.

4.2 Illumination-Invariant Face Recognition in the Presence of a Single Light Source

This section deals with illumination-invariant face recognition in the presence of a single light source, which serves as a main evaluation tool for the generalized photometric stereo algorithm.

We define in Section 4.2.1 recognition setting and report in Section 4.2.2 face recognition results using the PIE database.

4.2.1 Recognition setting

As mentioned earlier, we study an extreme recognition setting with the following features: there is no identity overlap between the training set and the gallery and probe sets; only one image per object is stored in the gallery set; the lighting conditions for the training, gallery and probe sets are completely unknown.

Our recognition strategy is as follows.

- Learn W from the training set using the recovery algorithm described in Section 4.1.4 or construct W if we have 3D face models available.
- With W given, learn the identity signature f's for both the gallery and probe sets using the recovery algorithm that solves the Problem A in Eq. (4.14) as described in Section 4.1.3, assuming no knowledge of illumination directions.

- Perform recognition using the nearest correlation coefficient. Suppose that a gallery image g has its signature $\mathtt{f}_g$ and a probe image p has its signature $\mathtt{f}_p$, their correlation coefficient is defined as

$$cc(p, g) = \frac{(\mathtt{f}_p, \mathtt{f}_g)}{\sqrt{(\mathtt{f}_p, \mathtt{f}_p)(\mathtt{f}_g, \mathtt{f}_g)}}, \tag{4.21}$$

where (x, y) is an inner-product such as $(\mathrm{x}, \mathrm{y}) = \mathrm{x}^{\mathsf{T}} \Sigma \mathrm{y}$ with Σ learned or given. We use Σ as an identity matrix.

Compared to the approached reviewed in Chapter 2, the proposed recognition scheme possesses the following properties: (i) It is able to recognize new objects not present in the training set; (ii) It is able to handle new lighting conditions not present in the training set; and (iii) No explicit 3D model and no prior knowledge about illumination conditions are needed. In other words, we combine the advantages of the subspace learning and reflectance model-based methods.

We use the PIE database [85] in our experiment. In particular, we use the 'illum' part of the PIE database that is close to the Lambertian model as in [77] while the 'light' part that includes an ambient light is used in [72]). Figure 4.3 shows the distribution of all 21 flashes used in PIE and their estimated positions using our algorithm. Since the flashes are almost symmetrically distributed about the head position, we only use 12 of them distributed on the right half of the unit sphere in Figure 4.3. More specifically, the flashes we used are f_{08}, f_{09}, f_{11}-f_{17}, and f_{20}-f_{22}. In total, we used $68 \times 12 = 816$ images in a fixed view as there are 68 subjects in the PIE database. Figure 4.4 displays one PIE object under the selected 12 illuminants.

Registration is performed by aligning the eyes and mouth to desired positions. No flow computation is carried on for further alignment as opposed to [72] . After the pre-processing step, the cropped out face image is of size 50 by 50, i.e. $d = 2500$. Also, we only study gray images by taking the average of the red, green, and blue channels of their color versions. We use all 68 images under one illumination to form a gallery set and under another illumination to form a probe set. The training set is taken from sources other than the PIE dataset. Thus, we have $12 \times 11 = 132$ tests, with each test giving rise to a recognition score.

4.2.2 Experiments and results

We assume that all the images have been captured in a frontal view, but we do not assume that the directions and intensities of the illuminants are known.

Yale training set

The training set is first taken as the Yale's illumination database [75]. There are only 10 subjects (i.e. $m = 10$) in this database and each subject has 64

Figure 4.4. The top row displays one PIE object under the selected 12 illuminants (from left to right, f_{08}, f_{09}, f_{11}-f_{17}, and f_{20}-f_{22}) and the bottom row one Yale object under 9 lights (most frontal lights) used in the training set.

Gly / *Prb*	f_{08}	f_{09}	f_{11}	f_{12}	f_{13}	f_{14}	f_{15}	f_{16}	f_{17}	f_{20}	f_{21}	f_{22}	*Avg*
f_{08}	-	96	96	87	66	60	46	29	22	85	78	53	65
f_{09}	94	-	96	96	90	87	56	40	24	84	96	68	75
f_{11}	94	91	-	97	72	72	38	28	16	F	94	51	69
f_{12}	88	94	97	-	88	93	57	41	28	94	F	76	78
f_{13}	56	87	59	85	-	F	90	71	50	54	87	F	76
f_{14}	51	85	63	93	F	-	90	66	49	59	91	99	77
f_{15}	33	40	37	49	85	88	-	93	78	32	49	97	62
f_{16}	19	26	26	32	59	44	84	-	93	26	31	63	46
f_{17}	14	28	19	26	50	41	68	94	-	19	26	44	39
f_{20}	90	85	99	97	65	69	38	26	21	-	93	53	67
f_{21}	79	94	93	F	88	94	62	49	28	91	-	76	78
f_{22}	43	65	46	75	99	99	97	76	59	43	74	-	70
Avg	60	72	66	76	78	77	66	56	42	63	74	71	67

Table 4.1. Recognition rate obtained by the generalized photometric stereo approach using the Yale's database as the training set. 'F' means 100 and 'f_{nn}' means flash no. nn.

images in frontal view illuminated by 64 different lights. We pick out images under 9 lights (mostly frontal) in order to cover up to second-order harmonic components [144]. Figure 4.3 shows one Yale object under $r = 9$ lights.

Table 4.1 lists the recognition rates for the PIE database using the Yale's database as the training set. Even with $m = 10$, we obtain quite good results, especially when the gallery and probe sets are close in terms of their flash positions. When the flashes of the gallery and probe sets become separated, the recognition rate decreases. The worst performance is with the gallery set at f_{08} and the probe set at f_{17}, two most separated flashes. In general, using images under frontal or near-frontal illuminants (e.g. f_{09}, f_{12}, and f_{21}) as gallery sets produces good results.

For comparison, we also implemented the 'Eigenface' approach (discarding the first 3 components) and the 'Fisherface' approach by training the subspace projection vectors from the same training set. The recognition rates are pre-

Gly	f_{08}	f_{09}	f_{11}	f_{12}	f_{13}	f_{14}	f_{15}	f_{16}	f_{17}	f_{20}	f_{21}	f_{22}	*Avg*
Prb													
f_{08}	-	F	90	66	21	9	1	9	4	60	60	1	38
f_{09}	F	-	72	94	59	31	10	24	13	51	84	13	50
f_{11}	97	91	-	F	29	24	13	15	10	F	94	19	54
f_{12}	93	97	F	-	93	90	56	59	35	96	F	69	81
f_{13}	19	62	22	68	-	97	82	F	68	13	84	81	63
f_{14}	9	15	12	62	F	-	F	84	82	12	72	F	59
f_{15}	0	3	1	4	76	F	-	74	76	1	18	F	41
f_{16}	6	25	3	31	82	65	71	-	F	3	41	57	44
f_{17}	4	12	3	31	51	56	81	F	-	3	28	59	39
f_{20}	88	76	F	99	28	28	15	12	16	-	99	19	53
f_{21}	84	97	97	F	96	88	57	74	46	96	-	71	82
f_{22}	3	4	3	13	72	F	F	50	57	3	24	-	39
Avg	46	53	46	61	64	62	53	54	46	40	64	54	54

Table 4.2. Recognition rate obtained by the 'Eigenface' approach discarding the first 3 components using the Yale's database as the training set. 'F' mean 100 and 'f_{nn}' means flash no. nn.

Gly	f_{08}	f_{09}	f_{11}	f_{12}	f_{13}	f_{14}	f_{15}	f_{16}	f_{17}	f_{20}	f_{21}	f_{22}	*Avg*
Prb													
f_{08}	-	97	97	93	63	56	29	16	9	94	85	29	61
f_{09}	99	-	97	99	96	88	38	21	12	91	96	57	72
f_{11}	99	96	-	99	62	63	29	16	12	F	94	41	65
f_{12}	96	99	F	-	93	91	40	22	13	99	F	69	75
f_{13}	74	93	69	84	-	F	71	37	16	62	87	97	72
f_{14}	66	88	74	93	F	-	76	34	19	71	93	F	74
f_{15}	22	34	24	35	71	66	-	82	46	28	44	99	50
f_{16}	12	21	13	18	28	26	74	-	85	18	22	47	33
f_{17}	6	7	9	13	15	18	40	81	-	13	16	24	22
f_{20}	93	88	F	96	63	68	32	19	13	-	96	43	65
f_{21}	87	94	F	F	93	99	51	22	15	99	-	84	77
f_{22}	41	65	43	62	96	F	F	56	29	46	71	-	64
Avg	63	71	66	72	71	70	53	37	24	65	73	63	61

Table 4.3. Recognition rate obtained by the 'Fisherface' approach using the Yale's database as the training set. 'F' mean 100 and 'f_{nn}' means flash no. nn.

sented in Tables 4.2 and 4.3. The 'Fisherface' approach outperforms the 'Eigenface' approach, but both perform worse than our approach. On the average, the

Gly	f_{08}	f_{09}	f_{11}	f_{12}	f_{13}	f_{14}	f_{15}	f_{16}	f_{17}	f_{20}	f_{21}	f_{22}	*Avg*
Prb													
f_{08}	-	F	99	99	97	97	79	72	43	99	97	93	88
f_{09}	F	-	99	99	99	99	97	91	60	97	97	97	94
f_{11}	99	99	-	F	F	F	90	76	65	F	F	99	93
f_{12}	99	99	F	-	F	F	F	93	76	F	F	F	97
f_{13}	99	99	F	F	-	F	F	F	88	99	F	F	99
f_{14}	99	99	F	F	F	-	F	F	96	99	F	F	99
f_{15}	84	94	93	F	F	F	-	F	F	88	F	F	96
f_{16}	69	87	78	90	F	F	F	-	F	69	90	F	89
f_{17}	44	60	51	71	84	91	99	F	-	56	75	94	75
f_{20}	97	97	F	F	F	F	90	74	68	-	F	99	93
f_{21}	97	97	F	F	F	F	F	97	82	F	-	F	98
f_{22}	90	97	96	F	F	F	F	F	99	97	F	-	98
Avg	89	93	92	96	98	99	96	91	80	91	96	98	93

Table 4.4. Recognition rate obtained by the generalized photometric stereo approach using the Yale's database (the left number in each cell) and the Vetter's database (the right number in each cell) as the training set. 'F' means 100 and 'f_{nn}' means flash no. nn.

proposed generalized photometric stereo approach is 10% better than the 'Fisherface' approach. This highlights the benefit of decoupling the illumination variation.

Vetter training set

Generalization capacity with $m = 10$ is rather restrictive. We now increase m from 10 to 100 by using Vetter's 3D face database [72]. As this is a 3D database, we actually have $\mathtt{W}$ available. However, we believe that using a training set of $m = 100$ from other sources can yield similar performances. Table 4.4 tabulates the recognition rates obtained by the proposed algorithm. Significant improvements have been achieved by increasing m. This seems to suggest that a moderate sample size of 100 is enough to span the entire face space under a fixed view. The comparison between our approach with Blanz and Vetter [72] is highlighted in Section 4.3.2.

Illuminant estimation

In the above process, we also achieve illuminant estimation. Figure 4.3 shows the estimated illuminant directions. It is quite accurate for estimation of directions of flashes near the frontal pose. But when the flashes are significantly off-frontal, accuracy slightly goes down.

4.3 Illumination-Invariant Face Recognition in the Presence of Multiple Light Sources

This section deals with face recognition in the presence of multiple light sources. It turns out that the nonlinearity in the Lambert's law is very important to this task. We extend our earlier analysis to directly incorporate the attached shadows rather than excluding them for computation.

4.3.1 How important is the nonlinearity in the Lambert's law?

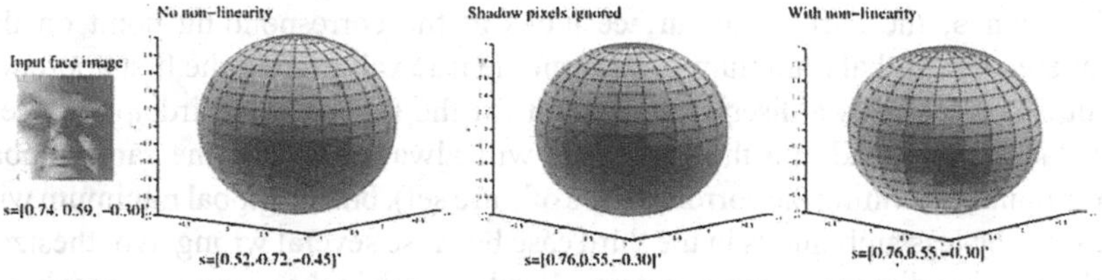

Figure 4.5. The error surfaces for the estimation of the light source direction given a face image of known shape and albedo. The three plots correspond to the three approaches described in the text. The lower the error is for a particular illumination direction, the darker the error sphere looks at the point corresponding to that direction. The true and estimated values of the illumination direction are listed along with the plots.

In general, objects like faces do not have all the surface points facing the illumination source which leads to the formation of attached shadows. The cast and attached shadows are often ignored from the analysis to keep the subspace of the observed images in a three [161] or with the addition of an ambient component [168], four dimensional linear subspace. This is also true for the proposed generalized photometric stereo algorithm. Therefore, these generative approaches either ignore this non-linearity completely or try to somehow ignore the shadow pixels. Here we present a simple illustration to highlight the role attached shadows can play.

Suppose the goal is to estimate the illumination source from a single face image given the shape and albedo of the face. We explore three approaches for this task: the first approach ignores the non-linearity completely, the second one uses the linear rule but ignores the shadow pixels and the last one uses the Lambert's Law in its pure form. The accuracy of the global minimum and its ambiguity on the error surface is taken as the criterion for the goodness of the method. The analytical expressions for the error function using the three options can be written as :

$$\text{Completely linear:} \qquad \mathcal{E}(\mathrm{s}) = \| \mathrm{h} - \rho \mathrm{n}^{\mathsf{T}} \mathrm{s} \|^2; \tag{4.22}$$

$$\text{Shadow pixels ignored:} \quad \mathcal{E}(\mathbf{s}) = \| \tau \circ (\mathbf{h} - \rho \mathbf{n}^{\mathsf{T}} \mathbf{s}) \|^2; \tag{4.23}$$

$$\text{Non-linear rule:} \quad \mathcal{E}(\mathbf{s}) = \| \mathbf{h} - \max(\rho \mathbf{n}^{\mathsf{T}} \mathbf{s}, 0) \|^2 . \tag{4.24}$$

Clearly, the linear method penalizes the correct illumination at the shadow pixels by having non-zero error values for those pixels. On the other hand, when shadows are ignored, the illuminations which produce wrong values for the shadow pixels do not get penalized there. As the set of all possible normals lies on the surface of a unit sphere, we use a sphere to display the computed error functions. Figure 4.5 shows the error surfaces for the three methods for a given face image. The lower the error is for a hypothesized illumination direction $\mathbf{s}$, the darker the surface looks at the corresponding point on the sphere. The global minimum is far from the true value using the first approach but is correct up to a discretization error for the second and third approaches. In fact, the second and third methods will always produce the same global minimum (assuming the correct values of τ are set), but the global minimum will always be less ambiguous in the third case because several wrong hypothesized illumination directions do not get penalized enough in the second approach due to the exclusion of the shadow pixels (Figure 4.5) .

The case of multiple light sources

The above analysis implicitly assumes that there is only one distant light source illuminating the face. Though the assumption is valid for datasets like PIE, it does not hold for most realistic scenarios. We now explore the impact of using the *linear* Lambert's law for images illuminated by multiple light sources. Using the *linear* Lambert's law, an image illuminated by k different light sources can be represented as:

$$\mathbf{h} = \sum_{i=1}^{k} \rho \mathbf{n}^{\mathsf{T}} \mathbf{s}_i = \rho \mathbf{n}^{T} \sum_{i=1}^{k} \mathbf{s}_i = \rho \mathbf{n}^{\mathsf{T}} \mathbf{s}^{\star}, \tag{4.25}$$

where $\mathbf{s}^{\star} = \sum_{i=1}^{k} \mathbf{s}_i$. This shows that under the linear assumption, multiple light sources can be replaced by a suitably placed single light source without having any effect on the image. This is a bit counter-intuitive as can be seen in a simple two-source scenario:

$$\mathbf{h} = \rho \mathbf{n}^{\mathsf{T}} \mathbf{s}_1 + \rho \mathbf{n}^{\mathsf{T}} \mathbf{s}_2. \tag{4.26}$$

Now if $\mathbf{s}_1 = -\mathbf{s}_2$

$$\mathbf{h} = \rho \mathbf{n}^{\mathsf{T}} (\mathbf{s}_1 - \mathbf{s}_2) = 0. \tag{4.27}$$

Thus the linear assumption can make the effect of light sources interfere in a destructive manner and give strange outcomes. Please note that the negativity comes because of the direction and not because of the intensity of the light source. Quite clearly, the harm done by the linearity assumption is proportional to the angle subtended by the light sources at the surface.

Though the above discussion concludes that the Lambert's law in its pure form is better suited for illumination estimation than the other variants, it is only of academic interest if inclusion of the non-linearity does not improve the recognition results. The following section proposes a variant of the generalized photometric approach taking the non-linearity into account. The improvement in the recognition accuracy highlights the importance of including the attached shadows in the analysis.

4.3.2 Face recognition in the presence of a single light source (revisited)

Gly	f_{08}	f_{09}	f_{11}	f_{12}	f_{13}	f_{14}	f_{15}	f_{16}	f_{17}	f_{20}	f_{21}	f_{22}	*Avg*
Prb													
f_{08}	-	F	F	F	96	97	81	72	50	F	97	84	90
f_{09}	F	-	F	F	F	99	97	96	75	F	F	97	97
f_{11}	F	F	-	F	F	97	94	78	63	F	99	94	94
f_{12}	F	F	F	-	F	F	F	99	90	F	F	F	99
f_{13}	97	F	F	F	-	F	F	F	96	F	F	F	99
f_{14}	94	F	F	F	F	-	F	F	99	F	F	F	99
f_{15}	88	97	97	F	F	F	-	F	F	97	F	F	98
f_{16}	74	90	81	93	F	F	F	-	F	76	97	F	93
f_{17}	59	74	63	87	99	99	F	F	-	71	94	F	87
f_{20}	99	F	F	F	F	99	96	82	71	-	F	97	95
f_{21}	97	F	F	F	F	F	F	99	96	F	-	F	99
f_{22}	93	F	99	F	F	F	F	F	99	99	F	-	99
Avg	92	97	95	98	F	99	97	94	87	95	99	98	96

Table 4.5. Recognition results on the PIE dataset. f_i denotes images taken with a particular flash ON as labeled in PIE. Each $(i, j)^{th}$ entry in the table shows the recognition rate obtained with the images from f_j as gallery while from f_i as probe.

We here extend the generalized photometric stereo approach to directly include attached shadows. Our main focus here is to highlight the importance of the non-linearity in the Lambert's law and not generalized photometric stereo. Therefore, we generate the shape-albedo matrix $\mathtt{W}$ using Vetter's 3D data for all our experiments.

The key derivation is Eq. (4.5), where the attached shadows are not considered. To take into account the inherent hard non-linearity present in the Lambert's law, we let $\mathtt{h}_i = \max(\mathtt{T}_i\mathtt{s}, 0)$ in Eq. (4.5) instead of $\mathtt{h}_i = \mathtt{T}_i\mathtt{s}$. Eq.

(4.5) can then be written as

$$\mathtt{h}_{d\times 1} = \sum_{i=1}^{m} f_i \mathtt{h}_i = \sum_{i=1}^{m} f_i \max(\mathtt{T}_i \mathtt{s}, 0). \quad (4.28)$$

Therefore, given shape-albedo matrix $\mathtt{W} = [\mathtt{T}_1, \mathtt{T}_2, \ldots, \mathtt{T}_m]$, the recovery of the identity vector $\mathtt{f}$ and illumination $\mathtt{s}$ can be posed as the following optimization problem:

$$[Problem\ B]\ \min_{\mathtt{f},\mathtt{s}} \mathcal{E}(\mathtt{f}, \mathtt{s}) = \| \mathtt{h} - \sum_{i=1}^{m} f_i \max(\mathtt{T}_i \mathtt{s}, 0) \|^2 + (\mathtt{1}^\mathsf{T}\mathtt{f} - 1)^2 \quad (4.29)$$

Please note that $\mathtt{s}$ is not a unit vector as it contains the intensity of the illumination source also. The main difference between Eq. (4.14) and Eq. (4.29) (or problems A and B) lies in that the shadow pixels are excluded in Eq. (4.14) but directly modeled in Eq. (4.29).

The minimization of Eq. (4.29) is performed using an iterative approach, fixing $\mathtt{f}$ for optimizing $\mathcal{E}$ w.r.t. $\mathtt{s}$ and fixing $\mathtt{s}$ for optimization w.r.t. $\mathtt{f}$. In each iteration, $\mathtt{f}$ can be estimated by solving a linear least-squares (LS) problem but a non-linear LS solution is required to estimate $\mathtt{s}$. The non-linear optimization is performed using the *lsqnonlin* function in MATLAB which is based on the interior-reflective Newton method. For most faces, the function value did not change much after 4-5 iterations. Therefore, the iterative optimization was always stopped after 5 iterations. The whole process took about 5-7 seconds per image on a normal desktop.

We perform recognition experiments across illumination using the frontal faces from the PIE dataset, following the same setting as in Section 4.2.1. Table 4.5 shows the recognition results obtained using this approach. Recognition is performed across illumination with images from one illumination condition from the PIE dataset forming the gallery set while images from another illumination condition forming the probe set. Each gallery/probe set contains one frontal image per subject taken in the presence of a particular light source (there are 68 subjects in each gallery/probe). Each entry in the table shows the recognition rate achieved for one such choice of gallery and probe. Compared with Table 4.4, the recognition performance with the inclusion of the non-linearity in the Lambert's law is almost always better or same. The overall average performance is up from 93% to 96%. The improvement is significant in cases involving difficult illumination conditions (with lots of shadows) like the flash f_{17} in the PIE dataset. This shows that though the estimation becomes slightly more difficult, the recognition rate improves with the inclusion of the non-linearity.

As an interesting comparison, Romdhani, Blanz, and Vetter [82] also reported detailed recognition rates across the illumination variation using the 3D morphable model. Using the 'light' part of the PIE database and only f_{12} as the gallery set, they recorded an average of 98% for color images. We matched their performance, an average of 98% using f_{12} as the gallery, using gray images. However, we used the 'illum' part of the PIE database, which lacks the ambient light source. The effect is that in our experiments, images captured under extreme lights are almost completely dark, which makes the recognition of these images nearly impossible. On the other hand, the challenge in the 'light' part is that people wear glasses. We believe that our performances can be boosted using the color images and finer alignment. In terms of computation, our approach is much faster than [82]. In principle, there are significant differences too. In [82] depths and texture maps of explicit 3D face models are used, while our image-based approach uses the concepts of albedo and surface normal and can recover the 3D models under the rank constraint.

4.3.3 Recognition in the presence of multiple light sources

One of the issues in handling multiple illumination case is the prior knowledge of the number of light sources. In the absence of this knowledge, one can hypothesize several different cases and choose the one with minimum residual error. This can be done in a manner very similar to the approach described for the single illumination case with the following change in the objective function:

$$\mathcal{E}(\mathtt{f}, \mathtt{s}) = \| \mathtt{h} - \sum_{i=1}^{m} f_i \sum_{j=1}^{k} \max(\mathtt{T}_i \mathtt{s}_j, 0) \|^2 + (\mathtt{1}^\mathsf{T} \mathtt{f} - 1)^2, \tag{4.30}$$

where k is the hypothesized number of light sources. The objective function can be minimized repeatedly for different values of k and the one with minimum error can be taken as the correct hypothesis. Figure 4.6 shows the variation of the error with k, for an image illuminated by three different light sources. As can be seen, the error more or less stabilizes for $k \geq 3$. Note that for the *linear* Lambert's law, such a curve will look more or less horizontal due to the equivalence of the single and multi-light source scenarios (Equation 4.25) under the linear assumption.

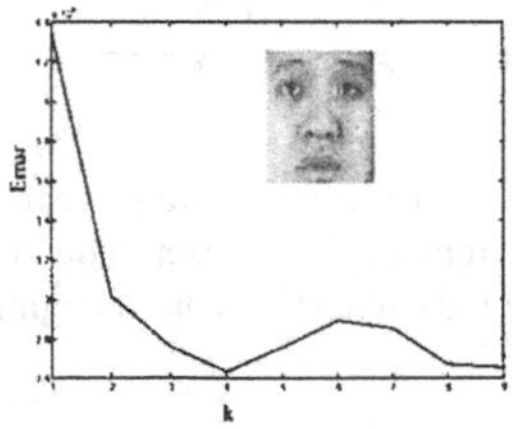

Figure 4.6. The error obtained for different hypothesized number of light sources for the face image shown. The face was illuminated using 3 light sources.

Though one can use this approach by varying k, it is both inelegant and computationally intensive. In our approach, we avoid the extra computations by making the following assumption. We assume that an image of an arbitrarily illuminated face can be approximated by a linear combination of the images of the same face in the same pose, illuminated by nine different light sources placed at pre-selected positions. Lee *et al.* [79] show that this approximation is quite good for a wide range of illumination conditions. Hence, a face image can be written as

$$\mathtt{h} = \sum_{j=1}^{9} \alpha_j \max(\mathtt{T}\hat{\mathtt{s}}_j, 0), \tag{4.31}$$

where $\{\hat{\mathtt{s}}_1, \hat{\mathtt{s}}_2, \ldots, \hat{\mathtt{s}}_9\}$ are the pre-specified illumination directions. As proposed in [79], we use the following directions for $\{\hat{\mathtt{s}}_1, \hat{\mathtt{s}}_2, \ldots, \hat{\mathtt{s}}_9\}$:

$$\begin{aligned} \phi &= \{0, 49, -68, 73, 77, -84, -84, 82, -50\}^\circ; \\ \theta &= \{0, 17, 0, -18, 37, 47, -47, -56, -84\}^\circ. \end{aligned} \tag{4.32}$$

Under this formulation, Eq. (4.30) changes to

$$[Problem\ C]\ \min_{\mathtt{f},\alpha} \mathcal{E}(\mathtt{f}, \alpha) = \| \mathtt{h} - \sum_{i=1}^{m} f_i \sum_{j=1}^{9} \alpha_j \max(\mathtt{T}_i\hat{\mathtt{s}}_j, 0) \|^2 + (\mathtt{1}^\mathsf{T}\mathtt{f} - 1)^2, \tag{4.33}$$

where $\mathtt{f} = [\Downarrow_{i=1}^{m} f_i]$ and $\alpha_{9\times 1} = [\Downarrow_{j=1}^{9} \alpha_i]$. This way one can potentially recover the illumination-free identity vector $\mathtt{f}$ without any prior knowledge of the number of light sources or any need to check different hypotheses for the same.

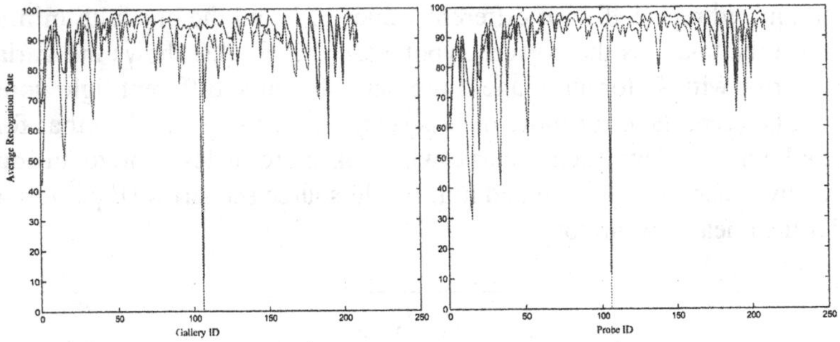

Figure 4.7. The per-gallery and per-probe average recognition rates on the 210 *doubly-illuminated* scenarios generated from the PIE dataset. The blue curve shows the performance of the proposed approach while the red curve shows the recognition rates obtained using the *linear* single light source approach.

Now the objective function is minimized with respect to $\mathtt{f}$ and α. This gives us the illumination-free identity vector $\mathtt{f}$ which is used for recognition.

The optimization is done in an iterative fashion by fixing one parameter and estimating the other and vice-versa.

By defining a $d \times m$ matrix $\mathtt{W_f}$ as

$$\mathtt{W_f} = \left[\Rightarrow_{i=1}^{m} (\sum_{j=1}^{9} \alpha_j \max(\mathtt{T}_i \hat{\mathtt{s}}_j, 0))\right],$$

it is easy to show that

$$\mathtt{f} = \begin{bmatrix} \mathtt{W_f} \\ \mathtt{1}^{\mathsf{T}} \end{bmatrix}^{\dagger} \begin{bmatrix} \mathtt{h} \\ 1 \end{bmatrix}. \tag{4.34}$$

where $\mathtt{h}_{d\times 1}$ is the vectorized input face image, $[.]^{\dagger}$ is the Moore-Penrose inverse, $\mathtt{1}_{m\times 1}$ is the m-dimensional vector of ones, included to handle scale ambiguity between $\mathtt{f}$ and α.

Looking carefully at the objective function (e.g. Eq. (4.33)), one can easily observe that α too can be estimated by solving a linear LS problem (as $\{\hat{\mathtt{s}}_1, \hat{\mathtt{s}}_2, \ldots \hat{\mathtt{s}}_9\}$ is known). This avoids the need for any nonlinear optimization here. Recall that nonlinear LS was required to estimate $\mathtt{s}$ in the approach proposed for the single light source case. The expression for α can be written as:

$$\alpha = \mathtt{W}_{\alpha}^{\dagger}\mathtt{h}, \tag{4.35}$$

where,

$$\mathtt{W}_{\alpha} = \left[\Rightarrow_{j=1}^{9} (\sum_{i=1}^{m} f_i \max(\mathtt{T}_i \hat{\mathtt{s}}_j, 0))\right]_{d\times 9}. \tag{4.36}$$

For most of the face images, the iterative optimization converged within 5-6 iterations. As there is no non-linear optimization involved, it took just 2-3 seconds to recover $\mathtt{f}$ and α from a given face image on a normal desktop. As the identity variable is estimated from an image by separating the effect of all the light sources in the form of α, it is used as the illumination-invariant representation for recognition across varying illumination. The correlation coefficient of the identity vectors is used as the similarity measure for recognition experiments.

4.3.4 Experiments and results

To begin with, we test this algorithm by running the same experiment as we do for the single light source approach. Though the PIE dataset is not suited to test the ability of this algorithm to handle arbitrarily illuminated images, a good performance here can be considered as a proof of concept. The overall average recognition rate for the experiment obtained using this algorithm is 95% which is higher than the generalized photometric stereo algorithm that gives 93%.

Due to the unavailability of a standard dataset containing face images with multiple light sources ON at a time, we generate such data using the PIE and

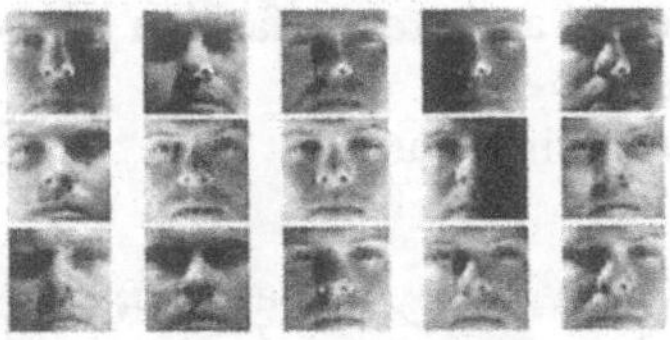

Figure 4.8. The *doubly-illuminated* images of a subject from the Yale database. Each image is generated by adding 2 images of the same subject illuminated by different light sources.

Yale datasets. Due to the controlled nature of the datasets, multiple images of a subject under different illuminations but same pose, are more or less aligned. If we ignore any camera gain, this allows us to add multiple images of a person taken under different illuminations to get one with the effect of an image captured with multiple lights ON. The images generated this way look pretty realistic (see Figure 4.8).

We report the results of experiments on the dataset created by adding images from two illumination conditions from PIE at a time. As PIE has 21 different illumination scenarios, we get a total of $\binom{21}{2} = 210$ different *doubly-illuminated* scenarios. Recognition was done across all 210 scenarios by taking one as the gallery and another one as the probe at a time to get 210×209 recognition scores. As it is difficult to show the recognition scores by drawing a 210×210 table, we show only the aggregated per-gallery and per-probe recognition rates (similar to the averages in Table 4.5) in Figure 4.7. The blue curve on the top shows the averages obtained by the proposed approach. For comparison, we show the recognition rates obtained on this dataset using the generalized photometric stereo algorithm that ignores shadow pixels under the single light source assumption (red curve). For ease of use, we will call this method as ISP-SLS (Ignores Shadow Pixels under Single Light Source Assumption). There exists a zero in the red curve because for one gallery/probe, the method ended up ignoring most of the pixels as shadows and thus was unable to recover the identity variable. The recognition rates obtained using the proposed approach are always better or same as compared to ISP-SLS. The increase in the recognition accuracy is more prominent for the cases where the two illumination sources combined to generate the doubly-illuminated scenario were far apart. This happens because the destructive interference of two light sources (due to the linearity assumption in ISP-SLS as described in Section 4.3.1) increases with an increase in the angle between the two.

We further test the algorithm by generating a similar *doubly-illuminated* data using Yale Face Database B [75]. Figure 4.9 shows the six challenging illumination conditions used to generate fifteen different scenarios (shown in

Figure 4.9. The 6 illumination conditions from the Yale face Database B used to generate the *doubly-illuminated* data.

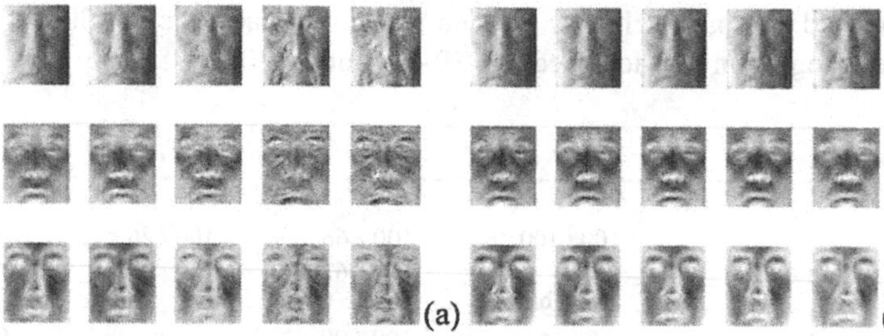

Figure 4.10. The reconstructed shapes of a face using (a) the ISP-SLS approach and (b) the proposed approach that takes into account nonlinearity. In each column, the three images display the three components of the reconstructed surface normals for the face. Columns 1-5 correspond to the five illumination scenarios with the number of light sources varying from 1-5, respectively. In (a), quite clearly, the quality of the reconstructed surface obtained by the ISP-SLS approach degrades as the number of light sources increase. In (b), we can see that there is hardly any difference in the reconstructed surfaces across various columns (which correspond to the 5 different illuminations scenarios with the number of light sources ranging from 1-5).

Figure 4.8) by pairing two at a time. The average recognition rate achieved on this difficult data (Figure 4.8 shows images of one subject under the 15 illumination conditions) using our algorithm is 77%. This is up by more that 25% compared to the accuracy achieved both by ISP-SLS method and the method which takes the non-linearity into account under the single light source assumption.

All the above experiments implicitly assume that the faces in the gallery and probe are illuminated by the same number of light sources. Clearly, the proposed algorithm does not impose any such restriction. Therefore, we perform another experiment to test the ability of the proposed approach to generalize across varying number of light sources. We generate five illumination scenarios using the PIE dataset with the number of light sources (added to create each scenario) ranging from 1-5. To avoid any bias, the combinations of the light sources are selected randomly from the 21 illumination sets in the PIE dataset. Recognition is performed across the five scenarios by considering one among them as the gallery and another one as the probe at a time. As before, each gallery/probe contains one image for each of the 68 subjects present in the PIE dataset. While the ISP-SLS approach performs poorly in this experiment, the proposed approach does a perfect job as shown in Table 4.6. Figure 4.10 shows the reconstructed surfaces for a face illuminated in the presence of the five illumination scenarios using the two approaches. The quality of the reconstructions explains the difference in the recognition accuracy obtained using the two methods. To confirm the authenticity of the results, we perform another similar experiment with 10 different scenarios with the number of randomly selected light sources (added to generate the 10 scenarios) ranging from 1-10. Here, the proposed approach achieves average recognition accuracy of 99.7% (The average recognition rate achieved by ISP-SLS here is 54%).

Gly	F_1	F_2	F_3	F_4	F_5
Prb					
F_1	- / -	100 / 100	100 / 66	100 / 26	100 / 26
F_2	100 / 100	- / -	100 / 62	100 / 28	100 / 25
F_3	100 / 93	100 / 91	- / -	100 / 72	100 / 74
F_4	100 / 62	100 / 66	100 / 90	- / -	100 / 93
F_5	100 / 66	100 / 66	100 / 93	100 / 93	- / -

$F_1 = \{f_{20}\}$; $F_2 = \{f_{05}, f_{22}\}$; $F_3 = \{f_{20}, f_{06}, f_{18}\}$; $F_4 = \{f_{21}, f_{06}, f_{07}, f_{03}\}$; $F_5 = \{f_{03}, f_{15}, f_{06}, f_{19}, f_{05}\}$.

Table 4.6. Recognition results on the multiply-illuminated data generated from the PIE dataset. The various scenarios differ in the number of light sources. The illumination conditions from the PIE dataset randomly selected to generate each scenario is shown in curly braces. The first number in each entry of the table shows the recognition accuracy obtained using the proposed approach while the second number shows the performance of the ISP-SLS method.

Chapter 5

ILLUMINATING LIGHT FIELD

State-of-the-art algorithms are not able to produce satisfactory recognition performance when confronted by pose and illumination variations. In general, pose variation is slightly more difficult to handle than illumination variation. The presence of both variations further challenges the recognition algorithms.

This chapter extends the generalized photometric stereo algorithm presented in Chapter 4 to handle pose variation. The way we handle pose variation is through the 'Eigen' light approach [76]. This unified approach is image-based, in the sense that, in the training set, only 2D images are used and no explicit 3D models are needed. The unification is achieved by exploiting the fact that both approaches use a subspace model for identity. The 'Eigen' light field approach combines subspace modeling with light field and offers a pose-invariant encoding of identity. The generalized photometric stereo algorithm combines the identity subspace with the illumination model and provides an illumination-invariant description. However, the 'Eigen' light field approach assumes a fixed illumination and cannot handle illumination variations, i.e., its pose-invariant identity encoding is not invariant to variations in illumination. The generalized photometric stereo algorithm assumes a fixed pose and cannot easily handle pose variations, i.e., its illumination-invariant identity description is not invariant to variations in pose. This motivates the integrated approach for handling both pose and illumination variations using an illumination- and pose-invariant identity signature.

Section 5.1 presents the principle of the illuminating light field approach. It begins by describing in Section 5.1.1 the 'Eigen' light field approach [76] that performs FR under pose variations, and then introduces in Section 5.1.2 our integrated approach. Section 5.1.3 presents algorithms for recovering the identity signature that is invariant to illumination and pose. Section 5.2 presents our experimental results on the PIE database [85] and comparisons with other approaches.

5.1 Principle of Illuminating Light Field

5.1.1 Pose-invariant identity signature

The light field measures the radiance in free space (free of occluding objects) as a 4D function of position and direction. An image is a 2D slice of the 4D light field. If the space is only 2D, the light field is then a 2D function. This is illustrated in Figure 5.1 (also see [76] for another illustration), where a camera conceptually moves along a circle, within which a square object with four differently colored sides resides. The 2D light field L is a function of θ and ϕ as properly defined in Figure 5.1. The image of the 2D object is just a vertical line. If the camera is allowed to leave the circle, then a curve is traced out in the light field to form the image, i.e. the light field is accordingly sampled. Even though the light field for a 3D object is a 4D function, we still use the notation $L(\theta, \phi)$ for the sake of simplification.

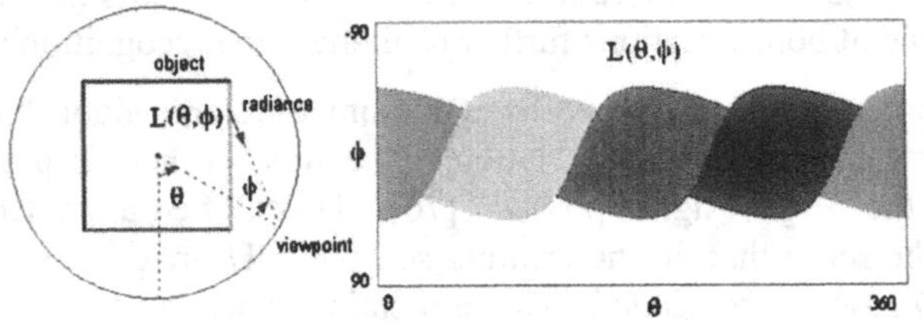

Figure 5.1. This figure illustrates the 2D light-field of a 2D object (a square with four differently colored sides), which is placed within an circle. The angles θ and ϕ are used to relate the viewpoint with the radiance from the object. The right image shows the actual light field for the square object.

Starting from the light fields $\{L_n(\theta, \phi);\ n = 1, ..., N\}$ of the training samples, the 'Eigen' light field approach conducts a PCA to find the eigenvectors $\{e_i(\theta, \phi);\ i = 1, ..., m\}$ which span a rank-m subspace. The 'Eigen' light field [76] is again motivated by the similarity among the human faces. Using the fact [50, 64] that: If $\mathrm{Y}^{\mathrm{T}}\mathrm{Y}$ has an eigenpair (λ, v), then YY^{T} has a corresponding eigenpair (λ, Yv), we know that $e_i(\theta, \phi)$ is just a linear combination of the $L_n(\theta, \phi)$'s, i.e., there exist a_{in}'s such that

$$e_i(\theta, \phi) = \sum_n a_{in} L_n(\theta, \phi). \tag{5.1}$$

For an arbitrary subject, its light field $L(\theta, \phi)$ lies in this rank-m subspace. In other words, there exists coefficients f_i's such that, $\forall(\theta, \phi)$,

$$L(\theta, \phi) = \sum_{i=1}^{m} f_i e_i(\theta, \phi) = \mathtt{e}(\theta, \phi)^{\mathsf{T}} \mathtt{f}, \tag{5.2}$$

where $\mathtt{e}(\theta, \phi) = [\Downarrow_{i=1}^{m} e_i(\theta, \phi)]_{m\times 1}$ and $\mathtt{f} = [\Downarrow_{i=1}^{m} f_i]_{m\times 1}$.

As mentioned earlier, to obtain an image $\mathtt{h}^v$ at a particular pose v (a collection of d pixels) one should sample the light field. Suppose that one pixel h^v is the point sample of the light field associated with the coordinate (θ^v, ϕ^v), i.e.,

$$h^v = L(\theta^v, \phi^v). \tag{5.3}$$

The image $\mathtt{h}^v$ can be expressed as

$$\mathtt{h}^v = [\Downarrow_{i=1}^{d} h_i^v] = [\Downarrow_{i=1}^{d} L(\theta_i^v, \phi_i^v)], \tag{5.4}$$

where (θ_i^v, ϕ_i^v) is the corresponding coordinate in the light field for the pixel h_i^v. Substituting Eqs. (5.2) into (5.4) yields

$$\mathtt{h}^v = [\Downarrow_{i=1}^{d} \mathtt{e}(\theta_i^v, \phi_i^v)^{\mathsf{T}}]\mathtt{f} = \mathtt{E}^v\mathtt{f}, \tag{5.5}$$

where $\mathtt{E}^v = [\Downarrow_{i=1}^{d} \mathtt{e}(\theta_i^v, \phi_i^v)^{\mathsf{T}}]_{d\times m}$.

Eq. (5.5) has an important implication: $\mathtt{f}$ is a pose-invariant identity signature because the pose information is encoded in $\mathtt{E}^v$. This is summarized in Theorem 5.1.

THEOREM 5.1 The identity signature $\mathtt{f}$ as derived in (5.5) is pose-invariant.

Constructing a light field is a practically difficult task. However, if only some specific poses are of interest with each pose sampling a subset of the light field, we can only focus on the portion of the light field that is equivalent to the union of these subsets. Suppose that the K poses are of interest are $\{v_1, ..., v_K\}$ and the corresponding images at these poses are $\{\mathtt{h}^{v_1}, \ldots, \mathtt{h}^{v_K}\}$ with $\mathtt{h}^{v_k}$ expressed as in (5.4), the portion of the light field of focus is nothing but $[\Downarrow_{k=1}^{K} [\Downarrow_{i=1}^{d} L(\theta_i^{v_k}, \phi_i^{v_k})]\ ]$, which is a 'long' $Kd \times 1$ vector obtained by stacking all the images at all these poses. The introduction of such a 'long' vector eases our computation: (i) If we are interested in a particular view v, we just simply take out those rows corresponding to this view. (ii) In this context, computing the 'Eigen' light field is equivalent to performing PCA on the ensemble consisting of a collection of such 'long' vectors.

The concept of light field was introduced in the computer graphics literature [219]. A strict assumption is that the scene be static. While characterizing the appearances of one object at given views using the concept of light field is legitimate, generalizing this to many objects is questionable since the lights fields belonging to different objects are not in correspondence, i.e. they are not shape-free in the terminology of [52, 87]. The mismatch in correspondence arises from differences in head sizes and locations in world coordinator system of different objects, and so on. Typically, correspondences between different objects are established using face normalization or registration is performed. Unfortunately, the normalization step ruins the static scene requirement in the light field theory. On the other hand, as argued in [52, 87], since the shape-free appearance is amenable for linear analysis, we can pursue PCA on the shape-free vector L, similar to the 'Eigen' light field approach [76]. This point is illustrated in [78]. Following [78], we also use the term light field in a loose sense.

5.1.2 Illumination- and pose-invariant identity signature

As mentioned earlier and in [219], the underlying assumption about the concept of light is one of fixed illumination. We now consider the light fields formed under varying illumination, i.e., illuminating the light field.

Clearly, the light field under a fixed illumination s, $L^s(\theta,\phi)$, follows the Lambertian reflectance model:

$$L^s(\theta,\phi) = \mathtt{t}(\theta,\phi)^{\mathsf{T}}\mathtt{s}, \tag{5.6}$$

where $\mathtt{t}(\theta,\phi)$ is the product of the albedo and the surface normal at a proper pixel and does not depend on $\mathtt{s}$. Combining Eq. (5.1) and Eq. (5.6) yields the 'Eigen' light field $e_i^s(\theta,\phi)$ under the illumination s as,

$$e_i^s(\theta,\phi) = \sum_n a_{in}\mathtt{t}_n(\theta,\phi)^{\mathsf{T}}\mathtt{s} = \mathtt{t}_{ei}(\theta,\phi)^{\mathsf{T}}\mathtt{s}, \tag{5.7}$$

where $\mathtt{t}_{ei}(\theta,\phi) = \sum_n a_{in}\mathtt{t}_n(\theta,\phi)$. Eq. (5.2) then becomes

$$L^s(\theta,\phi) = [\Downarrow_{i=1}^m \mathtt{t}_{ei}(\theta,\phi)^{\mathsf{T}}\mathtt{s}]^{\mathsf{T}}\mathtt{f} = \mathtt{W}(\theta,\phi)(\mathtt{f}\otimes\mathtt{s}), \tag{5.8}$$

where $\mathtt{W}(\theta,\phi) = [\Rightarrow_{i=1}^m \mathtt{t}_{ei}(\theta,\phi)]_{1\times 3m}$ does not depend on $\mathtt{s}$. This leads to a two-factor analysis [214].

A pixel h^{vs} under a pose v and an illumination s is a point sample of the light field $L^s(\theta,\phi)$ at coordinate (θ^v,ϕ^v), i.e.,

$$h^{vs} = L^s(\theta^v,\phi^v) = \mathtt{W}(\theta^v,\phi^v)(\mathtt{f}\otimes\mathtt{s}), \tag{5.9}$$

and an image $\mathbf{h}^{vs}$ under the pose v and illumination s, which traces a set of d samples of the light field under illumination s, is

$$\mathbf{h}^{vs} = [\Downarrow_{i=1}^d h_i^{vs}] = [\Downarrow_{i=1}^d \mathtt{W}(\theta_i^v,\phi_i^v)](\mathtt{f}\otimes\mathtt{s}) = \mathtt{W}^v(\theta,\phi)(\mathtt{f}\otimes\mathtt{s}), \tag{5.10}$$

where $\mathtt{W}^v(\theta,\phi) = [\Downarrow_{i=1}^{d} \mathtt{W}(\theta_i^v,\phi_i^v)]_{d\times 3m}$. Eq. (5.10) has an important implication: The coefficient vector $\mathbf{f}$ provides an identity signature invariant to both pose and illumination because the pose is absorbed in $\mathtt{W}^v(\theta,\phi)$ and the illumination is absorbed in $\mathbf{s}$.

THEOREM 5.2 The identity signature $\mathbf{f}$ as derived in (5.10) is illumination and pose-invariant.

The remaining questions are how to learn the basis matrix $\mathtt{W}(\theta,\phi)$ from a given training ensemble and how to compute the blending coefficient vector $\mathbf{f}$ as well as $\mathbf{s}$ for an arbitrary image $\mathbf{h}^{vs}$. The next section presents the algorithms in detail.

5.1.3 Learning algorithms

Learning the basis matrix $\mathtt{W}(\theta,\phi)$

Suppose that the training ensemble is given as $\{L_n^s(\theta,\phi);\ n=1,...N,\ s=1,...,S\}$, where $L_n^s(\theta,\phi)$ is the light field of the nth training object under illumination s (a $Kd\times 1$ vector as explained in Section 5.1.1). Learning $\mathtt{W}(\theta,\phi)$ (a $Kd\times mr$ matrix where m is the rank for the identity and r is the rank for the illumination) from the training ensemble is detailed in [214] and is further extended in [95] by imposing the integrability constraint. The main difference between [214] and [95] is the following: In [214], the recovered $\mathtt{W}(\theta,\phi)$ minimizes the approximation error in the mean square sense and not necessarily satisfies the integrability constraint. In other words, the hypothetical base objects in $\mathtt{W}(\theta,\phi)$ is not integrable. In [95], the recovered $\mathtt{W}(\theta,\phi)$ minimizes the above approximation error as well as a cost function invoked by violating the integrability constraint. As a consequence, [214] can only process the image ensemble consisting of different objects under the same set of illumination (e.g. the case considered here) while [95] can process the image ensemble consisting of different objects under completely different illumination. Here, we follow the approach in [214] to derive $\mathtt{W}(\theta,\phi)$ for simplicity. The basic underlying principle is to use a two-fold SVD algorithm that is reviewed below.

The following two matrices (A-type and B-type) are first constructed by grouping the 'long' vectors $\{L_n^s(\theta,\phi);\ n=1,...N,\ s=1,...,S\}$ in two ways:

$$\mathtt{A} = [\Downarrow_{n=1}^{N} [\Rightarrow_{s=1}^{S} L_n^s(\theta,\phi)]\,],\ \ \mathtt{B} = [\Downarrow_{s=1}^{S} [\Rightarrow_{n=1}^{N} L_n^s(\theta,\phi)]\,], \qquad (5.11)$$

where $\mathtt{A}$ is a $KNd\times S$ matrix whose rows stack together the light fields of different identities under the same illumination and whose columns correspond to different illumination and $\mathtt{B}$ is a $KSd\times N$ matrix whose rows stack together the light fields under different illumination for the same identity and whose columns correspond to different identities. It is obvious that we can convert from an A-type matrix to B-type and *vice versa*.

We perform the SVD for the $\mathtt{A}$ matrix as $\mathtt{A} = \mathtt{U}_{\mathtt{A}}\Lambda_{\mathtt{A}}\mathtt{V}_{\mathtt{A}}^{\mathsf{T}}$ and keep the top r rows of the column basis $\mathtt{V}_{\mathtt{A}}^{\mathsf{T}}$ for the illumination, denoted by $\mathtt{S}$. We do a similar operation on the $\mathtt{B}$ matrix and keep the top m rows of the column basis $\mathtt{V}_{\mathtt{B}}^{\mathsf{T}}$ for the identities, denoted by $\mathtt{F}$. Direct SVD of the $\mathtt{A}$ and $\mathtt{B}$ matrices is numerically inefficient or even prohibitive since they are extremely 'tall'. Also it is unnecessary to compute $\mathtt{U}$ and Λ as we are interested only in the $\mathtt{V}$ part of the SVD result. For computational savings, we observe that $\mathtt{V}_{\mathtt{A}}$ encodes the eigenvectors of $\mathtt{A}^{\mathsf{T}}\mathtt{A} = \mathtt{V}_{\mathtt{A}}\Lambda_{\mathtt{A}}^2\mathtt{V}_{\mathtt{A}}^{\mathsf{T}}$. Since the size of $\mathtt{A}^{\mathsf{T}}\mathtt{A}$ is only $S \times S$, computing its eigenvalues is numerically stable. Therefore, we simply first compute $\mathtt{A}^{\mathsf{T}}\mathtt{A}$ and then perform its 'Eigen' decomposition to find $\mathtt{V}_{\mathtt{A}}$. Similarly, we can compute $\mathtt{V}_{\mathtt{B}}$.

We now have the matrices $\mathtt{S}$ and $\mathtt{F}$ at our disposal. To find $\mathtt{W}(\theta, \phi)$, we first compute $\mathtt{A}' = \mathtt{A}\mathtt{S}^{\mathsf{T}}$, where $\mathtt{A}'$ is a $KNd \times r$ matrix. Notice that $\mathtt{A}'$ is still an $\mathtt{A}$-type matrix, so we can convert $\mathtt{A}'$ to a $\mathtt{B}$-type matrix $\mathtt{B}'$ following the strategy described in Eq. (5.11), where $\mathtt{B}'$ is a $Krd \times N$ matrix. Thirdly, we compute $\mathtt{W}' = \mathtt{B}'\mathtt{F}^{\mathsf{T}}$, where $\mathtt{W}'$ is a $Krd \times m$ matrix. The rest is to group $\mathtt{W}'$ to form a $Kd \times mr$ matrix $\mathtt{W}$.

Recovering the blending coefficient vector $\mathtt{f}$ from an image

Given $\mathtt{W}(\theta, \phi) = [\Rightarrow_{i=1}^{m} [\Rightarrow_{j=1}^{r} \mathtt{W}_{ij}(\theta, \phi)]\ ]_{Kd \times mr}$, where $\mathtt{W}_{ij}(\theta, \phi)$ denotes the $((i-1)*r+j)^{th}$ column of the $\mathtt{W}(\theta, \phi)$ matrix, computing $\mathtt{f}$ and $\mathtt{s}$ for an arbitrary image $\mathtt{h}^{vs}$ utilizes Eq. (5.10) iteratively [95]. Notice that we need only the portion of $\mathtt{W}(\theta, \phi)$ corresponding to the pose v, denoted by $\mathtt{W}^{v}(\theta, \phi) = [\Rightarrow_{i=1}^{m} [\Rightarrow_{j=1}^{r} \mathtt{W}_{ij}^{v}(\theta, \phi)]\ ]_{d \times mr}$.

If $\mathtt{f}$ is fixed, Eq. (5.10) is linear in $\mathtt{s}$ and its least square (LS) solution is

$$\mathtt{s} = [\Rightarrow_{j=1}^{r} ([\Rightarrow_{i=1}^{m} \mathtt{W}_{ij}^{v}(\theta, \phi)]\mathtt{f})\ ]^{\dagger}\mathtt{h}^{vs}, \tag{5.12}$$

where $[.]^{\dagger}$ is a matrix psuedo-inverse; if $\mathtt{s}$ is fixed, Eq. (5.10) is linear in $\mathtt{f}$ and its LS solution is

$$\mathtt{f} = \begin{bmatrix} [\Rightarrow_{i=1}^{m} ([\Rightarrow_{j=1}^{r} \mathtt{W}_{ij}^{v}(\theta, \phi)]\mathtt{s})\ ] \\ \mathtt{1}^{\mathsf{T}} \end{bmatrix}^{\dagger} \begin{bmatrix} \mathtt{h}^{vs} \\ 1 \end{bmatrix}, \tag{5.13}$$

where $\mathtt{1}$ is a vector of 1's. To obtain Eq. (5.13), we also impose $\mathtt{f}^{\mathsf{T}}\mathtt{1} = 1$ to normalize the solution to the same range, which facilitates the recognition task. We iterate this process until convergence. Meanwhile, we also take into account the pixels in shadows as in [95].

Recovering the blending coefficient vector $\mathtt{f}$ from a group of images

This iterative algorithm can be easily modified to handle a group of Q images $\{\mathtt{h}^{v_1 s_1}, \ldots, \mathtt{h}^{v_Q s_Q}\}$ having the same $\mathtt{f}$ but different $\mathtt{s}$'s since multiple equations like (5.10) can be formulated. To be specific, we have the following iterative equations:

$$\mathtt{s}_q = [\Rightarrow_{j=1}^{r} ([\Rightarrow_{i=1}^{m} \mathtt{W}_{ij}^{v_q}(\theta, \phi)]\mathtt{f})\,]^{\dagger}\mathtt{h}^{v_q s_q};\ \ q = 1, 2, \ldots, Q, \tag{5.14}$$

$$\mathtt{f} = \begin{bmatrix} [\Downarrow_{q=1}^{Q} [\Rightarrow_{i=1}^{m} ([\Rightarrow_{j=1}^{r} \mathtt{W}_{ij}^{v_q}(\theta, \phi)]\mathtt{s}_q)\,]\,] \\ \mathtt{1}^{\mathsf{T}} \end{bmatrix}^{\dagger} \begin{bmatrix} [\Downarrow_{q=1}^{Q} \mathtt{h}^{v_q s_q}] \\ 1 \end{bmatrix}. \tag{5.15}$$

In practice, using a group of images yields a robust estimate for $\mathtt{f}$.

The present of shadow pixels affects the learning algorithm. Handling shadows can be performed in the same fashion as in Chapter 4.

5.2 Face Recognition across Illumination and Poses

5.2.1 PIE database and recognition setting

We present the results on the 'illum' subset of the PIE database [85]. This subset has 68 subjects under 21 illumination and 13 poses. Out of 21 illumination configuration, we select 12 denoted by

$$F = \{f_{16}, f_{15}, f_{13}, f_{21}, f_{12}, f_{11}, f_{08}, f_{06}, f_{10}, f_{18}, f_{04}, f_{02}\}$$

as in [77], which typically span the set of variations. Out of the 13 poses, we select 9 denoted by

$$C = \{c_{22}, c_{02}, c_{37}, c_{05}, c_{27}, c_{29}, c_{11}, c_{14}, c_{34}\}$$

, which cover from the left profile to the right profile. In total, we have 68*12*9=7344 images. Figure 5.2 displays one PIE object under illumination and pose variations.

Registration is performed by aligning the eyes and mouth to desired positions. No flow computation is carried on for further alignment. After the pre-processing step, the used face image is of size 48 by 40, i.e. $d = 1920$. Also, we only use gray scale images by taking the average of the red, green, and blue channels of their color versions. We believe that our recognition rates can be boosted by using color images and finer registrations. Figure 5.2 shows some examples of the face images actually used in recognition.

We randomly divide the 68 subjects into two parts. The first 34 subjects are used in the training set and the remaining 34 subjects are used in the gallery and probe sets. It is guaranteed that there is no identity overlap between the training set and the gallery and probe sets. To form the light field, we use images at all available poses. Since the illumination model has generalization capability, we

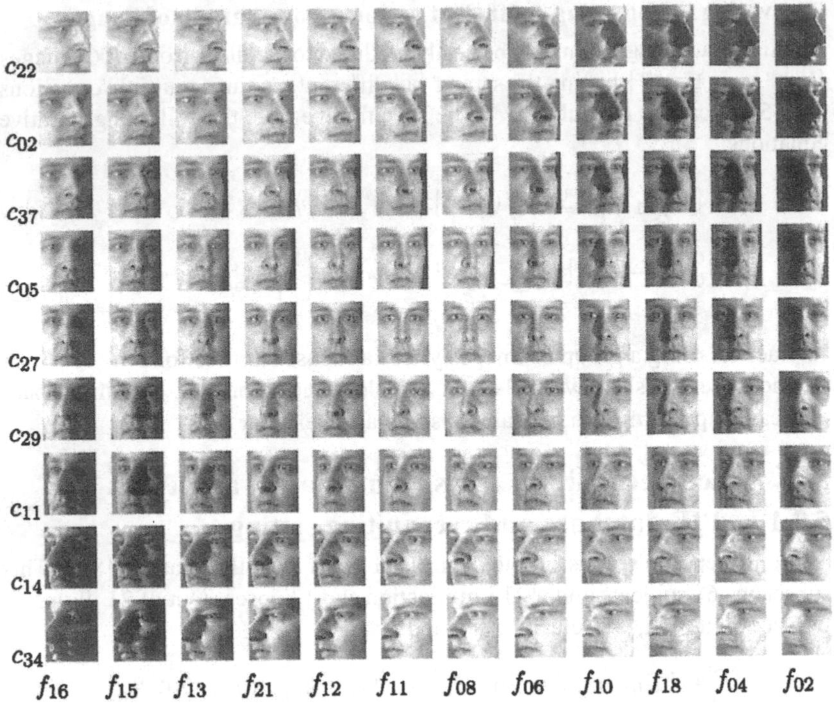

Figure 5.2. Examples of the face images of one PIE object (used in the testing stage) under selected illumination and poses .

can select a minimum of 3 illumination in the training set. In our experiments, the training set includes only 9 selected illumination to cover the second-order harmonic components [144]. Notice that this is not possible in the Fisher light field approach [77] that exhausts all illumination configurations.

The images belonging to the remaining 34 subjects are used in the gallery and probe sets. The construction of the gallery and probe sets conforms to the following two scenarios: (A) We use all the 34 images under one illumination s_p and one pose v_p to form a gallery set and under the other illumination s_g and the other pose v_g to form a probe set. There are three cases of interest: *same pose but different illumination*, *different pose but same illumination*, and *different pose and different illumination*. We mainly concentrate on the third case with $s_p \neq s_g$ and $v_p \neq v_g$. Also our approach reduces to the 'Eigen' light field approach [76] if $s_p = s_g$ and to the generalized photometric stereo approach [95] if $v_p = v_g$. Thus, we have $(9 * 12)^2 - (9 * 12) = 11,556$ tests, with each test giving rise to a recognition score. (B) We divide C into three sets: $C_1 = \{c_{22}, c_{02}, c_{37}\}$ (left-profile views), $C_2 = \{c_{05}, c_{27}, c_{29}\}$ (frontal views), and $C_3 = \{c_{11}, c_{14}, c_{34}\}$

(right-profile views) and F into 3 sets: $F_1 = \{f_{16}, f_{15}, f_{13}, f_{21}\}$ (left lights), $F_2 = \{f_{12}, f_{11}, f_{08}, f_{06}\}$ (frontal lights), and $F_3 = \{f_{10}, f_{18}, f_{04}, f_{02}\}$ (right lights). For each of the thirty four subjects, the gallery set contains all twelve images under the illumination in F_g and the poses in C_g and the probe set all twelve images under the illumination in F_p and the poses in C_g. We make sure that $(C_p, F_P) \neq (C_g, F_g)$. Thus, we have $(3 * 3)^2 - (3 * 3) = 72$ tests in this scenario that has no counterpart in the Fisher light field [77]. To make the recognition more difficult, we assume that the lighting conditions for the training, gallery and probe sets are completely unknown when recovering the identity signatures.

The testing strategy is similar to that described in Chapter 4.

1 Learn `W` from the training set using the bilinear learning algorithm [214, 95]. Figure 5.3 shows the `W` matrix obtained using the training set.

2 With `W` given, learn the identity signature `f`'s (as well as `s`'s) for all gallery and probe elements (an element is an image in Scenario A and a group of images in Scenario B) using the iterative algorithms in Section 5.1.3. Learning `f` and `s` from one single image takes about 1-2 seconds in a Matlab implementation. Figure 5.4 shows the reconstructed images using the learned `f` and `s`.

3 Perform recognition using the nearest correlation coefficient.

Gly	f_{16}	f_{15}	f_{13}	f_{21}	f_{12}	f_{11}	f_{08}	f_{06}	f_{10}	f_{18}	f_{04}	f_{02}	*Avg*
Prb													
c_{22}	56	41	62	68	71	71	53	65	41	44	38	21	52
c_{02}	71	76	76	91	88	94	94	94	85	71	50	32	77
c_{37}	79	82	82	94	94	97	94	94	76	65	65	50	81
c_{05}	68	85	97	100	100	97	97	97	91	82	71	44	86
c_{27}	94	100	100	100	100	–	100	100	100	97	94	76	97
c_{29}	74	82	91	100	100	100	97	97	94	91	88	65	90
c_{11}	50	53	68	79	85	97	97	88	79	82	71	62	76
c_{14}	15	24	44	71	76	82	74	82	82	74	79	56	63
c_{34}	18	18	47	50	56	65	62	56	44	44	41	38	45
Avg	58	62	74	84	86	88	85	86	77	72	66	49	74

Table 5.1. Recognition rates for all the probe sets with a fixed gallery set (c_{27},f_{11}).

5.2.2 Recognition performance

Scenario A

Table 5.1 shows the recognition results for all probe sets with a fixed gallery set (c_{27},f_{11}), whose gallery images are in a frontal pose and under a frontal illumination. Using this table we compare the three cases. The case of same pose but different illumination has an average rate 97% (i.e. the average of all 11 cells on the row c_{27}), the case of different pose but same illumination has an average rate 88% (i.e. the average of all 8 cells on the column f_{11}), the case of different pose and different illumination has an average rate 70% (i.e. the average of all 88 cells excluding the row c_{27} and the column f_{11}). This shows that illumination variation is easier to handle than pose illumination and variations in both pose and illumination are the most difficult to deal with.

Gly	f_{16}	f_{15}	f_{13}	f_{21}	f_{12}	f_{11}	f_{08}	f_{06}	f_{10}	f_{18}	f_{04}	f_{02}	Avg
Prb													
c_{22}	44	44	46	45	46	49	46	49	44	32	30	14	41
c_{02}	55	58	59	62	63	62	60	60	54	48	40	22	54
c_{37}	56	59	61	64	65	62	60	58	51	47	45	34	55
c_{05}	56	63	66	67	68	65	59	58	54	51	45	36	57
c_{27}	62	66	69	70	70	70	65	69	68	67	65	54	66
c_{29}	46	53	53	61	60	63	59	62	66	68	62	60	60
c_{11}	41	43	50	53	55	61	57	58	56	61	58	51	54
c_{14}	19	24	39	49	53	58	58	61	60	61	57	48	49
c_{34}	16	21	38	44	46	51	48	51	46	45	45	42	41
Avg	44	48	53	57	59	60	57	59	56	53	50	40	53

Table 5.2. Average recognition rates for all the gallery sets. For each cell, say the gallery set at ($v_g = c_{27}, s_g = f_{12}$), the average rate is taken over all probe sets (v_p, s_p) where $v_p \neq v_g$ and $s_p \neq s_g$. For example, the average rate for (c_{27}, f_{11}) is the average of the rates in Table 5.1 excluding the row c_{27} and the column f_{11}.

We now focus on the case of different pose and different illumination. For each gallery set, we average the recognition scores of all the probe sets with both pose and illumination different from the gallery set. Table 5.2 shows the average recognition rates for all the gallery sets. As an interesting comparison, the 'grand' average is 53% (the last cell in Table 5.2) while that of the Fisher light field approach [77] is 36%. In general, when the poses and illumination of the gallery and probe sets become far apart, the recognition rates decrease. The best gallery sets for recognition are those in frontal poses and under frontal illumination and the worst gallery sets are those in profile views and off-frontal illumination. As shown in Figures 1.4 and 5.2, the worst gallery sets consist of face images almost invisible (See for example the images (c_{22}, f_{02}), (c_{34}, f_{16}), etc.), on which recognition can be hardly performed.

Figure 5.5 presents the curves of the average recognition rates (i.e. the last columns and last rows of Tables 5.1 and 5.2) across poses and illumination. Clearly the effect of illumination variations is not as strong as due to pose variations in the sense that the curves of average recognition rates across illumination are flatter than those across poses. Figure 5.5 also shows the curves of the average recognition rates obtained based on the top 3 and top 5 matches. Using more matches increases the recognition rates significantly, which demonstrates the efficiency of our recognition scheme. For comparison, Figure 5.5 also plots the average rates obtained using the baseline PCA. These rates are well below ours. The 'grand' average is below 10% if the top 1 match is used.

Figure 5.3. The first nine columns of the learned W matrix.

Scenario B

This test scenario is designed for face recognition based on a group of images, which can be under different poses and different illumination. Table 5.3 lists the recognition rates, which are much higher than those in Tables 5.1 and 5.2. Also, similar observations can be made regarding the effects of illumination and pose variations.

5.2.3 Comparison with the 3D morphable model

The 3D morphable model (3DMM) [72] is the state-of-the-art approach to identify faces across illumination and poses. The proposed approach differs from the 3DMM approach mainly as follows:

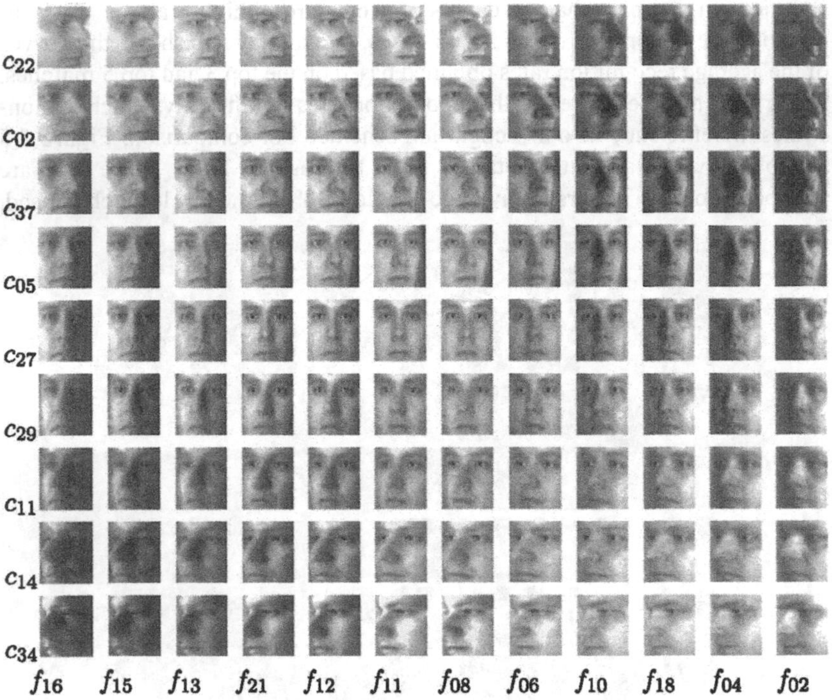

Figure 5.4. The reconstruction results of the object in Figure 5.2. Notice that only the f's and s's for the row c_{27} are used for reconstructing all the images.

Gallery	C_1F_1	C_1F_2	C_1F_3	C_2F_1	C_2F_2	C_2F_3	C_3F_1	C_3F_2	C_3F_3	*Average*
Probe										
C_1F_1	–	100	85	100	94	82	62	85	94	88
C_1F_2	100	–	100	100	100	85	71	82	94	92
C_1F_3	85	97	–	88	88	91	76	62	65	82
C_2F_1	97	94	71	–	100	85	71	85	76	85
C_2F_2	97	100	85	100	–	100	76	91	85	92
C_2F_3	79	82	76	97	100	–	74	88	91	86
C_3F_2	59	59	68	85	76	71	–	100	82	75
C_3F_2	74	85	62	91	94	82	100	–	100	86
C_3F_3	88	82	62	79	79	94	85	100	–	84
Average	85	88	76	93	92	86	77	87	86	85

Table 5.3. The recognition rates for test scenario B.

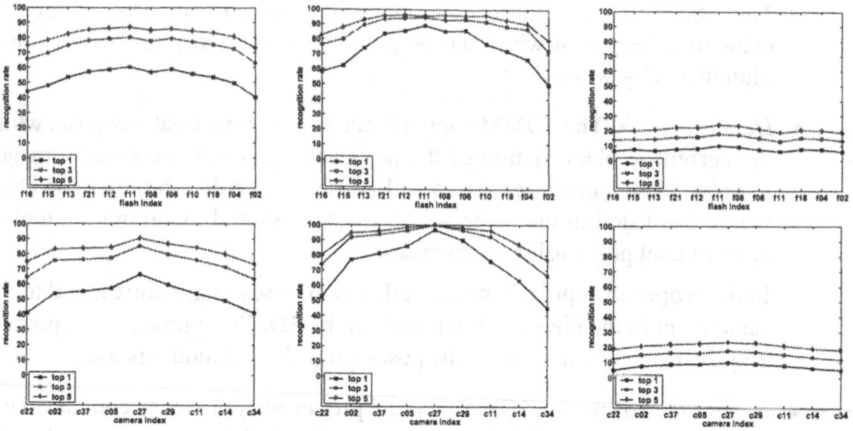

(a) (b) (c)

Figure 5.5. The average recognition rates across illumination (the top row) and across poses (the bottom row) for three cases. Case (a) shows the average recognition rate (averaging over all illumination/poses and all gallery sets) obtained by the proposed algorithm using the top n matches. Case (b) shows the average recognition rate (averaging over all illumination/poses for the gallery set (c_{27}, f_{11}) only) obtained by the proposed algorithm using the top n matches. Case(c) shows the average recognition rate (averaging over all illumination/poses and all gallery sets) obtained by the 'Eigenface' algorithm using the top n matches.

- *Model-based v.s. image-based.* The 3DMM approach requires prior 3D models while the proposed approach that is image-based needs only 2D images.

  Linear assumptions are used in both approaches. Two major components in the 3DMM approach are 3D depth and texture, respectively, and two independent linear models are assumed in both components. The major component in the proposed approach is the product of the albedo and surface normal and a single linear model is assumed. As in the 3DMM approach, it seems that the dimensionality of the proposed model can be 'decomposed' as the product (or the addition) of the dimensionality of the surface normals and that of the albedo field. However, empirical analysis shows [94] that such a decomposition is not necessary and might overfit the problem, thereby indicating that a subspace of rather low dimensionality can be used.

- *Handling illumination.* The Lambertian model is used in the proposed algorithm and pixels in shadows and specular reflection regions are inferred and excluded for consideration. The 3DMM approach uses the standard Phong model to directly model diffuse and specular reflection on the face surface.

The 3DMM also takes into account inputs illuminated by colored lights using color transformation while the proposed approach only processes inputs illuminated by white lights.

- *Handling pose.* The 3DMM approach can handle images at any pose, while the current implementation of the proposed approach can handle images sampled from a given set of poses. In order to handle arbitrary pose other than those listed in the given set, the system should incorporate a tool to render novel poses using given poses.

  In the proposed approach, pixels at different poses might correspond to the same point in the physical 3D model. In the 3DMM approach, one point is only represented once for all the poses since the 3D model is used.

- *Experiments* Both the 3DMM and the proposed approaches conducted experiments using the PIE database. However, different portions of the PIE database are used. The 3DMM approach worked on the 'lights' part, where an ambient light source is always present. The proposed approach worked on the 'illum' part with no ambient light source. As a consequence, some images appear almost dark (refer to Figure 5.2) and there is little hope of performing correct recognition based on these extreme images, explaining the relatively low recognition rates compared with those produced by the 3DMM approach.

  In terms of computational complexity, the proposed algorithm is more computationally efficient than the 3DMM approach. The proposed fitting algorithm, taking 1-2 seconds to process one input image using Matlab implementation, is simply linear (rather bilinear) and has a unique minimum; while the 3DMM approach, taking 4.5 minutes to process one input image, invokes a gradient descent algorithm that does not guarantee a global minimum. Also, the proposed algorithm is able to handle face images of very small size. In the reported experiments, gray-level images are normalized to size of 48×40. The size of color images used in the 3DMM approach is unclear, but typically much larger.

Chapter 6

FACIAL AGING

In this chapter, we focus on two research topics related to facial aging: age estimation and face recognition across aging progression.

6.1 Age Estimation

We attack the problem of age estimation using a general technique of image based regression (IBR). The problem of IBR is defined as follows: Given an image x, we are interested in inferring an entity y(x) that is associated with the image x. Since IBR is a general technique, the meaning of y(x) varies in different applications. Figure 6.1 illustrates three IBR tasks. For example, it could be a feature characterizing the image (e.g., the human age in the first problem A), a parameter related to the image (e.g., the position and anisotropic spread of the tumor in the second problem B), or other meaningful quantity (e.g., the location of the endocardial wall in the third problem C).

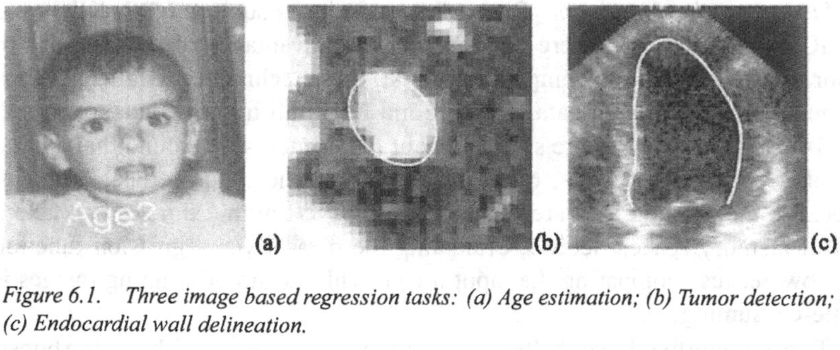

Figure 6.1. Three image based regression tasks: (a) Age estimation; (b) Tumor detection; and (c) Endocardial wall delineation.

IBR is an emerging challenge in the vision literature. In the article of Wang *et al.* [227], support vector regression was employed to infer the shape deformation parameter. In a recent work [207], Agarwal and Triggs used the relevance vector regression to estimate the 3D human pose from silhouettes. However, in the above two works, the inputs to the regressors are not images themselves, rather pre-processed entities, e.g., landmark locations in [227] and shape context descriptor in [207].

Numerous algorithms [9] have been proposed in the machine learning literature to attack the general regression problem. Chapter 2 briefly reviewed the data-driven regression techniques. However, it is often difficult or inefficient to directly apply them to vision applications due to the following challenges.

Curse of dimensionality. The input (i.e. image data) is of very high dimension, which manifests the phenomenon commonly referred to as the curse of dimensionality. Ideally, in order to adequately represent the sample space, the number of required image samples should be exponential to the cardinality of the input space. However, in practice, the number of training samples is often extremely sparse, compared with the cardinality of the input space.

Varying appearance. First, there are a lot of factors that affect the appearance of the foreground object of interest. Apart from the intrinsic differences among the objects, extrinsic factors include the camera system, imaging geometry, lighting conditions, makeup, etc. Second, the variation arises from the presence of background whose appearance varies too. The third variation is caused by alignment. The regression technique must either tolerate the alignment error (as in the problems A) or regress out the alignment parameter (as in the problems B and C).

Multiple output. The output variable is also of high dimensional. Most regression approaches, such as SVR, can deal with the single-output regression problem very robustly. Extending them to the multiple-output setting is sometime nontrivial as in the case of SVR. A naive practice of decoupling a multiple-output problem to several isolated single-output tasks ignores the statistical dependence among different dimensions of the output variable.

Storage and computation. Regression techniques such as NPR, KRR, and SVR are data-driven. There are two main disadvantages of the data-driven approaches: storage and computation. First, these techniques require storing a large amount of training data. In NPR and KRR, all training data are stored. In SVR, support vectors are stored. In our experiments, we found that a large number of support vectors, often 80%-100% of the training data, are kept. Because the training data are images, storing the training images can take a lot of memory space. Second, evaluating the data-driven regression function is slow because comparing the input image with the stored training images is time-consuming.

To overcome the above challenges, we propose an IBR algorithm using boosting methods [238, 240, 241, 254]. AdaBoosting is the state-of-the-art classification method. After its theoretic connection to forward stagewise additive modeling [241] was discovered, Friedman [242] used boosting as a greedy function approximation in a regression setting [242]. Multiple additive regression tree (MART) [9] was proposed as a boosting tree solution to a single-output regression problem. Duffy and Helmbold [238] also studied boosting methods for regression for a single-output setting. However, a multiple-output regression setting is rarely studied in the literature. In this chapter, we focus on this setting that takes images as inputs. Features of our approaches are:

1 We formulate the multiple-output regression problem in such way that an analytic solution is allowed at each round of boosting. No decoupling of the output dimension is performed. Also, we decrease overfitting using an image-based regularization term that can be interpreted as prior knowledge. In addition, the regularization allows an analytic solution.

2 We invoke the boosting framework to perform feature selection such that only relevant local features are preserved to conquer the variations in appearance. The use of decision stump as weak learner also makes it robust to appearance change.

3 We use the Haar-like simple features [197] that can be rapidly computed. As a result, we do not store the training data. The knowledge of the training data is absorbed in the weighting coefficients and the selected feature set. Also, we evaluate the regression function almost in no time.

4 We propose an efficient implementation to perform boosting training, which is usually a time-consuming process if a truly greedy feature selection procedure is used. In our implementation, we select the features incrementally over the dimension of the output variable.

6.1.1 Regression using boosting method

We now define the loss function and the regularization term that are appropriate for our purpose of developing regression algorithm using boosting method.

We focus on the L^2 loss function. To allow a general treatment and to deal with the scaling effort of different data dimensions, we use the normalized error cost:

$$\begin{aligned} L(\mathtt{y}(\mathtt{x}), \mathtt{g}(\mathtt{x})) &= [\mathtt{y}(\mathtt{x}) - \mathtt{g}(\mathtt{x})]^{\mathsf{T}} \mathtt{A} [\mathtt{y}(\mathtt{x}) - \mathtt{g}(\mathtt{x})] \\ &= \|\mathtt{y}(\mathtt{x}) - \mathtt{g}(\mathtt{x})\|^2_{\mathtt{A}}, \end{aligned} \tag{6.1}$$

where $\mathtt{A}_{q\times q}$ is a *normalization matrix* that must be positive definite.

Regularization exists in various forms. We focus on the following data-driven regularization term $\|\mu - \mathtt{g}(\mathtt{x})\|^2_{\mathtt{B}}$, where $\mathtt{B}_{q\times q}$ is a *normalization matrix* that must be positive definite. This regularization term has a subspace interpretation with μ being the mean and B^{-1} being the covariance matrix.

Hence, it boils down to the following cost function to be minimized.

$$\begin{aligned} J(g) &= \sum_{n=1}^{N} \|y(x_n) - g(x_n)\|_A^2 + \lambda \sum_{n=1}^{N} \|\mu - g(x_n)\|_B^2 \\ &= \sum_{n=1}^{N} \|r(x_n)\|_A^2 + \lambda \sum_{n=1}^{N} \|s(x_n)\|_B^2 \\ &= tr\{ARR^T\} + \lambda tr\{BSS^T\} \\ &= \|R\|_A^2 + \lambda \|S\|_B^2, \end{aligned} \tag{6.2}$$

where $r(x) = y(x) - g(x)$ is the *approximation error*, $s(x) = u - g(x)$ is the *deviation error*, and the matrices $R_{q \times N}$ and $S_{q \times N}$ are, respectively, defined as follows $R = [r(x_1), r(x_2), \ldots, r(x_N)]$, $S = [s(x_1), s(x_2), \ldots, s(x_N)]$.

We now resort to the influential framework of boosting to derive an *analytic* solution.

Boosting

In boosting method for regression, the regression output function $g(x) : \mathcal{R}^d \rightarrow \mathcal{R}^q$ is assumed to take a linear form:

$$g(x) = \sum_{t=1}^{T} \alpha_t h_t(x); \; h_t(x) \in \mathcal{H}, \tag{6.3}$$

where each $h_t(x)$ is a weak learner (or weaker function) and $g(x)$ is a strong learner (or strong function). Further, it is assumed that a weak function $h(x) : \mathcal{R}^d \rightarrow \mathcal{R}^q$ lies in a *dictionary* set or weak function set $\mathcal{H}$.

Boosting iteratively approximates the target function $y(x)$ by adding one more weak function using the additive form:

$$g'(x) = g(x) + \alpha h(x). \tag{6.4}$$

At each round of boosting, we select the function $\hat{h}$ and its weight coefficient $\hat{\alpha}$ that mostly decreases the cost function. In other words, the following problem is attacked.

$$(\hat{\alpha}, \hat{h}) = \arg \min_{\alpha, h \in \mathcal{H}} J(g + \alpha h). \tag{6.5}$$

THEOREM 6.1 *By adding a function $\alpha h(x)$ to the output function $g(x)$ as in Eq. (6.4), the new cost function $J(g')$ maximally decreases the cost function $J(g)$ by a factor of $(1 - \epsilon^2(h))$, with $|\epsilon(h)| \leq 1$.*

Proof: The cost function of $J(\mathrm{g}')$ is computed as

$$
\begin{aligned}
J(\mathrm{g}') &= \sum_{n=1}^{N} \|\mathrm{y}(\mathrm{x}_n) - \mathrm{g}'(\mathrm{x}_n)\|_{\mathrm{A}}^2 + \lambda \sum_{n=1}^{N} \|\mu - \mathrm{g}'(\mathrm{x}_n)\|_{\mathrm{B}}^2 \\
&= \sum_{n=1}^{N} \|\mathrm{y}(\mathrm{x}_n) - \mathrm{g}(\mathrm{x}_n) - \alpha \mathrm{h}(\mathrm{x}_n)\|_{\mathrm{A}}^2 + \\
&\quad \lambda \sum_{n=1}^{N} \|\mu - \mathrm{g}(\mathrm{x}_n) - \alpha \mathrm{h}(\mathrm{x}_n)\|_{\mathrm{B}}^2 \\
&= \sum_{n=1}^{N} \|\mathrm{r}(\mathrm{x}_n) - \alpha \mathrm{h}(\mathrm{x}_n)\|_{\mathrm{A}}^2 + \lambda \sum_{n=1}^{N} \|\mathrm{s}(\mathrm{x}_n) - \alpha \mathrm{h}(\mathrm{x}_n)\|_{\mathrm{B}}^2 \\
&= tr\{\mathrm{A}[\mathrm{R} - \alpha \mathrm{H}][\mathrm{R} - \alpha \mathrm{H}]^{\mathsf{T}}\} + \lambda tr\{\mathrm{B}[\mathrm{S} - \alpha \mathrm{H}][\mathrm{S} - \alpha \mathrm{H}]^{\mathsf{T}}\} \\
&= (tr\{\mathrm{ARR}^{\mathsf{T}}\} + \lambda tr\{\mathrm{BSS}^{\mathsf{T}}\}) - 2\alpha(tr\{\mathrm{ARH}^{\mathsf{T}}\} + \lambda tr\{\mathrm{BSH}^{\mathsf{T}}\}) \\
&\quad + \alpha^2(tr\{\mathrm{AHH}^{\mathsf{T}}\} + \lambda tr\{\mathrm{BHH}^{\mathsf{T}}\}) \\
&= J(\mathrm{g}) - 2\alpha\, tr\{(\mathrm{AR} + \lambda \mathrm{BS})\mathrm{H}^{\mathsf{T}}\} + \alpha^2 \|\mathrm{H}\|_{\mathrm{A}+\lambda\mathrm{B}}^2 \\
&= J(\mathrm{g}) - 2\alpha\, tr\{\mathrm{DH}^{\mathsf{T}}\} + \alpha^2 \|\mathrm{H}\|_{\mathrm{C}}^2, \qquad (6.6)
\end{aligned}
$$

where $\mathrm{C} = \mathrm{A} + \lambda\mathrm{B}$, $\mathrm{D} = \mathrm{AR} + \lambda\mathrm{BS}$, and $\mathrm{H}_{q\times N} = [\mathrm{h}(\mathrm{x}_1), \mathrm{h}(\mathrm{x}_2), \ldots, \mathrm{h}(\mathrm{x}_N)]$.

With the function h fixed, the cost function $J(\mathrm{g}')$ is quadratic in α so that there is a unique minimizer $\hat{\alpha}(\mathrm{h})$. By letting $\frac{\partial J(\mathrm{g}')}{\partial \alpha} = 0$, simple algebra yields that

$$\hat{\alpha}(\mathrm{h}) = \frac{tr\{\mathrm{DH}^{\mathsf{T}}\}}{\|\mathrm{H}\|_{\mathrm{C}}^2} = \frac{tr\{(\mathrm{AR} + \lambda\mathrm{BS})\mathrm{H}^{\mathsf{T}}\}}{\|\mathrm{H}\|_{\mathrm{A}+\lambda\mathrm{B}}^2}. \qquad (6.7)$$

The minimum cost $J(\mathrm{g}')$ is then calculated as

$$J(\mathrm{g}') = J(\mathrm{g}) - \frac{tr^2\{\mathrm{DH}^{\mathsf{T}}\}}{\|\mathrm{H}\|_{\mathrm{C}}^2} = J(\mathrm{g})(1 - \epsilon^2(\mathrm{h})), \qquad (6.8)$$

where

$$\epsilon(\mathrm{h}) = \frac{\hat{\alpha}(\mathrm{h})\sqrt{\|\mathrm{H}\|_{\mathrm{C}}^2}}{\sqrt{\|\mathrm{R}\|_{\mathrm{A}}^2 + \lambda\|\mathrm{S}\|_{\mathrm{B}}^2}} = \frac{tr\{\mathrm{DH}^{\mathsf{T}}\}}{\sqrt{\|\mathrm{H}\|_{\mathrm{C}}^2}\sqrt{\|\mathrm{R}\|_{\mathrm{A}}^2 + \lambda\|\mathrm{S}\|_{\mathrm{B}}^2}}. \qquad (6.9)$$

It is obvious that $|\epsilon(\mathrm{h})| \leq 1$ since the cost functions $J(\mathrm{g}')$ and $J(\mathrm{g})$ is nonnegative. *< E.O.F. >*

In practice, we can always assume $\epsilon(\mathrm{h}) \geq 0$ because, if $\epsilon(h) < 0$, we simply change the sign of the function h. Therefore, in the sequel, the absolute symbol $|.|$ is removed. Correspondingly, we have $\hat{\alpha}(\mathrm{h}) \geq 0$ because $\hat{\alpha}(\mathrm{h})$ and $\epsilon(\mathrm{h})$ have the same sign.

Therefore, each boosting round aims at finding the function $\mathtt{h}$ such that the cost function is maximally reduced. Equivalently, the value of $\epsilon(\mathtt{h})$ is maximized.

$$\hat{\mathtt{h}} = \arg \max_{\mathtt{h}\in\mathcal{H}} \epsilon(\mathtt{h}) = \arg \max_{\mathtt{h}\in\mathcal{H}} \frac{tr\{\mathtt{DH}^{\mathsf{T}}\}}{\sqrt{\|\mathtt{H}\|_{\mathtt{C}}^2}}. \tag{6.10}$$

Note that the term $\sqrt{\|\mathtt{R}\|_{\mathtt{A}}^2 + \lambda\|\mathtt{S}\|_{\mathtt{B}}^2}$ does not depend on $\mathtt{H}$ and hence can be ignored in the above. The corresponding value of α is $\hat{\alpha}(\hat{\mathtt{h}})$. Finally, the cost $J(\mathtt{g}')$ maximally decreases the cost $J(\mathtt{g})$ by a factor of $(1 - \epsilon(\hat{\mathtt{h}})^2)$.

Shrinkage

Shrinkage [235, 242] is another measure for reducing the effect of overfitting. The idea is very simple: at each round of boosting, simply shrink the newly selected function $\alpha\mathtt{h}(\mathtt{x})$ by a *shrinkage factor* $\eta \in [0, 1]$. The new updating rule is

$$\mathtt{g}'(\mathtt{x}) = \mathtt{g}(\mathtt{x}) + \eta\hat{\alpha}\hat{\mathtt{h}}(\mathtt{x}), \tag{6.11}$$

where $\hat{\alpha}$ and $\hat{\mathtt{h}}$ are the optimal solutions found above. In practice, we found that a modest choice of $\eta = 0.5$ gives good results.

Figure 6.2 summarizes the regression algorithm using boosting method.

1 Initialization $t = 0$.

(a) Set the fixed parameter values: μ (the mean vector), $\mathtt{A}$ and $\mathtt{B}$ (the normalization matrices), λ (the regularization coefficient), and η (the shrinkage factor).

(b) Set the values related to the stopping criteria: T_{max} (the maximum number of iterations), J_{min} (the minimum cost function), ϵ_{min}, and α_{min}.

(c) Set initial values for $t = 0$: $\mathtt{g}_0(\mathtt{x}) = 0$, $\mathtt{r}_0(x) = \mathtt{y}(\mathtt{x})$, and $\mathtt{s}_0(\mathtt{x}) = \mu$.

2 Iteration $t = 1, \ldots, T_{max}$

(a) Find $\hat{\mathtt{h}}_t = \arg \max_{\mathtt{h}\in\mathcal{H}} \epsilon_t(\mathtt{h})$ and its corresponding $\hat{\alpha}_t(\hat{\mathtt{h}}_t)$ and $\epsilon_t(\hat{\mathtt{h}}_t)$.

(b) Form the new function $\mathtt{g}_t(\mathtt{x}) = \mathtt{g}_{t-1}(\mathtt{x}) + \eta\hat{\alpha}_t\hat{\mathtt{h}}_t(\mathtt{x})$.

(c) Evaluate the approximation error $\mathtt{r}_t(\mathtt{x}) = \mathtt{y}(\mathtt{x}) - \mathtt{g}_t(\mathtt{x})$ and the deviation error $\mathtt{s}_t(\mathtt{x}) = \mu - \mathtt{g}_t(\mathtt{x})$.

(d) Evaluate the cost function $J(\mathtt{g}_t)$.

(e) Check convergence, e.g. see if $J(\mathtt{g}_t) < J_{min}$, $\alpha_t < \alpha_{min}$, $\epsilon_t < \epsilon_{min}$, or combination of them.

Figure 6.2. Regression algorithm using boosting method.

6.1.2 Image based regression

The image-related entity is the dictionary set $\mathcal{H}$, whose every element is based on the image x. Intuitively, this function set must be sufficiently large such that it allows rendering, through a linear combination, highly complex output function $y(\mathbf{x})$. Following the work of Viola and Jones [197], we use one-dimensional decision stumps as primitives to construct the weak function set $\mathcal{H}$. The advantages of using decision stumps include (i) that they are robust to appearance variation; (ii) that they are local features; (iii) that they are fast to evaluate using the so-called integral image [197]; and, most importantly, (iv) that they allows an incremental feature selection scheme that will be addressed later.

Weak function set

A one-dimensional (1D) decision stump $h(\mathbf{x})$ is associated with a Haar filter feature $f(\mathbf{x})$, a decision threshold θ, and a parity direction indicator p that takes a binary value of either $+1$ or -1.

$$h(\mathbf{x}) = \begin{cases} +1 & \text{if } pf(\mathbf{x}) \geq p\theta \\ -1 & \text{otherwise} \end{cases} \tag{6.12}$$

Each Haar filter $f(\mathbf{x})$ has its own attributes: type, window position, and window size. Given a moderate size of image, one can generate a huge number of Haar filters by varying the filter attributes. See [197] for details. Denote the number of Haar filters by M. By adjusting the threshold θ (say K even-spaced levels), for every Haar filter, one can further create K decision stumps. In total, we have $2KM$ 1-D decision stumps. Note that the number $2KM$ can be prohibitively large so that it can even create difficulty in storing all these decision stumps during training.

A weak function is constructed as a q-dimensional (q-D) decision stump $\mathbf{h}(\mathbf{x})$ that simply stacks q 1D decision stumps.

$$\mathbf{h}(\mathbf{x})_{q\times 1} = [h_1(\mathbf{x}), h_2(\mathbf{x}), ..., h_q(\mathbf{x})]^\mathsf{T}.$$

Note that each $h_j(\mathbf{x})$ in the above may be associated with a different parameter. Hence, one can construct a sufficiently large weak function set that contains $(2KM)^q$ weak functions!

Feature selection

Boosting operates as a feature selection oracle. At each round of boosting, the features that can maximally decrease the cost function are selected. However, to transform the boosting recipe in Figure 6.2 into an efficient IBR algorithm, there is a computational bottleneck, that is Step $(2a)$. This step necessitates a *greedy* feature selection scheme that is too expensive to evaluate because, in principle, it involves evaluating $(2MNK)^q$ decision stumps, a formidable computational task in practice.

One possible way is to break the q-D regression problem into q *independent* 1D regression problems, leading to an *independent* feature selection scheme. Consequently, only $2qMNK$ decision stumps are evaluated at each round of boosting. However, the independence assumption is too strong to be hold in real situations.

We propose an *incremental* feature selection scheme by breaking the q-D regression problem into q *dependent* 1D regression problems. Using the incremental vector

$$\mathtt{h}^i(\mathtt{x})_{i\times 1} = [h_1(\mathtt{x}), h_2(\mathtt{x}), ..., h_i(\mathtt{x})]^{\mathsf{T}} = [\mathtt{h}^{i-1}(\mathtt{x})^{\mathsf{T}}, h_i(\mathtt{x})]^{\mathsf{T}},$$

and the incremental matrices $\mathtt{C}^i$, $\mathtt{D}^i$, and $\mathtt{H}^i$,

$$\mathtt{C}^i = \begin{bmatrix} \mathtt{C}^{i-1} & \mathtt{c}^{i-1} \\ \mathtt{c}^{i-1\mathsf{T}} & c_i \end{bmatrix}, \ \mathtt{D}^i = \begin{bmatrix} \mathtt{D}^{i-1} \\ \mathtt{d}_i{}^{\mathsf{T}} \end{bmatrix}, \ \mathtt{H}^i = \begin{bmatrix} \mathtt{H}^{i-1} \\ \mathtt{h}_i{}^{\mathsf{T}} \end{bmatrix}$$

we define the incremental coefficient as

$$\epsilon^i(h) = tr\{\mathtt{D}^i \mathtt{H}^{i\mathsf{T}}\} / \sqrt{\|\mathtt{H}^i\|^2_{\mathtt{C}^i}}. \tag{6.13}$$

Therefore, we learn a 1D decision stump $h_i(\mathtt{x})$ at one time.

$$\hat{h}_i = \arg\max_{h \in \mathcal{H}} \epsilon^i(h).$$

In terms of computation, the incremental selection scheme requires evaluating $2qMNK$ decision stumps, the same as the independent selection scheme. Of course, compared with the independent scheme, there are overhead computations needed in the incremental scheme because we calculate matrix quantities like $tr\{\mathtt{D}^i \mathtt{H}^{i\mathsf{T}}\}$ and $\|\mathtt{H}^i\|^2_{\mathtt{C}^i}$; whereas in the independent feature selection scheme, the counterparts are vector inner products. Fortunately, there exist reusable computations. For example, it is easy to show that

$$\|\mathtt{H}^i\|^2_{\mathtt{C}^i} = \|\mathtt{H}^{i-1}\|^2_{\mathtt{C}^{i-1}} + 2\mathtt{h}_i^{\mathsf{T}} \mathtt{H}^{i-1\mathsf{T}} \mathtt{c}^{i-1} + c_i \mathtt{h}_i{}^{\mathsf{T}} \mathtt{h}_i.$$

$$tr\{\mathtt{D}^i \mathtt{H}^{i\mathsf{T}}\} = tr\{\mathtt{D}^{i-1} \mathtt{H}^{i-1\mathsf{T}}\} + \mathtt{d}_i^{\mathsf{T}} \mathtt{h}_i. \tag{6.14}$$

Although the incremental selection scheme in principle yields a suboptimal solution, it is better than the independence selection scheme because it utilizes the dependence among the output data dimensions to some extent. In fact, there exists special cases when the incremental feature selection yields the same solution as the greedy selection scheme. One such case is that when $\mathtt{C} = \beta\mathtt{I}$ (e.g. when $\mathtt{A} = \mathtt{B} = \mathtt{I}$). This makes the denominator term $\|\mathtt{H}^i\|^2_{\mathtt{C}^i}$ in Eq. (6.13) a constant value of $i\beta^2$, which does not vary with different choices of h functions. Therefore, $\epsilon^i(h)$ only depends on $tr\{\mathtt{D}^i\mathtt{H}^{i\mathsf{T}}\}$. But, according to Eq. (6.14), maximizing $tr\{\mathtt{D}^i\mathtt{H}^{i\mathsf{T}}\}$ can be done by maximizing the term $\mathtt{d}_i^{\mathsf{T}}\mathtt{h}_i$ in each incremental step.

To improve robustness and remove bias, we randomly permutate the order of the dimensions of the output variable. Other tricks to improve computational efficiency include: (i) randomly sampling the dictionary set, i.e. replacing M by a smaller M'; and (ii) randomly sampling the training data set, i.e., replacing N by a smaller N'.

Figure 6.3 presents the incremental feature selection scheme.

1 Initialization.

- Create a random permutation of $\{1, 2, \ldots, q\}$, yielding $\{<1>, <2>, \ldots, <q>\}$.

2 Iteration over the dimension of the output variable $i = 1, 2, \ldots, q$

- (optional) Sample M' Haar filters from the dictionary set and form the reduced set of weak functions $\mathcal{H}'$.
- (optional) Sample N' data points from the training set.
- Loop over the filter index $m = 1, 2, \ldots, M'$ and the threshold level index $k = 1, 2, \ldots, K$ to find $h_{<i>} = \arg\ \max_{h\in\mathcal{H}'} \epsilon^{<i>}(h)$.
- Form the new vector $\mathtt{h}^{<i>} = [\mathtt{h}^{<i-1>\mathsf{T}}, h_{<i>}]^{\mathsf{T}}$.
- Compute reusable quantities $tr\{\mathtt{D}^{<i>}\mathtt{H}^{<i>\mathsf{T}}\}$ and $tr\{\|\mathtt{H}^{<i>}\|^2_{\mathtt{C}^{<i>}}\}$.

Figure 6.3. Incremental feature selection.

6.1.3 Experiments

We tested the proposed IBR algorithm on the the problem of age estimation. For results on the other two problems mentioned in the beginning of the chapter, refer to [260]. For comparison, we also implemented NPR, KRR and SVR, all using the RBF kernel function. We used 5-fold cross-validation as the evaluation protocol and tuned the RBF kernel width for empirical best performance. Because SVR only works for the single-output regression problem, we decoupled the multiple-output regression problem to isolated single-output ones. For IBR, we simply set $\mathtt{A} = \mathtt{B} = \mathtt{I}$ and stopped learning after a maximum number of boosting rounds is reached.

Table 6.1 shows the error statistics and computational time for evaluating regression outputs of all testing images belonging to the 5 testing subsets used in the 5-fold cross validation. We used different error measurement that is meaningful to the data of interest. We collected the error statistics for all testing images and reported their mean, 25% percentile, median, and 75% percentile. We used C++ programs on a PC with 2.4GHz dual CPUs and 3GB memory to record the computational time.

Age estimation

Aging modeling [136] is important for face analysis and recognition. In this experiment, we focused on estimating the human age.

Data statistics: We used the FGnet aging database [42]. There are 1002 facial images in the database. Five random divisions with 800 for training and 202 for testing are formed. The age ranges from 0 to 69. Normalization was done by first aligning 68 landmark points provided by [42] and then performing a zero-mean-unit-variance operation. However, we kept sufficient number of background pixels.

Input/output: The input x is a 60×60 image; the output y is his/her normalized age. We converted the actual age to $y = log(y + 1)$ to avoid negative regressor output.

Variation: The face images involve all possible variations including illumination, pose, expression, beards, moustaches, spectacles, etc. Figure 6.4 shows sample images of one subject at different ages and with various appearance variations.

Performance: We computed the absolute age difference as the error measurement. The proposed IBR approach (with 500 weak functions, the regularization coefficient $\lambda = 0.1$ and the shrinkage factor $\eta = 0.5$) achieves the best performance and runs fastest. In [136], age estimation is performed on a smaller set with mostly frontal-view images. The reported mean absolute error in years is 7.48 using a pure appearance based regressor.

Figure 6.4. Sample images (before and after normalization) of one subject at different ages.

	NPR	*KRR*	*SVR*	*IBR*
mean err.	8.44	13.56	6.60	5.81
25% per. err.	2.54	3.99	1.38	1.26
median err.	5.50	10.80	4.39	3.15
75% per. err.	10.87	17.99	9.04	7.79
testing time(s)	- 3.6s	3.6s	3.3s	0.016s

Table 6.1. Comparison of different regressors for age estimation.

6.2 Face Recognition across Aging Progression

How does age progression affect facial similarity across a pair of images of an individual? Studying the above would have direct implications in passport renewal. Passports need to be renewed once in every 10 years and upon renewal, passports feature the individual's most recent image. Thus given a pair of age separated face images of an individual, what is the confidence measure in verifying his identity?

Our database comprises of 465 pairs (younger and most recent) of face images retrieved from the passports of many individuals. Table 6.2 summarizes the database. The individuals in our database ranged from 20 years to 70 years in age. Since passport images are taken generally under controlled environments, the pose of most of the face images were frontal. But there were quite a few passport images where we observed an uneven distribution of illumination. Moreover, age separated face images of an individual invariably differed in the nature of illumination. Thus to study the aging effects on face recognition, it would be crucial to reduce variations due to illumination and pose. We circumvent non-uniform illumination across the passport images by assuming facial symmetry and representing the face by just one half of the face that is better illuminated. We address this half as the 'PointFive' face[80].

Age Difference	*1-2 yrs*	*3-4 yrs*	*5-7 yrs*	*8-9 yrs*
# of pairs	165	104	81	115

Table 6.2. Database of passport images.

We formulate two approaches to studying facial similarity across time. The first one is a classifier based on a Bayesian framework and the second one is a direct similarity function across different age groups.

Figure 6.5. Age progressed images of individuals

6.2.1 Age difference classifier

We present a Bayesian age-difference classifier that is built on a probabilistic eigenspaces framework [56]. The classification based on age-differences, comprises of two stages. The first stage of classification deals with establishing the identity between a pair of age separated face images. In the second stage, the pairs of age separated face images across which identity has been established, are further classified based on their age differences. Since the dataset comprises of pairs of face images retrieved from passports, the age difference across each pair ranged from a year to 9 years. We consider the following four age difference categories in our formulation : $1 - 2\ yrs, 3 - 4\ yrs, 5 - 7\ yrs, 8 - 9\ yrs$.

Bayesian framework

Let $\mathrm{I}_{11}, \mathrm{I}_{12}, \mathrm{I}_{21}, \mathrm{I}_{22}, ..., \mathrm{I}_{M1}, \mathrm{I}_{M2}$ be the set of $N \times 1$ vectors formed by the lexicographic ordering of pixels in each of the M pairs of 'PointFive' faces. The intra-personal image differences $\{\mathrm{x}_i\}_{i=1}^{M}$ are obtained by the difference of two 'PointFive' faces of the same individual.

$$\mathrm{x}_i = \mathrm{I}_{i1} - \mathrm{I}_{i2} \tag{6.15}$$

Given the training data $\{\mathrm{x}_i\}_{i=1}^{M}$, its KLT basis vectors span the intra personal space Ω_I which in turn can be decomposed into two mutually exclusive and complementary subspaces F, the feature space (spanned by k basis vectors $\{\Phi_i\}_{i=1}^{k}$ the variance along each of which is maximum, extracted by principle component analysis) and $\bar{F}$, the orthogonal complement space (spanned by the basis vectors $\{\Phi\}_{i=k+1}^{N}$).

We assume that the intra-personal image difference samples are Gaussian distributed.The likelihood function for the data is estimated as :

$$\begin{aligned} P(\mathrm{x}|\Omega_I) &= \frac{\exp(-\frac{1}{2}(\mathrm{x}-\bar{\mathrm{x}})^{\mathsf{T}}\Sigma^{-1}(\mathrm{x}-\bar{\mathrm{x}}))}{(2\pi)^{N/2}|\Sigma|^{1/2}} = \frac{\exp(-\frac{1}{2}\sum_{i=1}^{N}\frac{y_i^2}{\lambda_i})}{(2\pi)^{N/2}\prod_{i=1}^{N}\lambda_i^{1/2}} \\ &\simeq \left[\frac{\exp(-\frac{1}{2}\sum_{i=1}^{k}\frac{y_i^2}{\lambda_i})}{(2\pi)^{k/2}\prod_{i=1}^{k}\lambda_i^{1/2}}\right] \cdot \left[\frac{\exp\left(-\frac{\epsilon^2(\mathrm{X})}{2\rho}\right)}{(2\pi\rho)^{(N-M)/2}}\right] \\ &= P_F(\mathrm{x}|\Omega_I)\,.\,\hat{P}_{\bar{F}}(\mathrm{x}|\Omega_I) \end{aligned} \tag{6.16}$$

where $y_i = \Phi_i^T(\mathrm{x}-\bar{\mathrm{x}})$ are the principal components,λ_i are the eigenvalues, $\epsilon^2(\mathrm{x}) = \sum_{i=k+1}^{N} y_i^2 = \|\tilde{\mathrm{x}}^2\| - \sum_{i=1}^{k} y_i^2$ is the PCA reconstruction error and ρ, the estimated variance along each dimension in the orthogonal subspace is $\rho = \frac{1}{N-k}\sum_{i=k+1}^{N}\lambda_i$. The sum $\sum_{i=k+1}^{N}\lambda_i$ is estimated by means of extrapolation of the cubic spline fit on the computed eigenvalues $\{\lambda_i\}_{i=1}^{k}$.

The extra-personal image differences $\{yz_i\}_{i=1}^{M}$ are obtained by the difference of two 'PointFive' faces of different individuals.

$$\mathrm{z}_i = I_{i1} - I_{j2}\ ,\ j \neq i,\ 1 \leq j \leq M \tag{6.17}$$

Again, the KLT basis on training data $\{\mathrm{z}_i\}_{i=1}^{M}$ spans the extra-personal space Ω_E which can be decomposed into two complementary spaces : the feature space and the orthogonal space. The density in the feature space is modeled using a mixture of Gaussians. We estimate the likelihood for the data as

$$\hat{P}(\mathrm{z}|\Omega_E) = P(\mathrm{y}|\Theta^*)\,.\,\hat{P}_{\bar{F}}(\mathrm{z}|\Omega_E) \tag{6.18}$$

where

$$P(\mathrm{y}|\Theta) = \sum_{i=1}^{N_c} w_i N(\mathrm{y};\mu_i,\Sigma_i) \tag{6.19}$$

$$\Theta^* = argmax\left[\prod_{i=1}^{M} P(\mathrm{y}_i|\Theta)\right] \tag{6.20}$$

$N(\mathrm{y};\mu_i,\Sigma_i)$ is Gaussian with parameters (μ_i,Σ_i) and w_i correspond to the mixing parameters such that $\sum_{i=1}^{N_c} w_i = 1$. We solve the estimation problem using the Expectation-Maximization algorithm.

During the first stage of the classification, we use the above formulation in building a classifier that establishes the identity between a pair of face images. Given a pair of age separated face images, we extract the 'PointFive' faces

I_1 and I_2 and compute the difference image $\text{x} = \text{I}_1 - \text{I}_2$. The *a posteriori* probability $P(\Omega_I|\text{x})$ is computed using the Bayes rule.

$$P(\Omega_I|\text{x}) = \frac{P(\text{x}|\Omega_I)P(\Omega_I)}{P(\text{x}|\Omega_I)P(\Omega_I) + P(\text{x}|\Omega_E)P(\Omega_E)} \tag{6.21}$$

The classification of the image difference as intra-personal or extra-personal is based on a maximum *a posteriori* (MAP) rule. For operational conditions, $P(\Omega_I)$ and $P(\Omega_E)$ are set equal and the difference image x is classified as intra personal if $P(\Omega_I|\text{x}) > \frac{1}{2}$.

During the second stage of classification, those pairs of face images that were classified as intra-personal, are further classified based on their intra age differences using the underlying formulation. Let Ω_1 ,Ω_2 ,Ω_3 ,Ω_4 be the space of intra personal difference images for age difference categories $1-2$ yrs, $3-4$ yrs, $5-7$ yrs and $8-9$ yrs respectively. We assume the underlying distribution of samples from each of the intra-personal spaces to be Gaussian.

Given a difference image x that has been classified as one belonging to the intrapersonal space Ω, we compute the *a posteriori* probability $P(\Omega_i|\text{x})$ with $i = 1, 2, 3, 4$ as :

$$P(\Omega_i|\text{x}) = \frac{P(\text{x}|\Omega_i)P(\Omega_i)}{\sum_{j=1}^{4} P(\text{x}|\Omega_j)P(\Omega_j)} \tag{6.22}$$

For operational conditions, $P(\Omega_i)$ were set equal. Thus if $P(\Omega_i|\text{x}) > P(\Omega_j|\text{x})$ for all $i \neq j$, $i, j = 1, 2, 3, 4$, then Ω_i is identified to be the class to which the difference image x belongs. Figure 6.6 illustrates the classifier.

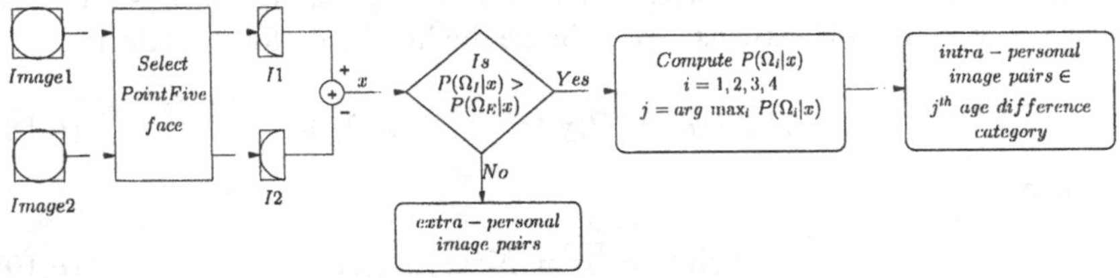

Figure 6.6. Age Difference Classifier

Experimental results

We selected pairs of 'PointFive' faces of 200 individuals from our database. We computed the intra personal difference images from the selected pairs and created the intra-personal subspace Ω. We computed the extra personal difference images (by randomly selecting two images of different individuals from the 200 pairs of images) and created the extra-personal subspace Ψ. Thus having created the two spaces, we created two sets of image differences : Set I comprised of intra-personal difference images computed from the 465 image pairs from our database and Set II comprised of 465 extra-personal difference images computed by the random selection of 'PointFive' faces of different individuals from our database. The results of the first stage of classification are as below :

- During the first stage of classification, 99 % of the difference images from Set I were correctly classified as intra-personal.
- 83 % of the difference images from Set II were correctly classified as extra-personal.
- It was observed that the image pairs from Set I that were misclassified as extra-personal differed from each other significantly either in facial hair or glasses. Moreover, their average age difference was 7.4 years.

During the second stage of classification, 50 pairs of 'PointFive' face images from each of the following age-difference categories $1-2\ yrs$, $3-4\ yrs$, $5-7\ yrs$ and $8-9\ yrs$ were randomly selected and their corresponding difference image subspaces namely Ω_1, Ω_2, Ω_3, Ω_4 were created. The image pairs from Set I that were classified as intra-personal were further classified into one of the above four age-difference categories using the formulation discussed in the previous subsection. The classification results are tabulated in Table 6.3. The bold entries in the table correspond to the percentage of image pairs that were correctly classified to their age-difference category.

	Ω_1	Ω_2	Ω_3	Ω_4
Ω_1	**51 %**	2 %	9 %	38 %
Ω_2	17 %	**37 %**	11	35 %
Ω_3	6 %	1 %	**61 %**	32 %
Ω_4	1 %	1 %	12 %	**86 %**

Table 6.3. Age-difference classifier results.

- When the image pairs from Set I that were correctly classified as intra-personal were classified further based on age-differences, it was observed that image pairs with little variations due to factors such as facial expressions, glasses and facial hair were more often classified correctly to their respective age-difference category.

- Image pairs belonging to age difference categories $1-2\ yrs$ or $3-4\ yrs$ or $5-7\ yrs$ with significant differences in facial hair or expressions or glasses, were misclassified under the category $8-9\ yrs$. The above trend is likely since Ω_4, the subspace of difference images from the age difference category $8-9\ yrs$, spans more intra pair variations than compared with other three age difference categories.

Thus, in applications such as passport renewal where the age difference between the pair of images is known *apriori*, if a pair of images are classified as intra-personal and further classified to their corresponding age-difference category, the identity across the image pair could be verified with low probability of error.

6.2.2 Similarity measure

We created an eigenspace using 200 'PointFive' faces retrieved from the database of passport images. The 465 pairs of 'PointFive' faces were projected onto the space of eigenfaces and were represented by the projections along the eigenfaces that correspond to 95% of the variance. Since illumination variations and pose variations across each pair of 'PointFive' faces is minimal, the similarity score between each pair would be affected by factors such as age progression, facial expression variations and occlusions due to facial hair and glasses. We divided our database into two sets : the first set comprised of those images where each pair of passport images had similar facial expressions and similar occlusions if any, due to glasses and facial hair. The second set comprised of those pairs of passport images where differences due to facial expressions or occlusions due to glasses and facial hair were significant.

The distribution of similarity scores across the age-difference categories namely $1-2\ yrs$, $3-4\ yrs$, $5-7\ yrs$ and $8-9\ yrs$ is plotted in Figure 6.7. The statistical variations in the similarity scores across each age-difference category and across each set of passport images are tabulated in Table 6.4.

Age Difference	*First Set*		*Second Set*					
			Expression		*Glasses*		*Facial Hair*	
	μ	σ^2	μ	σ^2	μ	σ^2	μ	σ^2
1-2 yrs	0.85	0.02	0.70	0.021	0.83	0.01	0.67	0.04
3-4 yrs	0.77	0.03	0.65	0.07	0.75	0.02	0.63	0.01
5-7 yrs	0.70	0.06	0.59	0.01	0.72	0.02	0.59	0.10
8-9 yrs	0.60	0.08	0.55	0.10	0.68	0.18	0.55	0.10

Table 6.4. Similarity Measure

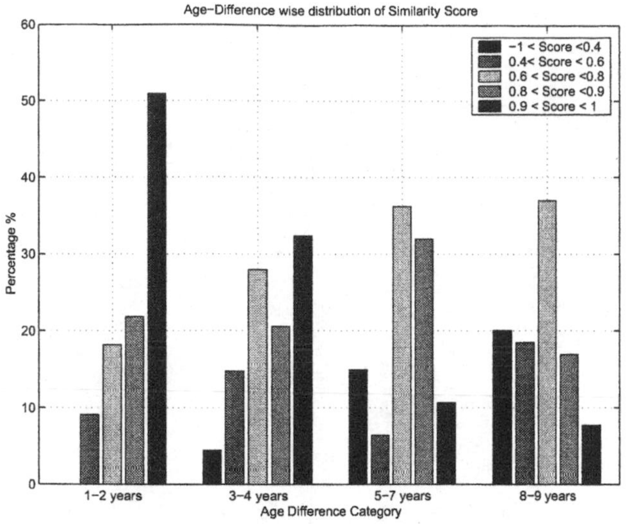

Figure 6.7. Age Difference Category

- From Figure 6.7 we note that as the age difference between the pairs of images increases, the proportion of images with high similarity scores decreases.
- While the distribution of similarity scores has a strong peak for category $1 - 2yrs$, it flattens out gradually as the age difference increases.
- From Table 6.4 we note that as the age difference increases, across both the sets of images and across all the variations such as expression, glasses and facial hair, the mean similarity score drops gradually and the variance of the similarity scores increases.
- Within each age-difference category, we see a notable drop in similarity scores when variations due expressions and facial hair are more pronounced.

PART III

FACE RECOGNITION VIA KERNEL LEARNING

Chapter 7

PROBABILISTIC DISTANCES IN REPRODUCING KERNEL HILBERT SPACE

Probabilistic distance measures, defined as the distances between two probability distributions, are important quantities and find their uses in many research areas such as probability and statistics, pattern recognition, information theory, communication and so on. In statistics, the probabilistic distances are often used in asymptotic analysis. In pattern recognition, pattern separability is usually calibrated using probabilistic distance measures [5] like Chernoff distance and Bhattarchayya distance because they provide bounds for probability of error in a pattern classification problem. In information theory, mutual information, a special example of Kullback-Leibler divergence or relative entropy [4] is a fundamental quantity related to the channel capacity. In communication, divergence and Bhattarchayya distance measures are used for signal selection [244].

Direct evaluation of probabilistic distances is nontrivial since they involve integrals. Only within certain parametric distributions, say the widely-used Gaussian density, we have analytic expressions for probability distances. However, the Gaussian density employs only up to second-order statistics and its modeling capacity is linear and hence rather limited when confronted with a nonlinear data structure. By nonlinear data structure, we mean that if conventional linear modeling techniques such as fitting the Gaussian density are used, the responses are inadequately approximated. To absorb the nonlinearity, mixture models or non-parametric densities are used in practice. For such cases, one has to resort to numerical methods for computing the probabilistic distances. Such computation is not robust in nature since two approximations are invoked: one in estimating the density and the other in evaluating the numerical integral.

In this chapter, we model the nonlinearity through a different approach: kernel methods. The essence of kernel methods is to combine a linear algorithm with a nonlinear embedding, which maps the data from the original vector space to the reproducing kernel Hilbert space (RKHS). But, we need not require any explicit knowledge of the nonlinear mapping function as long as we can cast our computations into dot product evaluations. Since a nonlinear function is used, albeit in an implicit fashion, we realize a new approach to study these distances and investigate their uses in a different space.

Clearly, our computation depends on the assumption that the data is Gaussian in RKHS. This assumption has been implicitly used in many kernel methods such as [263, 272]. In [272], PCA operates on the RKHS. Even though it seems that PCA needs only the covariance matrix without the Gaussianity assumption, it is the deviation of the data from Gaussianity in the original space that drives us to search for the principal components in the nonlinear feature space. In [263], discriminant analysis is performed in the feature space. Even for LDA, it is well known that it has ties to the optimal Bayesian classifier for a two-class problem, which assumes that each class is distributed as Gaussian with a common covariance matrix. Recently, the Gaussianity is directly adopted in the literature [261, 262, 266]. In [261, 262], it is used to compute the mutual information between two Gaussian random vectors in RKHS. In [266], it is used to construct the so-called Bhattacharyya kernel. In fact, the validity of this assumption boils down to a Gaussian process argument [266]. However, since the induced RKHS is certainly limited by the number of available samples, a regularized covariance matrix is needed in [261, 262]. We also propose a way to regularize the covariance matrix in this chapter.

This chapter is organized as follows. Section 7.1 introduces several probabilistic distances often used in the literature and Section 7.2 presents a method for estimating the first- and second-order statistics for the data in RKHS. Section 7.3 elaborates the derivations of the probabilistic distances in the RKHS and their limiting behavior. Section 7.4 demonstrates the feasibility and efficiency of the proposed measures using experiments on synthetic and real examples.

7.1 Probabilistic Distances in $\mathcal{R}^d$

Consider a two-class problem and suppose that class 1 has prior probability π_1 and class-conditional density $p_1(\mathbf{x})$ and class 2 has prior probability π_2 and class-conditional density $p_2(\mathbf{x})$, both defined on $\mathcal{R}^d$. Table 7.1 defines a list of probabilistic distance measures often found in the literature [5].

It is obvious that (i) the Bhattacharyya distance is a special case of the Chernoff distance with $\alpha = 1/2$; (ii) the Hellinger distance is related to the Bhattacharyya distance as follows:

$$J_T = \{2[1 - \exp(-J_B)]\}^{1/2}; \tag{7.1}$$

and (iii) the Kolmogorov distance is a special case of the Lissack-Fu distance with $\alpha = 1$. Some interesting properties of these distances can be found in [5, 244]

Distance Type	*Definition*
Chernoff distance [234]	$J_C(p_1, p_2) = -\log\{\int_{\mathbf{x}} p_1^{\alpha_2}(\mathbf{x})p_2^{\alpha_1}(\mathbf{x})d\mathbf{x}\}$
Bhattacharyya distance [233]	$J_B(p_1, p_2) = -\log\{\int_{\mathbf{x}} [p_1(\mathbf{x})p_2(\mathbf{x})]^{1/2}d\mathbf{x}\}$
Matusita distance [250]	$J_T(p_1, p_2) = \{\int_{\mathbf{x}} [\sqrt{p_1(\mathbf{x})} - \sqrt{p_2(\mathbf{x})}]^2 d\mathbf{x}\}^{1/2}$
Patrick-Fisher distance [252]	$J_P(p_1, p_2) = \{\int_{\mathbf{x}} [p_1(\mathbf{x})\pi_1 - p_2(\mathbf{x})\pi_2]^2 d\mathbf{x}\}^{1/2}$
Lissack-Fu distance [247]	$J_L(p_1, p_2) = \int_{\mathbf{x}} \|p_1(\mathbf{x})\pi_1 - p_2(\mathbf{x})\pi_2\|^{\alpha_1} p^{\alpha_2}(\mathbf{x})d\mathbf{x}$
Kolmogorov distance [230]	$J_K(p_1, p_2) = \int_{\mathbf{x}} \|p_1(\mathbf{x})\pi_1 - p_2(\mathbf{x})\pi_2\| d\mathbf{x}$
KL divergence [4]	$J_R(p_1 \| p_2) = \int_{\mathbf{x}} p_1(\mathbf{x}) \log\{\frac{p_1(\mathbf{x})}{p_2(\mathbf{x})}\}d\mathbf{x}$
Symmetric KL divergence [4]	$J_D(p_1, p_2) = \int_{\mathbf{x}} [p_1(\mathbf{x}) - p_2(\mathbf{x})] \log \frac{p_1(\mathbf{x})}{p_2(\mathbf{x})} d\mathbf{x}$

[a] $0 < \alpha_1, \alpha_2 < 1$ and $\alpha_1 + \alpha_2 = 1$.

Table 7.1. A list of probabilistic distances and their definitions.[a]

In particular, the symmetric divergence is of great interest in the information theory literature [4] and has a close connection with the famous Kullback-Leibler (KL) divergence [13]. The KL divergence or relative entropy between two densities $p_1(\mathbf{x})$ and $p_2(\mathbf{x})$ is given by

$$J_R(p_1 \| p_2) = \int_{\mathbf{x}} p_1(\mathbf{x}) \log\{\frac{p_1(\mathbf{x})}{p_2(\mathbf{x})}\}d\mathbf{x}. \tag{7.2}$$

However, the KL divergence is not a true metric because neither the symmetry constraint nor the triangle inequality is satisfied. The symmetric divergence, which is *symmetric*, is equal to

$$J_D(p_1, p_2) = J_R(p_1 \| p_2) + J_R(p_2 \| p_1). \tag{7.3}$$

As mentioned earlier, computing the above probabilistic distance measures is nontrivial. Only within certain parametric distributions, say the Gaussian density, we know how to analytically compute some of the distance measures defined above. Suppose that $\mathtt{N}(\mathbf{x}; \mu, \Sigma)$ is a multivariate Gaussian density defined as

$$\mathtt{N}(\mathbf{x}; \mu, \Sigma) = \frac{1}{\sqrt{(2\pi)^d |\Sigma|}} \exp\{-\frac{1}{2}(\mathbf{x} - \mu)^{\mathsf{T}} \Sigma^{-1}(\mathbf{x} - \mu)\}, \tag{7.4}$$

where $\mathbf{x} \in \mathcal{R}^d$ and $|.|$ denotes the matrix determinant. With $p_1(\mathbf{x}) = \mathtt{N}(\mathbf{x}; \mu_1, \Sigma_1)$ and $p_2(\mathbf{x}) = \mathtt{N}(\mathbf{x}; \mu_2, \Sigma_2)$, Table 7.2 lists analytic expressions of some probabilistic distances between two Gaussian densities. When the covariance matrices for two densities are same, i.e., $\Sigma_1 = \Sigma_2 = \Sigma$, the Bhattacharyya distance and the symmetric divergence reduce to the Mahalanobis distance [249]:

$$J_M = J_D = 8J_B.$$

Distance Type	*Analytic Expression*
Chernoff distance	$J_C(p_1, p_2) = \frac{1}{2}\alpha_1\alpha_2(\mu_1 - \mu_2)^\mathsf{T}[\alpha_1\Sigma_1 + \alpha_2\Sigma_2]^{-1}(\mu_1 - \mu_2) + \frac{1}{2}\log\frac{\lvert\alpha_1\Sigma_1+\alpha_2\Sigma_2\rvert}{\lvert\Sigma_1\rvert^{\alpha_1}\lvert\Sigma_2\rvert^{\alpha_2}}$;
Bhattacharyya distance	$J_B(p_1, p_2) = \frac{1}{8}(\mu_1 - \mu_2)^\mathsf{T}\Sigma^{-1}(\mu_1 - \mu_2) + \frac{1}{2}\log\frac{\lvert\Sigma\rvert}{\lvert\Sigma_1\rvert^{1/2}\lvert\Sigma_2\rvert^{1/2}}$;
Patrick-Fisher distance	$J_P(p_1, p_2) = [(2\pi)^d\lvert2\Sigma_1\rvert]^{-1/2} + [(2\pi)^d\lvert2\Sigma_2\rvert]^{-1/2} - 2[(2\pi)^d\lvert2\Sigma\rvert]^{-1/2}\exp\{-\frac{1}{2}(\mu_1 - \mu_2)^\mathsf{T}(2\Sigma)^{-1}(\mu_1 - \mu_2)\}$;
KL divergence	$J_R(p_1\lvert\rvert p_2) = \frac{1}{2}(\mu_1 - \mu_2)^\mathsf{T}\Sigma_2^{-1}(\mu_1 - \mu_2) + \frac{1}{2}\log\frac{\lvert\Sigma_2\rvert}{\lvert\Sigma_1\rvert} + \frac{1}{2}\mathtt{tr}[\Sigma_1\Sigma_2^{-1} - \mathbf{I}_d]$
Symmetric KL divergence	$J_D(p_1, p_2) = \frac{1}{2}(\mu_1 - \mu_2)^\mathsf{T}(\Sigma_1{}^{-1} + \Sigma_2{}^{-1})(\mu_1 - \mu_2) + \frac{1}{2}\mathtt{tr}[\Sigma_1{}^{-1}\Sigma_2 + \Sigma_2{}^{-1}\Sigma_1 - 2\mathbf{I}_d]$
Mahalanobis distance	$J_M(p_1, p_2) = (\mu_1 - \mu_2)^\mathsf{T}\Sigma^{-1}(\mu_1 - \mu_2)$

[a] $\Sigma = (\Sigma_1 + \Sigma_2)/2$.

Table 7.2. Analytic expressions of probabilistic distances between two normal densities. [a]

7.2 Mean and Covariance Marix in RKHS

7.2.1 First- and second-order statistics

Computing the probabilistic distance measures requires first- and second-order statistics in the RKHS, as shown in Section 7.1. In practice, we have to estimate these statistics from a set of training samples.

Suppose that $\{\mathbf{x}_1, \mathbf{x}_2, \ldots, \mathbf{x}_N\}$ are given observations in the original data space $\mathcal{R}^d$. We operate in the RKHS $\mathcal{R}^f$ induced by a nonlinear mapping function $\phi : \mathcal{R}^d \rightarrow \mathcal{R}^f$, where $f > d$ and f could even be infinite. The training samples in $\mathcal{R}^f$ are denoted by $\Phi_{f\times N} = [\phi_1, \phi_2, ..., \phi_N]$, where $\phi_n = \phi(\mathbf{x}_n) \in \mathcal{R}^f$.

Using the maximum likelihood estimate (MLE) principle, the mean μ and the covariance matrix Σ are estimated as

$$\mu = \frac{1}{N}\sum_{n=1}^{N}\phi(\mathbf{x}_n) = \Phi\mathbf{e};\ \Sigma = \frac{1}{N}\sum_{n=1}^{N}(\phi_n - \mu)(\phi_n - \mu)^\mathsf{T} = \Phi\mathbf{J}\mathbf{J}^\mathsf{T}\Phi^\mathsf{T} = \Psi\Psi^\mathsf{T}, \tag{7.5}$$

where the weight vector $\mathtt{e}_{N\times 1} = N^{-1}\mathtt{1}$ with $\mathtt{1}$ being a vector of 1's, $\Psi = \Phi\mathtt{J}$, and $\mathtt{J}$ is an $N \times N$ centering matrix given as

$$\mathtt{J} = N^{-1/2}(\mathtt{I}_N - \mathtt{e}\mathtt{1}^\mathsf{T}). \tag{7.6}$$

7.2.2 Covariance matrix approximation

The covariance matrix Σ in Eq. (7.5) is rank-deficient since $f > N$. Thus, inverting such a matrix is impossible and an approximation to the covariance matrix is necessary. Later in Section 7.3 we show a limiting behavior of this approximation.

Such an approximation $\mathtt{S}$ should possess the following features:

- It keeps the principal structure of the covariance matrix Σ. In other words, the dominant eigenvalues and eigenvectors of Σ and $\mathtt{S}$ should be the same.
- It is compact and regularized. The compactness is inspired by the fact that the smallest eigenvalues of the covariance matrix are very close to zero. The regularity is always desirable in the approximation theory.
- It is easy to invert.

We proposed to the following approximation form [276]:

$$\mathtt{S} = \rho\mathtt{I}_f + \Phi\mathtt{J}\mathtt{Q}\mathtt{Q}^\mathsf{T}\mathtt{J}^\mathsf{T}\Phi^\mathsf{T} = \rho\mathtt{I}_f + \Phi\mathtt{A}\Phi^\mathsf{T}, \tag{7.7}$$

where $\mathtt{Q}$ is an $N \times r$ matrix, $\mathtt{A} = \mathtt{J}\mathtt{Q}\mathtt{Q}^\mathsf{T}\mathtt{J}^\mathsf{T}$, and $\rho > 0$ is a pre-specified constant. Typically, $q << N << f$. Firstly, when

$$\mathtt{Q} = \mathtt{V}_q(\mathtt{I}_q - \rho\Lambda_q^{-1})^{1/2}\mathtt{R},$$

where $\mathtt{V}_q$ and Λ_q encode the top q eigenvectors and eigenvalues of the $\bar{\mathtt{K}}$ matrix, the top q eigenpairs of Σ are maintained and $\mathtt{R}$ is any $q \times q$ orthogonal matrix, i.e., $\mathtt{R}^\mathsf{T}\mathtt{R} = \mathtt{R}\mathtt{R}^\mathsf{T} = \mathtt{I}_q$. Without loss of generality, we set $\mathtt{R} = \mathtt{I}_q$. Hence, if $\rho = 0$, we exactly maintain the subspace containing the top q eigenpairs. Secondly, $\mathtt{S}$ is regularized and its compactness is achieved through the $\mathtt{Q}$ matrix. Finally, $\mathtt{S}$ can be easily inverted by using the Woodbury formula [8],

$$\mathtt{S}^{-1} = (\rho\mathtt{I}_f + \mathtt{W}\mathtt{W}^\mathsf{T})^{-1} = \rho^{-1}(\mathtt{I}_f - \mathtt{W}\mathtt{M}^{-1}\mathtt{W}^\mathsf{T}) = \rho^{-1}(\mathtt{I}_f - \Phi\mathtt{B}\Phi^\mathsf{T}), \tag{7.8}$$

where $\mathtt{B} = \mathtt{J}\mathtt{Q}\mathtt{M}^{-1}\mathtt{Q}^\mathsf{T}\mathtt{J}^\mathsf{T}$ and the matrix $\mathtt{M}_{q\times q}$ is

$$\mathtt{M} = \rho\mathtt{I}_q + \mathtt{W}^\mathsf{T}\mathtt{W} = \rho\mathtt{I}_q + \mathtt{Q}^\mathsf{T}\bar{\mathtt{K}}\mathtt{Q}. \tag{7.9}$$

After obtaining $\mathtt{Q}$, it is easy to check that the following equations hold:

$$\mathtt{M} = \Lambda_q, \quad |\mathtt{M}| = |\Lambda_q| = \prod_{i=1}^{q}\lambda_i, \quad \mathtt{M}^{-1} = \Lambda_q^{-1}, \quad |\mathtt{S}| = \rho^{f-q}|\Lambda_q|. \tag{7.10}$$

$$\mathtt{A} = \mathtt{J}\mathtt{V}_q(\mathtt{I}_q - \rho\Lambda_q^{-1})\mathtt{V}_q^\top\mathtt{J}^\top,\ \ \mathtt{B} = \mathtt{J}\mathtt{V}_q(\Lambda_q^{-1} - \rho\Lambda_q^{-2})\mathtt{V}_q^\top\mathtt{J}^\top. \tag{7.11}$$

$$\mathtt{tr}[\mathtt{AK}] = \mathtt{tr}[\Lambda_q] - \rho q,\ \ \mathtt{tr}[\mathtt{BK}] = q - \rho\mathtt{tr}[\Lambda_q^{-1}]. \tag{7.12}$$

7.3 Probabilistic Distances in RKHS

Since the probabilistic distances involve two densities p_1 and p_2, we need two sets of training samples: Φ_1 for p_1 and Φ_2 for p_2. For each density p_i, we can find its corresponding $\mathbf{e}_i$, $\mathtt{J}_i$, μ_i, Σ_i, $\mathtt{K}_i$, $\mathtt{S}_i$, $\mathtt{V}_{q_i,i}$, $\Lambda_{q_i,i} = \mathtt{D}[\lambda_{1,i}, \lambda_{2,i}, \ldots, \lambda_{q_i,i}]$, $\mathtt{A}_i$, $\mathtt{B}_i$, etc., by keeping the top q_i principal components. In general, we can have $q_1 \neq q_2$ and $N_1 \neq N_2$ with N_i being the number of samples for the ith density. In addition, we define the following dot product matrix:

$$\begin{bmatrix} \Phi_1^\top \\ \Phi_2^\top \end{bmatrix} [\Phi_1\ \Phi_2] = \begin{bmatrix} \Phi_1^\top\Phi_1 & \Phi_1^\top\Phi_2 \\ \Phi_2^\top\Phi_1 & \Phi_2^\top\Phi_2 \end{bmatrix} = \begin{bmatrix} \mathtt{K}_{11} & \mathtt{K}_{12} \\ \mathtt{K}_{21} & \mathtt{K}_{22} \end{bmatrix}, \tag{7.13}$$

where $\mathtt{K}_{ij} = \Phi_i^\top\Phi_j$ and $\mathtt{K}_{21} = \mathtt{K}_{12}^\top$.

7.3.1 The Chernoff distance and the Bhattarchayya distance

As mentioned before, the Bhattarchayya distance is a special case of Chernoff distance with $\alpha = 1/2$. Hence, we focus only on the Chernoff distance.

The key quantity in computing the Chernoff distance is $\alpha_1\mathtt{S}_1 + \alpha_2\mathtt{S}_2$ with $\alpha_1 + \alpha_2 = 1$. We now analyze this in detail.

$$\begin{aligned}
\alpha_1\mathtt{S}_1 + \alpha_2\mathtt{S}_2 &= \alpha_1\{\rho\mathtt{I}_f + \Phi_1\mathtt{A}_1\Phi_1^\top\} + \alpha_2\{\rho\mathtt{I}_f + \Phi_2\mathtt{A}_2\Phi_2^\top\} \\
&= \rho\mathtt{I}_f + \alpha_1\Phi_1\mathtt{A}_1\Phi_1^\top + \alpha_2\Phi_2\mathtt{A}_2\Phi_2^\top \\
&= \rho\mathtt{I}_f + [\Phi_1\ \Phi_2] \begin{bmatrix} \alpha_1\mathtt{A}_1 & 0 \\ 0 & \alpha_2\mathtt{A}_2 \end{bmatrix} \begin{bmatrix} \Phi_1^\top \\ \Phi_2^\top \end{bmatrix} \\
&= \rho\mathtt{I}_f + [\Phi_1\ \Phi_2] \begin{bmatrix} \alpha_1\mathtt{J}_1\mathtt{Q}_1\mathtt{Q}_1^\top\mathtt{J}_1^\top & 0 \\ 0 & \alpha_2\mathtt{J}_2\mathtt{Q}_2\mathtt{Q}_2^\top\mathtt{J}_2^\top \end{bmatrix} \begin{bmatrix} \Phi_1^\top \\ \Phi_2^\top \end{bmatrix} \\
&= \rho\mathtt{I}_f + [\Phi_1\ \Phi_2]\mathtt{A}_{ch} \begin{bmatrix} \Phi_1^\top \\ \Phi_2^\top \end{bmatrix},
\end{aligned} \tag{7.14}$$

where the matrix $\mathtt{A}_{ch}$ is rank-deficient since $\mathtt{A}_{ch} = \mathtt{P}\mathtt{P}^\top$ with

$$\mathtt{P}_{(N_1+N_2)\times(q_1+q_2)} = \begin{bmatrix} \sqrt{\alpha_1}\mathtt{J}_1\mathtt{Q}_1 & 0 \\ 0 & \sqrt{\alpha_2}\mathtt{J}_2\mathtt{Q}_2 \end{bmatrix}. \tag{7.15}$$

Therefore, the matrix $\alpha_1 S_1 + \alpha_2 S_2$ is of such a form that we can easily find its determinant and inverse.

The determinant $|\alpha_1 S_1 + \alpha_2 S_2|$ is given by

$$|\alpha_1 S_1 + \alpha_2 S_2| = \rho^{f-(q_1+q_2)} |\rho I_{q_1+q_2} + L| = \rho^{f-(q_1+q_2)} \prod_{i=1}^{q_1+q_2} (\tau_i + \rho), \quad (7.16)$$

where $\{\tau_i;\ i = 1, \ldots, q_1 + q_2\}$ are the eigenvalues of the L matrix. The L matrix is given by

$$\begin{aligned} L_{(q_1+q_2)\times(q_1+q_2)} &= P^T \begin{bmatrix} \Phi_1^T \\ \Phi_2^T \end{bmatrix} [\Phi_1\ \Phi_2] P = P^T \begin{bmatrix} K_{11} & K_{12} \\ K_{21} & K_{22} \end{bmatrix} P \\ &= \begin{bmatrix} \alpha_1 Q_1^T J_1^T K_{11} J_1 Q_1 & \sqrt{\alpha_1\alpha_2} Q_1^T J_1^T K_{12} J_2 Q_2 \\ \sqrt{\alpha_1\alpha_2} Q_2^T J_2^T K_{21} J_1 Q_1 & \alpha_2 Q_2^T J_2^T K_{22} J_2 Q_2 \end{bmatrix} \\ &= \begin{bmatrix} \alpha_1 \{\Lambda_{q_1,1} - \rho I_{q_1}\} & \sqrt{\alpha_1\alpha_2} L_{12} \\ \sqrt{\alpha_1\alpha_2} L_{12}^T & \alpha_2 \{\Lambda_{q_2,2} - \rho I_{q_2}\} \end{bmatrix}, \end{aligned} \quad (7.17)$$

with $L_{12} = Q_1^T J_1^T K_{12} J_2 Q_2$.

The inverse $\{\alpha_1 S_1 + \alpha_2 S_2\}^{-1}$ is given by

$$\{\alpha_1 S_1 + \alpha_2 S_2\}^{-1} = \rho^{-1}\{I_f - [\Phi_1\ \Phi_2] B_{ch} \begin{bmatrix} \Phi_1^T \\ \Phi_2^T \end{bmatrix} \}, P^T. \quad (7.18)$$

where

$$B_{ch} = P(\rho I_{q_1+q_2} + L)^{-1}. \quad (7.19)$$

We now show how to compute the following two terms needed for evaluating the Chernoff distance as shown in Table 7.2.

$$\begin{aligned} \mu_i^T \{\alpha_1 S_1 + \alpha_2 S_2\}^{-1} \mu_j &= e_i^T \Phi_i^T \rho^{-1} \{I_f - [\Phi_1\ \Phi_2] B_{ch} \begin{bmatrix} \Phi_1^T \\ \Phi_2^T \end{bmatrix} \} \Phi_j e_j \\ &= \rho^{-1} \{e_i^T K_{ij} e_j - e_i^T [K_{i1}\ K_{i2}] B_{ch} \begin{bmatrix} K_{1j} \\ K_{2j} \end{bmatrix} e_j\} \\ &= \rho^{-1} \xi_{ij}, \end{aligned} \quad (7.20)$$

$$\log \frac{|\alpha_1 S_1 + \alpha_2 S_2|}{|S_1|^{\alpha_1} |S_2|^{\alpha_2}} = \alpha_1 \sum_{i=1}^{q_1+q_2} \log \frac{\rho + \tau_i}{\lambda_{i,1}} + \alpha_2 \sum_{i=1}^{q_1+q_2} \log \frac{\rho + \tau_i}{\lambda_{i,2}}, \quad (7.21)$$

where $\{\lambda_{i,1}; i = 1, 2, ..., q_1\}$ and $\{\lambda_{i,2}; i = 1, 2, ..., q_2\}$ are eigenvalues for S_1 and S_2, respectively. Notice that (i) $\{\lambda_{i,1}; i = q_1 + 1, ..., q_1 + q_2\}$ and $\{\lambda_{i,2}; i = q_2 + 1, ..., q_1 + q_2\}$, all equal to ρ's, are introduced only for notational convenience; (ii) the infinite dimensionality f in Eq. (7.20) and Eq. (7.21) disappeared as needed; and (iii) all calculations are based on the Gram matrix defined in Eq. (7.13).

Finally, we compute the Chernoff distance as follows (with $\alpha_1 = 1 - \alpha$ and $\alpha_2 = \alpha$):

$$\begin{aligned} 2J_C(p_1, p_2) &= \rho^{-1}\alpha_1\alpha_2\{\xi_{11} + \xi_{22} - 2\xi_{12}\} + \alpha_1 \sum_{i=1}^{q_1+q_2} \log \frac{\rho + \tau_i}{\lambda_{i,1}} + \\ & \alpha_2 \sum_{i=1}^{q_1+q_2} \log \frac{\rho + \tau_i}{\lambda_{i,2}}. \end{aligned} \quad (7.22)$$

7.3.2 The KL divergence and the symmetric divergence

Computing the KL divergence in the RKHS is done by collecting terms like $\mu_i^{\mathsf{T}} \mathtt{S}_j^{-1} \mu_k$ and $\mathtt{tr}\{\mathtt{S}_i \mathtt{S}_j^{-1}\}$.

$$\begin{aligned} \mu_i^{\mathsf{T}} \mathtt{S}_j^{-1} \mu_k &= \mathtt{e}_i^{\mathsf{T}} \Phi_i^{\mathsf{T}} \rho^{-1}(\mathtt{I}_f - \Phi_j \mathtt{B}_j \Phi_j^{\mathsf{T}}) \Phi_k \mathtt{e}_k \\ &= \rho^{-1}(\mathtt{e}_i^{\mathsf{T}} \mathtt{K}_{ik} \mathtt{e}_k - \mathtt{e}_i^{\mathsf{T}} \mathtt{K}_{ij} \mathtt{B}_j \mathtt{K}_{jk} \mathtt{e}_k) = \rho^{-1}\theta_{ijk}. \end{aligned} \quad (7.23)$$

$$\begin{aligned} \mathtt{tr}[\mathtt{S}_i \mathtt{S}_j^{-1}] &= \mathtt{tr}[(\Phi_i \mathtt{A}_i \Phi_i^{\mathsf{T}} + \rho \mathtt{I}_f)\rho^{-1}(\mathtt{I}_f - \Phi_j \mathtt{B}_j \Phi_j^{\mathsf{T}})] \quad (7.24) \\ &= \rho^{-1}\mathtt{tr}[\Phi_i \mathtt{A}_i \Phi_i^{\mathsf{T}}] - \rho^{-1}\mathtt{tr}[\Phi_i \mathtt{A}_i \Phi_i^{\mathsf{T}} \Phi_j \mathtt{B}_j \Phi_j^{\mathsf{T}}] \\ & \quad + f - \mathtt{tr}[\Phi_j \mathtt{B}_j \Phi_j^{\mathsf{T}}] \\ &= \rho^{-1}\mathtt{tr}[\mathtt{A}_i \mathtt{K}_{ii}] - \rho^{-1}\mathtt{tr}[\mathtt{A}_i \mathtt{K}_{ij} \mathtt{B}_j \mathtt{K}_{ji}] + f - \mathtt{tr}[\mathtt{B}_j \mathtt{K}_{jj}] \\ &= \rho^{-1}\mathtt{tr}[\Lambda_{q_i,i}] - q_i - \rho^{-1}\mathtt{tr}[\mathtt{A}_i \mathtt{K}_{ij} \mathtt{B}_j \mathtt{K}_{ji}] \\ & \quad + f + \rho\,\mathtt{tr}[\Lambda_{q_j,j}^{-1}] - q_j \\ &= \rho^{-1}\{\mathtt{tr}[\Lambda_{q_i,i}] - \eta_{ij}\} + \rho\,\mathtt{tr}[\Lambda_{q_j,j}^{-1}] + f - (q_i + q_j), \end{aligned}$$

where

$$\eta_{ij} = \mathtt{tr}[\mathtt{A}_i \mathtt{K}_{ij} \mathtt{B}_j \mathtt{K}_{ji}].$$

Finally, we obtain the KL divergence and the symmetric divergence in the RKHS by substituting Eqs. (7.23) and (7.24) into the analytic expressions listed in Table 7.2 with d replaced by f,

$$\begin{aligned} 2J_R(p_1 || p_2) &= \rho^{-1}\{\theta_{121} + \theta_{222} - \theta_{122} - \theta_{221}\} \\ & \quad + \{\log |\Lambda_{q_2,2}| - \log |\Lambda_{q_1,1}|\} \\ & \quad + (q_1 - q_2)\log \rho + \rho^{-1}\{\mathtt{tr}[\Lambda_{q_1,1}] - \eta_{12}\} \\ & \quad + \rho\{\mathtt{tr}[\Lambda_{q_2,2}^{-1}]\} - (q_1 + q_2). \end{aligned} \quad (7.25)$$

$$\begin{aligned}
2J_D(p_1,p_2) &= \rho^{-1}\{\theta_{111}+\theta_{121}+\theta_{212}+\theta_{222} \\
&\qquad -\theta_{112}-\theta_{122}-\theta_{211}-\theta_{221}\} \\
&\quad +\rho^{-1}\{\mathtt{tr}[\Lambda_{q_1,1}]+\mathtt{tr}[\Lambda_{q_2,2}]-\eta_{12}-\eta_{21}\} \\
&\quad +\rho\{\mathtt{tr}[\Lambda_{q_1,1}^{-1}]+\mathtt{tr}[\Lambda_{q_2,2}^{-1}]\}-2(q_1+q_2). \qquad (7.26)
\end{aligned}$$

7.3.3 The Patrick-Fisher distance

Given the above derivations in Sections 7.3.1 and 7.3.2, computing the Patrick-Fisher distance $J_P(p_1,p_2)$ can be easily done by combining related terms.

$$\begin{aligned}
J_P(p_1,p_2) &= [2(2\pi)^f\rho^{f-q_1}\prod_{i=1}^{q_1}\lambda_{i,1}]^{-1/2}+[2(2\pi)^f\rho^{f-q_2}\prod_{i=1}^{q_2}\lambda_{i,2}]^{-1/2} \\
&\quad -2[2(2\pi)^f\rho^{f-q_1-q_2}\prod_{i=1}^{q_1+q_2}(\rho+\tau_i)]^{-1/2} * \\
&\quad \exp\{-\rho^{-1}(\xi_{11}+\xi_{22}-2\xi_{12})\}. \qquad (7.27)
\end{aligned}$$

where $\{\tau_i; i=1,2,\ldots,q_1+q_2\}$ are the eigenvalues of the $\mathtt{L}$ matrix defined in Eq. (7.17) with $\alpha = 1/2$.

7.3.4 Limiting behavior

It is interesting to study the behavior of the distances when ρ approaches to zero.

First,

$$\lim_{\rho\to 0}\mathtt{A}=\hat{\mathtt{A}}=\mathtt{J}\mathtt{V}_q\mathtt{V}_q^\mathsf{T}\mathtt{J}^\mathsf{T},\quad \lim_{\rho\to 0}\mathtt{B}=\hat{\mathtt{B}}=\mathtt{J}\mathtt{V}_q\Lambda_q^{-1}\mathtt{V}_q^\mathsf{T}\mathtt{J}^\mathsf{T}, \qquad (7.28)$$

Then,

$$\lim_{\rho\to 0}\theta_{ijk}=\hat{\theta}_{ijk}=\mathbf{e}_i^\mathsf{T}\mathtt{K}_{ik}\mathbf{e}_k-\mathbf{e}_i^\mathsf{T}\mathtt{K}_{ij}\hat{\mathtt{B}}_j\mathtt{K}_{jk}\mathbf{e}_k,\quad \lim_{\rho\to 0}\eta_{ij}=\hat{\eta}_{ij}=\mathtt{tr}[\hat{\mathtt{B}}_i\mathtt{K}_{ij}\hat{\mathtt{A}}_j\mathtt{K}_{ji}]. \qquad (7.29)$$

Similarly,

$$\lim_{\rho\to 0}\xi_{ij}=\hat{\xi}_{ij}==\mathbf{e}_i^\mathsf{T}\mathtt{K}_{ij}\mathbf{e}_j-\mathbf{e}_i^\mathsf{T}[\mathtt{K}_{i1}\;\mathtt{K}_{i2}]\hat{\mathtt{B}}_{ch}\begin{bmatrix}\mathtt{K}_{1j}\\ \mathtt{K}_{2j}\end{bmatrix}\mathbf{e}_j, \qquad (7.30)$$

where $\hat{\mathtt{B}}_{ch}=\lim_{\rho\to 0}\mathtt{B}_{ch}$.

Finally,

$$\lim_{\rho\to 0}\rho J_C(p_1,p_2)=\hat{J}_C(p_1,p_2), \qquad (7.31)$$

$$\lim_{\rho\to 0}\rho J_R(p_1||p_2)=\hat{J}_R(p_1||p_2), \qquad (7.32)$$

$$\lim_{\rho \to 0} \rho J_D(p_1, p_2) = \hat{J}_D(p_1, p_2), \tag{7.33}$$

where

$$2\hat{J}_C(p_1, p_2) = \alpha(1-\alpha)\{\hat{\xi}_{11} + \hat{\xi}_{22} - 2\hat{\xi}_{12}\}, \tag{7.34}$$

$$2\hat{J}_R(p_1 || p_2) = \hat{\theta}_{121} + \hat{\theta}_{222} - \hat{\theta}_{122} - \hat{\theta}_{221} + \mathtt{tr}[\Lambda_{q_1,1}] - \hat{\eta}_{12}, \tag{7.35}$$

$$\begin{aligned} 2\hat{J}_D(p_1, p_2) &= \hat{\theta}_{111} + \hat{\theta}_{121} + \hat{\theta}_{212} + \hat{\theta}_{222} - \hat{\theta}_{112} - \hat{\theta}_{122} - \hat{\theta}_{211} - \hat{\theta}_{221} \\ &\quad + \mathtt{tr}[\Lambda_{q_1,1}] + \mathtt{tr}[\Lambda_{q_2,1}] - \hat{\eta}_{12} - \hat{\eta}_{21}. \end{aligned} \tag{7.36}$$

When $\alpha = 1/2$, we obtain the limiting distance for the Bhattacharyya distance

$$2\hat{J}_B(p_1, p_2) = \frac{1}{4}\{\hat{\xi}_{11} + \hat{\xi}_{22} - 2\hat{\xi}_{12}\}. \tag{7.37}$$

The limiting behavior of the Patrick-Fisher distance $J_P(p_1, p_2)$ is not interesting since it involves f, thus we omit its discussion.

As mentioned earlier, when $\rho = 0$ and $q_1 = q_2 = q$, we actually use the subspace of the RKHS containing the top q eigenpairs. Therefore, the derived limiting distances calibrate the pattern separability on this subspace of the RKHS and carry many optimal features their original counterparts possess, yet additionally equipped with a nonlinear embedding.

7.3.5 Kernel for set

A set here is a collection of observations. A kernel for set is a two-input kernel function that takes the two sets as inputs and satisfies the requirement of positive definiteness.

Several kernels for set have emerged in the literature. In [275], Wolf and Shashua proposed the kernel principal angle. The principal angle is defined as the angle between the principal subspaces of the two input sets and then 'kernelized'. In [265], Jebara and Kondor showed that the Bhattacharyya coefficient [244] that operates the probability distribution defined on the original data space is a kernel. In [266], they extended the Bhattacharyya kernel to operate the probability distribution defined on the RKHS. In [269], Moreno *et. al.* proposed a kernel function based on the Kullback-Leibler divergence in the original data space.

It is obvious that our probabilistic distance measures can be adapted as kernel functions for set. First, the Bhattacharyya kernel defined in [265] differs from the Bhattacharyya distance by $-\log(.)$. Secondly, the adaptation can be in the sense of [269]. Other ways are possible by utilizing the construction rule of kernel functions.

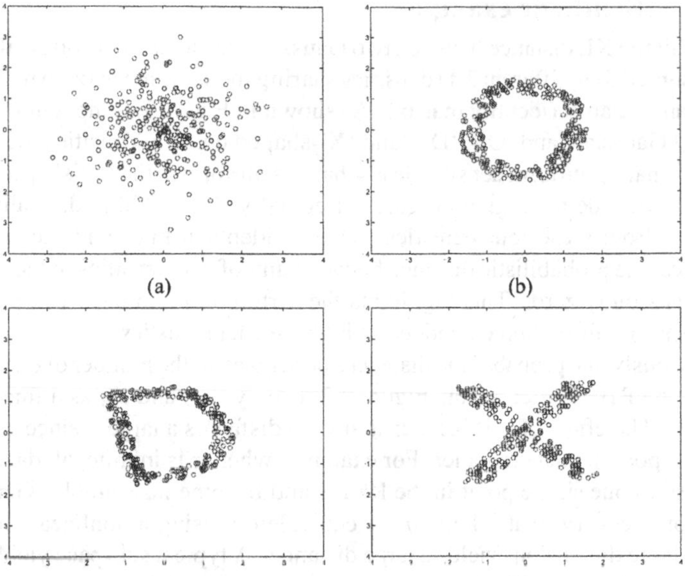

Figure 7.1. 300 i.i.d. realizations of four different densities with the same mean (zero mean) and covariance matrix (identity matrix). (a) 2-D Gaussian. (b) 'O'-shaped uniform.(c) 'D'-shaped uniform. (d) 'X'-shaped uniform.

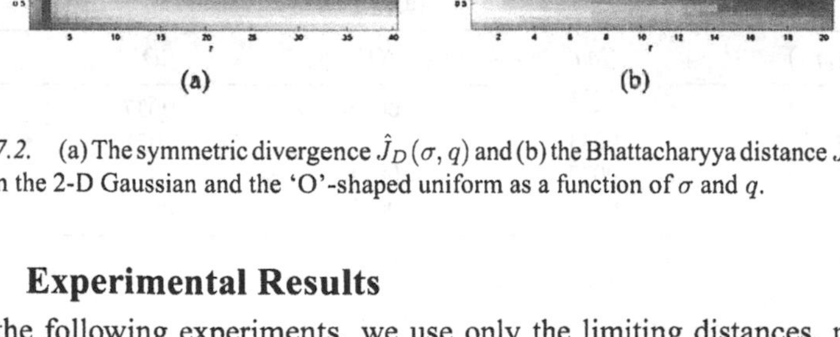

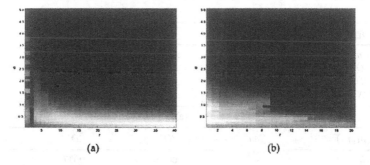

Figure 7.2. (a) The symmetric divergence $\hat{J}_D(\sigma, q)$ and (b) the Bhattacharyya distance $\hat{J}_B(\sigma, q)$ between the 2-D Gaussian and the 'O'-shaped uniform as a function of σ and q.

7.4 Experimental Results

In the following experiments, we use only the limiting distances, namely $\hat{J}_C(p_1, p_2)$ (or $\hat{J}_B(p_1, p_2)$), $\hat{J}_R(p_1||p_2)$, and $\hat{J}_D(p_1, p_2)$, since they do not depend on the choice ρ, which frees us from the burden of choosing ρ. Also, we set $q_1 = q_2 = q$.

7.4.1 Synthetic examples

To fail the KL distance between two Gaussian densities in the original space, we designed four different 2-D densities sharing the same mean (zero mean) and covariance matrix (identity matrix). As shown in Figure 7.1, the four densities are 2-D Gaussian, and 'O'-, 'D'-, and 'X'-shaped uniform densities, where say the 'O'-shaped uniform density means that it is uniform in the 'O'-shaped region and zero outside the region. Figure 7.1 actually shows 300 i.i.d. realizations sampled from these four densities. Due to identical first- and second-order statistics, the probabilistic distance between any of two densities in the original space is simply zero. This highlights the virtue of a nonlinear mapping that provides us information embedded in higher-order statistics.

Obviously, the probabilistic distances depend on q, the number of eigenpairs, and σ, the RBF kernel width. Figure 7.2 displays $\hat{J}_D$ and $\hat{J}_B$ as a function of q and σ. The effect of σ is biased: It always disfavors a large σ since a large σ tends to pool the data together. For example, when σ is infinite, all data points collapse to one single point in the RKHS and become inseparable. Generally, it is not necessary that a large q (or equivalently using a nonlinear subspace with a large dimension) yields a large distance. A typical subspace yielding the maximum distances is of low-dimensional.

Table 7.3 lists some computed values of the probabilistic distances. It is interesting to observe that when the shapes of two densities are close, their distance is small. For example, 'O' is closest to 'D' among all possible pairs. The closest density to the 2-D Gaussian is the 'O'-shaped uniform.

$\hat{J}_R(p_1\|\|p_2)$	*Gau*	*'O'*	*'D'*	*'X'*
Gau	-	.0740	.0782	.0808
'O'	.0584	-	.0281	.0523
'D'	.0670	.0295	-	.0436
'X'	.0944	.0505	.0417	-

(a)

$\hat{J}_B(p_1, p_2)$	*Gau*	*'O'*	*'D'*	*'X'*
Gau	-	.0033	.0037	.0048
'O'	.0033	-	.0021	.0099
'D'	.0037	.0021	-	.0086
'X'	.0048	.0099	.0086	-

(b)

Table 7.3. (a) The KL distances in the RKHS with $\sigma = 1$ and $q = 3$. (b) The Bhattacharyya distances in the RKHS with $\sigma = 0.5$ and $q = 1$. p_1 is listed in the first column and p_2 in the first row.

7.4.2 Face recognition from a group of images

The gallery set consists of 15 sets (one per person) while the probe set consists of 15 new sets of the same people (one per person). In these sets, the people can move their heads freely so that pose and illumination variations abound. The existence of these variations violates the Gaussianity assumption of the original data space used in [118]. Figure 7.3 shows some example faces of the in the 4th gallery person, the 9th gallery person, and the 4th probe person (whose identity is same as the 4th gallery person). The 32×32 face images are automatically cropped from video sequences (courtesy of [109]) using a flow-based tracking algorithm.

	Symmetric divergence	*Bhattacharyya distance*
$\hat{J}(p_1, p_2)$ *in the RKHS*	13/15	13/15
$J(p_1, p_2)$ *in the original space* $\mathcal{R}^d$	11/15	11/15

Table 7.4. The recognition score obtaining using the symmetric divergence and Bhattacharyya distance.

A generic PCA is performed to reduce the dimensionality to 300. Figure 7.3 also plots the first three PCA coefficients of the 4th gallery person, the 9th gallery person, and the 4th probe person. Clearly, the manifolds are highly nonlinear, which indicates a need for nonlinear modeling.

Table 7.4 reports the recognition rates. The top match with the smallest distance is claimed to be the winner. For comparison, we also implemented the approaches using the symmetric divergence [118] and the Bhattacharyya distance in the original space. Clearly, using the distances in RKHS yields better result. Out of 15 probe sets, we successfully classified 13 of them. In fact, Figure 7.3 shows a misclassification example in [118], where the 4th probe person is misclassified as the 9th gallery person, while our approach corrects this error.

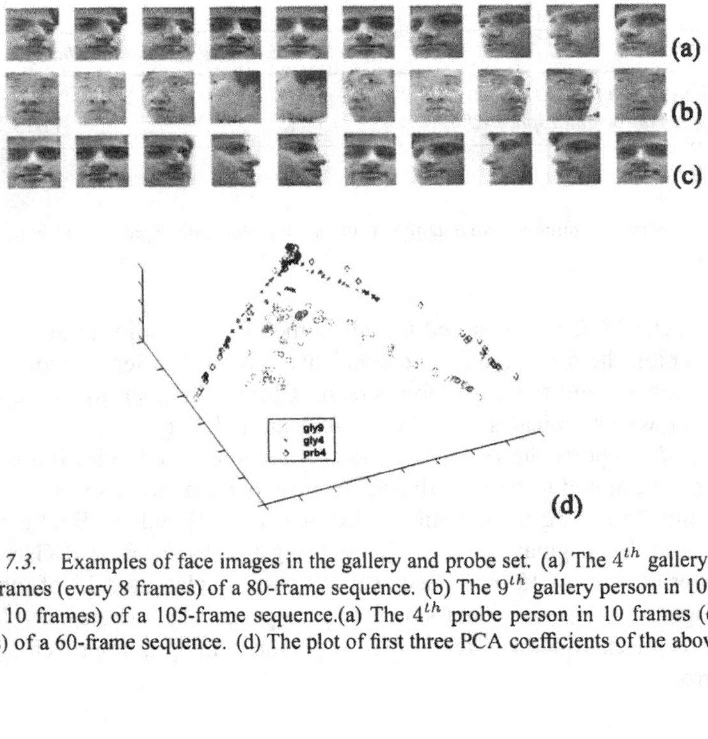

Figure 7.3. Examples of face images in the gallery and probe set. (a) The 4th gallery person in 10 frames (every 8 frames) of a 80-frame sequence. (b) The 9th gallery person in 10 frames (every 10 frames) of a 105-frame sequence.(a) The 4th probe person in 10 frames (every 6 frames) of a 60-frame sequence. (d) The plot of first three PCA coefficients of the above three sets.

Chapter 8

MATRIX-BASED KERNEL SUBSPACE ANALYSIS

Subspace methods are widely used in the face recognition literature due to the influential 'Eigenface' approach [64]. However, as mentioned in Chapter ??, subspace analysis in the original data space is very limited. Kernel method is one way to enhance its modeling capability.

It is a common practice that a matrix, the *de facto* image representation, is first converted into a vector before fed into subspace analysis or kernel method; however, the conversion ruins the spatial structure of the pixels that defines the image. In this chapter, we propose two kernel subspace methods that are directly based on the matrix representation, namely matrix-based kernel principal component analysis (matrix KPCA) and matrix-based kernel linear discriminant component analysis (matrix KLDA). We derive their principles in sections 8.1.1 and 8.1.2, respectively. Correspondingly, we call the vector-based kernel principal component analysis as vector KPCA and the vector-based linear discriminant analysis as vector KLDA.

We further show in section 8.2.1 that the matrix KPCA and matrix KLDA generalize the vector KPCA [272] and vector KLDA [263, 268]. In particular, the Gram matrix used in the vector KPCA and vector KLDA can be derived from the one used in the matrix KPCA and matrix KLDA. Therefore, matrix-based methods provide richer representations than vector-based counterparts. Our experiments in section 8.2.2 also demonstrate the advantages of matrix-based methods. Another advantage of the matrix-based methods is that they enable us to study the spatial statistics in the matrix.

To facilitate our analysis, we introduce the following quantity 'kernelized matrix'.

Kernelized matrix

For a matrix $X_{p\times q} = [\Rightarrow_{i=1}^{q} x_i]$, we define its *kernerlized matrix* $\phi(X)$ as

$$\phi(X)_{f\times q} = [\Rightarrow_{i=1}^{q} \phi(x_i)],$$

which maps each column of the matrix X to the nonlinear feature space. Note that the kernelized matrix is a hypothesized quantity introduced for analysis: we do not really compute this in practice. The dot product matrix $K_{q\times q}$ of two kernelized matrices X and Y is given as

$$K(X,Y)_{q\times q} = \phi(X)^{\mathsf{T}}\phi(Y) = [\Downarrow_{i=1}^{q} \; [\Rightarrow_{j=1}^{q} k(x_i, y_j)]\,].$$

Similarly, for the block matrix $\mathcal{X}_{p\times nq} = [\Rightarrow_{i=1}^{n} X_i]$ and its kernelized matrix

$$\phi(\mathcal{X})_{f\times nq} = [\Rightarrow_{i=1}^{n} \phi(X_i)],$$

we can compute the dot product matrix $\mathcal{K}_{nq\times nq}$ of the two kernerlized block matrices $\phi(\mathcal{X})$ and $\phi(\mathcal{Y})$ as

$$\mathcal{K}(\mathcal{X},\mathcal{Y}) = \phi(\mathcal{X})^{\mathsf{T}}\phi(\mathcal{Y}) = [\Downarrow_{i=1}^{n} \; [\Rightarrow_{j=1}^{n} K(X_i, Y_j)]\,].$$

The matrix $\mathcal{K}_{nq\times nq}$ is also a block matrix.

8.1 Matrix KPCA and Matrix KLDA

8.1.1 Matrix KPCA

Given a matrix $X_{p\times q}$ and its kernelized version $\phi(X)_{f\times q}$, the matrix KPCA attempts to find the projection matrix $U_{f\times r}$, i.e.,

$$Z_{r\times q} = U_{f\times r}^{\mathsf{T}}\phi(X)_{f\times q}, \tag{8.1}$$

such that the variation of the output matrix $Z_{r\times q}$ is maximized.

In the above definition, we note the following:

- We assume that the mean of the data (i.e. $\phi(X)$) is removed; otherwise, it contributes only a constant matrix to the output matrix Z in Eq. (8.1).
- Because each column is lifted from $\mathcal{R}^p$ to $\mathcal{R}^f$, we will call the above matrix KPCA as *column-lifted* matrix KPCA. To obtain a *row-lifted* matrix KPCA, we simply replace X with X^{T}.

$$Z_{p\times s} = \{V_{f\times s}^{\mathsf{T}}\psi(X^{\mathsf{T}})_{f\times p}\}^{\mathsf{T}} = \psi(X^{\mathsf{T}})^{\mathsf{T}}V.$$

- For one projection direction, the column-lifted matrix KPCA outputs a principal component vector whose dimensionality equals the number of the columns of the input matrix. In comparison, the vector KPCA [272] outputs a principal component value for one projection direction.

We start by finding the first project direction $u_{f\times 1}$ such that the variation of the output vector matrix $z_{1\times q} = u^T\phi(Y)$ is maximized. Mathematically, we have the following optimization problem:

$$\max_{||u||=1} ||z - E[z]||^2 = u^T\Sigma u,$$

where

$$\Sigma_{f\times f} = E[\{\phi(X) - E[\phi(X)]\}\{\phi(X) - E[\phi(X)]\}^T]$$

is *the total scatter matrix.* It is easy to show that the optimal vector u is the leading eigenvector of Σ corresponding to the largest eigenvalue.

In practice, we learn the projection vector u based on a training set $\mathcal{X} = [\Rightarrow_{i=1}^{n} X_i]$ that is kernelized to $\phi(\mathcal{X})_{f\times nq} = [\Rightarrow_{i=1}^{n} \phi(X_i)]$. The mean $E[\phi(X)]$ is estimated as

$$\overline{\phi(X)}_{f\times 1} = \frac{1}{n}\sum_{i=1}^{n}\phi(X_i) = \phi(\mathcal{X})\frac{1}{n}(e\otimes I_q)$$

where $e_{n\times 1} = [1, 1, \ldots, 1]^T$ is a column vector of 1's, and the total scatter matrix Σ is estimated as

$$\hat{\Sigma} = \frac{1}{n}\sum_{i=1}^{n}\{\phi(X_i) - \overline{\phi(X)}\}\{\phi(A_i) - \overline{\phi(X)}\}^T = \phi(\mathcal{X})\mathcal{J}\mathcal{J}^T\phi(\mathcal{X})^T \quad (8.2)$$

where $\mathcal{J}_{nq\times nq}$ plays the role of data centering.

$$\mathcal{J}_{nq\times nq} = \frac{1}{\sqrt{n}}J\otimes I_q,\ \ J_{n\times n} = I_n - \frac{1}{n}ee^T.$$

It remains to show how to compute the eigenvector of the $\hat{\Sigma}$ matrix. Usually, the matrix $\hat{\Sigma}$ is rank deficient because the cardinality of the nonlinear feature space is quite large. In the case of the RBF kernel, f is infinite. We follow the standard method given in [64] to calculate the leading eigenvectors for a rank deficient matrix.

Define the matrix $\bar{\mathcal{K}}_{nq\times nq}$ as

$$\bar{\mathcal{K}} = \mathcal{J}^T\phi(\mathcal{X})^T\phi(\mathcal{X})\mathcal{J} = \mathcal{J}^T\mathcal{K}(\mathcal{X},\mathcal{X})\mathcal{J},$$

where $\mathcal{K}(\mathcal{X},\mathcal{X})$ is the Gram matrix that is computable in practice. Suppose that (λ, v) is an eigenpair of the matrix $\bar{\mathcal{K}}$, i.e., $v_{nq\times 1}$ is an unit eigenvector with the corresponding eigenvalue λ or $\bar{\mathcal{K}}v = \lambda v$. Because

$$\phi(\mathcal{X})\mathcal{J}\bar{\mathcal{K}}v = \hat{\Sigma}\phi(\mathcal{X})\mathcal{J}v = \lambda\phi(\mathcal{X})\mathcal{J}v,$$

the vector $\mathrm{u}_{f\times 1} = \phi(\mathcal{X})\mathcal{J}\mathrm{v}$ is an eigenvector of the matrix $\hat{\Sigma}$ with the corresponding eigenvalue λ. To obtain a normalized vector u, we note that

$$\mathrm{u}^\top \mathrm{u} = \mathrm{v}^\top \mathcal{J}^\top \phi(\mathcal{X})^\top \phi(\mathcal{X})\mathcal{J}\mathrm{v} = \lambda \mathrm{v}^\top \mathrm{v} = \lambda. \tag{8.3}$$

Therefore, $(\lambda, \mathrm{u} = \frac{1}{\sqrt{\lambda}}\phi(\mathcal{X})\mathcal{J}\mathrm{v})$ is an eigenpair of the matrix $\hat{\Sigma}$.

For a given matrix $\mathrm{Y}_{p\times q} = [\Rightarrow_{i=1}^{q} \mathrm{y}_i]$, its principal component vector $\mathrm{z}_{1\times q} = \mathrm{u}^\top \phi(\mathrm{Y})$ is computed as

$$\mathrm{z} = \frac{1}{\sqrt{\lambda}} \mathrm{v}^\top \mathcal{J}^\top \phi(\mathcal{X})^\top \phi(\mathrm{Y}) = \frac{1}{\sqrt{\lambda}} \mathrm{v}^\top \mathcal{J}^\top [\Downarrow_{i=1}^{n} \mathrm{K}(\mathrm{X}_i, \mathrm{Y})]. \tag{8.4}$$

Similarly, we first obtain the top r eigenpairs $\{(\lambda_i, \mathrm{v}_i);\ i = 1, \ldots, r\}$ that are associated with the matrix $\bar{\mathcal{K}}$ and then convert them to those of the matrix $\hat{\Sigma}$. In a matrix form, the eigenvector matrix is given as

$$\mathrm{U}_{f\times r} = [\Rightarrow_{i=1}^{r} \mathrm{u}_i] = \phi(\mathcal{X})\mathcal{J}\mathrm{V}\Lambda^{-1/2},$$

where $\mathrm{V}_{nq\times r} = [\Rightarrow_{i=1}^{r} \mathrm{v}_i]$ encodes the top m eigenvectors v_i of the matrix $\bar{\mathcal{K}}$ and Λ is a diagonal matrix whose diagonal elements are $\{\lambda_i;\ i = 1, \ldots, r\}$. The matrix for all principal component vectors is

$$\mathrm{Z}_{r\times q} = [\Downarrow_{i=1}^{r} \mathrm{z}_i] = \Lambda^{-1/2} \mathrm{V}^\top \mathcal{J}^\top [\Downarrow_{j=1}^{n} \mathrm{K}(\mathrm{X}_i, \mathrm{Y})].$$

The column-lifted matrix KPCA is summarized in Figure 8.1. It should be noted that when the kernel function is $k(\mathrm{x}, \mathrm{y}) = \mathrm{x}^\top \mathrm{y}$, then matrix KPCA reduces to matrix PCA [66]. However, the 'kernel trick' substantially enhances the modeling capacity of the matrix PCA that is linear in nature.

8.1.2 Matrix KLDA

The matrix KLDA attempts to find the projection matrix $\mathrm{U}_{f\times r}$, i.e., $\mathrm{Z}_{r\times q} = \mathrm{U}^\top \phi(\mathrm{X})$, such that the within-class variation of the matrix Z is minimized while the between-class variation of the matrix Z is maximized. Again this is a column-lifted definition.

We only show how to find the first project direction $\mathrm{u}_{f\times 1}$; the rest just follows. Mathematically, we have the following optimization problem:

$$\max_{||\mathrm{u}||=1} \frac{\mathrm{u}^\top \Sigma_B \mathrm{u}}{\mathrm{u}^\top \Sigma_W \mathrm{u}},$$

where Σ_W is the *within-class scatter matrix* and Σ_B the *between-class scatter matrix*. The optimal vector is the leading eigenvector corresponding to a generalized eigenvalue problem,

$$\Sigma_B \mathrm{u} = \lambda \Sigma_W \mathrm{u}. \tag{8.5}$$

[*Training*]

- Compute the centering matrix $\mathcal{J}$, the Gram matrix $\mathcal{K}(\mathcal{X},\mathcal{X})$, and the matrix $\bar{\mathcal{K}}$.
- Find the leading r eigenpairs $\{(\lambda_i, \mathrm{v}_i);\ i = 1, 2, ..., r\}$ of the matrix $\bar{\mathcal{K}}$.
- The leading r eigenpairs for the matrix $\hat{\Sigma}$ is $\{(\lambda_i, \frac{1}{\sqrt{\lambda_i}}\phi(\mathcal{X})\mathcal{J}\mathrm{v}_i);\ i = 1, 2, ..., r\}$

[*Projection*]

- For an arbitrary input matrix $\mathtt{Y}$, find its ith principal component vector using Eq. (8.4), that is $\mathrm{z}_i = \frac{1}{\sqrt{\lambda_i}}\mathrm{v}_i^\mathsf{T}\mathcal{J}^\mathsf{T}[\Downarrow_{j=1}^{n} \mathtt{K}(\mathtt{X}_j, \mathtt{Y})]$.

Figure 8.1. Summary of matrix KPCA.

It is easy to show [7] that the total scatter matrix Σ can be written as $\Sigma = \Sigma_W + \Sigma_B$. Therefore, Eq. (8.5) is equivalent to

$$\Sigma_B \mathrm{u} = \lambda \Sigma \mathrm{u}, \tag{8.6}$$

except that there is a difference in the eigenvalue.

We assume that the training set is given as $\mathcal{X} = [\Rightarrow_{i=1}^{n} \mathtt{X}_i]$ and each data point $\mathtt{X}_i$ has its class label function $h(\mathtt{X}_i)$, taking a value in the class label set $\{1, 2, \ldots, C\}$. In section 8.1.1, we showed that the matrix Σ can be estimated as $\hat{\Sigma} = \phi(\mathcal{X})\mathcal{J}\mathcal{J}^\mathsf{T}\phi(\mathcal{X})^\mathsf{T}$, e.g., Eq. (8.2). We now derive the estimate for the matrix Σ_B, denoted by $\hat{\Sigma}_B$.

Without loss of generality, we further assume that the data points are already ordered by class labels. The number of data points belonging to the class c is given as $n_c = \sum_{i=1}^{n} I[h(\mathtt{X}_i) = c]$, where $I[.]$ is an indicator function.

The mean for the class c is estimated as

$$\overline{\phi_c(\mathtt{X})} = \frac{\sum_{i=1}^{n} \phi(\mathtt{X}_i) I[h(\mathtt{X}_i) = c]}{\sum_{i=1}^{n} I[h(\mathtt{X}_i) = c]} = \phi(\mathcal{X})\frac{1}{n_c}(\mathsf{e}_c \otimes \mathtt{I}_q),$$

where e_c is a column vector of size $n \times 1$ given as $\mathsf{e}_c = [\Downarrow_{i=1}^{n} I[h(\mathtt{X}_i) = c]]$.

The between-class scatter matrix Σ_B is estimated as

$$\hat{\Sigma}_B = \frac{n_c}{n}\sum_{c=1}^{C}\{\overline{\phi_c(\mathtt{X})} - \overline{\phi(\mathtt{X})}\}\{\overline{\phi_c(\mathtt{X})} - \overline{\phi(\mathtt{X})}\}^\mathsf{T} = \phi(\mathcal{X})\mathcal{W}\phi(\mathcal{X})^\mathsf{T},$$

where $\mathcal{W}_{nq\times nq} = \mathtt{W}_{n\times n} \otimes \mathtt{I}_q$ and

$$\mathtt{W}_{n\times n} = \frac{n_c}{n}\sum_{c=1}^{C}\{(\frac{\mathtt{e}_c}{n_c} - \frac{\mathtt{e}}{n})\}\{(\frac{\mathtt{e}_c}{n_c} - \frac{\mathtt{e}}{n})\}^{\mathsf{T}}.$$

It is easy to show that $\mathtt{W}_{n\times n} = \mathtt{J}_{n\times n}\mathtt{B}_{n\times n}\mathtt{J}_{n\times n}$ where

$$\mathtt{B}_{n\times n} = \begin{bmatrix} \frac{1}{n_1}\mathtt{I}_{n_1} & & \\ & \cdots & \\ & & \frac{1}{n_C}\mathtt{I}_{n_C} \end{bmatrix}.$$

Therefore,

$$\mathcal{W} = (\mathtt{JBJ}) \otimes \mathtt{I}_q = \mathcal{J}_{nq\times nq}\mathcal{B}_{nq\times nq}\mathcal{J}_{nq\times nq},$$

where

$$\mathcal{J}_{nq\times nq} = \mathtt{J}_{n\times n} \otimes \mathtt{I}_q, \;\; \mathcal{B}_{nq\times nq} = \mathtt{B}_{n\times n} \otimes \mathtt{I}_q.$$

Combining the above derivations together, we have

$$\hat{\Sigma}_B = \phi(\mathcal{X})\mathcal{J}\mathcal{B}\mathcal{J}^{\mathsf{T}}\phi(\mathcal{X})^{\mathsf{T}}. \tag{8.7}$$

Substituting the ensemble estimators of the scatter matrices, i.e., Eqs. (8.2) and (8.7), into Eq. (8.6) yields

$$\phi(\mathcal{X})\mathcal{J}\mathcal{B}\mathcal{J}^{\mathsf{T}}\phi(\mathcal{X})^{\mathsf{T}}\mathtt{u} = \lambda\phi(\mathcal{X})\mathcal{J}\mathcal{J}^{\mathsf{T}}\phi(\mathcal{X})^{\mathsf{T}}\mathtt{u}, \tag{8.8}$$

The eigenvector $\mathtt{u}_{f\times 1}$ of Eq. (8.8) is in the form of

$$\mathtt{u} = \phi(\mathcal{X})\mathcal{J}\mathtt{v},$$

where $\mathtt{v}_{nq\times 1}$ is the leading eigenvector that satisfies

$$\bar{\mathcal{K}}(\mathcal{X},\mathcal{X})\mathcal{B}\bar{\mathcal{K}}(\mathcal{X},\mathcal{X})\mathtt{v} = \lambda\bar{\mathcal{K}}(\mathcal{X},\mathcal{X})\bar{\mathcal{K}}(\mathcal{X},\mathcal{X})\mathtt{v}.$$

To normalize the eigenvector u, we obtain

$$\mathtt{u} = \frac{1}{\sqrt{\xi}}\phi(\mathcal{X})\mathcal{J}\mathtt{v}, \;\; \xi = \mathtt{v}^{\mathsf{T}}\bar{\mathcal{K}}(\mathcal{X},\mathcal{X})\mathtt{v} = \mathtt{v}^{\mathsf{T}}\mathcal{J}^{\mathsf{T}}\mathcal{K}(\mathcal{X},\mathcal{X})\mathcal{J}\mathtt{v}.$$

For an arbitrary matrix $\mathtt{Y}_{p\times q}$, its discriminative vector is computed as

$$\mathtt{z}_{1\times q} = \mathtt{u}^{\mathsf{T}}\phi(\mathtt{Y}) = \frac{1}{\sqrt{\xi}}\mathtt{v}^{\mathsf{T}}\mathcal{J}^{\mathsf{T}}[\Downarrow_{i=1}^{n} \mathtt{K}(\mathtt{X}_i,\mathtt{Y})].$$

8.2 Discussions and Experimental Results

8.2.1 Discussions

It is insightful to compare the (column-lifted) matrix KPCA with the vector KPCA. This is especially important because the current practice usually vectorizes a matrix to a vector.

The vector KPCA [272] is based on the Gram matrix $\mathtt{K}(\mathcal{X},\mathcal{X})_{n\times n}$ whose ij^{th} element is $k(vec(\mathtt{X}_i), vec(\mathtt{X}_j))$, i.e.,

$$\mathtt{K}(\mathcal{X},\mathcal{X})_{n\times n} = [\Downarrow_{i=1}^{n} [\Rightarrow_{j=1}^{n} k(vec(\mathtt{X}_i), vec(\mathtt{X}_j))]],$$

whereas the block Gram matrix

$$\mathcal{K}(\mathcal{X},\mathcal{X})_{nq\times nq} = [\Downarrow_{i=1}^{n} [\Rightarrow_{j=1}^{n} \mathtt{K}(\mathtt{X}_i,\mathtt{X}_j)]]$$

is used in the matrix KPCA. First, these two Gram matrices have different sizes. The matrix $\mathcal{K}$ has a much bigger size than the matrix $\mathtt{K}$. As a consequence, the vector KPCA finds maximally $(n-1)$ eigenpairs, whereas the matrix KPCA has maximally $(n-1)q$ eigenpairs. Also, the vector KPCA outputs a vector of maximum size $(n-1)\times 1$ while the matrix KPCA outputs a matrix of maximum size $(n-1)q\times q$. In term of training complexity, matrix KPCA is more computationally involved than vector KPCA. Table 8.1 summarizes the above comparisons.

	Vector KPCA	*Column-lifted matrix KPCA*
Input	$pq\times 1$ vector	$p\times q$ matrix
Number of training samples	n	n
Gram matrix size	$n\times n$	$nq\times nq$
Maximum # of principal components	$(n-1)$	$(n-1)q$
Output of maximum size	$(n-1)\times 1$ vector	$(n-1)q\times q$ matrix

Table 8.1. Comparison between vector KPCA and matrix KPCA.

Second, the two Gram matrices are closely related. We compare the ij^{th} element of $\mathtt{K}(\mathcal{X},\mathcal{X})$, or $k(vec(\mathtt{X}_i), vec(\mathtt{X}_j))$, with the ij^{th} block of $\mathcal{K}(\mathcal{X},\mathcal{X})$, or $\mathtt{K}(\mathtt{X}_i,\mathtt{X}_j)$. For convenience, we let $\mathtt{X}_i = \mathtt{A} = [\Rightarrow_{i=1}^{q} \mathtt{a}_i]$ and $\mathtt{X}_j = \mathtt{B} = [\Rightarrow_{i=j}^{q} \mathtt{b}_j]$. Using the RBF kernel $k(\mathtt{a},\mathtt{b}) = \exp\{-\theta^{-1}||\mathtt{a}-\mathtt{b}||^2\}$, the quantities $k(vec(\mathtt{A}), vec(\mathtt{B}))$ (or $k(\mathtt{A},\mathtt{B})$ in short) and $\mathtt{K}(\mathtt{A},\mathtt{B})_{q\times q}$ are computed as follows.

$$k(\mathtt{A},\mathtt{B}) = \prod_{i=1}^{q} k(\mathtt{a}_i,\mathtt{b}_i), \quad \mathtt{K}(\mathtt{A},\mathtt{B}) = [\Downarrow_{i=1}^{q} [\Rightarrow_{j=1}^{q} k(\mathtt{a}_i,\mathtt{b}_j)]].$$

The scalar $k(vec(\mathtt{A}), vec(\mathtt{B}))$ is just the product of the diagonal elements of the matrix $\mathtt{K}(\mathtt{A},\mathtt{B})_{q\times q}$. The Gram matrix $\mathtt{K}(\mathcal{X},\mathcal{X})_{n\times n}$ can be completely derived from the block Gram matrix $\mathcal{K}(\mathcal{X},\mathcal{X})_{nq\times nq}$. In general, the above relationship between the two Gram matrices holds. Because the mapping from $\mathcal{K}(\mathcal{X},\mathcal{X})$ to $\mathtt{K}(\mathcal{X},\mathcal{X})$ is many-to-one, the block matrix $\mathcal{K}(\mathcal{X},\mathcal{X})$ contains more information than the matrix $\mathtt{K}(\mathcal{X},\mathcal{X})$. Thus, the matrix KPCA provides a richer representation than the vector KPCA.

More importantly, $\mathtt{K}(\mathtt{A},\mathtt{B})$ can be viewed as encoding the column-wise statistics, because its ij^{th} element $k(\mathtt{a}_i,\mathtt{b}_j)$ compares two columns. Spatial statistics of higher order between columns are somewhat captured. However, this property is typically lost in $k(vec(\mathtt{A}),vec(\mathtt{B}))$. For example, in the RBF kernel, there is no comparison between the two columns $\mathtt{a}_i$ and $\mathtt{b}_j$ when $i\neq j$.

Another advantage of the matrix KPCA is that in the matrix KPCA we can interchange the role of row and column. This can be done by simply replacing a matrix $\mathtt{X}$ by its transpose $\mathtt{X}^{\mathsf{T}}$. Alternatively, we can perform the following recursive procedure.

$$\begin{aligned}\mathtt{X}_{p\times q} &\longmapsto_{(1)} \mathtt{Y}_{r\times q}=\mathtt{U}^{\mathsf{T}}_{f\times r}\phi(\mathtt{X})_{f\times q}\\ &\longmapsto_{(2)} \mathtt{Z}_{r\times s}=\psi(\mathtt{Y}^{\mathsf{T}})^{\mathsf{T}}_{f\times r}\mathtt{V}_{f\times s}=\psi(\phi(\mathtt{X})^{\mathsf{T}}\mathtt{U})^{\mathsf{T}}\mathtt{V},\end{aligned}\tag{8.9}$$

where '$\longmapsto_{(1)}$' means the column-lifted matrix KPCA and '$\longmapsto_{(2)}$' means the row-lifted matrix KPCA. Through the above procedure that is similar to bilinear analysis [214], we essentially perform the matrix KPCA first along the column and then along the row to capture both column-wise and row-wise statistics of higher order.

Similar observations can be made when comparing the matrix KLDA and the vector KLDA.

8.2.2 Experimental results

In this section, we show two applications of the kernel methods developed above.

Visualization

We applied the matrix KPCA to 200 images of the digit 'three'. Figure 8.2(a) shows ten example images of size 16×16. The digit 'three' manifests a spatially nonlinear pattern. To capture it, methods able to handle both nonlinearity and spatial statistics are required.

The column-lifted matrix KPCA is first applied along the column direction using the kernel function $k(\mathrm{x},\mathrm{y})=\exp\{-32^{-1}||\mathrm{x}-\mathrm{y}||^2\}$. We kept only the top 16 principal components that are displayed in Figure 8.2(b). Note that each output matrix is again of size 16×16. Next, we further applied the row-lifted matrix KPCA, with a different kernel function $k(\mathrm{x},\mathrm{y})=\exp\{-||\mathrm{x}-\mathrm{y}||^2\}$, along the row direction (of those in Figure 8.2(b)), Again, we kept only the top 16 principal components. The outputs are shown in Figure 8.2(c). It is interesting to observe that there is a distinctive white line characterizing all these images.

We adopted the local linear embedding (LLE) [251] to visualize the data in different representations. Figure 8.2(d) visualizes the original images, where a triangle structure appears. In Figure 8.2(e), the vector KPCA representation, obtained using the kernel function $k(\mathrm{x}, \mathrm{y}) = \exp\{-128^{-1}||\mathrm{x} - \mathrm{y}||^2\}$, is displayed. Note that the structure in Figure 8.2(e) is only slightly tighter than that in Figure 8.2(d), meaning that vector KPCA does not change the distribution of the data too much.

Figure 8.2(f) visualizes the data representation after the column-lifted matrix KPCA with the kernel function $k(\mathrm{x}, \mathrm{y}) = \exp\{-||\mathrm{x} - \mathrm{y}||^2\}$ is applied along the column vector. The data becomes very clustered. The row-lifted matrix KCPA with the same kernel function is further applied along the row direction and its output is visualized in Figure 8.2(g). The data is even more clustered after high-order row and column statistics are somewhat captured. However, it is not fully captured because the data still form a tight nonlinear manifold. It should be noted that changing the kernel function does not affect the structure presented in the figure.

Face recognition

One main application of subspace analysis is face recognition [64, 65, 66, 29]. We also tested the matrix KPCA and KLDA for this task. In particular, we focused on variations in pose and illumination.

The AT&T database has 40 subjects with 10 images for each subject. Figure 8.3(a) shows one subject at 10 poses. While pose variations ruin the pixel correspondence required for vector-based method, matrix-based methods are relatively immune to this problem. We randomly divided 10 images of one subject into two sets, M images for training and N images for testing ($M+N = 10$). Such a random division was repeated for every subject. Table 8.2(a) shows the average recognition rate of 10 simulations. Here 'Matrix ($q = n$)' means the following: When $q = 2$ for example, the image is converted to a matrix with 2 columns, the first column for the left part of the image and the second column for the right part. Hence in this case we can characterize the statistical dependence between the left and right parts of the face image.

We repeated the same experiment for the PIE database [85] that consists of 68 subjects. Here we focused only on the illumination variation and selected 12 lighting conditions. Figure 8.3(b) shows one subject under these 12 illumination conditions. As PCA is known to be inadequate in handling illumination variation, we only considered LDA [44]. For comparison, we implemented the illumination subspace approach [144] that is physical-model-based and hence effective for modeling illumination variations. In [144], a separate linear sub-

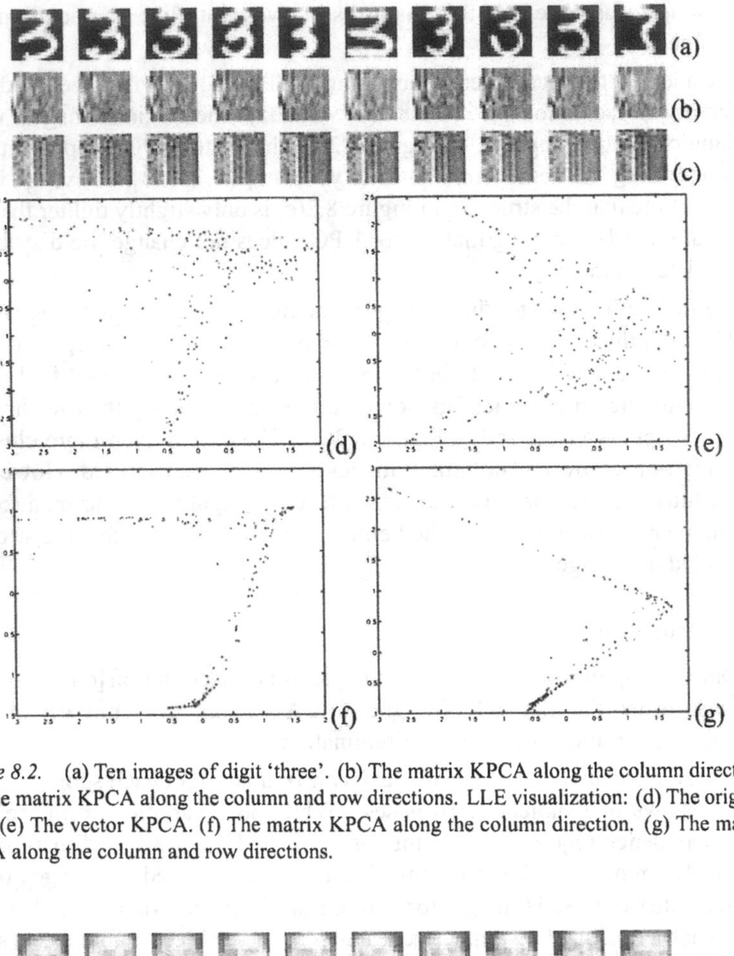

Figure 8.2. (a) Ten images of digit 'three'. (b) The matrix KPCA along the column direction. (c) The matrix KPCA along the column and row directions. LLE visualization: (d) The original data. (e) The vector KPCA. (f) The matrix KPCA along the column direction. (g) The matrix KPCA along the column and row directions.

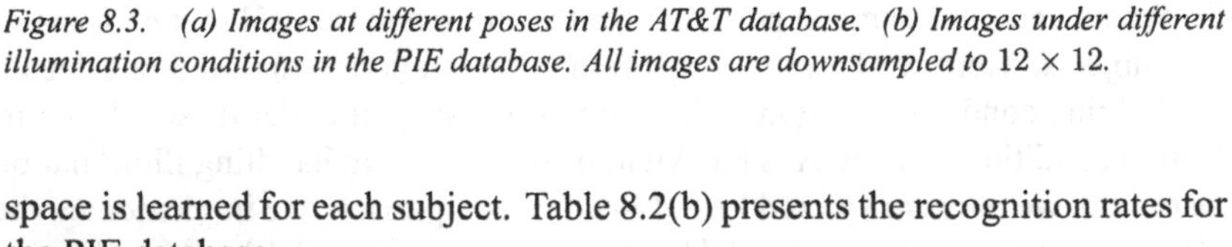

Figure 8.3. (a) Images at different poses in the AT&T database. (b) Images under different illumination conditions in the PIE database. All images are downsampled to 12×12.

space is learned for each subject. Table 8.2(b) presents the recognition rates for the PIE database.

From Table 8.2, we make the following observations:

1 The matrix-based analysis almost always outperforms the vector-based analysis, highlighting the virtue of the matrix KPCA and matrix KLDA.

2 The matrix KLDA consistently outperforms the matrix KPCA because the former is a supervised approach.

3 Using more samples in the training set increases the recognition performance.

4 Kernel methods almost always outperforms their non-kernel counterparts.

5 When dealing with the illumination variation, the matrix KLDA algorithm that is learning-based even outperforms, in small-sample cases, the illumination approach that is physical-model-based and needs more data to learn the model.

Polynomial kernel ($\theta = 1, d = 3$)	$M = 2$ $N = 8$	$M = 3$ $N = 7$	$M = 4$ $N = 6$	$M = 5$ $N = 5$
matrix KPCA ($q = 4$)	**73.4±2.6**	**75.7±2.0**	**78.1±1.4**	**80.6±2.6**
matrix KPCA ($q = 2$)	71.2±3.1	72.4±1.9	75.9±2.4	78.3±2.9
vector KPCA ($q = 1$)	65.9±3.1	68.5±2.5	75.3±2.4	78.3±1.8
matrix KLDA ($q = 4$)	73.6±2.5	82.1±3.0	87.4±3.0	89.8±3.4
matrix KLDA ($q = 2$)	**76.0±2.5**	**83.9±3.7**	**88.1±2.6**	**92.0±2.9**
vector KLDA ($q = 1$)	76.0±3.0	82.7±2.8	87.5±3.2	90.5±2.4

(a)

Polynomial kernel ($\theta = 1, d = 3$)	$M = 2$ $N = 10$	$M = 4$ $N = 8$	$M = 6$ $N = 6$	$M = 8$ $N = 4$	$M = 10$ $N = 2$
matrix KLDA ($q = 2$)	55.4±2.1	82.6±2.4	**93.0±1.5**	**96.5±1.5**	98.2±1.1
vector KLDA ($q = 1$)	**64.3±3.7**	81.3±2.5	81.2±2.6	80.2±2.2	71.0±4.3
vector LDA ($q = 1$)	49.2±3.7	66.1±3.5	74.8±1.9	80.0±3.3	83.6±2.7
Illumination subspace	53.1±2.5	**85.0±2.2**	92.3±1.5	96.1±1.3	**98.5±1.1**

(b)

Table 8.2. Face recognition rates for (a) the AT&T database and (b) the PIE database.

PART IV

FACE TRACKING AND RECOGNITION FROM VIDEOS

Chapter 9

ADAPTIVE VISUAL TRACKING

Particle filtering [179, 245, 248, 237, 6] is an inference technique [3, 20] for estimating the unknown motion state, θ_t, from a noisy collection of observations, $\mathrm{y}_{1:t} = \{\mathrm{y}_1, ..., \mathrm{y}_t\}$ arriving in a sequential fashion. A state space time series model is often employed to accommodate such a time series. As mentioned in Chapter 2, two important components of a time series are state transition and observation models.

The state transition model characterizes the motion change between frames. In a visual tracking problem, it is ideal to have an exact motion model governing the kinematics of the object. In practice, however, approximate models are used. There are two types of approximations commonly found in the literature. (i) One is to learn a motion model directly from a training video [183, 189]. However such a model may overfit the training data and may not necessarily succeed when presented with testing videos containing objects arbitrarily moving at different times and places. Also one cannot always rely on the availability of training data. (ii) Secondly, a fixed constant-velocity model with fixed noise variance is fitted as in [174, 198, 208, 129].

$$\theta_t = \theta_{t-1} + \nu_t + \mathrm{u}_t, \tag{9.1}$$

where ν_t is a constant velocity, i.e. $\nu_t = \nu_0$, and u_t has a fixed noise variance of the form $\mathrm{u}_t = r_0 * \mathrm{u}_0$ with r_0 a fixed constant measuring the extent of noise and u_0 a 'standardized' random variable/vector Consider the scalar case for example. If u_t is distributed as $\mathtt{N}(0, \sigma^2)$, we can write $\mathrm{u}_t = \sigma \mathrm{u}_0$ where u_0 is standard normal $\mathtt{N}(0, 1)$. This also applies to multivariate cases. Since a constant ν_0 has difficulty in handling arbitrary movement, ν_0 is typically set to be $\nu_0 = 0$. If r_0 is small, it is very hard to model rapid movements; if r_0 is large, it is computationally inefficient since many more particles are needed to accommodate the large noise variance. All these factors make such a model ineffective. In this chapter, we overcome this by introducing an adaptive-velocity model.

While contour is the visual cue used in many tracking algorithms [183], another class of tracking approaches [180, 192, 129] exploits an appearance model $\mathtt{A}_t$. In its simplest form, we have the following observation equation. For the sake of simplicity, we denote: $\mathbf{z}_t = \mathcal{T}\{\mathbf{y}_t; \theta_t\}, \mathbf{z}_t^{(j)} = \mathcal{T}\{\mathbf{y}_t; \theta_t^{(j)}\}, \hat{\mathbf{z}}_t = \mathcal{T}\{\mathbf{y}_t; \hat{\theta}_t\}$. Also, we can always vectorize the 2-D image by a lexicographical scanning of all pixels and denote the number of pixels by d.

$$\mathbf{z}_t = \mathcal{T}\{\mathbf{y}_t; \theta_t\} = \mathtt{A}_t + \mathbf{v}_t, \tag{9.2}$$

where $\mathbf{z}_t$ is the image patch of interest in the video frame $\mathbf{y}_t$, parameterized by θ_t. In [180], a fixed template, $\mathtt{A}_t = \mathtt{A}_0$, is matched with observations to minimize a cost function in the form of sum of squared distance (SSD). This is equivalent to assuming that the noise $\mathbf{v}_t$ is a normal random vector with zero mean and a diagonal (isotropic) covariance matrix. At the other extreme, one could use a rapidly changing model [192], say, $\mathtt{A}_t = \hat{\mathbf{z}}_{t-1}$, i.e., the 'best' patch of interest in the previous frame. However, a fixed template cannot handle appearance changes in the video, while a rapidly changing model is susceptible to drift. Thus, it is necessary to have a model which is a compromise between these two cases. In [185], Jepson *et. al.* proposed an online appearance model (OAM) for a robust visual tracker, which is a mixture of three components. Two EM algorithms are used, one for updating the appearance model and the other for deriving the tracking parameters.

Our approach to visual tracking is to make both observation and state transition models adaptive in the framework of a particle filter, with provisions for handling occlusion. The main features of our tracking approach are as follows:

- Appearance-based. The only visual cue used in our tracker is the 2-D appearance; i.e., we employ only image intensities, though in general features derived from image intensities, such as the phase information of the filter responses [185] or the Gabor feature graph presentation [111], are also applicable. No prior object models are invoked. In addition, we only use gray scale images.

- Adaptive observation model. We adopt an appearance-based approach. The original OAM is modified and then embedded in our particle filter. Therefore, the observation model is adaptive as the appearance $\mathtt{A}_t$ involved in (9.2) is adaptive.

- Adaptive state transition model. Instead of using a fixed model, we use an adaptive-velocity model, where the adaptive motion velocity ν_t is predicted using a first-order linear approximation based on the appearance difference between the incoming observation and the previous particle configuration.

We also use an adaptive noise component, i.e, $u_t = r_t * u_0$, whose magnitude r_t is a function of the prediction error. It is natural to vary the number of particles based on the degree of uncertainty r_t in the noise component.

- Handling occlusion. Occlusion is handled using robust statistics [11, 180, 173]. We robustify the likelihood measurement and the adaptive velocity estimate by downweighting the 'outlier' pixels. If occlusion is declared, we stop updating the appearance model and estimating the motion velocity.

This chapter is organized as follows. We examine the details of an adaptive observation model in Section 9.1.1, with a special focus on the adaptive appearance model, and of an adaptive state transition model in Section 9.1.2 with a special focus on how to calculate the motion velocity. Handling occlusion is discussed in Section 9.1.3, and experimental results on tracking vehicles and human faces are presented in Section 9.2.

9.1 Appearance-Adaptive Models

9.1.1 Adaptive observation model

The adaptive observation model arises from the adaptive appearance model A_t. We use a modified version of OAM as developed in [185]. The differences between our appearance model and the original OAM are highlighted below.

Mixture appearance model

The original OAM assumes that the observations are explained by different causes, thereby indicating the use of a mixture density of components. In the original OAM presented in [185], three components are used, namely the W-component characterizing the two-frame variations, the S-component depicting the stable structure within all past observations (though it is slowly-varying), and the L-component accounting for outliers such as occluded pixels.

We modify the OAM to accommodate our appearance analysis in the following aspects. (i) We directly use the image intensities while they use phase information derived from image intensities. Direct use of image intensities is computationally more efficient than using the phase information that requires filtering and visually more interpretable. (ii) As an option, in order to further stabilize the tracker one could use an F-component which is a fixed template that one is expecting to observe most often. For example, in face tracking this could be just the facial image as seen from a frontal view. In the sequel, we derive the equations as if there is an F-component. However, the effect of this component can be ignored by setting its initial mixing probability to zero. (iii) We embed the appearance model in a particle filter to perform tracking while they use the EM algorithm. (iv) In our implementation, we do not incorporate the L-component because we model the occlusion in a different manner (using robust statistics) as discussed in Section 9.1.3.

We now describe the mixture appearance model. The appearance model at time t,

$$\mathtt{A}_t = \{\mathtt{W}_t, \mathtt{S}_t, \mathtt{F}_t\},$$

is a time-varying one that models the appearances present in all observations up to time $t-1$. It obeys a mixture of Gaussians, with $\mathtt{W}_t, \mathtt{S}_t, \mathtt{F}_t$ as mixture centers $\{\mu_{i,t};\ i = w, s, f\}$ and their corresponding variances $\{\sigma^2_{i,t};\ i = w, s, f\}$ and mixing probabilities $\{m_{i,t};\ i = w, s, f\}$. Notice that

$$\{m_{i,t}, \mu_{i,t}, \sigma^2_{i,t};\ i = w, s, f\}$$

are 'images' consisting of d pixels that are assumed to be independent of each other.

In summary, the observation likelihood is written as

$$p(\mathbf{y}_t|\theta_t) = p(\mathbf{z}_t|\theta_t) = \prod_{j=1}^{d}\{\sum_{i=w,s,f} m_{i,t}(j)\mathtt{N}(\mathbf{z}_t(j); \mu_{i,t}(j), \sigma^2_{i,t}(j))\}, \quad (9.3)$$

where $\mathtt{N}(x; \mu, \sigma^2)$ is a normal density

$$\mathtt{N}(x; \mu, \sigma^2) = (2\pi\sigma^2)^{-1/2}\exp\{-\rho(\frac{x-\mu}{\sigma})\},\ \rho(x) = \frac{1}{2}x^2. \quad (9.4)$$

Model update

To keep the chapter self-contained, we show how to update the current appearance model $\mathtt{A}_t$ to $\mathtt{A}_{t+1}$ after $\hat{\mathbf{z}}_t$ becomes available, i.e., we want to compute the new mixing probabilities, mixture centers, and variances for time $t+1$,

$$\{m_{i,t+1}, \mu_{i,t+1}, \sigma^2_{i,t+1};\ i = w, s, f\}.$$

It is assumed that the past observations are exponentially 'forgotten' with respect to their contributions to the current appearance model. Denote the exponential envelop by $\alpha\exp(-\tau^{-1}(t-k))$ for $k \le t$, where $\tau = n_h/\log 2$, n_h is the half-life of the envelope in frames, and $\alpha = 1 - \exp(-\tau^{-1})$ to guarantee that the area under the envelope is 1. We just sketch the updating equations as follows and refer the interested readers to [185] for technical details and justifications.

The expectation maximization (EM) algorithm [236] is invoked. Since we assume that the pixels are independent of each other, we can deal with each pixel separately. The following computation is valid for $j = 1, 2, \ldots, d$ where d is the number of pixels in the appearance model.

First, the posterior responsibility probabilities are computed as

$$o_{i,t}(j) \propto m_{i,t}(j)\mathtt{N}(\hat{\mathbf{z}}_t(j); \mu_{i,t}(j), \sigma^2_{i,t}(j)); \;\; i = w, s, f, \;\; \& \sum_{i=w,s,f} o_{i,t}(j) = 1. \tag{9.5}$$

Then, the mixing probabilities are updated as

$$m_{i,t+1}(j) = \alpha \, o_{i,t}(j) + (1-\alpha)\, m_{i,t}(j); \;\; i = w, s, f, \tag{9.6}$$

and the first- and second-moment images $\{\mathtt{M}_{p,t+1};\ p = 1, 2\}$ are evaluated as

$$\mathtt{M}_{p,t+1}(j) = \alpha \, \hat{\mathbf{z}}^p_t(j) o_{s,t}(j) + (1-\alpha)\, \mathtt{M}_{p,t}(j); \;\; p = 1, 2. \tag{9.7}$$

Finally, the mixture centers and the variances are updated as:

$$\mathtt{S}_{t+1}(j) = \mu_{s,t+1}(j) = \frac{\mathtt{M}_{1,t+1}(j)}{m_{s,t+1}(j)}, \;\; \sigma^2_{s,t+1}(j) = \frac{\mathtt{M}_{2,t+1}(j)}{m_{s,t+1}(j)} - \mu^2_{s,t+1}(j). \tag{9.8}$$

$$\mathtt{W}_{t+1}(j) = \mu_{w,t+1}(j) = \hat{\mathbf{z}}_t(j), \;\; \sigma^2_{w,t+1}(j) = \sigma^2_{w,1}(j), \tag{9.9}$$

$$\mathtt{F}_{t+1}(j) = \mu_{f,t+1}(j) = \mathtt{F}_1(j), \;\; \sigma^2_{f,t+1}(j) = \sigma^2_{f,1}(j). \tag{9.10}$$

Model initialization

To initialize $\mathtt{A}_1$, we set $\mathtt{W}_1 = \mathtt{S}_1 = \mathtt{F}_1 = \mathtt{T}_0$ (with $\mathtt{T}_0$ supplied by a detection algorithm or manually), $\{m_{i,1}, \sigma^2_{i,1};\ i = w, s, f\}$, and $\mathtt{M}_{1,1} = m_{s,1}\mathbf{z}_0$ and $\mathtt{M}_{2,1} = m_{s,1}\sigma^2_{s,1} + \mathtt{T}^2_0$.

9.1.2 Adaptive state transition model

The state transition model we use incorporates a term for modeling adaptive velocity. The adaptive velocity is calculated using a first-order linear prediction method based on the appearance differences between two successive frames. The previous particle configuration is incorporated in the prediction scheme.

Construction of the particle configuration involves the costly computation of image warping (in the experiments reported here, it usually accounts for about half of the computations). In a conventional particle filtering algorithm, the particle configuration is used only to update the weight, i.e., computing weight for each particle by comparing the warped image with the online appearance model using the observation equation. But, our approach in addition uses the particle configuration in the state transition equation. In some sense, we 'maximally' utilize the information contained in the particles (without wasting the costly computation of image warping) since we use it in both state and observation models.

In [193], random samples are guided by deterministic search. Momentum for each particle is computed as the sum of absolute difference between two frames. If the momentum is below a threshold, a deterministic search is first performed using a gradient descent method and a small number of offsprings is then generated using stochastic diffusion; otherwise, stochastic diffusion is performed to generate a large number of offsprings. The stochastic diffusion is based on a second-order autoregressive process. But, the gradient descent method does not utilize the previous particle configuration in its entirety. Also, the generated particle configuration could severely deviate from the second-order autoregressive model, which clearly implies the need for an adaptive model.

Adaptive velocity

With the availability of the sample set $\Theta_{t-1} = \{\theta_{t-1}^{(j)}\}_{j=1}^{J}$ and the image patches of interest $\mathcal{Z}_{t-1} = \{\mathbf{z}_{t-1}^{(j)}\}_{j=1}^{J}$, for a new observation $\mathbf{y}_t$, we can predict the shift in the motion vector (or adaptive velocity) $\nu_t = \theta_t - \hat{\theta}_{t-1}$ using a first-order linear approximation [172, 180, 186, 188], which essentially comes from the constant brightness constraint, i.e., there exists a θ_t such that

$$\mathcal{T}\{\mathbf{y}_t; \theta_t\} \simeq \hat{\mathbf{z}}_{t-1}. \tag{9.11}$$

Approximating $\mathcal{T}\{\mathbf{y}_t; \theta_t\}$ using a first-order Taylor series expansion around $\tilde{\theta}_t$ (we set $\tilde{\theta}_t = \hat{\theta}_{t-1}$) yields

$$\mathcal{T}\{\mathbf{y}_t; \theta_t\} \simeq \mathcal{T}\{\mathbf{y}_t; \tilde{\theta}_t\} + \mathsf{C}_t(\theta_t - \tilde{\theta}_t) = \mathcal{T}\{\mathbf{y}_t; \tilde{\theta}_t\} + \mathsf{C}_t\nu_t, \tag{9.12}$$

where C_t is the Jacobian matrix.

Combining (9.11) and (9.12) gives

$$\hat{\mathbf{z}}_{t-1} \simeq \mathcal{T}\{\mathbf{y}_t; \tilde{\theta}_t\} + \mathsf{C}_t\nu_t, \tag{9.13}$$

i.e.,

$$\nu_t = \theta_t - \tilde{\theta}_t \simeq -\mathsf{B}_t(\mathcal{T}\{\mathbf{y}_t; \tilde{\theta}_t\} - \hat{\mathbf{z}}_{t-1}), \tag{9.14}$$

where B_t is the pseudo-inverse of the C_t matrix, which can be efficiently estimated from the available data Θ_{t-1} and $\mathcal{Z}_{t-1}$.

Specifically, to estimate B_t we stack into matrices the differences in motion vectors and image patches, using $\hat{\theta}_{t-1}$ and $\hat{\mathbf{z}}_{t-1}$ as pivotal points:

$$\delta\Theta_{t-1} = [\theta_{t-1}^{(1)} - \hat{\theta}_{t-1}, \ \ldots, \ \theta_{t-1}^{(J)} - \hat{\theta}_{t-1}], \tag{9.15}$$

$$\delta\mathcal{Z}_{t-1} = [\mathbf{z}_{t-1}^{(1)} - \hat{\mathbf{z}}_{t-1}, \ \ldots, \ \mathbf{z}_{t-1}^{(J)} - \hat{\mathbf{z}}_{t-1}]. \tag{9.16}$$

The least square (LS) solution for B_t is

$$\mathsf{B}_t = (\delta\Theta_{t-1}\delta\mathcal{Z}_{t-1}^{\mathsf{T}})(\delta\mathcal{Z}_{t-1}\delta\mathcal{Z}_{t-1}^{\mathsf{T}})^{-1}. \tag{9.17}$$

However, it turns out that the matrix $\delta\mathcal{Z}_{t-1}\delta\mathcal{Z}_{t-1}^{\mathsf{T}}$ is very often rank-deficient due to the high dimensionality of the data (unless the number of the particles at least exceeds the data dimension). To overcome this, we use the SVD as

$$\delta\mathcal{Z}_{t-1} = \mathtt{U}\Lambda\mathtt{V}^{\mathsf{T}} \tag{9.18}$$

It can be easily shown that

$$\mathtt{B}_t = \delta\Theta_{t-1}\mathtt{V}\Lambda^{-1}\mathtt{U}^{\mathsf{T}}. \tag{9.19}$$

To gain some computational efficiency, we can further approximate

$$\mathtt{B}_t = \delta\Theta_{t-1}\mathtt{V}_q\Lambda_q^{-1}\mathtt{U}_q^{\mathsf{T}}, \tag{9.20}$$

by retaining the top q components. Notice that if only a fixed template is used [186], the $\mathtt{B}$ matrix is fixed and pre-computable. But, in our case, the appearance is changing so that we have to compute the $\mathtt{B}_t$ matrix in each time step.

In practice, one may run several iterations till $\tilde{\mathtt{z}}_t = \mathcal{T}\{\mathtt{y}_t; \tilde{\theta}_t + \nu_t\}$ stabilizes, i.e., the error ϵ_t defined below is small enough.

$$\epsilon_t = \phi(\tilde{\mathtt{z}}_t, \mathtt{A}_t) = \frac{2}{d}\sum_{j=1}^{d}\{\sum_{i=w,s,f} m_{i,t}(j)\rho(\frac{\tilde{\mathtt{z}}_t(j) - \mu_{i,t}(j)}{\sigma_{i,t}(j)})\}. \tag{9.21}$$

In (9.21), ϵ_t measures the distance between $\mathcal{T}\{\mathtt{y}_t; \tilde{\theta}_t + \nu_t\}$ and the updated appearance model $\mathtt{A}_t$. The iterations proceed as follows: We initially set $\tilde{\theta}_t^1 = \hat{\theta}_{t-1}$. For the first iteration, we compute ν_t^1 as usual. For the kth iteration, we use the predicted $\tilde{\theta}_t^k = \tilde{\theta}_t^{k-1} + \nu_t^{k-1}$ as a pivotal point for the Taylor expansion in (9.12) and the rest of the calculation then follows. It is rather beneficial to run several iterations especially when the object moves very fast in two successive frames since $\hat{\theta}_{t-1}$ might cover the target in $\mathtt{y}_t$ in a small portion. After one iteration, the computed ν_t might be not accurate, but indicates a good minimization direction. Using several iterations helps to find ν_t (compared to $\hat{\theta}_{t-1}$) more accurately.

We use the following adaptive state transition model

$$\theta_t = \hat{\theta}_{t-1} + \nu_t + \mathtt{u}_t, \tag{9.22}$$

where ν_t is the predicted shift in the motion vector. The choice of $\mathtt{u}_t$ is discussed below. One should note that we are not using (9.22) as a proposal function to draw particles, which requires using (2.11) to compute the particle weight. Instead we directly use it as the state transition model and hence use (2.8) to compute the particle weight. Our model can be easily interpreted as a time-varying state model.

It is interesting to note that the approach proposed in [196] also uses motion cues as well as color parameter adaptation. Our approach is different from [196] in that: (i) We use the motion cue in the state transition model while they use it as part of observations; (ii) We only use the gray images without using the color cue which is used in [196]; and (iii) We use an adaptive appearance model which is updated by the EM algorithm while they use an adaptive color model which is updated by a stochastic version of the EM algorithm.

Adaptive noise

The value of ϵ_t determines the quality of prediction. Therefore, if ϵ_t is small, which implies a good prediction, we only need noise with small variance to absorb the residual motion; if ϵ_t is large, which implies a poor prediction, we then need noise with large variance to model the potentially large jumps in the motion state.

To this end, we use u_t of the form $\mathrm{u}_t = r_t * \mathrm{u}_0$, where r_t is a function of ϵ_t. Since ϵ_t defined in (9.21) is a 'variance'-type measure, we use

$$r_t = \max(\min(r_0\sqrt{\epsilon_t}, r_{max}), r_{min}), \tag{9.23}$$

where r_{min} is the lower bound to maintain a reasonable sample coverage and r_{max} is the upper bound to constrain the computational load.

Adaptive number of particles

If the noise variance r_t is large, we need more particles, while conversely, fewer particles are needed for noise with small variance r_t. Based on the principle of asymptotic relative efficiency (ARE) [3], we adjust the particle number J_t in a similar fashion, i.e.,

$$J_t = J_0 r_t / r_0. \tag{9.24}$$

Fox [239] also presents an approach to improve the efficiency of particle filters by adapting the particle numbers on-the-fly. His approach is to divide the state space into bins and approximate the posterior distribution by a multinomial distribution. A small number of particles is used if the density is focused on a small part of the state space and a large number of particles if the uncertainty in the state space is high. In this way, the error between the empirical distribution and the true distribution (approximated as a multinomial in his analysis) measured by Kullback-Leilber distance is bounded. However, in his approach, since the state space (only 2D) is exhaustively divided, the number of particles is at least several thousand, while our approach uses at most a few hundred. Our attempt is not to explore the state space (6-D affine space) exhaustively, but only regions that have high potential for the object to be present.

Comparison between the adaptive velocity model and the zero velocity model

We demonstrate the necessity of the adaptive velocity model by comparing it with the zero velocity model. Figure 9.1 shows the particle configurations created from the adaptive velocity model (with $J_t < J_0$ and $r_t < r_0$ computed as above) and the zero velocity model (with $J_t = J_0$ and $r_t = r_0$). Clearly, the adaptive-velocity model generates particles very efficiently, i.e, they are tightly centered around the object of interest so that we can easily track the object at time t; while the zero-velocity model generates more particles widely spread to explore larger regions, leading to unsuccessful tracking as widespread particles often lead to a local minimum.

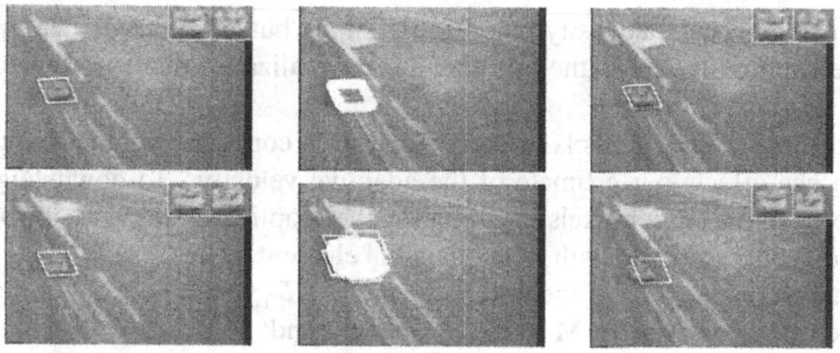

Tracking result at $t-1$ Particle configuration at t Tracking result at t

Figure 9.1. Particle configurations from (top row) the adaptive velocity model and (bottom row) the zero-velocity model.

9.1.3 Handling occlusion

Occlusion is usually handled in two ways. One way is to use joint probabilistic data associative filter (JPDAF) [2, 191]; and the other one is to use robust statistics [11]. We use robust statistics here.

Robust statistics

We assume that occlusion produces large image differences which can be treated as 'outliers'. Outlier pixels cannot be explained by the underlying process and their influences on the estimation process should be reduced. Robust statistics provide such mechanisms.

We use the $\hat{\rho}$ function defined as follows:

$$\hat{\rho}(x) = \begin{cases} \frac{1}{2}x^2 & \text{if } |x| \le c \\ cx - \frac{1}{2}c^2 & \text{if } |x| > c \end{cases}, \tag{9.25}$$

where x is normalized to have unit variance and the constant c controls the outlier rate. In our experiment, we take $c = 1.435$ based on experimental experience. If $|x| > c$ is satisfied, we declare the corresponding pixel as an outlier.

Robust likelihood measure and adaptive velocity estimate

The likelihood measure defined in Eq. (9.3) involves a multi-dimensional normal density. Since we assume that each pixel is independent, we consider the one-dimensional normal density. To make the likelihood measure robust, we replace the one-dimensional normal density $\mathtt{N}(x; \mu, \sigma^2)$ by

$$\hat{\mathtt{N}}(x; \mu, \sigma^2) = (2\pi\sigma^2)^{-1/2} \exp(-\hat{\rho}(\frac{x-\mu}{\sigma})). \tag{9.26}$$

Note that this is not a density function any more, but since we are dealing with discrete approximation in the particle filter, normalization makes it a probability mass function.

Existence of outlier pixels severely violates the constant brightness constraint and hence affects our estimate of the adaptive velocity. To downweight the influence of the outlier pixels in estimating the adaptive velocity, we introduce a $d \times d$ diagonal matrix $\mathtt{L}_t$ with its ith diagonal element being $\mathtt{L}_t(i) = \eta(x_i)$ where x_i is the pixel intensity of the difference image $(\mathcal{T}\{\mathtt{y}_t; \tilde{\theta}_t\} - \hat{\mathtt{z}}_{t-1})$ normalized by the variance of the OAM stable component and

$$\eta(x) = \frac{1}{x}\frac{d\hat{\rho}(x)}{dx} = \begin{cases} 1 & if \quad |x| \le c \\ c/|x| & if \quad |x| > c \end{cases}, \tag{9.27}$$

Eq. (9.14) becomes

$$\nu_t \simeq -\mathtt{B}_t\mathtt{L}_t(\mathcal{T}\{\mathtt{y}_t; \hat{\theta}_{t-1}\} - \hat{\mathtt{z}}_{t-1}). \tag{9.28}$$

This is similar in principle to the weighted least square algorithm.

Occlusion declaration

If the number of the outlier pixels in $\hat{\mathtt{z}}_t$ (compared with the OAM), say d_{out}, exceeds a certain threshold, i.e., $d_{out} > \lambda d$ where $0 < \lambda < 1$ (we take $\lambda = 0.15$), we declare occlusion. Since the OAM has more than one component, we count the number of outlier pixels with respect to every component and take the maximum.

If occlusion is declared, we stop updating the appearance model and estimating the motion velocity. Instead, we (i) keep the current appearance model, i.e., $\mathtt{A}_{t+1} = \mathtt{A}_t$ and (ii) set the motion velocity to zero, i.e., $\nu_t = 0$ and use the maximum number of particles sampled from the diffusion process with largest variance, i.e., $r_t = r_{max}$, and $J_t = J_{max}$.

The adaptive particle filtering algorithm with occlusion analysis is summarized in Figure 9.2.

Initialize *a sample set* $S_0 = \{\theta_0^{(j)}, 1/J_0\}_{j=1}^{J_0}$ *according to prior distribution* $p(\theta_0)$.
Initialize *the appearance model* A_1.
Set $OCC_{FLAG} = 0$ *to indicate no occlusion.*
For $t = 1, 2, \ldots$
    If *(*$OCC_{FLAG} == 0$*)*
        Calculate *the state estimate* $\hat{\theta}_{t-1}$ *by Eq. (2.9) or (2.10), the adaptive velocity* ν_t *by Eq. (9.14), the noise variance* r_t *by Eq. (9.23), and the particle number* J_t *by Eq. (9.24).*
    Else
        $r_t = r_{max}$, $J_t = J_{max}$, $\nu_t = 0$.
    End
    For $j = 1, 2, \ldots, J_t$
        Draw *the sample* $u_t^{(j)}$ *for* u_t *with variance* r_t.
        Construct *the sample* $\theta_t^{(j)} = \hat{\theta}_{t-1} + \nu_t + u_t^{(j)}$ *by Eq. (9.22).*
        Compute *the transformed image* $z_t^{(j)}$.
        Update *the weight using* $w_t^{(j)} = p(y_t|\theta_t^{(j)}) = p(z_t^{(j)}|\theta_t^{(j)})$.
    End
    Normalize *the weight using* $w_t^{(j)} = w_t^{(j)} / \sum_{j=1}^{J} w_t^{(j)}$.
    Set OCC_{FLAG} *according to the number of the outlier pixels in* $\hat{z}_t$.
    If *(*$OCC_{FLAG} == 0$*)*
        Update *the appearance model* A_{t+1} *using* $\hat{z}_t$.
    End
End

Figure 9.2. The proposed visual tracking algorithm with occlusion handling.

9.2 Experimental Results on Visual Tracking

In our implementation, we used the following choices. We consider affine transformation only, i.e., the motion is depicted by $\theta = (a_1, a_2, a_3, a_4, t_x, t_y)$ where $\{a_1, a_2, a_3, a_4\}$ are deformation parameters and $\{t_x, t_y\}$ denote the 2-D translation parameters. Even though significant pose/illumination changes are present in the video, we believe that our adaptive appearance model can easily absorb them and therefore for our purposes the affine transformation is a reasonable approximation. Regarding photometric transformations, only a zero-mean-unit-variance normalization is used to partially compensate for contrast variations. The complete image transformation $\mathcal{T}\{y; \theta\}$ is implemented as follows: affine transform y using $\{a_1, a_2, a_3, a_4\}$, crop out the region of interest at position $\{t_x, t_y\}$ with the same size as the still template in the appearance model, and perform zero-mean-unit-variance normalization.

We demonstrate our algorithm by tracking a disappearing car, a moving tank acquired by a camera mounted on a micro air vehicle, and a moving face under occlusion. Table 9.1 summarizes some statistics about the video sequences and the appearance model size used.

We initialize the particle filter and the appearance model with a detector algorithm (we actually used the face detector described in [197] for the face

Video	*Car*	*Tank*	*Face*
# of frames	500	300	800
Frame size	576x768	240x360	240x360
A_t size	24x30	24x30	30x26
Occlusion	No	No	Yes (twice)
'adp'	o	o	x
'fa'	o	o	x
'fm'	x	x	x
'fb'	x	x	x
'adp & occ'	o	o	o

Table 9.1. Comparison of tracking results obtained by particle filters with different configurations. 'A_t size' means pixel size in the component(s) of the appearance model. 'o' means success in tracking. 'x' means failure in tracking.

sequence) or a manually specified image patch in the first frame. r_0 and J_0 are also manually set, depending on the sequence.

9.2.1 Car tracking

We first test our algorithm to track a vehicle with the F-component but without occlusion analysis. The result of tracking a fast moving car is shown in Figure 9.3 (column 1). The tracking result is shown with a bounding box. We also show the stable and wandering components separately (in a double-zoomed size) at the corner of each frame. The video is captured by a camera mounted on the car. In this footage the relative velocity of the car with respect to the camera platform is very large, and the target rapidly decreases in size. Our algorithm's adaptive particle filter successfully tracks this rapid change in scale. Figure 9.4(a) plots the scale estimate (calculated as $\sqrt{(a_1^2 + a_2^2 + a_3^2 + a_4^2)/2}$) recovered by our algorithm. It is clear that the scale follows a decreasing trend as time proceeds. The pixels located on the car in the final frame are about 12 by 15 in size, which makes the vehicle almost invisible. In this sequence we set $J_0 = 50$ and $r_0 = 0.25$. The algorithm implemented in a standard Matlab environment processes about 1.2 frames per second (with $J_0 = 50$) running on a PC with a PIII 650 CPU and 512M memory.

9.2.2 Object tracking in an aerial video

Figure 9.5 shows our results on tracking a tank in an aerial video with degraded image quality due to motion blur. Also, the movement of the tank is very jerky and arbitrary because of platform motion, as seen in Figure 9.4(b) which plots the 2-D trajectory of the centroid of the tracked tank every 10 frames,

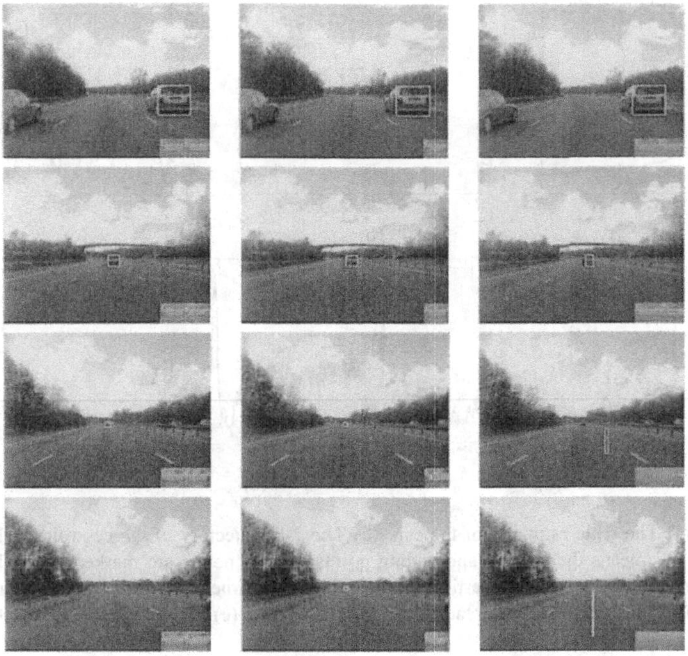

Figure 9.3. The car sequence. Notice the fast scale change present in the video. Column 1: the tracking results obtained with an adaptive motion model and an adaptive appearance model ('adp'). Column 2: the tracking results obtained with an adaptive motion model but a fixed appearance model ('fa'). In this case, the corner shows the tracked region. Column 3: the tracking results obtained with an adaptive appearance model but a fixed motion model ('fm').

covering from the left to the right in 300 frames. Although the tank moved about 100 pixels in column index in a certain period of 10 frames, the tracking is still successful.

Figure 9.4(c) displays the plot of actual number of particles J_t as a function of time t. The average number of particle is about 83, where we set J_0 to be 100, which means that in this case we actually saved about 20% in computation by using an adaptive J_t instead of a fixed number of particles.

To further illustrate the importance of the adaptive appearance model, we computed the mean square error (MSE) invoked by two particle filter algorithms, one (referred as 'adp' in Section 9.2.4) using the adaptive appearance model and the other (referred as 'fa' in Section 9.2.4) using a fixed appearance model. Computing the MSE for the 'fa' algorithm is straightforward, with T_0 denoting

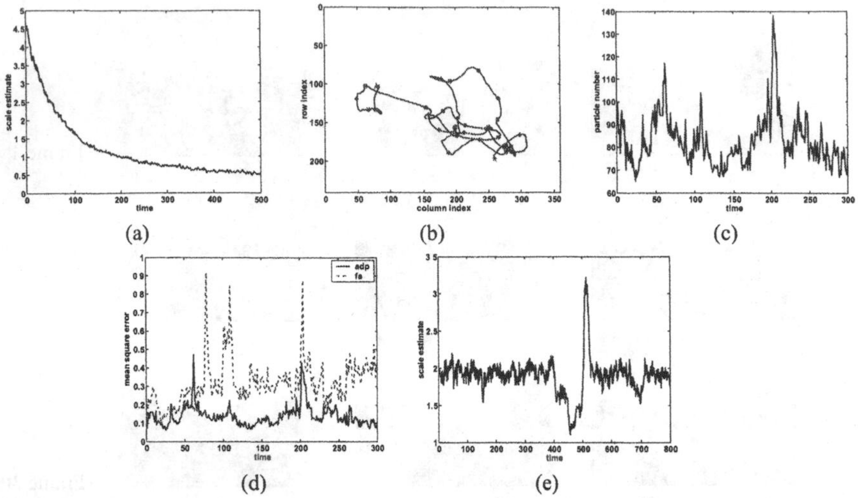

Figure 9.4. (a) The scale estimate for the car. (b) The 2-D trajectory of the centroid of the tracked tank. '*' means the starting and ending points and '.' points are marked along the trajectory every 10 frames. (c) The particle number J_t against time t obtained when tracking the tank. (d) The MSE invoked by the 'adp' and 'fa' algorithms. (e) The scale estimate for the face sequence.

Figure 9.5. Tracking a moving tank in a video acquired by an airborne camera.

the fixed template,

$$MSE_{fa}(t) = d^{-1} \sum_{j=1}^{d} (\hat{\mathbf{z}}_t(j) - \mathrm{T}_0(j))^2. \tag{9.29}$$

Computing the MSE for the 'adp' algorithm is as follows:

$$MSE_{adp}(t) = d^{-1}\sum_{j=1}^{d}\{\sum_{i=w,s,f} m_{i,t}(\hat{z}_t(j) - \mu_{i,t}(j))^2\}. \tag{9.30}$$

Figure 9.4(d) plots the functions of $MSE_{fa}(t)$ and $MSE_{adp}(t)$. Clearly, using the adaptive appearance model invokes smaller MSE for almost all 300 frames. The average MSE for the 'adp' algorithm is 0.1394while that for the 'fa' algorithm is 0.3169! Note that the range of MSE is very reasonable since we are using image patches after the zero-mean-unit-variance normalization not the raw image intensities.

9.2.3 Face tracking

We present one example of successful tracking of a human face using a hand-held video camera in an office environment, where both camera and object motion are present.

Figure 9.6 presents the tracking results on the video sequence featuring the following variations: moderate lighting variations, quick scale changes (back and forth) in the middle of the sequence, and occlusion (twice). The results are obtained by incorporating the occlusion analysis in the particle filter, but we did not use the F-component. Notice that the adaptive appearance model remains fixed during occlusion.

Figure 9.7 presents the tracking results obtained using the particle filter without occlusion analysis. We have found that the predicted velocity actually accounts for the motion of the occluding hand since the outlier pixels (mainly on the hand) dominate the image difference $(\mathcal{T}\{\mathbf{y}_t; \tilde{\theta}_t\} - \hat{\mathbf{z}}_{t-1})$. Updating the appearance model deteriorates the situation.

Figure 9.4(e) plots the scale estimate against time t. We clearly observe a rapid scale change (a sudden increase followed by a decrease within about 50 frames) in the middle of the sequence (though hard to display the recovered scale estimates are in perfect synchrony with the video data).

9.2.4 Comparison

We illustrate the effectiveness of our adaptive approach ('adp') by comparing the particle filter either with (a) an adaptive motion model but a fixed appearance model ('fa'), or with (b) a fixed motion model but an adaptive appearance model ('fm'); or with (c) a fixed motion model and a fixed appearance model ('fb'). Table 9.1 lists the tracking results obtained using particle filters under the above situations, where 'adp & occ' refers to the adaptive approach with occlusion handling. Figure 9.3 also shows the tracking results on the car sequence when the 'fa' and 'fm' options are used.

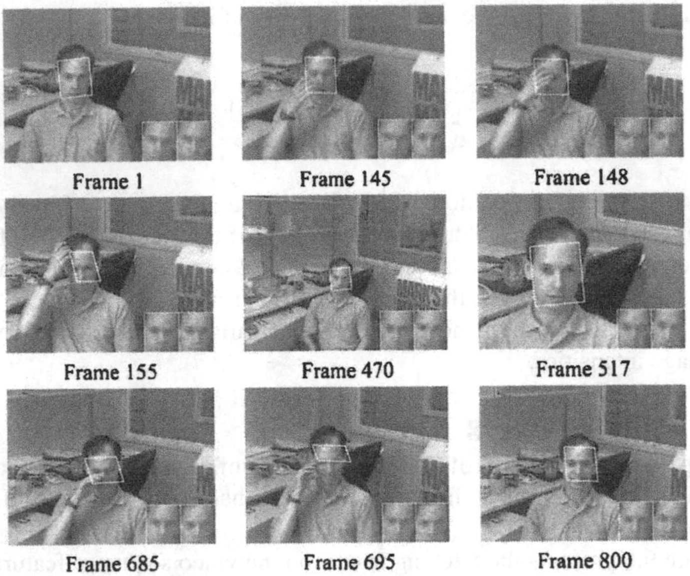

Figure 9.6. The face sequence. Frames 145, 148, and 155 show the first occlusion. Frames 470 and 517 show the smallest and largest face observed. Frames 685, 690, and 710 show the second occlusion.

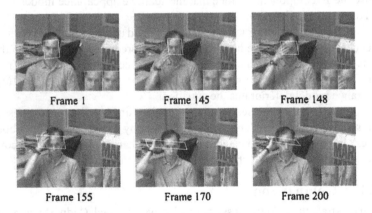

Figure 9.7. Tracking results on the face sequence using the adaptive particle filter without occlusion analysis.

Table 9.1 seems to suggest that the adaptive motion model plays a more important role than the adaptive appearance model since 'fa' always yields successful tracking while 'fm' fails, the reasons being that (i) the fixed motion model is unable to adapt to quick motion present in the video sequences, and

(ii) the appearance changes in the video sequences, though significant in some cases, are still within the range of the fixed appearance model. However, as seen in the videos, 'adp' produces much smoother tracking results than 'fa', demonstrating the power of the adaptive appearance model.

Chapter 10

SIMULTANEOUS TRACKING AND RECOGNITION

Following [60], we define a *still-to-video* scenario: the gallery consists of still facial templates and the probe set consists of video sequences containing the facial region. Denote the gallery as $\mathcal{G} = \{\mathbf{g}_1, \mathbf{g}_2, \ldots, \mathbf{g}_N\}$, indexed by the identity variable n, which lies in a finite sample space $\mathcal{N} = \{1, 2, \ldots, N\}$. Though significant research has been conducted on the still-to-still face recognition problem, research efforts on still-to-video recognition, are relatively fewer due to the following challenges [29] in typical surveillance applications: poor video quality, significant illumination and pose variations, and low image resolution. Most existing video-based recognition systems [103] attempt the following: the face is first detected and then tracked over time. Only when a frame satisfying certain criteria (size, pose) is acquired, recognition is performed using still-to-still recognition technique. For this, the face part is cropped from the frame and transformed or registered using appropriate transformations. This *tracking-then-recognition* approach attempts to resolve uncertainties in tracking and recognition *sequentially and separately*.

There are several unresolved issues in the *tracking-then-recognition* approach: criteria for selecting good frames and estimation of parameters for registration. Also, still-to-still recognition does not effectively exploit temporal information. A common strategy that selects several good frames, performs recognition on each frame and then votes on these recognition results for a final solution is rather *ad hoc*.

To overcome these difficulties, we propose a *tracking-and-recognition* approach, which attempts to resolve uncertainties in tracking and recognition *simultaneously* in a unified probabilistic framework. To fuse temporal information, the time series state space model is adopted to characterize the evolving kinematics and identity in the probe video. Three basic components of the model are:

- a *motion equation* governing the kinematic behavior of the tracking motion vector,
- an *identity equation* governing the temporal evolution of the identity variable,
- an *observation equation* establishing a link between the motion vector and the identity variable.

Using the SIS [179, 183, 237, 245, 248] technique, the joint posterior distribution of the motion vector and the identity variable, i.e., $p(n_t, \theta_t | \mathbf{y}_{0:t})$. is estimated at each time instant and then propagated to the next time instant governed by motion and identity equations. Note that here for notational convenience, e.g. in (10.5) and (10.6), we introduce in this chapter a dummy variable $\mathbf{y}_0$. The marginal distribution of the identity variable, i.e., $p(n_t | \mathbf{y}_{0:t})$, is estimated to provide a recognition result. An SIS algorithm is presented to approximate the distribution $p(n_t | \mathbf{y}_{0:t})$ in the still-to-video scenario. It achieves computational efficiency over its CONDENSATION counterpart by considering the discrete nature of the identity variable.

It is worth emphasizing that (i) our model can take advantage of any still-to-still recognition algorithm [44, 47, 51, 64] by embedding distance measures used therein in our likelihood measurement; and (ii) it allows a variety of image representations and transformations. Section 10.2.4 presents an enhancement technique by incorporating the sophisticated appearance-based models in Chapter 9. The appearance models are used for tracking (modeling inter-frame appearance changes) and recognition (modeling appearance changes between video frames and gallery images), respectively. Table 10.1 summarizes the proposed approach and others, in term of using temporal information.

Process	*Operation*	*Temporal information*
Visual tracking	Modeling the inter-frame differences	Used in tracking
Visual recognition	Modeling the difference between probe and gallery images	Not applicable
Tracking-then-recognition	Combining tracking and recognition sequentially	Used only in tracking
Tracking-and-recognition	Unifying tracking and recognition	Used in both tracking and recognition

Table 10.1. Use of temporal information in various tracking/recognition processes.

The organization of the chapter is as follows: Section 10.1 introduces the time series state space model for recognition and establishes the time-evolving behavior of $p(n_t|\mathrm{y}_{0:t})$. Section 10.1.3 briefly reviews the SIS principles from the viewpoint of a general state space model and develops a SIS algorithm to solve the still-to-video recognition problem, with special emphasis on its computational efficiency. Section 10.2 describes the experimental scenarios for still-to-video recognition and presents results using data collected at UMD, NIST/USF, and CMU (MoBo database) as part of the DARPA HumanID effort.

10.1 Stochastic Models and Algorithms for Recognition from Video

In this section, we present the details on the propagation model for recognition and discuss its impact on the posterior distribution of identity variable.

10.1.1 Time series state space model

Motion equation

In its most general form, the motion model can be written as

$$\theta_t = \mathtt{f}(\theta_{t-1}, \mathrm{u}_t); \quad t \geq 1, \tag{10.1}$$

where u_t is *noise* in the motion model, whose distribution determines the motion state transition probability $p(\theta_t|\theta_{t-1})$. The function g(.,.) characterizes the evolving motion and it could be a function learned offline or given a priori. One of the simplest choice is an additive function, i.e., $\theta_t = \theta_{t-1} + \mathrm{u}_t$, which leads to a first-order Markov chain.

Choice of θ_t is application dependent. Affine motion parameters are often used when there is no significant pose variation available in the video sequence. However, if a 3-D face model is used, then the 3-D motion parameters should be used accordingly.

Identity equation

$$n_t = n_{t-1}; \quad t \geq 1, \tag{10.2}$$

assuming that the identity does not change as time proceeds.

Observation equation

By assuming that the transformed observation is a noise-corrupted version of some still template in the gallery, the observation equation can be written as

$$\mathrm{z}_t = \mathcal{T}\{\mathrm{y}_t; \theta_t\} = \mathrm{g}_{n_t} + \mathrm{v}_t; \quad t \geq 1, \tag{10.3}$$

where v_t is *observation noise* at time t, whose distribution determines the observation likelihood $p(\mathrm{y}_t|n_t, \theta_t)$, and $\mathcal{T}\{\mathrm{y}_t; \theta_t\}$ is a transformed version of the observation y_t. This transformation could be either geometric or photometric or both. However, when confronting sophisticated scenarios, this model is far from sufficient. One should use the complicated likelihood measurement as shown in Section 10.2.2.

We assume statistical independence between all noise variables and prior knowledge on the distributions $p(\theta_0|\mathbf{y}_0)$ and $p(n_0|\mathbf{y}_0)$. Using the overall state vector $\mathbf{x}_t = (n_t, \theta_t)$, Eq. (10.1) and (10.2) can be combined into one state equation (in a normal sense) which is completely described by the overall state transition probability

$$p(\mathbf{x}_t|\mathbf{x}_{t-1}) = p(n_t|n_{t-1})p(\theta_t|\theta_{t-1}) \,. \tag{10.4}$$

Given this model, our goal is to compute the posterior probability $p(n_t|\mathbf{y}_{0:t})$. It is in fact a probability mass function (PMF) since n_t only takes values from $\mathcal{N} = \{1, 2, ..., N\}$, as well as a marginal probability of $p(n_t, \theta_t|\mathbf{y}_{0:t})$, which is a mixed-type distribution. Therefore, the problem is reduced to computing the posterior probability.

10.1.2 Posterior probability of identity variable

The evolution of the posterior probability $p(n_t|\mathbf{y}_{0:t})$ as time proceeds is very interesting to study as the identity variable does not change by assumption, i.e., $p(n_t|n_{t-1}) = \delta(n_t - n_{t-1})$, where $\delta(.)$ is a discrete impulse function at zero.

Using time recursion, Markov properties, and statistical independence embedded in the model, we can easily derive:

$$\begin{aligned} & p(n_{0:t}, \theta_{0:t}|\mathbf{y}_{0:t}) \\ = \ & p(n_{0:t-1}, \theta_{0:t-1}|\mathbf{y}_{0:t-1}) \frac{p(\mathbf{y}_t|n_t, \theta_t)p(n_t|n_{t-1})p(\theta_t|\theta_{t-1})}{p(\mathbf{y}_t|\mathbf{y}_{0:t-1})} \\ = \ & p(n_0, \theta_0|\mathbf{y}_0) \prod_{s=1}^{t} \frac{p(\mathbf{y}_s|n_s, \theta_s)p(n_s|n_{s-1})p(\theta_s|\theta_{s-1})}{p(\mathbf{y}_s|\mathbf{y}_{0:s-1})} \\ = \ & p(n_0|\mathbf{y}_0)p(\theta_0|\mathbf{y}_0) \prod_{s=1}^{t} \frac{p(\mathbf{y}_s|n_s, \theta_s)\delta(n_s - n_{s-1})p(\theta_s|\theta_{s-1})}{p(\mathbf{y}_s|\mathbf{y}_{0:s-1})} . \end{aligned} \tag{10.5}$$

Therefore, by marginalizing over $\theta_{0:t}$ and $n_{0:t-1}$, we obtain

$$p(n_t = l|\mathbf{y}_{0:t}) = p(l|\mathbf{y}_0) \int_{\theta_0} \cdots \int_{\theta_t} p(\theta_0|\mathbf{y}_0) \prod_{s=1}^{t} \frac{p(\mathbf{y}_s|l, \theta_s)p(\theta_s|\theta_{s-1})}{p(\mathbf{y}_s|\mathbf{y}_{0:s-1})} \mathrm{d}\theta_t \ldots \mathrm{d}\theta_0 . \tag{10.6}$$

Thus $p(n_t = l|\mathbf{y}_{0:t})$ is determined by the prior distribution $p(n_0 = l|\mathbf{y}_0)$ and the product of the likelihood functions, $\prod_{s=1}^{t} p(\mathbf{y}_s|l, \theta_s)$. If a uniform prior is assumed, then $\prod_{s=1}^{t} p(\mathbf{y}_s|l, \theta_s)$ is the only determining factor.

In the appendix, we show that, under some minor assumptions, the posterior probability for the correct identity l, $p(n_t = l|\mathbf{y}_{0:t})$, is lower-bounded by an increasing curve which converges to 1.

To measure the evolving uncertainty remaining in the identity variable as observations accumulate, we use the notion of entropy [4]. In the context of this problem, conditional entropy $H(n_t|\mathrm{y}_{0:t})$ is used. However, the knowledge of $p(\mathrm{y}_{0:t})$ is needed to compute $H(n_t|\mathrm{y}_{0:t})$. We assume that it degenerates to an impulse at the actual observations $\tilde{\mathrm{y}}_{0:t}$ since we observe only this particular sequence, i.e., $p(\mathrm{y}_{0:t}) = \delta(\mathrm{y}_{0:t} - \tilde{\mathrm{y}}_{0:t})$. Thus,

$$H(n_t|\mathrm{y}_{0:t}) = -\sum_{n_t=1}^{N} p(n_t|\tilde{\mathrm{y}}_{0:t}) \log_2 p(n_t|\tilde{\mathrm{y}}_{0:t}). \tag{10.7}$$

Under the assumptions listed in the appendix, we expect that $H(n_t|\mathrm{y}_{0:t})$ decreases as time proceeds since we start from an equi-probable distribution to a degenerate one.

10.1.3 SIS algorithms and computational efficiency

Consider a general time series state space model fully determined by (i) the overall state transition probability $p(\mathrm{x}_t|\mathrm{x}_{t-1})$, (ii) the observation likelihood $p(\mathrm{y}_t|\mathrm{x}_t)$, and (iii) prior probability $p(\mathrm{x}_0)$ and statistical independence among all the noise variables. We wish to compute the posterior probability $p(\mathrm{x}_t|\mathrm{y}_{0:t})$.

If the model is linear with Gaussian noise, it is analytically solvable by a Kalman filter which essentially propagates the mean and variance of a Gaussian distribution over time. For nonlinear and non-Gaussian cases, an extended Kalman filter (EKF) and its variants have been used to arrive at an approximate analytic solution [1]. Recently, the SIS technique or particle filter algorithm, a special case of Monte Carlo method, [183, 237, 245, 248] has been used to provide a numerical solution and propagate an arbitrary distribution over time. However, since we are dealing with a mixed-type distribution, additional properties are available to be exploited when developing the SIS algorithms.

First, two following two lemmas are useful.

LEMMA 10.1 *When $\pi(x)$ is a PMF defined on a finite sample space, the proper sample set should exactly include all samples in the sample space.*

LEMMA 10.2 *If a set of weighted random samples $\{(x^{(m)}, y^{(m)}, w^{(m)})\}_{m=1}^{M}$ is proper with respect to $\pi(x, y)$, then a new set of weighted random samples $\{(y'^{(k)}, w'^{(k)})\}_{k=1}^{K}$, which is proper with respect to $\pi(y)$, the marginal of $\pi(x, y)$, can be constructed as follows:*
1) Remove the repetitive samples from $\{y^{(m)}\}_{m=1}^{M}$ to obtain $\{y'^{(k)}\}_{k=1}^{K}$, where all $y'^{(k)}$'s are distinct;
2) Sum the weight $w^{(m)}$ belonging to the same sample $y'^{(k)}$ to obtain the weight $w'^{(k)}$, i.e.,

$$w'^{(k)} = \sum_{m=1}^{M} w^{(m)} \delta(y^{(m)} - y'^{(k)}) \tag{10.8}$$

In the context of this framework, the posterior probability $p(n_t, \theta_t | \mathrm{y}_{0:t})$ is represented by a set of *indexed and weighted* samples

$$S_t = \{(n_t^{(m)}, \theta_t^{(m)}, w_t^{(m)})\}_{m=1}^{M} \tag{10.9}$$

with n_t as the above index. By Lemma 10.2, we can sum the weights of the samples belonging to the same index n_t to obtain a proper sample set $\{n_t, \beta_{n_t}\}_{n_t=1}^{N}$ with respect to the posterior PMF $p(n_t | \mathrm{y}_{0:t})$.

A straightforward implementation of the particle filter algorithm (Figure 10.1) for simultaneous tracking and recognition is not efficient in terms of its computational load. Since $\mathcal{N} = \{1, 2, \ldots, N\}$ is a countable sample space, we need N samples for the identity variable n_t according to Lemma 10.1. Assume that, for each identity variable n_t, J samples are needed to represent θ_t. Hence, we need $M = J * N$ samples in total. Further assume that one resampling step takes T_r seconds (s), one predicting step T_p s, computing one transformed image T_t s, evaluating likelihood once T_l s, one updating step T_u s. Obviously, the bulk of computation is $J * N * (T_r + T_p + T_t + T_l)$ s to deal with one video frame as the computational time for the normalizing step and the marginalizing step is negligible. It is well known that computing the transformed image is much more expensive than other operations, i.e., $T_t >> \max(T_r, T_p, T_l)$. Therefore, as the number of templates N grows, the computational load increases dramatically.

Initialize *a sample set* $\mathcal{S}_0 = \{(n_0^{(m)}, \theta_0^{(m)}, 1)\}_{m=1}^{M}$ *according to prior distributions* $p(n_0 | \mathrm{y}_0)$ *and* $p(\theta_0 | \mathrm{y}_0)$.
For $t = 1, 2, \ldots$
  For $m = 1, 2, \ldots, M$
    Resample $\mathcal{S}_{t-1} = \{(n_{t-1}^{(m)}, \theta_{t-1}^{(m)}, w_{t-1}^{(m)})\}_{m=1}^{M}$ *to obtain a new sample* $(n_{t-1}^{'(m)}, \theta_{t-1}^{'(m)}, 1)$.
    Predict *a sample by drawing* $(n_t^{(m)}, \theta_t^{(m)})$ *from* $p(n_t | n_{t-1}^{'(m)})$ *and* $p(\theta_t | \theta_{t-1}^{'(m)})$.
    Compute *the transformed image* $z_t^{(m)} = \mathcal{T}\{y_t; \theta_t^{(m)}\}$.
    Update *the weight using* $\alpha_t^{(m)} = p(y_t | n_t^{(m)}, \theta_t^{(m)})$.
  End
  Normalize *each weight using* $w_t^{(m)} = \alpha_t^{(m)} / \sum_{m=1}^{M} \alpha_t^{(m)}$.
  Marginalize *over* θ_t *to obtain the weight* β_{n_t} *for* n_t.
End

Figure 10.1. The conventional particle filter algorithm for simultaneous tracking and recognition.

There are various approaches in the literature to reduce the computational cost of the conventional particle filter algorithm. In [193], random particles are guided by deterministic search. Assumed density filtering approach [231], different from particle filter, is even more efficient. Those approaches are general and do not explicitly exploit the special structure of the distribution in this setting: a mixed distribution of continuous and discrete variables. To this end, we propose the following algorithm.

As the sample space $\mathcal{N}$ is countably finite, an exhaustive search of sample space $\mathcal{N}$ is possible. Mathematically, we release the random sampling in the identity variable n_t by constructing samples as follows: for each $\theta_t^{(j)}$,

$$(1, \theta_t^{(j)}, w_{t,1}^{(j)}), (2, \theta_t^{(j)}, w_{t,2}^{(j)}), \ldots, (N, \theta_t^{(j)}, w_{t,N}^{(j)}).$$

We in fact use the following notation for the sample set,

$$\mathcal{S}_t = \{(\theta_t^{(j)}, w_t^{(j)}, w_{t,1}^{(j)}, w_{t,2}^{(j)}, \ldots, w_{t,N}^{(j)})\}_{j=1}^J, \tag{10.10}$$

with $w_t^{(j)} = \sum_{n=1}^N w_{t,n}^{(j)}$. The proposed algorithm is summarized in Figure 10.2.

Initialize *a sample set* $S_0 = \{(\theta_0^{(j)}, N, 1, ..., 1)\}_{j=1}^J$ *according to prior distribution* $p(\theta_0|z_0)$.
For $t = 1, 2, \ldots$
  For $j = 1, 2, \ldots, J$
  Resample $\mathcal{S}_{t-1} = \{(\theta_{t-1}^{(j)}, w_{t-1}^{(j)})\}_{j=1}^J$ *to obtain a new sample* $(\theta_{t-1}^{'(j)}, 1, w_{t-1,1}^{'(j)}, \ldots, w_{t-1,N}^{'(j)})$, *where* $w_{t-1,n}^{'(j)} = w_{t-1,n}^{(j)}/w_{t-1}^{(j)}$ *for* $n = 1, 2, \ldots, N$.
    Predict *a sample by drawing* $(\theta_t^{(j)})$ *from* $p(\theta_t|\theta_{t-1}^{'(j)})$.
    Compute *the transformed image* $z_t^{(m)} = \mathcal{T}\{y_t; \theta_t^{(m)}\}$.
    For $n = 1, \ldots, N$
      Update *the weight using* $\alpha_{t,n}^{(j)} = w_{t-1,n}^{'(j)} * p(y_t|n, \theta_t^{(j)})$.
    End
  End
  Normalize *each weight using* $w_{t,n}^{(j)} = \alpha_{t,n}^{(j)} / \sum_{n=1}^N \sum_{j=1}^J \alpha_{t,n}^{(j)}$ *and* $w_t^{(j)} = \sum_{n=1}^N w_{t,n}^{(j)}$.
  Marginalize *over* θ_t *to obtain the weight* β_{n_t} *for* n_t.
End

Figure 10.2. The computationally efficient particle filter algorithm for simultaneous tracking and recognition.

The crux of this algorithm lies in the fact that, instead of propagating random samples on both motion vector and identity variable, we can keep the samples on the identity variable fixed and let those on the motion vector be random. Although we propagate only the marginal distribution for motion tracking, we still propagate the joint distribution for recognition purposes.

The bulk of computation of the proposed algorithm is $J * (T_r + T_p + T_t) + J * N * T_l$ s, a tremendous improvement over the conventional particle filter when dealing with a large database since the majority computational time $J * T_t$ does not depend on N.

10.2 Still-to-Video Face Recognition Experiments

In this section we describe the still-to-video scenarios used in our experiments and their practical model choices, followed by a discussion of experiments. Three databases are used in the still-to-video experiments.

Database-0 was collected outside a building. Subjects walked straight towards a video camera in order to simulate typical scenarios in visual surveillance. Database-0 includes one face gallery, and one probe set. The images in the gallery are listed in Figure 10.3. The probe contains 12 videos, one for each individual. Figure 10.3 gives some frames in a probe video.

In Database-1, we have video sequences with subjects walking in a slant path towards the camera. There are 30 subjects, each having one face template. There are one face gallery and one probe set. The face gallery is shown in Figure 10.4. The probe contains 30 video sequences, one for each subject. Figure 10.4 gives some example frames extracted from one probe video. As far as imaging conditions are concerned, the gallery is very different from the probe, especially in lighting. This is similar to the 'FC' test protocol of the FERET test [60]. These images/videos were collected, as part of the HumanID project, by National Institute of Standards and Technology and University of South Florida researchers.

Database-2, Motion of Body (MoBo) database, was collected at the Carnegie Mellon University [105] under the HumanID project. There are 25 different individuals in total. The video sequences show the individuals walking on a tread-mill so that they move their heads naturally. Different walking styles have been simulated to assure a variety of conditions that are likely to appear in real life: *walking slowly*, *walking fast*, *inclining* and *carrying an object*. Therefore, four videos per person and 99 videos in total (with one *carrying* video missing) are available. However, the probe set we use in this section includes only 25 *slowWalk* videos. Some example images of the videos (*slowWalk*) are shown in Figure 10.5. Figure 10.5 also shows the face gallery in Database-2 with face images in almost frontal view cropped from probe videos and then normalized using their eye positions.

Table 10.2 summaries the features of the three databases.

10.2.1 Results for Database-0

We consider an affine transformation. Specifically, the motion is characterized by $\theta = (a_1, a_2, a_3, a_4, t_x, t_y)$ where $\{a_1, a_2, a_3, a_4\}$ are deformation parameters and $\{t_x, t_y\}$ are 2-D translation parameters. It is a reasonable approximation since there is no significant out-of-plane motion as the subjects walk towards the camera. Regarding the photometric transformation, only zero-mean-unit-variance operator is performed to partially compensate for contrast variations. The complete transformation $\mathcal{T}\{\mathrm{y}; \theta\}$ is processed as follows:

Database	*Database*-0	*Database*-1	*Database*-2
No. of subjects	12	30	25
Gallery	Frontal face	Frontal face	Frontal face
Motion in probe	Walking straight towards the camera	Walking in an angle towards the camera	Walking on tread-mill
Illumination variation	No	Large	No
Pose variation	No	Slight	Large

Table 10.2. Summary of three databases experimented.

Figure 10.3. Database-0. The 1st row: the face gallery with image size being 30×26. The 2nd and 3rd rows: 4 example frames in one probe video with image size being 320×240 while the actual face size ranges approximately from 30×30 in the first frame to 50×50 in the last frame. Notice that the sequence is taken under a well-controlled condition so that there are no illumination or pose variations between the gallery and the probe.

affine transform y using $\{a_1, a_2, a_3, a_4\}$, crop out the interested region at posi-

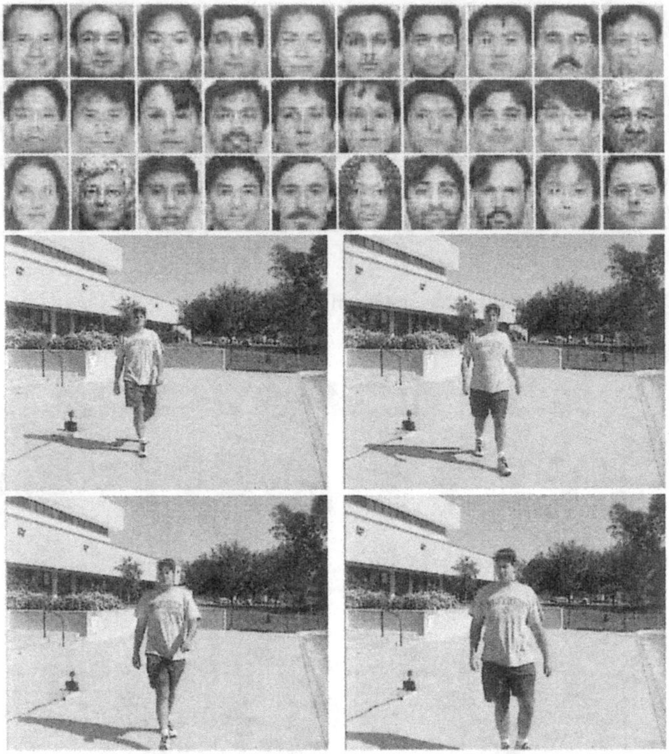

Figure 10.4. Database-1. The 1st row: the face gallery with image size being 30×26. The 2nd and 3rd rows: 4 example frames in one probe video with image size being 720×480 while the actual face size ranges approximately from 20×20 in the first frame to 60×60 in the last frame. Notice the significant illumination variations between the probe and the gallery.

tion $\{t_x, t_y\}$ with the same size as the still template in the gallery, and perform zero-mean-unit-variance operation.

Prior distribution $p(\theta_0|\mathbf{y}_0)$ is assumed to be Gaussian, whose mean comes from the initial detector and whose covariance matrix is manually specified.

A time-invariant first-order Markov Gaussian model with constant velocity is used for modeling motion transition. Given the scenario that the subject is walking towards the camera, the scale increases with time. However, under perspective projection, this increase is no longer linear, causing the constant-velocity model to be not optimal. However, experimental results show that as long as the samples of θ can cover the motion, this model is sufficient.

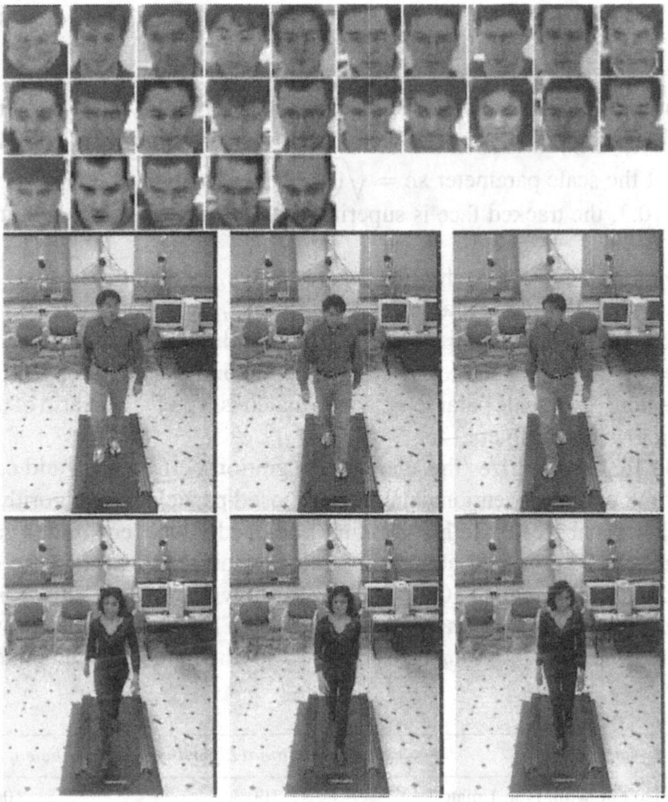

Figure 10.5. Database-2. The 1st row: the face gallery with image size being 30 × 26. The 2nd and 3rd rows: some example frames in one probe video (*slowWalk*). Each video consists of 300 frames (480 × 640 pixels per frame) captured at 30 Hz. The inner face regions in these videos contain between 30 × 30 and 40 × 40 pixels. Notice the significant pose variation available in the video.

The likelihood measurement is simply set as a 'truncated' Laplacian:

$$p_1(\mathrm{y}_t|n_t, \theta_t) = Lap(\|\mathcal{T}\{\mathrm{y}_t; \theta_t\} - \mathrm{g}_{n_t}\|_1; \sigma_1, \tau_1) \tag{10.11}$$

where, $\|.\|_1$ is sum of absolute distance, σ_1 and λ_1 are manually specified, and

$$Lap(x; \sigma, \tau) = \begin{cases} \sigma^{-1}\exp(-x/\sigma) & \text{if } x \leq \tau\sigma \\ \sigma^{-1}\exp(-\tau) & \text{otherwise} \end{cases} \tag{10.12}$$

Gaussian distribution is widely used as a noise model, accounting for sensor noise, digitization noise, etc. However, given the observation equation: $\mathrm{v}_t = \mathcal{T}\{\mathrm{y}_t; \theta_t\} - \mathrm{g}_{n_t}$, the dominant part of v_t becomes the high-frequency residual if θ_t is not proper, and it is well known that the high-frequency residual of natural images is more Laplacian-like. The 'truncated' Laplacian is used to give a 'surviving' chance for samples to accommodate abrupt motion changes.

Figure 10.6 presents the plot of the posterior probability $p(n_t|\mathbf{y}_{0:t})$, the conditional entropy $H(n_t|\mathbf{y}_{0:t})$ and the minimum mean square error (MMSE) estimate of the scale parameter $sc = \sqrt{(a_1^2 + a_2^2 + a_3^2 + a_4^2)/2}$, all against t. In Figure 10.3, the tracked face is superimposed on the image using a bounding box.

Suppose the correct identity for Figure 10.3 is l. From Figure 10.6, we can easily observe that the posterior probability $p(n_t = l|\mathbf{y}_{0:t})$ increases as time proceeds and eventually approaches 1, and all others $p(n_t = j|\mathbf{y}_{0:t})$ for $j \neq l$ go to 0. Figure 10.6 also plots the decrease in conditional entropy $H(n_t|\mathbf{y}_{0:t})$ and the increase in scale parameter, which matches with the scenario of a subject walking towards a camera.

Table 10.3 summarizes the average recognition performance and computational time of the conventional and the proposed particle filter algorithm when applied to Database-0. Both algorithms achieved 100% recognition rate with top match. The proposed algorithm is much more efficient than the conventional one. It is more than 10 times faster as shown in Table I. This experiment was implemented in C++ on a PC with P-III 1G CPU and 512M RAM with the number of motion samples J chosen to be 200, the number of templates in the gallery N to be 12.

Algorithm	*Conventional algorithm*	*Efficient algorithm*
Recognition rate within top 1 match	100%	100%
Time per frame	7s	0.5s

Table 10.3. Recognition performance of algorithms when applied to Database-0.

10.2.2 Results for Database-1

Case 1: Tracking and Recognition using Laplacian Density

We first investigate the performance using the same setting as described in Section 10.2.1. In other words, we still use the affine transformation, first-order Markov Gaussian state transition model, 'truncated' Laplacian observation likelihood, etc.

Table 10.4 shows that the recognition rate is very poor, only 13% are correctly identified using top match. The main reason is that the 'truncated' Laplacian density is far from sufficient to capture the appearance difference between the probe and the gallery, thereby indicating a need for a different appearance mod-

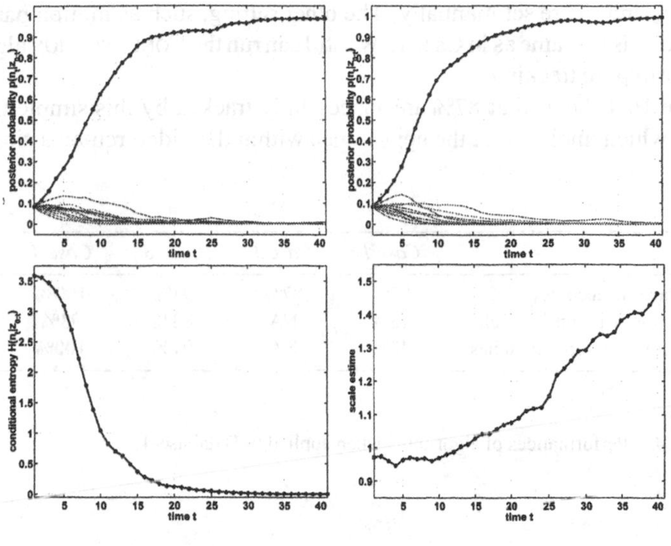

Figure 10.6. Posterior probability $p(n_t|\mathbf{y}_{0:t})$ against time t, obtained by the CONDENSATION algorithm (top left) and the proposed algorithm (top right). Conditional entropy $H(n_t|\mathbf{y}_{0:t})$ (bottom left) and MMSE estimate of scale parameter sc (bottom right) against time t. The conditional entropy and the MMSE estimate are obtained using the proposed algorithm.

eling. Nevertheless, the tracking accuracy is reasonable with 83% successfully tracked because we are using multiple face templates in the gallery to track the specific face in the probe video. After all, faces in both the gallery and the probe belong to the same class of human face and it seems that the appearance change is within the class range. To count the tracking accuracy, we manually inspect the tracking results by imposing the MMSE motion estimate on the final frame as shown in Figs. 10.3 and 10.4 and determine if tracking is successful or not for this sequence. This is done for all sequences and tracking accuracy is defined as the ratio of the number of sequences successfully tracked to the total number of all sequences.

Case 2: Pure Tracking using Laplacian Density

In Case 2, we measure the appearance change within the probe video as well as the noise in the background. To this end, we introduce a dummy template T_0, a cut version in the first frame of the video. Define the observation likelihood for tracking as

$$p_2(\mathbf{y}_t|\theta_t) = Lap(\|\mathcal{T}\{\mathbf{y}_t;\theta_t\} - \mathrm{T}_0\|;\sigma_2,\tau_2), \qquad (10.13)$$

where σ_2 and τ_2 are set manually. The other setting, such as motion parameter and model, is the same as in Case 1. We still can run the CONDENSATION algorithm to perform pure tracking.

Table 10.4 shows that 87% are successfully tracked by this simple tracking model, which implies that the appearance within the video remains similar.

	Case 1	*Case 2*	*Case 3*	*Case 4*	*Case 5*
Tracking accuracy	83%	87%	93%	100%	NA
Recognition w/in top 1 match	13%	NA	83%	93%	57%
Recognition w/in top 3 matches	43%	NA	97%	100%	83%

Table 10.4. Performances of algorithms when applied to Database-1.

Case 3: Tracking and Recognition using Probabilistic Subspace Density
As mentioned in Case 1, we need a new appearance model to improve the recognition accuracy. As reviewed in Chapter 2, there are various approaches in the literature. We decided to use the approach suggested by Moghaddam et al. [57] due to its computational efficiency and high recognition accuracy. However, in our implementation, we model only intra-personal variations instead of both intra/extra-personal variations for simplicity.

We need at least two facial images for one identity to construct the intra-personal space (IPS). Apart from the available gallery, we crop out the second image from the video ensuring no overlap with the frames actually used in probe videos. Figure 10.7 (top row) shows a list of such images. Compare with Figure 10.4 to see how the illumination varies between the gallery and the probe.

We then fit a probabilistic subspace density [58] on top of the IPS. It proceeds as follows: a regular PCA is performed for the IPS. Suppose the eigensystem for the IPS is $\{(\lambda_i, \mathbf{e}_i)\}_{i=1}^{d}$, where d is the number of pixels and $\lambda_1 \geq ... \geq \lambda_d$. Only top s principal components corresponding to top s eigenvalues are then kept while the residual components are considered as isotropic. We refer the reader to the original paper [58] for the full details. Figure 10.7 (middle row) shows the eigenvectors for the IPS. The density is written as follows:

$$Q_{IPS}(\mathbf{x}) = \{\frac{exp(-\frac{1}{2}\sum_{i=1}^{s}\frac{\alpha_i^2}{\lambda_i})}{(2\pi)^{s/2}\prod_{i=1}^{s}\lambda_i^{1/2}}\}\{\frac{exp(-\frac{\epsilon^2}{2\rho})}{(2\pi\rho)^{(d-s)/2}}\}, \quad (10.14)$$

where α_i (the ith principal component of x), ϵ^2 (the reconstruction error), and the coefficient ρ are defined as follows:

$$\alpha_i = \mathbf{e}_i^T \mathbf{x};\ \ \epsilon^2 = \|\mathbf{x}\|^2 - \sum_{i=1}^{s} \alpha_i^2;\ \ \rho = \frac{1}{d-q}(\sum_{i=s+1}^{d} \lambda_i).$$

It is easy to write the likelihood as follows:

$$p_3(\mathbf{y}_t|n_t, \theta_t) = Q_{IPS}(\mathcal{T}\{\mathbf{y}_t; \theta_t\} - \mathbf{g}_{n_t}). \tag{10.15}$$

Table 10.4 lists the performance by using this new likelihood measurement. It turns out that the performance is significantly better that in Case 1, with 93% tracked successfully and 83% recognized within top 1 match. If we consider the top 3 matches, 97% are correctly identified.

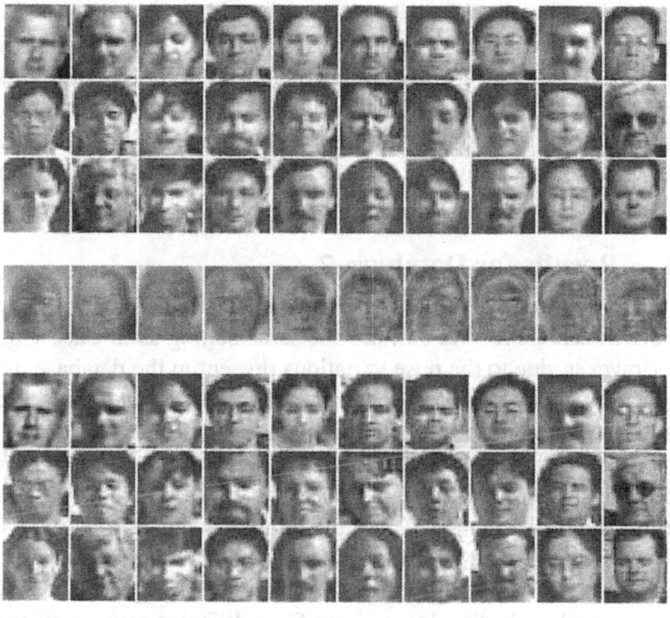

Figure 10.7. Database-1. Top row: the second facial images for estimating probabilistic density. Middle row: top 10 eigenvectors for the IPS. Bottom row: the facial images cropped out from the largest frontal view.

Case 4: Tracking and Recognition using Combined Density

In Case 2, we have studied appearance changes within a video sequence. In Case 3, we have studied the appearance change between the gallery and the probe. In Case 4, we attempt to take advantage of both cases by introducing a combined likelihood defined as follows:

$$p_4(\mathbf{y}_t|n_t, \theta_t) = p_3(\mathbf{y}_t|n_t, \theta_t)p_2(\mathbf{y}_t|\theta_t) \tag{10.16}$$

Again, all other setting is the same as in Case 1. We now obtain the best performance so far: no tracking error, 93% are correctly recognized as the first match, and no error in recognition when top 3 matches are considered.

Case 5: Still-to-still Face Recognition

To make a comparison, we also performed an experiment on still-to-still face recognition. We selected the probe video frames with the best frontal face view (i.e. biggest frontal view) and cropped out the facial region by normalizing with respect to the eye coordinates manually specified. This collection of images is shown in Figure 10.7 (bottom row) and it is fed as probes into a still-to-still face recognition system with the learned probabilistic subspace as in Case 3. It turns out that the recognition result is 57% correct for the top one match, and 83% for the top 3 matches. The cumulative match curves for Case 1 and Cases 3-5 are presented in Figure 10.8. Clearly, Case 4 is the best among all. We also implemented the original algorithm by Moghaddam et al. [58], i.e., both intra/extra-personal variations are considered, the recognition rate is similar to that obtained in Case 5.

10.2.3 Results for Database-2

The recognition result for Database-2 is presented in Figure 10.8, using the cumulative match curve. We still use the same setting as in Case 1 of section 10.2.2. However, due to the pose variations present in the database, using one frontal view is not sufficient to represent all the appearances under different poses and the recognition rate is hence not so high, 56% when only the top match is considered and 88% when top 3 matches are considered. We do not use probabilistic subspace modeling for this database because such modeling requires manually cropping out multiple templates for each individual. Also, pre-selecting video frames from the same probe video and ensuring that they do not overlap with the probe frames is time-consuming. What is desirable is to automatically select such templates from different sources other than the probe video. Since we have multiple videos available for one individual in Database-2, this motivates us to obtain more representative views for one face class, leading to the discussions in [124].

10.2.4 Enhanced results

Visual tracking models the inter-frame appearance differences and visual recognition models the appearance differences between video frames and gallery

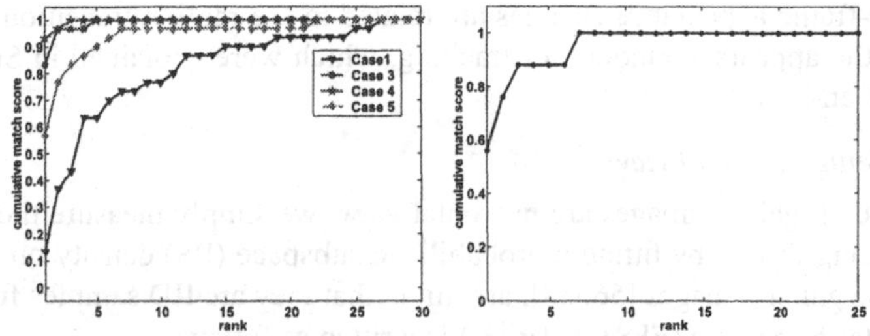

Figure 10.8. Cumulative match curves for Database-1 (left) and Database-2 (right).

images. Simultaneous tracking and recognition provides a mechanism of jointly modeling inter-frame appearance differences and the appearance differences between video frames and gallery images. As in Section 10.2.2, this joint modeling of appearance differences in both tracking and recognition in one framework actually improves both tracking and recognition accuracies over approaches that separate tracking and recognition as two tasks. The more effective the model choices are, improved performance in tracking and recognition is expected. We explore this avenue by incorporating the models used in Chapter 9.

We use the same adaptive-velocity motion model (9.22) and the same identity equation (10.2). The observation likelihood is modified to combine contributions (or scores) from both tracking and recognition in the likelihood yields the best performance in both tracking and recognition.

To compute the tracking score $p_a(\mathbf{y}_t|\theta_t)$ which measures the inter-frame appearance changes, we use the appearance model introduced in Section 9.1.1 and the quantity defined in (9.3) as $p_a(\mathbf{y}_t|\theta_t)$.

To compute the recognition score which measures the appearance changes between probe videos and gallery images, we assume the same model as in (10.3), i.e., the transformed observation is a noise-corrupted version of some still template in the gallery, and the noise distribution determines the recognition score $p_n(\mathbf{y}_t|n_t, \theta_t)$. We will physically define this quantity below.

To fully exploit the fact that all gallery images are in frontal view, we also compute below how likely the patch $\mathbf{z}_t$ is in frontal view and denote this score by $p_f(\mathbf{y}_t|\theta_t)$. If the patch is in frontal view, we accept a recognition score; otherwise, we simply set the recognition score as equiprobable among all identities, i.e., $1/N$. The complete likelihood $p(\mathbf{y}_t|n_t, \theta_t)$ is now defined as

$$p(\mathbf{y}_t|n_t, \theta_t) \propto p_a \left\{ p_f \, p_n + (1 - p_f) \, N^{-1} \right\}. \tag{10.17}$$

Model components in detail

- *A. Modeling inter-frame appearance changes*

Inter-frame appearance changes are related to the motion transition model and the appearance model for tracking, which were explained in Sections 9.1.1 and 9.1.2.

- *B. Being in frontal view*

  Since all gallery images are in frontal view, we simply measure the extent of being frontal by fitting a probabilistic subspace (PS) density on the top of the gallery images [56, 58], assuming that they are IID samples from the frontal face space (FFS). $p_f(\mathbf{y}_t|\theta_t)$ is written as follows:

$$p_f(\mathbf{y}_t|\theta_t) = Q_{FFS}(\mathbf{z}_t), \qquad (10.18)$$

  where the density $q(.)$ is defined same as that in (10.14) and $\mathbf{z}_t = \mathcal{T}\{\mathbf{y}_t; \theta_t\}$.

- *C. Modeling appearance changes between probe video frames and gallery images*

  We adopt the MAP rule developed in [58] for computing the recognition score $p_n(\mathbf{y}_t|n_t, \theta_t)$. Two subspaces are constructed to model appearance variations. The IPS is meant to cover all the variations in appearances belonging to the same person while the EPS is used to cover all the variations in appearances belonging to different people. More than one facial image per person is needed to construct the IPS. Apart from the available gallery, we crop out four images from the video ensuring no overlap with frames used in probe videos. The above PS density estimation method is applied separately to the IPS and the EPS, yielding two different eigensystems. The recognition score $p_n(\mathbf{y}_t|n_t, \theta_t)$ is finally computed as, assuming equal priors on the IPS and the EPS,

$$p_n(\mathbf{y}_t|n_t, \theta_t) = \frac{Q_{IPS}(\mathbf{z}_t - \mathbf{g}_{n_t})}{Q_{IPS}(\mathbf{z}_t - \mathbf{g}_{n_t}) + Q_{EPS}(\mathbf{z}_t - \mathbf{g}_{n_t})}. \qquad (10.19)$$

D. Proposed algorithm

We adjust the particle number J_t based on the following considerations. (i) The first issue is same as (9.24) based on the prediction error. (ii) As shown above, the uncertainty in the identity variable n_t is characterized by an entropy measure H_t for $p(n_t|\mathbf{y}_{1:t})$ and H_t is a non-increasing function (under one weak assumption). Accordingly, we increase the number of particles by a fixed amount J_{fix} if H_t increases; otherwise we deduct J_{fix} from J_t. Combining these two, we have

$$J_t = J_0 \frac{r_t}{r_0} + J_{fix} * (-1)^{i[H_{t-1} < H_{t-2}]}\}, \qquad (10.20)$$

where $i[.]$ is an indication function.

Initialize *a sample set* $\mathcal{S}_0 = \{\theta_0^{(j)}, w_0^{(j)} = 1/J_0)\}_{j=1}^{J_0}$ *according to prior distribution* $p(\theta_0)$.
Set $\beta_{0,l} = 1/N$. *Initialize the appearance mode* A_1.
For $t = 1, 2, \ldots$
 Calculate *the MAP estimate* $\hat{\theta}_{t-1}$, *the adaptive motion shift* ν_t *by Eq. (9.14), the noise variance* r_t *by Eq. (9.23), and particle number* J_t *by Eq. (10.20).*
 For $j = 1, 2, \ldots, J_t$
  Draw *the sample* $\mathrm{u}_t^{(j)}$ *for* u_t *with variance* R_t.
  Construct *the sample* $\theta_t^{(j)}$ *by Eq. (9.22).*
  Compute *the transformed image* $\mathrm{z}_t^{(j)}$.
  For $l = 1, 2, ..., N$
   Update *the weight using* $\alpha_{t,l}^{(j)} = \beta_{t-1,l}p(\mathrm{y}_t|l, \theta_t^{(j)}) = \beta_{t-1,l}p(\mathrm{z}_t^{(j)}|l, \theta_t^{(j)})$ *by Eq. (10.17).*
  End
 End
 Normalize *the weight using* $w_{t,l}^{(j)} = \alpha_{t,l}^{(j)} / \sum_{j,l} \alpha_{t,l}^{(j)}$ *and compute* $w_t^{(j)} = \sum_j w_{t,l}^{(j)}$ *and* $\beta_{t,l} = \sum_j w_{t,l}^{(j)}$.
 Update *the appearance model* A_{t+1} *using* $\hat{\mathrm{z}}_t$.
End

Figure 10.9. The visual tracking and recognition algorithm.

The proposed particle filtering algorithm for simultaneous tracking and recognition is summarized in Figure 10.9, where $w_{t,l}^{(j)}$ is the weight of the particle $(n_t = l, \theta_t = \theta_t^{(j)})$ for the posterior density $p(n_t, \theta_t|\mathrm{y}_{1:t})$; $w_t^{(j)}$ is the weight of the particle $\theta_t = \theta_t^{(j)}$ for the posterior density $p(\theta_t|\mathrm{y}_{1:t})$; and $\beta_{t,l}$ is the weight of the particle $n_t = l$ for the posterior density $p(n_t|\mathrm{y}_{1:t})$. Occlusion analysis can also be included in Figure 10.9.

Figure 10.10. Row 1-3: the gallery set with 29 subjects in frontal view. Rows 4, 5, and 6: the top 10 eigenvectors for FFS, IPS, and EPS, respectively.

Experimental results on visual tracking and recognition

We have applied our algorithm for tracking and recognition of human faces captured by a hand-held video camera in office environments. There are 29 subjects in the database. Figure 10.10 lists all the images in the galley set and the top 10 eigenvectors for FFS, IPS, and EPS, respectively. Figure 10.11 presents some frames (with tracking results) in the video sequence for 'Subject-2' featuring quite large pose variations, moderate illumination variations, and quick scale changes (back and forth toward the end of the sequence).

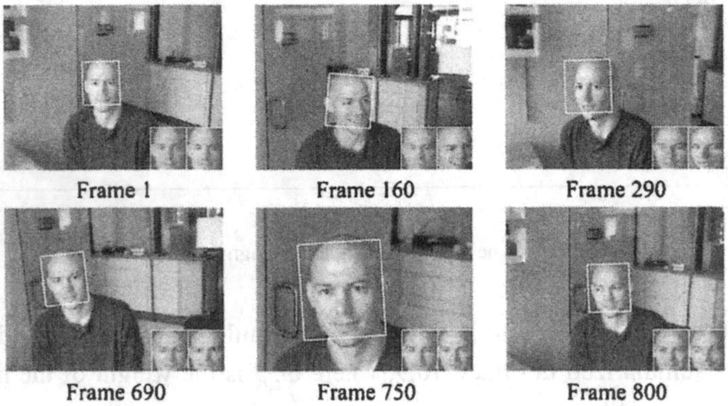

Figure 10.11. Example images in 'Subject-2' probe video sequence and the tracking results.

Tracking is successful for all video sequences and 100% recognition rate is achieved, while early approaches fail to track in several video sequences due to its inability to handle significant appearance changes caused by pose and illumination variations. The posterior probabilities $p(n_t|\mathbf{y}_{1:t})$ with $n_t = 1, 2, ...N$ obtained for the 'Subject-2' sequence are plotted in Figure 10.12(a). We start from a uniform prior for the identity variable, i.e., $p(n_0) = N^{-1}$ for $n_0 = 1, 2, ...N$. It is very fast, taking about less than 10 frames, to reach above 0.9 level for the posterior probability corresponding to 'Subject-2', while all other posterior probabilities corresponding to other identities approach zero. This is mainly attributed to the discriminative power of the MAP recognition score induced by IPS and EPS modeling. The previous approach [129] usually takes about 30 frames to reach 0.9 level since only intra-personal modeling is adopted. Figure 10.12(b) captures the scale change in the 'Subject-2' sequence.

10.3 Appendix

Derivation of the lower bound for the posterior probability of identity

Suppose that the following two assumptions hold:

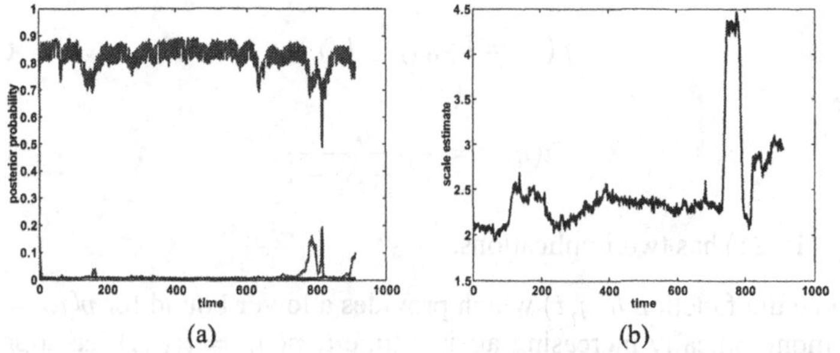

Figure 10.12. Results on the 'Subject-2' sequence. (a) Posterior probabilities against time t for all identities $p(n_t|\mathbf{y}_{1:t})$, $n_t = 1, 2, ..., N$. The line close to 1 is for the true identity. (b) Scale estimate against time t.

- (A) The prior probability for each identity is same,

$$p(n_0 = j|\mathbf{y}_0) = 1/N; \quad j \in \mathcal{N}, \tag{10.21}$$

- (B) for the correct identity $l \in \mathcal{N}$, there exists a constant $\eta > 1$ such that,

$$p(\mathbf{y}_t|n_t = l, \theta_t) \geq \eta p(\mathbf{y}_t|n_t = j, \theta_t); \quad t \geq 1, j \in \mathcal{N}, j \neq l. \tag{10.22}$$

Substitution of Eq. (10.21) and (10.22) into Eq. (10.6) gives rise to

$$\begin{aligned}
& p(n_t = l|\mathbf{y}_{0:t}) \\
= \; & \frac{1}{N}\int_{\theta_0}\cdots\int_{\theta_t} p(\theta_0|\mathbf{y}_0)\prod_{s=1}^{t}\frac{p(\mathbf{y}_s|n_s = l, \theta_s)p(\theta_s|\theta_{s-1})}{p(\mathbf{y}_s|\mathbf{y}_{0:s-1})}\mathrm{d}\theta_t\ldots\mathrm{d}\theta_0 \\
\geq \; & \frac{1}{N}\int_{\theta_0}\cdots\int_{\theta_t} p(\theta_0|\mathbf{y}_0)\prod_{s=1}^{t}\frac{\eta p(\mathbf{y}_s|n_s = j, \theta_s)p(\theta_s|\theta_{s-1})}{p(\mathbf{y}_s|\mathbf{y}_{0:s-1})}\mathrm{d}\theta_t\ldots\mathrm{d}\theta_0 \\
= \; & \frac{\eta^t}{N}\int_{\theta_0}\cdots\int_{\theta_t} p(\theta_0|z_0)\prod_{s=1}^{t}\frac{p(\mathbf{y}_s|n_s = j, \theta_s)p(\theta_s|\theta_{s-1})}{p(\mathbf{y}_s|\mathbf{y}_{0:s-1})}\mathrm{d}\theta_t\ldots\mathrm{d}\theta_0 \\
= \; & \eta^t p(n_t = j|\mathbf{y}_{0:t}); \quad j \in \mathcal{N}, j \neq l,
\end{aligned} \tag{10.23}$$

where $\eta^t = \prod_{s=1}^{t}\eta$.

More interestingly, from Eq. (10.23), we have

$$(N-1)p(n_t = l|\mathbf{y}_{0:t}) \geq \eta^t \sum_{j=1, j\neq l}^{N} p(n_t = j|\mathbf{y}_{0:t}) = \eta^t(1 - p(n_t = l|\mathbf{y}_{0:t})), \tag{10.24}$$

i.e.,

$$p(n_t = l|\mathbf{y}_{0:t}) \geq h(\eta, t), \tag{10.25}$$

where

$$h(\eta, t) = \frac{\eta^t}{\eta^t + N - 1}. \tag{10.26}$$

Eq. (10.25) has two implications.

1 Since the function $h(\eta, t)$ which provides a lower bound for $p(n_t = l|\mathbf{y}_{0:t})$ is monotonically increasing against time t, $p(n_t = l|\mathbf{y}_{0:t})$ has a probable trend of increase over t, even though not in a monotonic manner.

2 Since $\eta > 1$ and $p(n_t = l|\mathbf{y}_{0:t}) \leq 1$,

$$\lim_{t\to\infty} p(n_t = l|\mathbf{y}_{0:t}) = 1, \tag{10.27}$$

implying that $p(n_t = l|\mathbf{y}_{0:t})$ degenerates in the identity l for some sufficiently large t.

However, all these derivations are based on assumptions (A) and (B). Though it is easy to satisfy (A), difficulty arises in practice in order to satisfy (B) for all the frames in the sequence. Fortunately, as we have seen in the experiment in Section 10.2, numerically this degeneracy is still reached even if (B) is satisfied only for most but not all frames in the sequence.

More on assumption (B)

A trivial choice for η is the lower bound on the likelihood ratio, i.e.,

$$\eta = \inf_{t\geq 1, j\neq l, \theta_t \in \Theta} \frac{p(\mathbf{y}_t|n_t = l, \theta_t)}{p(\mathbf{y}_t|n_t = j, \theta_t)}. \tag{10.28}$$

This choice is of theoretical interest. In practice, how good is the assumption (B) satisfied? Figure 10.13 plots against the logarithm of the scale parameter, the 'average' likelihood of the correct identity,

$$\frac{1}{N} \sum_{n\in\mathcal{N}} p(\mathbf{g}_n|n, \theta),$$

and that of the incorrect identities,

$$\frac{1}{N(N-1)} \sum_{m\in\mathcal{N}, n\in\mathcal{N}, m\neq n} p(\mathbf{g}_m|n, \theta),$$

of the face gallery as well as the 'average' likelihood ratio, i.e., the ratio between the above two quantities. The observation is that only within a narrow 'band' the condition (B) is well satisfied. Therefore, the success of SIS algorithm depends on how good the samples lie in a similar 'band' in the high-dimensional affine space. Also, the lower bound η in assumption (B) is too strict. If we take the mean of the 'average' likelihood ratio shown in Figure 10.13 as an estimate of η (roughly 1.5), Eq. (10.25) shows that, after 20 frames, the probability $p(l|\mathbf{y}_{0:t})$ reaches 0.99! However, this is not reached in the experiments due to noise in the observations and incomplete parameterization of transformations.

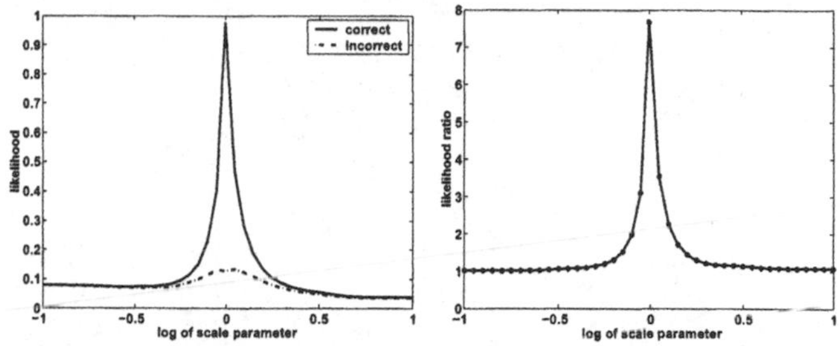

Figure 10.13. Left: The 'average' likelihood of the correct hypothesis and incorrect hypotheses against the log of scale parameter. Right: The 'average' likelihood ratio against the log of scale parameter.

Chapter 11

PROBABILISTIC IDENTITY CHARACTERIZATION

Even though a lot of research has been carried out, state-of-the-art face recognizers still yield unsatisfactory results especially when confronted with pose and illumination variations. Another aspect is the nature of input to the face recognition system. While single-still-image based face recognition has been investigated for a long time, there is a growing trend of using multiple still images or video sequences as input. In addition, the recognizers are further complicated by the registration requirement as the images that the recognizers process contain transformed appearances of the object. Below, we simply use the term 'transformation' to model all the variations due to misregistration, or pose and illumination variations.

In the literature, these covariants are treated rather independently. In this chapter, we propose a general framework called probabilistic identity characterization to unify the different approaches to face recognition. The unified framework possesses the following features:

- It processes either a single image or a group of images. Here a group of images include two types. In terms of the transformations embedded in the group or the temporal continuity between the transformations, the group can be either independent or not. Examples of the independent group (I-group) are face databases that store multiple appearances for one object. Examples of the dependent group are video sequences. If the temporal information is stripped, video sequences reduce to I-groups. In this chapter, whenever we mention video sequences, we mean dependent groups of images.

- It handles the localization problem, illumination and pose variations.

- The identity description could be either discrete or continuous. The continuous identity encoding typically arises from subspace modeling.

- It is probabilistic and integrates all the available evidence.

In Section 11.1 we introduce the generic framework which provides a probabilistic characterization of the object identity. In Section 11.2 we address issues and challenges arising in this framework. In Section 11.3 we focus on how to achieve an identity encoding which is invariant to localization, illumination and pose variations. In Section 11.3.2, we present some efficient computational methods. In Section 11.3.3, we present experimental results.

11.1 Principle of Probabilistic Identity Characterization

Suppose α is the identity signature, which represents the identity in an abstract manner. It can be either discrete- or continuous- valued. If we have an N-class problem, α is discrete taking value in $\{1, 2, ..., N\}$. If we associate the identity with image intensity or feature vectors derived from say subspace projections, α is continuous-valued. Given a group of images $\mathbf{y}_{1:T} \doteq \{\mathbf{y}_1, \mathbf{y}_2, ..., \mathbf{y}_T\}$ containing the appearances of the same but unknown identity, *probabilistic identity characterization is equivalent to finding the posterior probability* $p(\alpha|\mathbf{y}_{1:T})$.

As the image only contains a transformed version of the object, we also need to associate it a transformation parameter θ, which lies in a transformation space Θ. The transformation space Θ is usually application dependent. Affine transformation is often used to compensate for the localization problem. To handle illumination variation, the lighting direction is used. If pose variation is involved, 3D transformation is needed or a discrete set is used if we quantize the continuous view space.

We assume that the prior probability of α is $\pi(\alpha)$, which is assumed to be, in practice, a *non-informative* prior. A non-informative prior is uniform in the discrete case and treated as a constant, say 1, in the continuous case.

The key to our probabilistic identity characterization is as follows:

$$\begin{aligned} p(\alpha|\mathbf{y}_{1:T}) &\propto \pi(\alpha)p(\mathbf{y}_{1:T}|\alpha) \\ &= \pi(\alpha)\int_{\theta_{1:T}} p(\mathbf{y}_{1:T}|\theta_{1:T},\alpha)p(\theta_{1:T})d\theta_{1:T} \\ &= \pi(\alpha)\int_{\theta_{1:T}} \prod_{t=1}^{T} p(\mathbf{y}_t|\theta_t,\alpha)p(\theta_t|\theta_{1:t-1})d\theta_{1:T}, \end{aligned} \tag{11.1}$$

where the following rules, namely (a) *observational conditional independence* and (b) *chain rule*, are applied:

$$(a)\ p(\mathbf{y}_{1:T}|\theta_{1:T},\alpha) = \prod_{t=1}^{T} p(\mathbf{y}_t|\theta_t,\alpha); \tag{11.2}$$

$$(b)\ p(\theta_{1:T}) = \prod_{t=1}^{T} p(\theta_t|\theta_{1:t-1});\ p(\theta_1|\theta_0) \doteq p(\theta_1). \tag{11.3}$$

Eq. (11.1) involves two key quantities: the *observation likelihood* $p(\mathrm{y}_t|\theta_t, \alpha)$ and the *state transition probability* $p(\theta_t|\theta_{1:t-1})$. The former is essential to a recognition task, the ideal case being that it possesses a discriminative power in the sense that it always favors the correct identity and disfavors the others; the latter is also very helpful especially when processing video sequences, which constrains the search space.

We now study two special cases of $p(\theta_t|\theta_{1:t-1})$.

11.1.1 Independent group (I-group)

In this case, the transformations $\{\theta_t;\ t = 1, \ldots, T\}$ are independent of each other, i.e.

$$p(\theta_t|\theta_{1:t-1}) = p(\theta_t). \tag{11.4}$$

Eq. (11.1) becomes

$$p(\alpha|\mathrm{y}_{1:T}) \propto \pi(\alpha) \prod_{t=1}^{T} \int_{\theta_t} p(\mathrm{y}_t|\theta_t, \alpha) p(\theta_t) d\theta_t. \tag{11.5}$$

In this context, the probability $p(\theta_t)$ can be regarded as a prior for θ_t, which is often assumed to be Gaussian with mean $\hat{\theta}$ or non-informative.

The most widely studied case in the literature is $T = 1$, i.e. there is only a single image in the group. Due to its importance, sometimes we will distinguish it from the I-group (with $T > 1$) depending on the context. We will present in Section 11.2 the shortcomings of many contemporary approaches.

It all boils down to how to compute the integral in Eq. (11.5) in real applications. In the sequel, we show how to efficiently approximate it.

11.1.2 Video sequence

In the case of video sequence, temporal continuity between successive video frames implies that the transformations $\{\theta_t;\ t = 1, \ldots, T\}$ follow a Markov chain. Without loss of generality, we assume a first-order Markov chain, i.e.

$$p(\theta_t|\theta_{1:t-1}) = p(\theta_t|\theta_{t-1}). \tag{11.6}$$

Eq. (11.1) becomes

$$p(\alpha|\mathrm{y}_{1:T}) \propto \pi(\alpha) \int_{\theta_{1:T}} \prod_{t=1}^{T} p(\mathrm{y}_t|\theta_t, \alpha) p(\theta_t|\theta_{t-1}) d\theta_{1:T}. \tag{11.7}$$

The difference between Eq. (11.5) and Eq. (11.7) is whether the product lies inside or outside the integral. In Eq. (11.5), the product lies outside the integral, which divides the quantity of interest into 'small' integrals that can be computed efficiently; while Eq. (11.7) does not have such a decomposition, causing computational difficulty.

11.1.3 Difference from Bayesian estimation

Our framework is very different from the traditional Bayesian parameter estimation setting, where a certain parameter β should be estimated from the i.i.d. observations $\{\mathbf{x}_1, \mathbf{x}_2, ..., \mathbf{x}_T\}$ generated from a parametric density $p(\mathbf{x}|\beta)$. If we assume that β has a prior probability $\pi(\beta)$, then the posterior probability $p(\beta|\mathbf{x}_{1:T})$ is computed as

$$p(\beta|\mathbf{x}_{1:T}) \propto \pi(\beta)p(\mathbf{x}_{1:T}|\beta) = \pi(\beta)\prod_{t=1}^{T} p(\mathbf{x}_t|\beta) \quad (11.8)$$

and used to derive the parameter estimate $\hat{\beta}$. One should not confuse our transformation parameter θ with the parameter β. Notice that β is fixed in $p(\mathbf{x}_t|\beta)$ for different t's. However, each $\mathbf{y}_t$ is associates with a θ_t. Also, α is different from β in the sense that α describes the identity and β helps to describe the parametric density.

To make our framework more general, we can also incorporate the parameter β by letting the observation likelihood be $p(\mathbf{y}|\theta, \alpha, \beta)$. Eq. (11.1) then becomes

$$\begin{aligned} & p(\alpha|\mathbf{y}_{1:T}) \propto \pi(\alpha)p(\mathbf{y}_{1:T}|\alpha) \quad (11.9) \\ = & \ \pi(\alpha)\int_{\beta,\theta_{1:T}} p(\mathbf{y}_{1:T}|\theta_{1:T}, \alpha, \beta)p(\theta_{1:T})\pi(\beta)d\theta_{1:T}d\beta \\ = & \ \pi(\alpha)\int \prod_{t=1}^{T} p(\mathbf{y}_t|\theta_t, \alpha, \beta)p(\theta_t|\theta_{1:t-1})\pi(\beta)d\theta_{1:T}d\beta, \end{aligned}$$

where $\theta_{1:T}$ and β are assumed to be statistically independent. In this chapter, we will focus only on Eq. (11.1) as if we already know the true parameter β in Eq. (11.9). This greatly simplifies our computation.

11.2 Recognition Setting and Issues

Eq. (11.1) lays a theoretical foundation, which is universal for all recognition settings: (i) recognition is based on a single image (an I-group with $T = 1$), an I-group with $T \geq 2$, or a video sequence; (ii) the identity signature is either discrete- or continuous-valued; and (iii) the transformation space takes into account all available variations, such as localization and variations in illumination and pose.

11.2.1 Discrete identity signature

In a typical pattern recognition scenario, say an N-class problem, the identity signature for $\mathrm{y}_{1:T}$, $\hat{\alpha}$, is determined by the Bayesian decision rule:

$$\hat{\alpha} = \arg \max_{\{1,2,\ldots,N\}} p(\alpha|\mathrm{y}_{1:T}). \tag{11.10}$$

Usually $p(\mathrm{y}|\theta, \alpha)$ is a class-dependent density, either pre-specified or learned. This is a well studied problem and we will not focus on this.

11.2.2 Continuous identity signature

If the identity signature is continuous-valued, two recognition schemes are possible. The first is to derive a point estimate $\hat{\alpha}$ (e.g. conditional mean, mode) from $p(\alpha|\mathrm{y}_{1:T})$ to represent the identity of image group $\mathrm{y}_{1:T}$. Recognition is performed by matching $\hat{\alpha}$'s belonging to different groups of images using a metric $k(.,.)$. Say, $\hat{\alpha}_1$ is for group 1 and $\hat{\alpha}_2$ for group 2, the point distance

$$\hat{k}_{1,2} \doteq k(\hat{\alpha}_1, \hat{\alpha}_2)$$

is computed to characterize the difference between groups 1 and 2.

Instead of comparing the point estimates, the second scheme directly compares different distributions that characterize the identities for different groups of images. Therefore, for two groups 1 and 2 with the corresponding posterior probabilities $p(\alpha_1)$ and $p(\alpha_2)$, we use the following expected distance [199]

$$\bar{k}_{1,2} \doteq \int_{\alpha_1}\int_{\alpha_2} k(\alpha_1, \alpha_2)p(\alpha_1)p(\alpha_2)d\alpha_1 d\alpha_2.$$

Ideally, we wish to compare the two probability distributions using quantities such as the Kullback-Leibler distance [4]. However, computing such quantities is numerically prohibitive.

The second scheme is preferred as it utilizes the complete statistical information, while in the first one, point estimates use partial information. For examples, if only the conditional mean is used, the covariance structure or higher-order statistics is thrown away. However, there are circumstances when the first scheme makes sense: for instance, when the posterior distribution $p(\alpha|\mathrm{y}_{1:T})$ is highly peaked or even degenerate at $\hat{\alpha}$. This might occur when (i) the variance parameters are taken to be very small; or (ii) we let T go to ∞, i.e. keep observing the same object for a long time.

11.2.3 The effects of the transformation

Even though recognition based on single images has been studied for a long time, most efforts assume only one alignment parameter $\hat{\theta}$ and compute the probability $p(\mathrm{y}|\hat{\theta}, \alpha)$. Any recognition algorithm computing some distance measures can be thought of as using a properly defined Gibbs distribution. The underlying assumption is that

$$p(\theta) = \delta(\theta - \hat{\theta}), \tag{11.11}$$

where $\delta(.)$ is an impulse function. Using Eq. (11.11), Eq. (11.5) becomes

$$p(\alpha|\mathrm{y}) \propto \pi(\alpha) \int_\theta p(\mathrm{y}|\theta, \alpha)\delta(\theta - \hat{\theta})d\theta = \pi(\alpha)p(\mathrm{y}|\hat{\theta}, \alpha). \tag{11.12}$$

Incidentally, if the Laplace's method is used to approximate the integral (refer to the Appendix for detail) and the maximizer $\hat{\theta}_\alpha = \arg\max_\theta p(\mathrm{y}|\theta, \alpha)p(\theta)$ does not depend on α, say $\hat{\theta}_\alpha = \hat{\theta}$, then

$$\begin{aligned} p(\alpha|\mathrm{y}) &\propto \pi(\alpha) \int_\theta p(\mathrm{y}|\theta, \alpha)p(\theta)d\theta \\ &\simeq \pi(\alpha)p(\mathrm{y}|\hat{\theta}, \alpha)p(\hat{\theta})\sqrt{(2\pi)^r/|\mathrm{J}(\hat{\theta})|}. \end{aligned} \tag{11.13}$$

This gives rise to the same decision rule as implied by Eq. (11.12) and also partly explains why the simple assumption Eq. (11.11) can work in practice.

The alignment parameter is therefore very crucial for a good recognition performance. Even a slightly erroneous $\hat{\theta}$ may affect the recognition system significantly. It is very beneficial to have a continuous density $p(\theta)$ such as Gaussian or even a non-informative one since marginalization of $p(\theta, \alpha|\mathrm{y})$ over θ yields a robust estimate of $p(\alpha|\mathrm{y})$.

In addition, our Bayesian framework also provides a way to estimate the best alignment parameter through the posterior probability:

$$p(\theta|\mathrm{y}) \propto \int_\alpha p(\mathrm{y}|\theta, \alpha)\pi(\alpha)d\alpha. \tag{11.14}$$

11.2.4 Asymptotic behaviors

When we have an I-group or a video sequence, we are often interested in discovering the asymptotic (or large-sample) behaviors of the posterior distribution $p(\alpha|\mathrm{y}_{1:T})$ when T is large. In [129], the discrete case of α in a video sequence is studied. However it is very challenging to extend this study to a continuous case. Experimentally (refer to Section 11.3.3), we find that $p(\alpha|\mathrm{y}_{1:T})$ becomes more and more peaked as N increase, which seems to suggest a degenerancy in the true value α_{true}.

11.3 Subspace Identity Encoding

The main challenge is to specify the likelihood $p(\mathrm{y}|\theta, \alpha)$. Practical considerations require that (i) the identity encoding coefficient α is compact so that our target space where α resides is of low dimensional; and (ii) α should be invariant to transformations and tightly clustered so that we can safely focus on a small portion of the spaces.

Inspired by the popularity of subspace analysis, we assume that the observation y can be well explained by a subspace, whose basis vectors are encoded in a matrix denoted by B, i.e. there exists linear coefficient α such that $y \approx B\alpha$. Clearly, α naturally encodes the identity. However, the observation under the transformation condition (parameterized by θ) deviates from the canonical condition (parameterized by say $\bar{\theta}$) under which the B matrix is defined. To achieve an identity encoding that is invariant to the transformation, there are two possible ways. One way is to inverse-warp the observation y from the transformation condition θ to the canonical condition $\bar{\theta}$ and the other way is to warp the basis matrix B from the canonical condition $\bar{\theta}$ to the transformation condition θ. In practice, inverse-warping is typically difficult. For example, we cannot easily warp an off-frontal view to a frontal view without explicit 3D depth information that may not be available. Hence, we follow the second approach, which is also known as *analysis-by-synthesis* approach. We denote the basis matrix under the transformation condition θ by B_θ.

11.3.1 Invariant to localization, illumination, and pose

The localization parameter, denoted by ε, includes the face location, scale and in-plane rotation. Typically, an affine transformation is used. We absorb the localization parameter ε in the observation using $\mathcal{T}\{y; \varepsilon\}$, where the $\mathcal{T}\{.; \varepsilon\}$ is a localization operator, extracting the region of interest and normalizing it to match with the size of the basis.

The illumination parameter, denoted by λ, is a vector specifying the illuminant direction (and intensity if required). The pose parameter, denoted by υ, is a continuous-valued random variable. However, practical systems [73, 76] often discretize this due to the difficulty in handling 3D to 2D projection. Suppose the quantized pose set is $\{1, \ldots, V\}$. To achieve pose invariance, we concatenate all the images [76] $\{y^1, \ldots, y^V\}$ under all the views and a fixed illumination λ to form a high-dimensional vector $Y^\lambda = [y^{1,\lambda}, ..., y^{V,\lambda}]^T$. To further achieve invariance to illuminations, we invoke the Lambertian reflectance model, ignoring shadow pixels. Now, λ is actually a 3-D vector describing the illuminant. We now follow Chapter 5 to perform a bilinear analysis; the results of which are summarized below.

Since all y^υ's are illuminated by the same λ, the Lambertian model gives,

$$Y^\lambda = W\lambda. \tag{11.15}$$

Following [95], we assume that

$$\mathtt{W} = \sum_{i=1}^{m} \alpha_i \mathtt{W}_i, \tag{11.16}$$

and we have

$$\mathtt{Y}^{\lambda} = \sum_{i=1}^{m} \alpha_i \mathtt{W}_i \lambda, \tag{11.17}$$

where $\mathtt{W}_i$'s are illumination-invariant bilinear basis and $\alpha = [\alpha_1, \ldots, \alpha_m]^{\mathsf{T}}$ provides an illuminant-invariant identity signature. Those bilinear basis can be easily learned as shown in [214, 94]. Thus α is also pose-invariant because, for a given view v, we take the part in $\mathtt{Y}$ corresponding to this view and still have

$$\mathtt{y}^{\lambda,v} = \sum_{i=1}^{m} \alpha_i \mathtt{W}_i^v \lambda. \tag{11.18}$$

In summary, the basis matrix $\mathtt{B}_\theta$ for $\theta = (\varepsilon, \lambda, v)$ with ε absorbed in y is expressed as $\mathtt{B}_{\lambda,v} = [\mathtt{W}_1^v \lambda, \ldots, \mathtt{W}_m^v \lambda]$.

We focus on the following likelihood:

$$\begin{aligned} p(\mathtt{y}|\theta) &= p(\mathtt{y}|\varepsilon, \lambda, v, \alpha) \\ &= \mathtt{Z}_{\lambda,v,\alpha}^{-1} \exp\{-d(\mathcal{T}\{\mathtt{y};\varepsilon\}, \mathtt{B}_{\lambda,v}\alpha)\}, \end{aligned} \tag{11.19}$$

where $\mathtt{D}(\mathtt{y}, \mathtt{B}_\theta \alpha)$ is some distance measure and $\mathtt{Z}_{\lambda,v,\alpha}$ is the so-called partition function which plays a normalization role. In particular, if we take d as

$$d(\mathcal{T}\{\mathtt{y};\varepsilon\}, \mathtt{B}_{\lambda,v}\alpha) = (\mathcal{T}\{\mathtt{y};\varepsilon\} - \mathtt{B}_{\lambda,v}\alpha)^{\mathsf{T}} \Sigma^{-1} (\mathcal{T}\{\mathtt{y};\varepsilon\} - \mathtt{B}_{\lambda,v}\alpha)/2, \tag{11.20}$$

with a given Σ (say $\Sigma = \sigma^2 \mathtt{I}$ where $\mathtt{I}$ is an identity matrix), then Eq. (11.19) becomes a multivariate Gaussian and the partition function $\mathtt{Z}_{\lambda,v,\alpha}$ does not depend on the parameters any more. However, even though Eq. (11.19) is a multivariate Gaussian, the posterior distribution $p(\alpha|\mathtt{y}_{1:T})$ is no longer Gaussian.

11.3.2 Computational issues

The integral

If the transformation space Θ is discrete, it is easy to evaluate the integral $\int_\theta p(\mathtt{y}|\theta, \alpha)p(\theta)d\theta$, which becomes a sum. Note that here we drop the subscript $[.]_t$ notation as this is a general treatment. If Θ is continuous, in general, computing integral $\int_\theta p(\mathtt{y}|\theta, \alpha)p(\theta)d\theta$ is a difficult task. Many techniques are available in the literature. Here we mainly focus on two techniques: Monte Carlo simulation [14, 16] and Laplace's method [16, 210].

Monte Carlo simulation. The underlying principle is the law of large number (LLN). If $\{\mathtt{x}^{(1)}, \mathtt{x}^{(2)}, \ldots, \mathtt{x}^{(K)}\}$ are K IID samples drawn from the density $p(\mathtt{x})$, for any bounded function $h(\mathbf{x})$,

$$\lim_{K\to\infty} \frac{1}{K}\sum_{k=1}^{K} h(\mathbf{x}^{(k)}) = \int_{\mathbf{x}} h(\mathbf{x})p(\mathbf{x})d\mathbf{x} = \mathrm{E}_p[h]. \tag{11.21}$$

Alternatively, when drawing i.i.d. samples from $p(\mathbf{x})$ is difficult, we can use importance sampling [14, 16]. Suppose that the *importance function* $q(\mathbf{x})$ has i.i.d. realizations $\{\mathbf{x}^{(1)}, \mathbf{x}^{(2)}, \ldots, \mathbf{x}^{(K)}\}$. The pdf $p(\mathbf{x})$ can be represented by a weighted sample set $\{(\mathbf{x}^{(k)}, w_p^{(k)})\}_{k=1}^{K}$, where the weight for the sample $\mathbf{x}^{(k)}$ is

$$w_p^{(k)} = p(\mathbf{x}^{(k)})/q(\mathbf{x}^{(k)}), \tag{11.22}$$

in the sense that for any bounded function $h(\mathbf{x})$,

$$\lim_{K\to\infty} \sum_{k=1}^{K} w_p^{(k)} h(\mathbf{x}^{(k)}) = \sum_{k=1}^{K} \frac{p(\mathbf{x}^{(k)})}{q(\mathbf{x}^{(k)})} h(\mathbf{x}^{(k)}) = \mathrm{E}_p[h]. \tag{11.23}$$

Laplace's method [16, 210]. The general approach of this method is presented in Appendix. This is a good approximation to the integral only if the integrand is uniquely peaked and reasonably mimics the Gaussian function.

In our context, we use importance sampling (or IID sampling if possible) for ε and the Laplace's method for λ and enumerate v. We draw i.i.d. samples $\{\varepsilon^{(1)}, \varepsilon^{(2)}, \ldots, \varepsilon^{(K)}\}$ from $q(\varepsilon)$ and, for each sample $\varepsilon^{(k)}$, compute the weight $w_{\varepsilon^{(k)}} = p(\varepsilon^{(k)})/q(\varepsilon^{(k)})$. If the i.i.d. sampling is used, the weights are always ones. Putting things together, we have (assuming $\pi(\alpha)$ is a non-informative prior)

$$\begin{aligned} p(\alpha|\mathbf{y}) &\propto \int_{\varepsilon,\lambda,v} p(\mathbf{y}|\varepsilon,\lambda,v,\alpha)p(\varepsilon)p(\lambda)p(v)d\varepsilon d\lambda dv \\ &\simeq \frac{1}{K}\sum_{k=1}^{K} w_{\varepsilon^{(k)}} \frac{1}{V}\sum_{v=1}^{V} p(\mathbf{y}|\varepsilon^{(k)}, \hat{\lambda}_{\varepsilon^{(k)},v,\alpha}, v, \alpha) \times \\ &\qquad p(\hat{\lambda}_{\varepsilon^{(k)},v,\alpha})\sqrt{(2\pi)^r/|\mathrm{J}(\hat{\lambda}_{\varepsilon^{(k)},v,\alpha})|}, \end{aligned} \tag{11.24}$$

where $\hat{\lambda}_{\varepsilon^k,v,\alpha}$ is the maximizer

$$\hat{\lambda}_{\varepsilon^{(k)},v,\alpha} = \arg\min_{\lambda} p(\mathbf{y}|\varepsilon^{(k)}, \lambda, v, \alpha)p(\lambda), \tag{11.25}$$

r is the dimensionality of λ, and $\mathrm{J}(\hat{\lambda}_{\varepsilon,v,\alpha})$ is a properly defined matrix. Refer to Appendix for computing $\hat{\lambda}_{\varepsilon,v,\alpha}$ and $\mathrm{J}(\hat{\lambda}_{\varepsilon,v,\alpha})$ if the likelihood is given as Eq. (11.19) and Eq. (11.20) and a non-informative prior $p(\lambda)$ is assumed. Similar derivations can be conducted for an I-group of observations $\mathbf{y}_{1:T}$.

The distances $\bar{k}$ and $\hat{k}$

To evaluate the expected distance $\bar{k}$, we use the Monte Carlo method. In our context, the target distribution is $p(\alpha|\mathbf{y}_{1:T})$. Based on the above derivations, we know how to evaluate the target distribution, but not to draw sample from it. Therefore, we use importance sampling. Other sampling techniques such as Monte Carlo Markov chain [14, 16] can also be applied.

Suppose that, say for group 1, the importance function is $q_1(\alpha_1)$, and weighted sample set is $\{\alpha_1^{(i)}, w_1^{(i)}\}_{i=1}^{I}$, the expected distance is approximated as

$$\bar{k}_{1,2} \simeq \frac{\sum_{i=1}^{I}\sum_{j=1}^{J} w_1^{(i)} w_2^{(j)} k(\alpha_1^{(i)}, \alpha_2^{(j)})}{\sum_{i=1}^{I} w_1^{(i)} \sum_{j=1}^{J} w_2^{(j)}}. \tag{11.26}$$

The point distance is approximated as

$$\hat{k}_{1,2} \simeq k\left(\frac{\sum_{i=1}^{I} w_1^{(i)} \alpha_1^{(i)}}{\sum_{i=1}^{I} w_1^{(i)}}, \frac{\sum_{j=1}^{J} w_2^{(j)} \alpha_2^{(j)}}{\sum_{j=1}^{J} w_2^{(j)}}\right). \tag{11.27}$$

11.3.3 Experimental results

We use the 'illum' subset of the PIE database [85] in our experiments. This subset has 68 subjects under 21 illumination configurations and 13 poses. Out of the 21 illumination configurations, we select 12 of them denoted by F,

$$F = \{f_{16}, f_{15}, f_{13}, f_{21}, f_{12}, f_{11}, f_{08}, f_{06}, f_{10}, f_{18}, f_{04}, f_{02}\},$$

which typically span the set of variations. Out of the 13 poses, we select 9 of them denoted by C,

$$C = \{c_{22}, c_{02}, c_{37}, c_{05}, c_{27}, c_{29}, c_{11}, c_{14}, c_{34}\},$$

which cover from the left profile to the frontal to the right profile. In total, we have $68 * 12 * 9 = 7344$ images. Fig 5.2 displays one PIE object under the illumination and pose variations.

We randomly divide the 68 subjects into two parts. The first 34 subjects are used in the training set and the remaining 34 subjects are used in the gallery and probe sets. It is guaranteed that there is no identity overlap between the training set and the gallery set.

During training, the images are pre-preprocessed by aligning the eyes and mouth to desired positions. No flow computation is carried on for further alignment. After the pre-processing step, the used face image is of size 48 by 40, i.e. $d = 48 * 40 = 1920$. Also, we only study gray images by taking the average of the red, green, and blue channels of their color versions.

The training set is used to learn the basis matrix $\mathtt{B}_\theta$ or the bilinear basis $\mathtt{W}_i$'s. As mentioned before, θ includes the illumination direction λ and the view pose

υ, where λ is a continuous-valued random vector and υ is a discrete random variable taking values in $\{1, \ldots, V\}$ with $p = 9$ (corresponding to C).

The images belonging to the remaining 34 subjects are used in the gallery and probe sets. The construction of the gallery and probe sets conforms the following: To form a gallery set of the 34 subjects, for each subject, we use an I-group of 12 images under all the illuminations under one pose υ_p; to form a probe set, we use I-groups under the other pose υ_g. We mainly concentrate on the case with $\upsilon_p \neq \upsilon_g$. Thus, we have $9 * 8 = 72$ tests, with each test giving rise to a recognition score. The 1-NN (nearest neighbor) rule is applied to find the identity for a probe I-group.

During testing, we no longer use the pre-processed images and therefore the unknown transformation parameter includes the affine localization parameter, the light direction, and the discrete view pose. The prior distribution $p(\varepsilon_t)$ is assumed to be a Gaussian, whose mean is found by a background subtraction algorithm and whose covariance matrix is manually specified. We use i.i.d. sampling from $p(\varepsilon_t)$ since it is Gaussian. The metric $k(.,.)$ actually used in our experiments is the correlation coefficient:

$$k(\mathbf{x}, \mathbf{y}) = \{(\mathbf{x}^\mathsf{T}\mathbf{y})^2\}/\{(\mathbf{x}^\mathsf{T}\mathbf{x})(\mathbf{y}^\mathsf{T}\mathbf{y})\}.$$

Figure 11.1 shows the marginal posterior distribution of the first element α^1 of the identity variable α, i.e., $p(\alpha^1|\mathbf{y}_{1:T})$, with different N's. From Figure 11.1, we notice that (i) the posterior probability $p(\alpha^1|\mathbf{y}_{1:T})$ has two modes, which might fail those algorithms using the point estimate, and (ii) it becomes more peaked and tightly-supported as T increases, which empirically supports the asymptotic behavior mentioned in Section 11.2.

Figure 11.2 shows the recognition rates for all the 72 tests. In general, when the poses of the gallery and probe sets are far apart, the recognition rates decrease. The best gallery sets for recognition are those in frontal poses and the worst gallery sets are those in profile views. These observation are similar to those made in Chapter 5.

For comparison, Table 11.1 shows the average recognition rates for four different methods: our two probabilistic approaches using $\bar{k}$ and $\hat{k}$, respectively, the PCA approach [64], and the statistical approach [118] using the KL distance. When implementing the PCA approach, we learned a generic face subspace from all the training images, stripping their illumination and pose conditions; while implementing the KL approach, we fit a Gaussian density on every I-group and the learning set is not used. Our approaches outperform the other two approaches significantly due to the transformation-invariant subspace modeling. The KL approach [118] performs even worse than the PCA approach simply because no illumination and pose learning is used in the KL approach while the PCA approach has a learning algorithm based on image ensembles taken under different illuminations and poses (though this specific information is stripped).

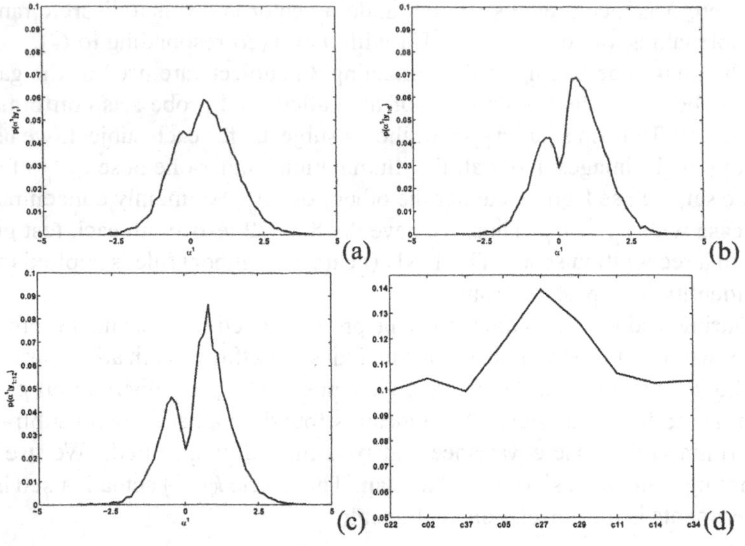

Figure 11.1. The posterior distributions $p(\alpha^1|\mathbf{y}_{1:T})$ with different T's: (a) $p(\alpha^1|\mathbf{y}_1)$; (b) $p(\alpha^1|\mathbf{y}_{1:6})$; and (c) $p(\alpha^1|\mathbf{y}_{1:12})$, and (d) the posterior distribution $p(v|\mathbf{y}_{1:12})$. Notice that $p(\alpha^1|\mathbf{y}_{1:T})$ has two modes and becomes more peaked as T increases.

Method	$\bar{k}$	$\hat{k}$	*PCA*	*KL [118]*
Rec. Rate (top 1)	82%	76%	36%	6%
Rec. Rate (top 3)	94%	91%	56%	15%

Table 11.1. Recognition rates of different methods.

As earlier mentioned in Section 11.2.3, we can infer the transformation parameters using the posterior probability $p(\theta|\mathbf{y}_{1:T})$. Figure 11.1 also shows the obtained $p(v|\mathbf{y}_{1:12})$ for one probe I-group. In this case, the actual pose is $v = 5$ (i.e. camera c_{27}), which has the maximum probability in Figure 11.1(d). Similarly, we can find an estimation for ε, which is quite accurate as the back ground subtraction algorithm already provides a clean position.

11.4 Appendix

Laplace's method

We are interested in computing the following integral $H = \int p(\theta)d\theta$, for $\theta = [\theta_1, \theta_2, \ldots, \theta_r]^{\mathsf{T}} \in \mathcal{R}^r$. Suppose that $\hat{\theta}$ is the maximizer of $p(\theta)$ or

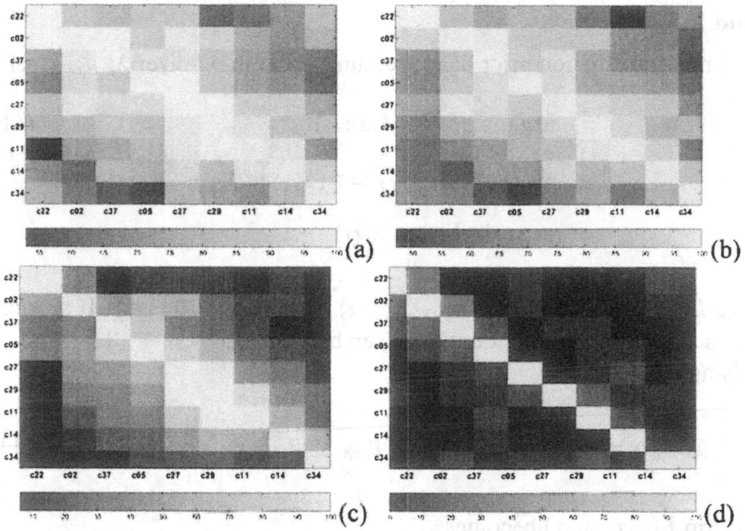

Figure 11.2. The recognition rates of all tests. (a) Our method based on $\bar{k}$. (b) Our method based on $\hat{k}$. (c) The PCA approach [64]. (d) The KL approach. Notice the different ranges of values for different methods and the diagonal entries should be ignored.

equivalently $\log p(\theta)$ which satisfies

$$\frac{\partial p(\theta)}{\partial \theta}|_{\hat{\theta}} = 0 \; or \; \frac{\partial \log p(\theta)}{\partial \theta}|_{\hat{\theta}} = 0. \tag{11.28}$$

We expand $\log p(\theta)$ around $\hat{\theta}$ using a Taylor series:

$$\log p(\theta) \sim \log p(\hat{\theta}) - \frac{1}{2}(\theta - \theta^*)^\top \mathtt{J}(\hat{\theta})(\theta - \hat{\theta}), \tag{11.29}$$

where $\mathtt{J}(\theta)$ is an $r \times r$ matrix whose ij^{th} element is

$$\mathtt{J}_{ij}(\theta) = -\frac{\partial^2 \log p(\theta)}{\partial \theta_i \partial \theta_j}. \tag{11.30}$$

Note that the first-order term in Eq. (11.29) is zero by virtue of Eq. (11.28). If $p(\theta)$ is a pdf function with parameter θ, then $\mathtt{J}(\theta)$ is the famous Fisher information matrix [16]. Substituting Eq. (11.29) into $H = intp(\theta)d\theta$ gives

$$\begin{aligned} H &\simeq p(\hat{\theta}) \int \exp\{-\frac{1}{2}(\theta - \hat{\theta})^\top \mathtt{J}(\hat{\theta})(\theta - \hat{\theta})\} d\theta \\ &= p(\hat{\theta})\sqrt{(2\pi)^r / |\mathtt{J}(\hat{\theta})|}. \end{aligned} \tag{11.31}$$

About $\hat{\lambda}_{\varepsilon,\upsilon,\alpha}$

If a non-information prior $p(\lambda)$ is assumed, the maximizer $\hat{\lambda}_{\varepsilon,\upsilon,\alpha}$ satisfies

$$\begin{aligned} \hat{\lambda}_{\varepsilon,\upsilon,\alpha} &= \arg\max_{\lambda} p(\mathrm{y}|\varepsilon,\lambda,\upsilon,\alpha) \\ &= \arg\min_{\lambda} (\mathcal{T}\{\mathrm{y};\varepsilon\} - \mathrm{B}_{\lambda,\upsilon}\alpha)^{\mathsf{T}}(\mathcal{T}\{\mathrm{y};\varepsilon\} - \mathrm{B}_{\lambda,\upsilon}\alpha) \\ &= \arg\min_{\lambda} L(\varepsilon,\upsilon,\lambda,\alpha) \end{aligned} \tag{11.32}$$

where $L(\varepsilon,\upsilon,\lambda,\alpha) \doteq (\mathcal{T}\{\mathrm{y};\varepsilon\} - \mathrm{B}_{\lambda,\upsilon}\alpha)^{\mathsf{T}}(\mathcal{T}\{\mathrm{y};\varepsilon\} - \mathrm{B}_{\lambda,\upsilon}\alpha)$. If a Gaussian prior is assumed, a similar derivation can be carried.

Using the fact that

$$\mathrm{B}_{\lambda,\upsilon}\alpha = [\mathrm{W}_1^{\upsilon}\lambda,\ldots,\mathrm{W}_m^{\upsilon}\lambda]\alpha = \mathrm{B}_{\alpha,\upsilon}\lambda;\ \mathrm{B}_{\alpha,\upsilon} \doteq \sum_{i=1}^{m}\alpha_i \mathrm{W}_i^{\upsilon}, \tag{11.33}$$

The term $L(\varepsilon,\upsilon,\lambda,\alpha)$ becomes

$$L(\varepsilon,\upsilon,\lambda,\alpha) = (\mathcal{T}\{\mathrm{y};\varepsilon\} - \mathrm{B}_{\alpha,\upsilon}\lambda)^{\mathsf{T}}(\mathcal{T}\{\mathrm{y};\varepsilon\} - \mathrm{B}_{\alpha,\upsilon}\lambda), \tag{11.34}$$

which is quadratic in λ. The optimum $\hat{\lambda}_{\varepsilon,\upsilon,\alpha}$ is unique and its value is

$$\hat{\lambda}_{\varepsilon,\upsilon,\alpha} = (\mathrm{B}_{\alpha,\upsilon}{}^{\mathsf{T}}\mathrm{B}_{\alpha,\upsilon})^{-1}\mathrm{B}_{\alpha,\upsilon}{}^{\mathsf{T}}\mathrm{y} = \mathrm{B}_{\alpha,\upsilon}{}^{\dagger}\mathcal{T}\{\mathrm{y};\varepsilon\}. \tag{11.35}$$

where $[.]^{\dagger}$ is the pseudo-inverse. Substituting Eq. (11.35) into $L(\varepsilon,\upsilon,\lambda,\alpha)$ yields

$$L(\varepsilon,\upsilon,\hat{\lambda}_{\varepsilon,\upsilon,\alpha},\alpha) = \mathcal{T}\{\mathrm{y};\varepsilon\}^{\mathsf{T}}(\mathrm{J}_d - \mathrm{B}_{\alpha,\upsilon}\mathrm{B}_{\alpha,\upsilon}{}^{\dagger})\mathcal{T}_{\varepsilon}\{\mathrm{y}\}. \tag{11.36}$$

It is easy to show that $\mathrm{J}(\lambda)$ is no longer a function of λ and equals to

$$\mathrm{J} = \sigma^{-2}\mathrm{B}_{\alpha,\upsilon}{}^{\mathsf{T}}\mathrm{B}_{\alpha,\upsilon}. \tag{11.37}$$

PART V

SUMMARY AND FUTURE RESEARCH DIRECTIONS

Chapter 12

SUMMARY AND FUTURE RESEARCH DIRECTIONS

12.1 Summary

This monograph addressed several approaches for unconstrained face recognition from three aspects. The first aspect is to directly model illumination and pose variations. The second aspect is to use nonlinear kernel learning to characterize the face appearance manifold. The third aspect is to perform recognition using video sequences.

We summarize some of the major concepts made in the book:

- The general theory of symmetric SFS in Chapter 3 incorporates the lateral symmetric cue into an SFS problem. By doing this, we derived a unique solution of both shape and albedo. We also showed the use of self-ratio image in robust estimation of illumination direction and the extensions of symmetric SFS and applications of symmetry cue for image synthesis and view-synthesis of face images.

- In the generalized photometric stereo approach presented in Chapter 4, we proposed a rank constraint on the product of albedo and surface normal that provides a very compact yet efficient encoding of the identity. In the literature, usually two separate linear subspaces [46, 72] are constructed for shape and texture, respectively, assuming the independence between them. This assumption might result in an overfit for the problem [94].

  By using the integrability and symmetry constraints, we designed a linearized algorithm that recovers the *class-specific* albedos and surface normals under the most general and hence most difficult setting, i.e., the observation matrix consists of different objects under different illuminations. In particular, this algorithm takes into account the effect of varying albedo field in the integrability term.

- The illuminating light field approach in Chapter 5 is image-based and requires no explicit 3D model. It is computationally efficient and able to deal with images of small size. In contrast, the 3D model-based approach [72] is computationally intense and needs image of large size.

- In Chapter 6, age estimation is solved using a regression algorithm based on boosting to select relevant features from the image. Since the regressor does not depend the training data, it is efficient in both storage and computation. An efficient training algorithm that performs incremental feature selection was also presented. For face recognition across aging progression, we had proposed two approaches to studying facial similarity across time. The method proposed in this chapter, is very relevant to applications such as renewal of passports. During renewal of passports, the age difference between the image pairs is known *a priori*. Given a pair of age-separated face images of an individual, the age difference classifier establishes the identity between the image pairs and further classifies them to their corresponding age difference category. Moreover, the similarity scores computed between two images of an individual when compared with the scores tabulated in Table 6.4 of help in identifying outliers, if any.

- Computing the probabilistic distance measures (e.g. the Chernoff distance, the Bhatacharyya distance, the KL distance, and the divergence distance) between two Gaussian densities in the RKHS is presented in Chapter 7. Since the RKHS might be infinite-dimensional, we derive a limiting distance which can be easily computed. This leads to a novel paradigm for studying pattern separability, especially for visual pattern lying in a nonlinear manifold.

- Chapter 8 presented two matrix-based kernel subspace methods: matrix KPCA and matrix KLDA. The proposed matrix-based kernel subspace methods generalize their vector-based counterparts, e.g. vector KPCA and vector KLDA, in the sense that the matrix KPCA and matrix KLDA provide richer representations and capture spatial statistics to some extent. This comes from the fact the Gram matrix used in the vector-based kernel methods can be derived from that used in the proposed matrix-based kernel methods.

- Presented in Chapter 9 is an adaptive method for visual tracking which stabilizes the tracker by embedding deterministic linear prediction into stochastic diffusion. Numerical solutions have been provided using particle filters with the adaptive observation model arising from the adaptive appearance model, adaptive state transition model, and adaptive number of particles. Occlusion analysis is also embedded in the particle filter.

- A systematic method for face recognition from a probe video, compared with a gallery of still templates is introduced in Chapter 10. A time series state space model is used to accommodate the video and SIS algorithms provide the numerical solutions to the model. This probabilistic framework, which overcomes many difficulties arising in conventional recognition approaches using video, is registration-free and poses no need for selecting good frames. It turns out that an immediate recognition decision can be made in our framework due to the degeneracy of the posterior probability of the identity variable. The conditional entropy can also serve as a good indication for the convergence.

- We presented in Chapter 11 a generic framework of modeling human identity for a single image, a group of images, or a video sequence . This framework provides a complete statistic description of the identity. Various current recognition schemes are just instances of this generic framework.

12.2 Future Research Directions

Unconstrained face recognition can be expanded in a multitude of ways. The following just lists some potential avenues to explore in the context of the proposed approaches:

- For the symmetric SFS in Chapter 3, ideally we would like to handle symmetric objects under different lighting, viewing conditions and projections, for example, to handle rotated symmetric objects. Moreover, we expect to be able to handle partially symmetric objects by integrating traditional SFS and symmetric SFS. The following is a list of future research directions: (i) developing symmetric SFS algorithms to handle arbitrarily varying albedo and (ii) extending the Lambertian model to more general models, such as including specular reflections and multiple lighting sources.

- In Chapters 4 and 5, we used a Lambertian reflectance model to describe the illumination phenomenon. However, the Lambertian reflectance model is a rather simple model and unable to handle cast shadows and specular regions. Although we employed a simple technique to exclude pixels in cast shadow and specular regions, it turns out when the light comes from extreme directions (e.g. highly off-frontal ones), the recognition performance drops quickly. We need to investigate these lighting conditions. Alternatively, a complex illumination model providing a better illumination description can be used.

- In the illuminating light field approach of Chapter 5, we need an image-based rendering technique to handle novel poses. Some promising works along this line are [73, 175, 176].

- The boosted regressor proposed in Chapter 6 is very general and can be applied to other regression problems. The choices of feature functions are crucial to many applications. All these issues should be further investigated. Also, understanding aging of faces is important to the success of face recognition systems. It is of great interest to derive a robust model for facial aging across all age categories.

- Regarding the probability distances on RKHS, possible future works include (i) how to design or select the kernel function for a given task, be it classification or modeling; (ii) evaluating the kernels for set based on the derived probabilistic distances (as argued in Section 7.3.5) in a classification device such as an SVM for various applications; (iii) utilizing probabilistic distances for ICA as in [261].

- The key quantity in Chapter 8 is the extended Gram matrix. Using this Gram matrix, one can construct reproducing kernel functions that take matrix as inputs. For example, it is easy to show that the trace and determinant of the extended Gram matrix are positive-definite and hence legitimate reproducing kernels. Other constructions are also feasible.

- The visual tracking algorithm of Chapter 9 can be extended in many ways [202, 204]. (i) Combining shape information into appearance. Appearance and shape are two very important visual cues arguably presented in a complementary fashion [198]. (ii) Utilizing appearance from multiple views. Using multiple views can overcome some difficulty in a single view. For example, an object might be occluded in one view but not the other one. Using the multiview geometry, we can infer the movement of the object in the occluded view [203]. (iii) Here we mostly model the movement of the foreground object. Joint modeling of foreground and background movements is very promising [204, 205] since the stabilization obtained by background modeling significantly reduces the clutter in the background that confuses the foreground tracking algorithm.

- In simultaneous tracking and recognition of Chapter 10, many issues exist. (i) Robustness. Generally speaking, our approach is more robust than still-image-based approach since we essentially compute the recognition score based on all video frames and, in each frame, all kinds of transformed versions of the face part corresponding to the sample configurations that are considered. However, since we take no explicit measure when handling frames with outlier or other unexpected factors, recognition scores based on those frames might be low. But, this is a problem for other approaches too. The assumption that the identity does not change as time proceeds, i.e., $p(n_t|n_{t-1}) = \delta(n_t - n_{t-1})$, could be relaxed by having nonzero transition probabilities between different identity variables. Using nonzero transition probabilities will enable us an easier transition to the correct choice in case that the initial choice is incorrectly chosen, making the algorithm more robust.

(ii) Resampling. In the recognition algorithm, the marginal distribution $\{(\theta_{t-1}^{(j)}, w_{t-1}^{\prime(j)})\}_{j=1}^{J}$ is sampled to obtain the sample set $\{(\theta_t^{(j)}, 1)\}_{j=1}^{J}$. This may cause problems in principle since there is no conditional independence between θ_t and n_t given $\mathbf{y}_{0:t}$. However, in a practical sense, this is not a big disadvantage because the purpose of resampling is to 'provide chances for the good streams (samples) to amplify themselves and hence rejuvenate the sampler to produce better results for future states as the system evolves' [248]. The resampling scheme can either be simple random sampling with weights (like in CONDENSATION), residual sampling, or local Monte Carlo methods.

- Further, in the experimental part of Chapter 11, we can extend our approach to perform recognition from video sequences with localization, illumination, and pose variations. Again, the SIS methods can be used to accommodate temporal continuity. This leads to a very high-dimensional state space to explore. Efficient simulation techniques are desired. In fact, the issue of computation load also exist for the efficient algorithm in Chapter 10. There, two important numbers affecting the computation are J, the number of motion samples, and N, the size of the database. (i) The choice of J is an open question in the statistics literature. In general, larger J produces more accurate results. (ii) The choice of N depends on application. Since a small database is used in this experiment, it is not a big issue here. However, the computational burden may be excessive if N is large. One possibility is to use a continuous parameterized representation, say α as in Chapter 11, instead of discrete identity variable n. Now the task reduces to computing $p(\alpha_t, \theta_t|\mathbf{y}_{0:t})$.

The approaches taken in this book by no means cover the whole spectrum of the unconstrained face recognition problem and address only a small portion of all the relevant issues. Some possible important issues, other than those addressed in the book, include the following:

- *3D model-based face matching.* 2D-appearance-based face recognition is in principle limited because a 2D image is a projection of a 3D model. An emerging trend is to directly utilize 3D model in the face matching process [132]. A lot of open issues are available: How to capture and represent the 3D model? How to do matching based on the 3D model?

- *Aging.* Aging is a very important topic in unconstrained face recognition. Often the stored gallery images are taken well before the probe images. For example, passengers hold passports with photos taken when the passport was issued years ago. While one solution is to maintain the gallery images up-to-date, a systematic solution is theoretical modeling of the generic affect of aging. This modeling is very difficult due to the individualized variation. Presented in [136, 138] are some preliminary attempts. So, more research efforts are certainly worthwhile.

- *Expression.* Facial expression analysis and modeling has attracted a lot of attention [45, 62, 63] and some approaches [62] focus on expression recognition, i.e., identifying different modalities of facial expression such as happy, angry, disgust, etc. Face recognition under expression variation has not been fully explored. Clearly expression recognition and face recognition under expression variation are two related topics. Expression recognition and modeling is a crucial component for accurate face recognition under expression variation.

  Further, facial expressions manifest themselves in a temporal dimension. The manner that an individual poses expressions (in natural contexts) captures certain behavioral aspect of the face biometric. Utilizing temporal information embedded in facial expression for face recognition under expression variation is an interesting research topic.

- *Distorted imagery.*

  Images as one main digital media are to be compressed, stored, transmitted and so on. Compression schemes sacrifice image quality for fewer bits to encode the image, storage devices are susceptible to various damages, transmission channels are often noisy. All these results in distorted images. How to perform face recognition accounting for sources of distortions [128] is a very practical research topic that needs to be explored.

- *Fusion with other biometrics* Even the best face recognition system cannot perform a perfect job under unconstrained conditions. Fusion of face biometrics and other biometrics will boost the overall performance because more information is available. Moreover, different biometrics are complementary. For example, acquisition of iris and fingerprint needs participant's cooperation while face and gait can be captured in an noninvasive manner. Face is mostly usable in frontal view while gait is most usable in side view.

- *Face recognition system*

  To build a reliable and robust face recognition system, one has to consider various issues. (i) Computation and storage. How to do the matching in real time? How to represent, manage, and store a large scale face database? (ii) System engineering. Given a limited budget of resources in camera, network, power, etc., how to maximize the performance gain by a smart distributing of these resources? (iii) Security issue. How to store the face database in a secure manner? How to avoid fake face image to break in to the system? How to securely transmit the face image over the network? For this, we should leverage knowledge from multimedia and network security, cryptography, etc.

References

[Books on general topics]

[1] B. Anderson and J. Moore, *Optimal Filtering*. New Jersey: Prentice Hall, Engle-wood Cliffs, 1979.

[2] Y. Bar-Shalom and T. Fortmann, *Tracking and Data Association*. Academic Press, 1988.

[3] G. Casella and R. L. Berger, *Statistical Inference*. Duxbury, 2002.

[4] T.M. Cover and J.A. Thomas, *Elements of Information Theory*. Wiley, 1991.

[5] P. Devijver and J. Kittler, *Pattern Recognition: A Statistical Approach*. Prentice Hall International, 1982.

[6] A. Doucet, N. d. Freitas, and N. Gordon (Eds.), *Sequential Monte Carlo Methods in Practice*. Springer-Verlag, New York, 2001.

[7] R. O. Duda, P. E. Hart, and D. G. Stork, *Pattern Classification*. Wiley-Interscience, 2001.

[8] G. H. Golub and C. F. Van Loan, *Matrix Computations*. The Johns Hopkins University Press, 1996.

[9] T. Hastie, R. Tibshirani, and J. Friedman, *The Elements of Statistical Learning: Data Mining, Inference, and Prediction*. Springer-Verlag, New York, 2001.

[10] B. Horn and M. Brooks (Eds.) *Shape from Shading*. MIT Press, 1989.

[11] P.J. Huber, *Robust statistics*. Wiley, 1981.

[12] I. T. Jolliffe, *Principal Component Analysis*. New York: Springer-Verlag, 2002.

[13] Kullback, *Information Theory and Statistics*. Wiley, New York, 1959.

[14] J.S. Liu, *Monte Carlo Strtegies in Scientific Computing*. Springer, 2001.

[15] K. V. Mardia, J. T. Kent, and J. M. Bibby, *Multivariate Analysis*. Academic Press, 1979.

[16] C. Robert and G. Casella, *Monte Carlo Statistical Methods*. Springer, 1999.

[17] W.J. Rugh, *Linear System Theory*. Pearson Education, 1995.

[18] B. Schölkopf and A. Smola, *Support Vector Learning*. Press, 2002.

[19] J. Shawe-Taylor and N. Cristianini, *Kernel Methods for Pattern Analysis*. Cambridge University Press, 2004.

[20] M.A. Tanner, *Tools for Statistical Inference: Methods for the Exploration of Posterior Distributions and Likelihood Functions*. Springer, 1996.

[21] V. N. Vapnik, *The Nature of Statistical Learning Theory*. Springer-Verlag, New York, ISBN 0-387-94559-8, 1995.

[**Books and review papers on face recognition**]

[22] M.S.Bartlett, *Face Image Analysis by Unsupervised Learning*. Kluwer Academic Publishers, 2001.

[23] R. Chellappa, C. L. Wilson, and S. Sirohey, "Human and machine recognition of faces: A survey," *Proceedings of IEEE*, vol. 83, pp. 705–740, 1995.

[24] S. Gong, S.J. McKenna, *Dynamic Vision: From Images to Face Recognition*. Imperial College Press, 2000.

[25] P.W. Hallinan, G. Gordon, A. Yuille, P. Giblin, and D. Mumford, *Two- and Three-Dimensional Patterns of the Face*. A. K. Peters, Ltd., 1999.

[26] T. Kanade, *Computer Recognition of Human Faces*. Birhauser, Basel, Switzerland, and Stuggart, Germany, 1973.

[27] S.Z. Li, A.K. Jain (Eds.), *Handbook of Face Recognition*. Springer-Verlag, 2004.

[28] H. Wechsler, P.J. Phillips, V. Bruce, F.F. Soulie, and T.S. Huang (Eds.), *Face Recognition: From Theory to Applications*. Springer-Verlag, 1998.

[29] W. Zhao, R. Chellappa, A. Rosenfeld, and J. Phillips, "Face recognition: A literature survey," *ACM Computing Surveys*, vol. 12, 2003.

[**Biometrics**]

[30] Biometric Catalog. http://www.biomtricscatalog.org.

[31] Biometric Consortium. http://www.biometrics.org.

[32] Deparment of Homeland Security (DHS), US-VISIT Program. http://www.dhs.goc/dhspublic/interapp/editorial/editorial_0333.xml.

[33] National Institue of Standards and Technologies (NIST), Biometrics Web Site. http://www.nist.gov/biometrics.

[34] D.M. Blackburn, "Biometrics 101 (version 3.1)" http://www.biometricscatalog.org/biometrics/Introduction.asp, March 2004.

[35] R. Hietmeyer, "Biometric identification promises fast and secure processings of airline passengers," *The Internationl Civil Aviation Organization Journal*, vol. 55, no. 9, pp. 10-11, 2000.

[36] P.J. Phillips, R.M. McCabe, and R. Chellappa, "Biometric image processing and recognition," *Proceedings of European Signal Processing Conference*, 1998.

[Psychophysical and neural aspects]

[37] I. Biederman and P. Kalocsai, "Neural and psychophysical analysis of object and face recognition," In *Face Recognition: From Theory to Applications*, H. Wechsler, P.J. Phillips, V. Bruce, F.F. Soulie, and T.S. Huang (Eds.), Springer-Verlag, 1998.

[38] V. Bruce, *Recognizing Faces*. Lawrence Erlbaum Associates, London, U.K., 1988.

[39] V. Bruce, P.J.B. Hancock, and A.M. Burton, "Human face perception and identification," In *Face Recognition: From Theory to Applications*, H. Wechsler, P.J. Phillips, V. Bruce, F.F. Soulie, and T.S. Huang (Eds.), Springer-Verlag, 1998.

[40] A.J. O'Toole, "Psychological and neural perspectives on human faces recognition," In *Handbook of Face Recognition*, S.Z. Li and A.K. Jain (Eds.), Springer, 2004.

[41] B. Knight and A. Johnston, "The role of movement in face recognition," *Visual Cognition*, vol. 4, pp. 265-274, 1997.

[Face recognition from a single still image]

[42] http://sting.cycollege.ac.cy/~alanitis/fgnetaging/index.htm.

[43] M.S. Barlett, H.M. Ladesand, and T.J. Sejnowski, "Independent component representations for face recognition," *Proceedings of SPIE 3299*, pp. 528-539, 1998.

[44] P. N. Belhumeur, J. P. Hespanha, and D. J. Kriegman, "Eigenfaces vs. fisherfaces: Recognition using class specific linear projection," *IEEE Trans. Pattern Analysis and Machine Intelligence*, vol. 19, pp. 711–720, 1997.

[45] M.J. Black and Y. Yacoob, "Recognizing facial expressions in image sequences using local paramterized models of image motion," *International Journal of Computer Vision*, vol. 25, pp. 23-48, 1997.

[46] T. Cootes, G. Edwards, and C. Taylor, "Active appearance model," *European Conference on Computer Vision*, 1998.

[47] K. Etemad and R. Chellappa, "Discriminant analysis for recognition of human face images," *Journal of Optical Society of America A*, pp. 1724–1733, 1997.

[48] T. Huang, Z. Xiong, and Z. Zhang, "Face recognition applications," *Handbook of Face Recognition*, S. Li and A. K. Jain (Eds.), Springer, 2004.

[49] M.D. Kelly, "Visual identification of people by computer," *Tech. rep. AI-130*, Stanford AI project, Stanform, CA, 1970.

[50] M. Kirby and L. Sirovich, "Application of Karhunen-Loéve procedure of the characterization of human faces," *IEEE Trans. on Pattern Analysis and Machine Intelligence*, vol. 12, pp. 103–108, 1990.

[51] M. Lades, J.C. Vorbruggen, J. Buhmann, J. Lange, C. v. d. Malsburg, R.P. Wurtz, and W. Konen, "Distortion invariant object recognition in the dynamic link architecture," *IEEE Trans. Computers*, vol. 42, no. 3, pp. 300–311, 1993.

[52] A. Lanitis, C.J. Taylor, and T.F. Cootes, "Automatic interpretation and coding of face images using flexible models," *IEEE Trans. Pattern Analysis and Machine Intelligence*, vol. 19, no. 7, pp. 442-455, 1997.

[53] S.H. Lin, S.Y. Kung, and J.J. Lin, "Face recognition/detection by probabilistic decision based neural network," *IEEE Trans. Neural Networks*, vol. 9, pp. 114-132, 1997.

[54] C. Liu and H. Wechsler, "Evolutionary pursuit and its applications to face recognition," *IEEE Trans. Pattern Analysis and Machine Intelligence*, vol. 22, pp. 570-582, 2000.

[55] M.J. Lyons, J. Biudynek, and S. Akamatsu, "Automatic classification of single facial images," *IEEE Trans. Pattern Analysis and Machine Intelligence*, vol. 21, no. 12, pp. 1357-1362, 1999.

[56] B. Moghaddam and A. Pentland, "Probabilistic visual learning for object representation," *IEEE Trans. on Pattern Analysis and Machine Intelligence*, vol. PAMI-19, no. 7, pp. 696–710, 1997.

[57] B. Moghaddam, T. Jebara, and A. Pentland, "Bayesian modeling of facial similarity," *Advances in Neural Information Processing Systems*, vol. 11, pp. 910–916, 1999.

[58] B. Moghaddam, "Principal manifolds and probabilistic subspaces for visual recognition," *IEEE Trans. Pattern Analysis and Machine Intelligence*, vol. 24, pp. 780–788, 2002.

[59] P.J. Phillips, "Support vector machines applied to face recognition," *Advances in Neural Information Processing Systems*, vol. 11, pp. 803-809, 1998.

[60] P.J. Phillips, H. Moon, S. Rizvi, and P.J. Rauss, "The FERET evaluation methodology fro face-recognition algorithms," *IEEE Trans. attern Analysis and Machine Intelligence*, vol. 22, pp. 1090–1104, 2000.

[61] P.J. Phillips, P. Grother, R.J. Micheals, D.M. Blackburn, E. Tabbssi, and M. Bone, "Face recognition vendor test 2002: evaluation report" *NISTIR 6965*, http://www.frvt.org, 2003.

[62] Y. Tian, T. Kanade, and J. Cohn, "Recognizing action units of facial expression analysis," *IEEE Trans. Pattern Analysis and Machine Intelligence*, vol. 23, pp. 1-19, 2001.

[63] Y. Tian, T. Kanade, and J. Cohn, "Recognizing action units of facial expression analysis," In *Handbook of Face Recognition*, S.Z. Li and A.K. Jain (Eds.), Springer, 2004.

[64] M. Turk and A. Pentland, "Eigenfaces for recognition," *Journal of Cognitive Neuroscience*, vol. 3, pp. 72–86, 1991.

[65] M.-H. Yang, "Kernel eigenfaces vs. kernel Fisherfaces: Face recognition using kernel methods," *Proceedings of International Conference on Automatic Face and Gesture Recognition*, 2002.

[66] J. Yang *et al.*, "Two-dimensional PCA: A new approach to appearance-based face representation and recognition," *IEEE Trans. Pattern Analysis and Machine Intelligence*, vol. 26, no. 1, 2004.

[67] W. Zhao, R. Chellappa, and A. Krishnaswamy, "Discriminant analysis of principal components for face recognition," *Proceedings of International Conference on Automatic Face and Gesture Recognition*, pp. 361-341, Nara, Japan, 1998.

[68] J. Li, S. Zhou, and C. Shekhar, "A comparison of subspace analysis for face recognition," *Proceedings of IEEE International Conference on Acoustics, Speech, and Signal Processing*, 2003.

[69] S. Zhou, R. Chellappa, and B. Moghaddam, "Intra-personal kernel space for face recognition," *Proceedings of International Conference on Automatic Face and Gesture Recognition*, Seoul, Korea, May 2004.

[70] S. Zhou and R. Chellappa, "Multiple-exemplar discriminant analysis for face recognition," *Proceedings of International Conference on Pattern Recognition*, Cambridge, UK, August 2004.

[Face recognition across illumination and poses]

[71] J. Atick, P. Griffin, and A. Redlich, "Statistical approach to shape from shading: Reconstrunction of 3-dimensional face surfaces from single 2-dimentional images," *Neural Computation*, vol. 8, pp. 1321–1340, 1996.

[72] V. Blanz and T. Vetter, "Face recognition based on fitting a 3D morphable model," *IEEE Trans. on Pattern Analysis and Machine Intelligence*, vol. 25, pp. 1063–1074, 2003.

[73] T. Cootes, K. Walker, and C. Taylor, "View-based Active appearance models," *Proceedings of International Conference on Automatic Face and Gesture Recognition*, 2000.

[74] T. Dovgard and R. Basri, "Statistical Symmetric Shape from Shading for 3D Structure Recovery of Faces," *Proceedings of European Conference on Computer Vision*, Prague, Czech, May 2004.

[75] A. S. Georghiades, P. N. Belhumeur, and D. J. Kriegman, "From few to many: Illumination cone models for face recognition under variable lighting and pose," *IEEE Trans. Pattern Analysis and Machine Intelligence*, vol. 23, pp. 643 –660, 2001.

[76] R. Gross, I. Matthews, and S. Baker, "Eigen light-fields and face recognition across pose," *Proceedings of Intenational Conference on Automatic Face and Gesture Recognition*, Washington D.C., 2002.

[77] R. Gross, I. Matthews, and S. Baker, "Fisher light-fields for face recognition across pose and illumination," *Proceedings of the German Symposium on Pattern Recognition*, Washington D.C., 2002.

[78] R. Gross, I. Matthews, and S. Baker, "Appearance-based face recognition and light-fields," *IEEE Transactions on Pattern Analysis and Machine Intelligence*, vol. 26, no. 4, pp. 449 - 465, April, 2004.

[79] K. C. Lee, J. Ho, and D. Kriegman, "Nine points of light: acquiring subspaces for face recognition under variable lighting," *IEEE Conference on Computer Vision and Pattern Recognition*, pp. 519–526, December 2001.

[80] N. Ramanathan, A. Roy-Chowdhury and R. Chellappa, "Facial Similarity across Age, Disguise, Illumination and Pose," *IEEE International Conference on Image Processing*, Oct 2004.

[81] A. Pentland, B. Moghaddam, and T. Starner, "View-based and modular eigenspaces for face recognition," *Proceedings of IEEE Computer Society Conference on Computer Vision and Pattern Recognition*, Seattle, WA, 1994.

[82] S. Romdhani, V. Blanz, and T. Vetter, "Face identification by fitting a 3D morphable model using linear shape and texture errror functions," *Proc. European Conference on Computer Vision*, 2002.

[83] S. Romdhani and T. Vetter, "Efficient, robust and accurate fitting of a 3D morphable model," *Proceedings of IEEE Internationl Conference on Computer Vision*, pp. 59-66, Nice, France, 2003.

[84] A. Shashua and T. R. Raviv, "The quotient image: Class based re-rendering and recognition with varying illuminations," *IEEE Trans. Pattern Analysis and Machine Intelligence*, vol. 23, pp. 129–139, 2001.

[85] T. Sim, S. Baker, and M. Bast, "The CMU pose, illuminatin, and expression (PIE) database," *Proceedings of International Conference on Automatic Face and Gesture Recognition*, pp. 53–58, Washington D.C., 2002.

[86] B.V.H. Saxberg, "A modern differential geometric approach to shape from shading," *MIT Artificial Intelligence Laboratory, Technical Report 1117*, 1989.

[87] T. Vetter and T. Poggio, "Linear object classes and image synthesis from a single example image," *IEEE Transactions on Pattern Analysis and Machine Intelligence*, vol. 11, pp. 733–742, 1997.

[88] M.A.O. Vasilescu and D. Terzopoulos, "Multilinear analysis of image ensembles: Tensorfaces," *European Conference on Computer Vision*, vol. 2350, pp. 447-460, Copenhagen, Denmark, May 2002.

[89] M. Vasilescu and D. Terzopoulos, "Multilinear image analysis for facial recognition," *Proceedings of International Conference on Pattern Recognition*, Quebec City, Canada, 2002.

[90] L. Zhang and D. Samaras, "Face recognition under variable lighting using harmonic image exemplars," *Proceedings of IEEE Computer Society Conference on Computer Vision and Pattern Recognition*, pp. 19–25, Madison, WA, 2003.

[91] W. Zhao and R. Chellappa, "Illumination-insensitive face recognition using symmetric shape-from-shading," *Proceedings of IEEE Computer Society Conference on Computer Vision and Pattern Recognition*, pp. 286-293, 2000.

[92] W. Zhao and R. Chellappa, "SFS based view synthesis for robust face recognition," *Proceedings of International Conference on Automatic Face and Gesture Recognition*, 2000.

[93] W. Zhao and R. Chellappa, "Symmetric shape-from-shading using self-ratio images," *International Journal of Computer Vision*, vol. 45, pp. 55-75, 2001.

[94] S. Zhou and R. Chellappa, "Rank constrained recognition under unknown illuminations," *IEEE Intl. Workshop on Analysis and Modeling of Faces and Gestures*, Nice, France, 2003.

[95] S. Zhou, R. Chellappa, and D. Jacobs, "Characterization of human faces under illumination variations using rank, integrability, and symmetry constraints," *European Conference on Computer Vision*, Prague, Czech, May 2004.

[96] S. Zhou and R. Chellappa, "Illuminating light field: Image-based face recognition across illuminations and poses," *Proceedings of International Conference on Automatic Face and Gesture Recognition*, Seoul, Korea, May 2004.

[97] S. Zhou and R. Chellappa, "Image-based face recognition under illumination and pose variantons," *Journal of the Optical Society of America*, vol. 22, pp. 217-229, 2005.

[Face recognition from multiple stills, videos, or 3D models]

[98] O. Arandjelović and R. Cipolla, "Face recognition from face motion manifolds using robust kernel resistor-average distance," *IEEE Workshop on Face Processing in Video*, Washington D.C., USA, 2004.

[99] O. Arandjelović, G. Shakhnarovich, J. Fisher, R. Cipolla, and T. Darrell, "Face Recognition with Image Sets using Manifold Density Divergence," *Proc. IEEE Conference on Computer Vision and Pattern Recognition*, vol. 1, pages 581-588, San Diego, USA, June 2005.

[100] G. Aggarwal, A. Roy-Chowdhury, and R. Chellappa, "A system identification approach for video-based face recognition," *Proceedings of International Conference on Pattern Recognition*, Cambridge, UK, August 2004.

[101] C. Beumie and M.P. Acheroy, "Automatic face authentication from 3D surface," *Proc. of British Machine Vision Conference*, pp. 449-458, 1998.

[102] A.M. Bronstein, M.M. Bronstein and R. Kimmel, "Expression-invariant 3D face recognition," *Proc. Audio and Video-based Biometric Personal Authentication*, pp. 62-69, 2003.

[103] T. Choudhury, B. Clarkson, T. Jebara, and A. Pentland, "Multimodal person recognition using unconstrained audio and video," *Proceedings of International Conference on Audio- and Video-Based Person Authentication*, pp. 176–181, Washington D.C., 1999.

[104] A. Fitzgibbon and A. Zisserman, "Joint manifold distance: a new approach to appearance based clustering," *Proceedings of IEEE Conference on Computer Vision and Pattern Recognition*, Madison, WI, 2003.

[105] R. Gross and J. Shi, "The CMU Motion of Body (MoBo) Database," *CMU-RI-TR-01-18*, 2001.

[106] H. Gupta, *Contour Based 3D Face Modeling From Monocular Video*. Master Thesis, University of Maryland, College Park, MD, 2003.

[107] A. Howell and H. Buxton, "Face recognition using radial basis function neural networks," *Proceedings of British Machine Vision Conference*, pp. 455–464, 1996.

[108] T. Jebara and A. Pentland, "Parameterized structure from motion for 3D adaptive feedback tracking of faces," *Proceedings of IEEE Computer Society Conference on Computer Vision and Pattern Recognition*, pp. 144 –150, Puerto Rico, 1997.

[109] K. Lee, M. Yang, and D. Kriegman, "Video-based face recognition using probabilistic appearance manifolds," *Proceedings of IEEE Computer Society Conference on Computer Vision and Pattern Recognition*, Madison, WI, 2003.

[110] K. Lee and D. Kriegman, "Online Learning of Probabilistic Appearance Manifolds for Video-based Recognition and Tracking," *IEEE Conf. on Computer Vision and Pattern Recognition*, San Diego, USA, June 2005.

[111] B. Li and R. Chellappa, "Face verification through tracking facial features," *Journal of Optical Society of America A*, vol. 18, no. 12, pp. 2969–2981, 2001.

[112] B. Li and R. Chellappa, "A generic approach to simultaneous tracking and verification in video," *IEEE Transaction on Image Processing*, vol. 11, no. 5, pp. 530–554, 2002.

[113] Y. Li, S. Gong, and H. Liddell, "Modelling faces dynamically across views and over time," *Proceedings of International Conference on Computer Vision*, pp. 554 –559, Hawaii, 2001.

[114] Y. Li, S. Gong, and H. Liddell, "Constructing facial identity surfaces in a nonlinear discriminant space," *Proceedings of IEEE Computer Society Conference on Computer Vision and Pattern Recognition*, Hawaii, 2001.

[115] X. Liu and T. Chen, "Video-based face recognition using adaptive hidden markov models," *Proceedings of IEEE Conference on Computer Vision and Pattern Recognition*, Madison, WI, 2003.

[116] M. Mavridis *et al.*, "The HISCORE face recognition applicaiton: Affordable desktop face recognition based on a novel 3D camera," *Proc. of Intl. Conference on Augmented Virtual Environments and 3D Imaging*, 2001.

[117] S. McKenna and S. Gong, "Non-intrusive person authentication for access control by visual tracking and face recognition," *Proceedings of International Conference on Audio- and Video-based Biometric Person Authentication*, pp. 177–183, Crans-Montana, Switzerland, 1997.

[118] G. Shakhnarovich, J. Fisher, and T. Darrell, "Face recognition from long-term observations," *Proc. European Conference on Computer Vision*, Copenhagen, Denmark, 2002.

[119] J. Steffens, E. Elagin, and H. Neven, "Personspotter - fast and robust system for human detection, tracking, and recognition," *Proceedings of Internationl Conference on Automatic Face and Gesture Recognition*, pp. 516–521, Nara, Japan, 1998.

[120] H. Wechsler, V. Kakkad, J. Huang, S. Gutta, and V. Chen, "Automatic video-based person authentication using the RBF network," *Proceedings of International Conference on Audio- and Video-based Biometric Person Authentication*, pp. 85–92, Crans-Montana, Switzerland, 1997.

[121] O. Yamaguchi, K. Fukui and K. Maeda, "Face recognition using temporal image sequence," *Proceedings of International Conference on Automatic Face and Gesture Recognition*, Nara, Japan, 1998.

[122] S. Zhou, V. Krueger, and R. Chellappa, "Face recgnition from video: A condensation approach," *Proceedings of International Conference on Automatic Face and Gesture Recognition*, Washington, D.C., USA, May 2002.

[123] S. Zhou and R. Chellappa, "Probabilistic human Recognition from video," *European Conference on Computer Vision*, vol. 3, pp. 681-697, Copenhagen, Denmark, May 2002.

[124] V. Krueger and S. Zhou, "Exemplar-based face recgnition from video," *European Conference on Computer Vision*, Copenhagen, Denmark, 2002.

[125] R. Chellappa, S. Zhou, and B. Li, "Bayesian methods for probabilistic human recgnition from video," *Proceedings of IEEE International Conference on Acoustic, Speech, and Signal Processing*, Orlando, Florida, USA, 2002.

[126] S. Zhou and R. Chellappa, "A robust algorithm for probabilistic human recognition from video," *Proceedings of International Conference on Pattern Recognition*, Quebec City, Canada, 2002.

[127] R. Chellappa, V. Krueger, and S. Zhou, "Probabilistic recognition of human faces from video," *Proceedings of IEEE International Conference on Image Processing*, Rochester, NY, 2002.

[128] S. Zhou and R. Chellappa, "Simultaneous tracking and recognition of human faces from video," *Proceedings of IEEE International Conference on Acoustic, Speech, and Signal Processing*, 2003.

[129] S. Zhou, V. Krueger, and R. Chellappa, "Probabilistic recognition of human faces from video," *Computer Vision and Image Understanding*, vol. 91, pp. 214–245, 2003.

[130] J. Li and S. Zhou, "Probabilistic face recognition with compressed imagery," *Proceedings of IEEE International Conference on Acoustics, Speech, and Signal Processing*, Montreal, Canada, May 2004.

[131] S. Zhou and R. Chellappa, "Probabilistic identity characterization for face recognition," *Proceedings of IEEE Computer Society Conference on Computer Vision and Pattern Recognition*, Washington D.C., USA, June 2004.

[132] S. Zhou, "Face recognition using more than one image: What is more?" *Sinobiometrics*, 2004.

[133] R. Chellappa and S. Zhou, "Face tracking and recognition from video," *Handbook of Face Recognition*, S. Li and A. K. Jain (Eds.), Springer-Verlag, 2005.

[134] S. Zhou and R. Chellappa, "Face recognition from still images and videos," *Handbook of Image and Video Processing*, A. Bovik (Ed.), Academic Press, 2005.

[Facial aging]

[135] G. Givens, J.R. Beveridge, B.A. Draper, P. Grother, and P.J. Phillips, "How Features of the Human Face Affect Recognition: a Statitical Comparison of Three Face Recognition Algorithms," *Proceedings of IEEE Computer Society Conference on Computer Vision and Pattern Recognition*, vol. 2, pp. 381-388, Washington D.C., USA, June 2004.

[136] A. Lanitis, C.J. Taylor, and T.F. Cootes, "Toward automatic simulation of aging affects on face images," *IEEE Trans. Pattern Analysis and Machine Intelligence*, vol. 24, pp. 442-455, 2002.

[137] A. Lanitis, C. Draganova, and C. Christodoulou, "Comparing Different Classifiers for Automatic Age Estimation," *IEEE Transactions on Systems, Man and Cybernetics - Part B*, vol. 34, no. 1, pp. 621-628, February, 2004.

[138] N. Ramanathan and R. Chellappa, "Face Verification across Age Progression," *Proceedings of IEEE Computer Society Conference on Computer Vision and Pattern Recognition*, San Diego, USA, June 2005.

[139] A.J. O'Toole, T. Vetter, H. Volz, and M.E. Salter, "Three-Dimensional caricatures of human heads: distinctiveness and the perception of facial age," *Perception*, vol. 26, pp. 719-732, 1997.

[140] J.B. Pittenger and R.E. Shaw, "Aging Faces as Viscal-Elastic Events : Implications for a Theory of Nonrigid Shape Perception," *Journal of Experimental Psychology : Human Perception and Performance*, vol. 1, no. 4, pp. 374-382, 1975.

[141] B.Tiddeman, M. Burt, and D. Perret, "Prototyping and Transforming Facial Texture for Perception Research," *Computer Graphics and Applications, IEEE*, vol. 21, no. 5, pp. 42-50, July-August, 2001.

[142] Y. Wu, N.M. Thalmann, and D. Thalmann, "A Dynamic wrinkle model in facial animation and skin aging," *Journal of Visualization and Computer Animation*, vol. 6, pp. 195-205, 1995.

[Lighting, illumination, and shape from shading]

[143] R. Basri and D. Jacobs, "Photometric stereo with general, unknown lighting," *Proceedings of IEEE Conference on Computer Vision and Pattern Recognition*, vol. II, pp. 374–381, Hawaii, 2001.

[144] R. Basri and D. Jacobs, "Lambertian reflectance and linear subspaces," *IEEE Transactions on Pattern Analysis and Machine Intelligence*, vol. 25, pp. 218–233, 2003.

[145] P.N. Belhumeur and D.J. Kriegman, "What is the set of images of an object under all possible illumination conditions?" *International Journal of Computer Vision*, vol. 28, pp. 245–260, 1998.

[146] P. Belhumeur, D. Kriegman, and A. Yuille, "The bas-relief ambiguity," *International Journal of Computer Vision*, vol. 35, pp. 33–44, 1999.

[147] M. Bichsel and A. Pentland, "A Simple Algorithm for Shape from Shading," *Proceedings of IEEE Conference on Computer Vision and Pattern Recognition*, pp. 459-465, 1992.

[148] P. Dupuis and J. Oliensis, "Direct Method for Reconstructing Shape from Shading," *Proc. Conference on Computer Vision and Pattern Recognition*, pp. 453-458, 1992.

[149] R. T. Frankot and R. Chellappa, "A method for enforcing integrability in shape from shaging problem," *IEEE Trans. Pattern Analysis and Machine Intelligence*, vol. 10, pp. 439–451, 1988.

[150] H. Hayakawa, "Photometric stereo under a light source with arbitrary motion," *Journal of Optical Society of America, A*, vol. 11, 1994.

[151] B.K.P. Horn, *Shape from Shading: A Method for Obtaining the Shape of a Smooth Opaque Object from One View*. PhD Thesis, Massachusetts Institute of Technology, 1970.

[152] B.K.P. Horn, "Height and Gradient from Shading," *Int. Journal of Computer Vision*, vol. 5, pp. 37-75, 1990.

[153] K. Ikeuchi and B.K.P. Horn, "Numerical Shape from Shading and Occluding Boundaries," *Artificial Intelligence*, vol. 17, pp. 141-184, 1981.

[154] D.W. Jacobs, P.N. Belhumeur, and R. Basri, "Comparing Images under Variable Illumination," *Proc. Conference on Computer Vision and Pattern Recognition*, pp. 610-617, 1998.

[155] C.H. Lee and A. Rosenfeld, "Improved Methods of Estimating Shape from Shading Using the Light Source Coordinate System," *Shape from Shading*. Eds. B.K.P. Horn and M.J. Brooks, MIT Press: Cambridge, MA, pp. 323-569, 1989.

[156] S.K. Nayar, K. Ikeuchi, and T. Kanade, "Surface Reflection: Physical and Geometrical Perspectives," *IEEE Trans. on Pattern Analysis and Machine Intelligence*, vol. 13, pp. 611-634, 1991.

[157] J. Oliensis, "Uniqueness in Shape from Shading," *Int. Journal of Computer Vision*, vol. 6, pp. 75-104, 1991.

[158] R. Onn and A. Bruckstein, "Integrability Disambiguates Surface Recovery in Two-Image Photometric Stereo," *Int. Journal of Computer Vision*, vol. 5, pp. 105-113, 1990.

[159] A.P. Pentland, "Finding the Illumination Directions," *Journal of the Optical Society of America A*, vol. 72, pp. 448-455, 1982.

[160] R. Ramamoothi and P. Hanrahan, "On the relationship between radiance and irradiance: Determining the illumination from images of a convex lambertian object," *Journal of the Optical Society of America (JOSA A)*, vol. 18, pp. 2448–2459, 2001.

[161] A. Shashua, "On photometric issues in 3d visual recognition from a single 2D image," *International Journal of Computer Vision*, vol. 21, pp. 99–122, 1997.

[162] I. Shimshoni, Y. Moses, and M. Lindenbaum, "Shape reconstruction of 3D bilaterally symmetric surfaces," *International Journal of Computer Vision*, vol. 39, pp. 97–100, 2000.

[163] P.S. Tsai and M. Shah, "Shape from shading using linear approximation," *Journal of Image and Vision Computing*, vol. 12, pp. 487-498, 1994.

[164] G.Q. Wei and G. Hirzinger, "Parametric shape-from-shading by radial basis functions," *IEEE Transactions on Pattern Analysis and Machine Intelligence*, vol. 19, pp. 353-365, 1997.

[165] L.B. Wolff and E. Angelopoulou, "3-D stereo using photometric ratios," *Proc. European Conference on Computer Vision*, pp. 247-258, 1994.

[166] R. Woodham, "Photometric method for determining surface orientation from multiple images," *Optical Engineering*, vol. 19, pp. 139-144, 1980.

[167] Z. Yue and R. Chellappa, "Pose-normailzed view synthesis of a symmetric object using a single image," *Proceedings of Asian Conference on Computer Vision*, 2004.

[168] A.L. Yuille, D. Snow, R. Epstein, and P.N. Belhumeur, "Determining generative models of objects under varying illumination: Shape and albedo from multiple images using svd and integrability," *Internationl Journal of Computer Vision*, vol. 35, pp. 203–222, 1999.

[169] R. Zhang, P.S. Tsai, J.E. Cryer, and M. Shah, "Shape from Shading: a survey", *IEEE Transactions on Pattern Analysis and Machine Intelligence*, vol. 21, pp. 690-706, 1999.

[170] Q. F. Zheng and R. Chellappa, "Estimation of illuminant direction, albedo and shape from shading," *IEEE Transactions on Pattern Analysis and Machine Intelligence*, vol. 13, pp. 680–702, 1991.

[Tracking, detection, and registration]

[171] A. Azarbayejani and A. Pentland, "Recursive estimation of motion, structure, and focal length," *IEEE Trans. Pattern Analysis and Machine Intelligence*, vol. 17, pp. 562–575, 1995.

[172] A. Bergen, P. Anadan, K. Hanna, and R. Hingorani, "Hierarchical model-based motion estimation," *European Conference on Computer Vision*, pp. 237–252, Stockholms, Sweden, 1992.

[173] M.J. Black and A.D. Jepson, "Eigentracking: Robust matching and tracking of articulated objects using a view-based representation," *European Conference on Computer Vision*, vol. 1, pp. 329–342, Cambridge, UK, 1996.

[174] M.J. Black and D.J. Fleet, "Probabilistic detection and tracking of motion discontinuities," *Proceedings of International Conference on Computer Vision*, vol. 2, pp. 551–558, Greece, 1999.

[175] M.E. Brand, "Morphable 3D Models from Video," *Proceedings of IEEE Conference on Computer Vision and Pattern Recognition*, Hawaii, 2001.

[176] C. Bregler, A. Hertzmann, and H. Biermann, "Recovering nonrigid 3D shape fomr image streams," *Proceedings of IEEE Conference on Computer Vision and Pattern Recognition*, Hilton Head, SC, 2000.

[177] T. J. Broida, S. Chandra, and R. Chellappa, "Recursive techniques for estimation of 3-d translation and rotation parameters from noisy image sequences," *IEEE Trans. Aerospace and Electronic Systems*, vol. AES-26, pp. 639–656, 1990.

[178] D. Comaniciu, V. Ramesh, and P. Meer, "Real-time tracking of non-rigid objects using mean shift," *Proceedings of IEEE Computer Society Conference on Computer Vision and Pattern Recognition*, vol. 2, pp. 142–149, Hilton Head, SC, 2000.

[179] N.J. Gordon, D.J. Salmond, and A.F.M. Smith, "Novel approach to nonlinear/non-gaussian bayesian state estimation," *IEE Proceedings on Radar and Signal Processing*, vol. 140, pp. 107–113, 1993.

[180] G. D. Hager and P. N. Belhumeur, "Efficient region tracking with parametric models of geometry and illumination," *IEEE Trans. on Pattern Analysis and Machine Intelligence*, vol. 20, pp. 1025–1039, 1998.

[181] M. Irani, "Multi-frame optical flow estimation using subspace constraints," *Proceedings of International Conference on Computer Vision*, pp. 626-633, Greece, 1999.

[182] M. Irani and P. Anandan, "Factorization with Uncertainty," *European Conference on Computer Vision*, pp. 539-553, Dublin, Ireland, 2000.

[183] M. Isard and A. Blake, "Contour tracking by stochastic propagation of conditional density," *European Conference on Computer Vision*, pp. 343–356, Cambridge, UK, 1996.

[184] M. Isard and A. Blake, "ICONDENSATION: Unifying low-level and high-level tracking in a stochastic framework," *Euporean Conference on Computer Vision*, vol. 1, pp. 767–781, Freiburg, Germany, 1998.

[185] A. D. Jepson, D. J. Fleet, and T. El-Maraghi, "Robust online appearance model for visual tracking," *Proceedings of IEEE Computer Society Conference on Computer Vision and Pattern Recognition*, vol. 1, pp. 415–422, Hawaii, 2001.

[186] F. Jurie and M. Dhome, "A simple and efficient template matching algorithm," *Proceedings of International Conference on Computer Vision*, vol. 2, pp. 544–549, Vancouver, BC, 2001.

[187] Q. Ke and T. Kanade, "A subspace approach to layer extraction," *Proceedings of IEEE Conference on Computer Vision and Pattern Recognition*, Hawaii, 2001.

[188] B. Lucas and T. Kanade, "An iterative image registration technique with an application to stereo vision," *International Joint Conference on Artifical Intelligence*, 1981.

[189] B. North, A. Blake, M. Isard, and J. Rittscher, "Learning and classification of complex dynamics," *IEEE Trans. Pattern Analysis and Machine Intelligence*, vol. 22, pp. 1016–1034, 2000.

[190] G. Qian and R. Chellappa, "Structure from motion using sequential monte carlo methods," *Proceedings of International Conference on Computer Vision*, pp. 614 –621, Vancouver, BC, 2001.

[191] C. Rasmussen and G. Hager, "Probabilistic data association methods for tracking complex visual objects," *IEEE Transactions on Pattern Analysis and Machine Intelligence*, vol. 23, no. 6, pp. 560–576, 2001.

[192] H. Sidenbladh, M. J. Black, and D. J. Fleet, "Stochastic tracking of 3d human figures using 2d image motion," *European Conference on Computer Vision*, vol. 2, pp. 702–718, Copenhagen, Denmark, 2002.

[193] J. Sullivan and J. Rittscher, "Guiding random particle by deterministic search," *Proceedings of International Conference on Computer Vision*, vol. 1, pp. 323 –330, Vancouver, BC, 2001.

[194] C. Tomasi and T. Kanade, "Shape and motion from image streams under orthography: a factorization method," *International Journal of Computer Vision*, vol. 9, no. 2, pp. 137–154, 1992.

[195] K. Toyama and A. Blake, "Probabilistic tracking in a metric space," *Proceedings of International Conference on Computer Vision*, pp. 50–59, Vancouver, BC, 2001.

[196] J. Vermaak, P. Peraz, M. Gangnet, and A. Blake, "Towards improved obsevation models for visual tracking: selective adaption," *European Conference on Computer Vision*, pp. 645–660, Copenhagen, Denmark, 2002.

[197] P. Voila and M. Jones, "Robust real-time object detection," *Second Intl. Workshop on Stat. and Comp. Theories of Vision*, Vancouver, BC, 2001.

[198] Y. Wu and T. S. Huang, "A co-inference approach to robust visual tracking," *Proceedings of International Confererence on Computer Vision*, vol. 2, pp. 26–33, Vancouver, BC, 2001.

[199] C. Yang, R. Duraiswami, A. Elgammal, and L. Davis, "Real-time kernel-based tracking in joint feature-spatial spaces," *Tech. Report CS-TR-4567, Univ. of Maryland*, 2004.

[200] S. Zhou, R. Chellappa, and B. Moghaddam, "Adaptive visual tracking and recognition using particle filters," *Proceedings of IEEE International Conference on Multimedia & Expo*, Baltimore, USA, 2003.

[201] S. Zhou, R. Chellappa, and B. Moghaddam, "Appearance tracking using adaptive models in a particle filter," *Proceedings of Asian Conference on Computer Vision*, Korea, January 2004.

[202] J. Shao, S. Zhou, and R. Chellappa, "Appearance-based visual tracking and recognition with trilinear tensor," *Proceedings of IEEE International Conference on Acoustics, Speech, and Signal Processing*, Montreal, Canada, May 2004.

[203] Z. Yue, S. Zhou, and R. Chellappa, "Robust two-camera visual tracking with homography," *Proceedings of IEEE International Conference on Acoustics, Speech, and Signal Processing*, Montreal, Canada, May 2004.

[204] J. Shao, S. Zhou, and Q. Zheng, "Robust appearance-based tracking of moving object from moving platform," *Proceedings of International Conference on Pattern Recognition*, Cambridge, UK, August 2004.

[205] J. Shao, S. Zhou, and R. Chellappa, "Simultaneous background and foreground modeling for tracking in surveillance video," *Proceedings of IEEE International Conference on Image Processing*, Singapore, October 2004.

[206] S. Zhou, R. Chellappa, and B. Moghaddam, "Visual tracking and recognition using appearance-adaptive models in particle filters," *IEEE Transactions on Image Processing*, vol. 11, pp. 1434-1456, November 2004.

[Others in computer vision and graphics]

[207] A. Agarwal and B. Triggs, "3D human pose from silhouette by revelance vector regression," *Proceedings of IEEE Computer Society Conference on Computer Vision and Pattern Recognition*, 2004.

[208] M. J. Black and A. D. Jepson, "A probabilistic framework for matching temporal trajectories," *Proceedings of International Conference on Computer Vision*, pp. 176–181, Greece, 1999.

[209] M. Bertero, T. Poggio, and V. Torre, "Ill-posed Problems in Early Vision," *MIT Artificial Intelligence Laboratory, Technical Report 924*, 1987.

[210] R. Bolle and D. Cooper, "On optimally combining pieces of information with application to estimating 3-d complex-object position from range data," *IEEE Trans. on Pattern Analysis and Machine Intelligence*, vol. 8, pp. 619–638, 1986.

[211] A.R. Bruss, "The Eikonal Equation: Some Results Applicable to Computer Vision," *Journal of Mathmetical Physics*, vol. 23, pp. 890-896, 1982.

[212] T.F. Cootes, G.J. Edwards, and C.J. Taylor, "Active appearance models," *IEEE Trans. on Pattern Analysis and Machine Intelligence*, vol. 23, no. 6, pp. 681-685, 2001.

[213] D. Forsyth, "Shape from texture and integrability," *Proc. International Conference on Computer Vision*, pp. 447–453, Vancouver, BC, 2001.

[214] W. T. Freeman and J. B. Tenenbaum, "Learning bilinear models for two-factor problems in vision," *Proceedings of IEEE Conference on Computer Vision and Pattern Recognition*, Puerto Rico, 1997.

[215] P. Fua, "Regularized bundle adjustment to model heads from image sequences without calibrated data," *Internationl Journal of Computer Vision*, vol. 38, pp. 153-157, 2000.

[216] S.J. Gortler, R. Grzeszczuk, R. Szeliski, and M. Cohen, "The lumigraph," *Proceedings of SIGGRAPH*, pp. 43-54, New Orleans, LA, USA, 1996.

[217] D. Jacobs, "Linear fitting with missing data for structure-from-motion," *Computer Vision and Image Understanding*, vol. 82, pp. 57–81, 2001.

[218] A. Laurentini, "The visual hull concept for silhouette-based image understanding," *IEEE Trans. Pattern Analysis and Machine Intelligences*, vol. 16, no. 2, pp. 150-162, 1994.

[219] M. Levoy and P. Hanrahan, "Light field rendering," *Proceedings of ACM SIGGRAPH*, New Orleans, LA, USA, 1996.

[220] J. Liu, J. Mundy, and A. Zisserman, "Grouping and Structure Recovery for Images of Objects with Finite Rotational Symmetry," Proceedings of the Asian Conference on Computer Vision, 1995.

[221] W. Matusik, C. Buehler, R. Raskar, S. Gortler, and L. McMillan, "Image-based visual hulls," *Proceedings of SIGGRAPH*, pp. 369 - 374, New Orleans, LA, USA, 2000.

[222] K. Okada, D. Comaniciu, and A. Krishanan, "Scale selection for anisotropic scale-space: Application for volumetric tumor characterization," *Proceedings of IEEE Computer Society Conference on Computer Vision and Pattern Recognition*, vol. 1, pp. 594-601, Washington D.C., 2004.

[223] C. Poelman and T. Kanade, "A paraperpective factorization method for shape and motion recovery," *IEEE Trans. Pattern Analysis and Machine Intelligence*, vol. 19, no. 3, pp. 206-218, 1997.

[224] A. Roy Chowdhury and R. Chellappa, "Face reconstruction from video using uncertainty analysis and a generic model," *Computer Vision and Image Understanding*, vol. 91, pp. 188-213, 2003.

[225] X.S. Zhou *et al.*, "A unified framework for uncertainty propagation in automatic shape tracking," *Proceedings of IEEE Computer Society Conference on Computer Vision and Pattern Recognition*, Washington D.C., 2004

[226] Y. Shan, Z. Liu, and Z. Zhang "Model-based bundle adjustment with applicaiton to face modeling," *Proceedings of Internationl Conference on Computer Vision*, pp. 645–651, Vancouver, BC, 2001.

[227] S. Wang, W. Zhu, and Z. Liang, "Shape deformation: SVM regression and application to medical image segmentation," *Proceedings of International Conference on Computer Vision*, 2001.

[228] J. Xiao, J. Chai, and T. Kanade, "A closed-form solution to non-rigid shape and motion recovery," *European Conference on Computer Vision*, 2004.

[229] J. Xiao, S. Baker, I. Matthews, and T. Kanade, "Real-time combined 2D+3D active appearance models," *IEEE Computer Society Conference on Computer Vision and Pattern Recognition*, Washington, DC, 2004.

[Statistical analysis and computing]

[230] B. Adhikara and D. Joshi, "Distance discrimination et resume exhaustif," *Publs. Inst. Statis.*, vol. 5, pp. 57–74, 1956.

[231] X. Boyen and D. Koller, "Tractable inference for complex stochastic processes," *Proceedings of the 14th Annual Conference on Uncertainty in AI (UAI)*, pp. 33 – 42, Madison, Wisconsin, 1998.

[232] M. Brand, "Incremental singular value decomposition of uncertain data with missing values," *European Conference on Computer Vision*, pp. 707–720, Copenhagen, Denmark, 2002.

[233] A. Bhattacharyya, "On a measure of divergence between two statistical populations defined by their probability distributions," *Bull. Calcutta Math. Soc.*, vol. 35, pp. 99–109, 1943.

[234] H. Chernoff, "A measure of asymptotic efficiency of tests for a hypothesis based on a sum of observations," *Annals of Math. Stat.*, vol. 23, pp. 493–507, 1952.

[235] H. Copas, "Regression, prediction, and shrinkage," *J. R. Statist. Soc. B*, vol. 45, pp.311-354, 1983.

[236] A. P. Dempster, N. M. Laird, and D. B. Rubin, "Maximum likelihood from incomplete data via the em algorithm." *J. Roy. Statist. Soc. B*, vol. 39, 1977.

[237] A. Doucet, S. J. Godsill, and C. Andrieu, "On sequential monte carlo sampling methods for bayesian filtering," *Statistics and Computing*, vol. 10, no. 3, pp. 197–209, 2000.

[238] N. Duffy and D. Helmbold, "Boosting methods for regression," *Machine Learning*, vol. 47, pp. 153-200, 2002.

[239] D. Fox, "KLD-sampling: Adaptive particle filters and mobile robot localization," *Neural Information Processing Systems (NIPS)*, 2001.

[240] Y. Freund and R. Schapire, "A decision-theoretic generalization of on-line learning and an application to boosting," *J. of Computer and System Sciences*, vol. 55, no. 1, pp. 119-139, 1997.

[241] J. Friedman, T. Hastie, and R. Tibshirani, "Additive logistive regression: A statistical view of boosting," *The Annals of Statistics*, vol. 28, no. 2, pp. 337-374, 2000.

[242] J. Friedman, "Greedy function approxiamtion: A gradient boosting machine," *The Annals of Statistics*, vol. 28, no. 2, 2001.

[243] A. Hyvarinen, "Survey on Independent Component Analysis," *Neural Computing Surveys*, vol. 2, pp. 94-128, 1999.

[244] T. Kailath, "The divergance and Bhattacharyya distance measures in signal selection," *IEEE Trans. on Comm. Tech.*, vol. COM-15, pp. 52–60, 1967.

[245] G. Kitagawa, "Monte carlo filter and smoother for non-gaussian nonlinear state space models," *J. Computational and Graphical Statistics*, vol. 5, pp. 1–25, 1996.

[246] R. Kondor and T. Jebara,"A Kernel Between Sets of Vectors," *Proc. of International Conference on Machine Learning, ICML*, 2003.

[247] T. Lissack and K. Fu, "Error estimation in pattern recognition via L-distance between posterior density functions," *IEEE Trans. Information Theory*, vol. 22, pp. 34–45, 1976.

[248] J. S. Liu and R. Chen, "Sequential monte carlo for dynamic systems," *Journal of the American Statistical Association*, vol. 93, pp. 1031–1041, 1998.

[249] P. Mahalanobis, "On the generalized distance in statistics," *Proc. National Inst. Sci. (India)*, vol. 12, pp. 49–55, 1936.

[250] K. Matusita, "Decision rules based on the distance for problems of fit, two samples and estimation," *Ann. Math. Stat.*, vol. 26, pp. 631–640, 1955.

[251] S. Roweis and L. Saul, "Nonlinear dimensionality reduction by locally linear embedding," *Science*, vol. 290, no. 5500, pp. 2323–2326, Dececember 2000.

[252] E. Patrick and F. Fisher, "Nonparametric feature selection," *IEEE Trans. Information Theory*, vol. 15, pp. 577–584, 1969.

[253] P. Penev and J. Atick, "Local feature analysis: A general statistical theory for object representation," *Networks: Computations in Neural Systems*, vol. 7, pp. 477-500, 1996.

[254] R. Schapire, Y. Freund, P. Bartlett, and W.S. Lee, "Boosting the margin: A new explanation for the effectiveness of voting methods," *The Annals of Statistics*, vol. 26, pp. 1651-1686, 1998.

[255] H. Shum, K. Ikeuchi, and R. Reddy, "Principal component analysis with missing data and its applications to polyhedral object modeling," *IEEE Trans. Pattern Analysis and Machine Intelligence*, vol. 17, pp. 854–867, 1995.

[256] J.B. Tenenbaum, V. de Silva, and J.C. Langford, "A Global Geometric Framework for Nonlinear Dimensionality Reduction," *Science*, vol. 290, no. 5500, pp. 2319-2323, December 2000.

[257] M. E. Tipping and C. M. Bishop, "Mixtures of probabilistic principal component analysers," *Neural Computation*, vol. 11, no. 2, pp. 443–482, 1999.

[258] M. E. Tipping and C. M. Bishop, "Probabilistic principal component analysis," *Journal of the Royal Statistical Society, Series B*, vol. 61, pp. 611–622, 1999.

[259] T. Wiberg, "Computation of principal components when data are missing," *Proc. Second Symp. Computational Statistics*, pp. 229–236, 1976.

[260] S. Zhou, B. Georgescu, X.S. Zhou, and D. Cominiciu, "Image based regression using boosting method," *Proceedings of International Conference on Compuer Vision*, Beijing, China 2005.

[Machine learning and kernel methods]

[261] F. Bach and M. I. Jordan, "Kernel independent component analysis," *Journal of Machine Learning Research*, vol. 3, pp. 1–48, 2002.

[262] F. Bach and M. I. Jordan, "Learning graphical models with Mercer kernels," *Advances in Neural Information Processing Systems*, 2002.

[263] G. Baudat and F. Anouar, "Generalized discriminant analysis using a kernel approach," *Neural Computation*, vol. 12, pp. 2385–2404, 2000.

[264] F. Girosi, M. Jones, and T. Poggio, "Regularization theory and neutral networks architectures," *Neural Computation*, vol. 7, pp. 219–269, 1995.

[265] T. Jebara and R. Kondor, "Bhattarcharyya and expected likelihood kernels," *Conference on Learning Theory (COLT)*, 2003.

[266] R. Kondor and T. Jebara, "A kernel between sets of vectors," *Intenational Conference on Machine Learning (ICML)*, 2003.

[267] J. Mercer, "Functions of positive and negative type and their connection with the thoery of integral equations," *Philos. Trans. Roy. Soc. London*, vol. A 209, pp. 415–446, 1909.

[268] S. Mika, G. Rätsch, J. Weston, B. Schölkopf, and K.-R. Müller, "Fisher discriminant analysis with kernels," in *Neural Networks for Signal Processing IX*, Y.-H. Hu, J. Larsen, E. Wilson, and S. Douglas, Eds. IEEE, 1999, pp. 41–48.

[269] P. Moreno, P. Ho, and N. Vasconcelos, "A Kullback-Leibler divergence based kernel for svm classfication in multimedia applications," *Neural Information Processing Systems*, 2003.

[270] K.R. Müller, S. Mika, G. Rätsch, K. Tsuda, and B. Schölkopf, "An introducation to kernel-based learning algorithms," *IEEE Trans. Neutral Networks*, vol. 12, pp. 181–202, 2001.

[271] A. Ng, M. Jordan, and Y. Weiss, "On spectral clustering: analysis and an algorithm," *Neural Information Processing Systems*, 2002.

[272] B. Schölkopf, A. Smola, and K.-R. Müller, "Nonlinear component analysis as a kernel eigenvalue problem," *Neural Computation*, vol. 10, pp. 1299–1319, 1998.

[273] M. Tipping, "Sparse kernel prinicipal component analysis," *Neural Information Processing Systems*, 2001.

[274] C. K. I. Williams, "On a connection between kernel PCA and metric multidimensional scaling," *Neural Information Processing Systems*, 2001.

[275] L. Wolf and A. Shashua, "Kernel principal angles for classification machines with applications to image sequence interpretation," *IEEE Computer Society Conference on Computer Vision and Pattern Recognition*, Madison, WI, 2003.

[276] S. Zhou, "Probabilistic analysis of kernel principal components: classification and mixture modeling," *CfAR Technial Report, CAR-TR-993*, 2003.

[277] S. Zhou and R. Chellappa, "From sample similarity to ensemble similarity: Probabilistic distance measures in reproducing kernel Hilbert space," *SCR Technical Report SCR-05-TR-774*, 2005.

[278] S. Zhou, "Matrix-based kernel methods," *SCR Technical Report SCR-05-TR-773*, 2005.

Index